This volume examines the process of political and cultural mobilization in the face of industrialized mass death during the First World War. Comparing Britain, France, Germany, Italy and Austria-Hungary, the book generates arguments on mobilization and 'total war' which have wider relevance.

The book explores 'national ideals' which cast the war as a crusade, the inclusive 'self-mobilization' of sectional identities and private organizations behind national efforts, and the exclusion of suspect groups (the 'enemy within') from the mobilization process. It also highlights the importance, and difficulty, of assessing the limits of mobilization as well as the differing capacities of the state to sustain it, factors related to prior degrees of national integration and political legitimacy. Mobilization in this sense was an important factor which helped determine the outcome and legacy of the war.

State, society and mobilization in Europe during the
First World War

Studies in the Social and Cultural History of Modern Warfare

General Editor
Jay Winter *Pembroke College, Cambridge*

Advisory Editors
Paul Kennedy *Yale University*
Antoine Prost *Université de Paris-Sorbonne*
Emmanuel Sivan *The Hebrew University of Jerusalem*

In recent years the field of modern history has been enriched by the exploration of two parallel histories. These are the social and cultural history of armed conflict, and the impact of military events on social and cultural history.

Studies in the Social and Cultural History of Modern Warfare
intends to present the fruits of this growing area of research, reflecting both the colonization of military history by cultural historians, and the reciprocal interest of military historians in social and cultural history, to the benefit of both. The series will reflect the latest scholarship in European and non-European events from the 1850s to the present day.

Titles in the series

1 *Sites of memory, sites of mourning*
The Great War in European cultural history
Jay Winter
ISBN 0 521 49682 9

2 *Capital cities at war: Paris, London and Berlin 1914–1919*
Jay Winter and Jean-Louis Robert
ISBN 0 521 57171 5

3 *State, society and mobilization in Europe during the First World War*
Edited by John Horne
ISBN 0 521 56112 4

State, society and mobilization in Europe during the First World War

Edited by

John Horne

Trinity College, Dublin

CAMBRIDGE
UNIVERSITY PRESS

PUBLISHED BY THE PRESS SYNDICATE OF THE UNIVERSITY OF CAMBRIDGE
The Pitt Building, Trumpington Street, Cambridge, United Kingdom

CAMBRIDGE UNIVERSITY PRESS
The Edinburgh Building, Cambridge CB2 2RU, UK
40 West 20th Street, New York NY 10011–4211, USA
477 Williamstown Road, Port Melbourne, VIC 3207, Australia
Ruiz de Alarcón 13, 28014 Madrid, Spain
Dock House, The Waterfront, Cape Town 8001, South Africa

http://www.cambridge.org

First published 1997
First paperback edition 2002

Typeface Plantin 10/12 pt.

A catalogue record for this book is available from the British Library

Library of Congress Cataloguing in Publication data
State, society, and mobilization in Europe during the First World War / edited
by John Horne.
       p.   cm. – (Studies in the Social and Cultural History of Modern Warfare: 3)
ISBN 0 521 56112 4 (hardcover)
1. World War, 1914–1918 – Europe.   2. Preparedness.
3. World War, 1914–1918 – Social Aspects – Europe.
4. War and society.   I. Horne, John N.   II. Series.
D523.S685   1997
940.3′1–dc20   96-44927   CIP

ISBN 0 521 56112 4 hardback
ISBN 0 521 52266 8 paperback

Contents

Contributors

Stéphane Audoin-Rouzeau is Professor of History at the University of Picardie–Jules Verne and co-director of the Research Centre of the Historial de la Grande Guerre at Péronne (Somme). His publications include *Men at War, 1914–1918* (1986; English translation, Providence and Oxford: Berg, 1992); *1870. La France dans la guerre* (Paris: Colin, 1989); *La Guerre des enfants (1914–1918)* (Paris: Colin, 1993); *L'Enfant de l'ennemi (1914–1918). Viols, avortement, infanticide pendant la grande guerre* (Paris: Aubier, 1995); and, with Jean-Jacques Becker, *La France, la nation, la guerre (1850–1920)* (Paris: SEDES, 1995).

Richard Bessel is Senior Lecturer in History at the Open University and co-editor of the journal *German History*. His publications include *Political Violence and the Rise of Nazism: the Storm Troopers in Eastern Germany, 1925–1934* (New Haven and London: Yale University Press, 1984); (ed.), *Life in the Third Reich* (Oxford: Oxford University Press, 1987); *Germany after the First World War* (Oxford: Oxford University Press, 1993); and (ed.), *Fascist Italy and Nazi Germany: Comparisons and Contrasts* (Cambridge: Cambridge University Press, 1996).

Paul Corner is Professor of European History at the University of Siena. He has published widely on Italian fascism and on various aspects of Italian industrialization, including *Fascism in Ferrara, 1915–25* (Oxford: Oxford University Press, 1975) and *Contadini e industrializzazione. Società rurale e impresa in Italia dal 1840 al 1940* (Rome/Bari: Laterza, 1993).

Mark Cornwall lectures in Eastern European History at the University of Dundee. Prior to that he was a Research Fellow at Wolfson College, Oxford. He has researched widely in eastern Europe and has published a range of articles on the collapse of the Habsburg empire, the Sudeten problem and the creation of Yugoslavia. In 1990 he edited and contributed to *The Last Years of Austria-Hungary 1908–1918* (Exeter:

Exeter University Press, 1990, second edn forthcoming, 1997). He was awarded the BP prize lectureship by the Royal Society of Edinburgh in 1995 in recognition of his contribution to modern eastern European history. He is currently completing *The Undermining of Austria-Hungary. The Role of Military Propaganda 1914–1918* (forthcoming).

Wilhelm Deist was Chief Historian at the Militärgeschichtliches Forschungsamt (Research Institute for Military History), Freiburg (1988–93), and is Professor at the University of Freiburg. Publications include *Militär und Innenpolitik im Weltkrieg 1914–1918* (Düsseldorf: Droste, 1970), a source book; *Flottenpolitik und Flottenpropaganda. Das Nachrichtenbureau des Reichsmarineamtes 1897–1914* (Stuttgart: DVA, 1976); (with M. Messerschmidt, H.-E. Volkmann and W. Wette), *The Build-up of German Aggression* (1979; English translation, Oxford: Oxford University Press, 1990); *The Wehrmacht and German Rearmament* (London: Macmillan, 1981); (with V. R. Berghahn), *Rüstung im Zeichen der wilhelminischen Weltpolitik. Grundlegende Dokumente* (Düsseldorf: Droste, 1988); *Militär, Staat und Gesellschaft. Studien zur preußisch-deutschen Militärgeschichte* (Munich: Oldenbourg, 1991). He has also edited *The German Military in the Age of Total War* (Leamington Spa: Berg, 1985).

David Englander is Senior Lecturer in European Humanities at the Open University. He is co-author of *Mr Charles Booth's Inquiry: Life and Labour of the People in London Reconsidered* (London: Hambledon, 1992), and co-editor of *Retrieved Riches: Social Investigation in Britain, 1840–1914* (London: Scolar Press, 1995). He is currently preparing a comparative study of war service in the First and Second World Wars.

Andrea Fava is Researcher in Contemporary History in the Department of Political Science at the University of 'La Sapienza', Rome, and teaches history at the Educational Institute of the University LUMSA in Rome. He has written on the history of fascism and poverty, and especially on patriotic propaganda in early twentieth-century Italy, the memory of the Great War, and the infusion of the primary school system with a nationalist culture under fascism. His publications include (ed., with others), *La storia dei poveri. Pauperismo e assistenza nell'età moderna* (Rome: Studium, 1985) and the exhibition catalogue, *Fronte Interno. Propaganda e mobilitazione civile nell'Italia della Grande Guerra* (Rome: Biblioteca di Storia Moderna e Contemporanea, 1988).

Christhard Hoffmann is a former Research Assistant at the Centre for Research into Anti-semitism at the Technische Universität, Berlin and, since 1994, a visiting DAAD Professor in German Studies at the history department, University of California at Berkeley. His publications include (ed. with H. A. Strauss), *Juden und Judentum in der Literatur* (Munich: Deutscher Taschenbuch Verlag, 1985); *Juden und Judentum im Werk deutscher Althistoriker des 19. und 20. Jahrhunderts* (Leiden: Brill, 1988); (ed., with others), *Der Antisemitismus der Gegenwart* (Frankfurt-am-Main and New York: Campus, 1990); (ed. with others), *Eduard Meyer und Viktor Ehrenberg. Ein Briefwechsel (1914–1930)* (Berlin: Akademie Verlag and Stuttgart: Teubner, 1990); and (ed., with others), *Die Emigration der Wissenschaften nach 1933. Disziplingeschichtliche Studien* (Munich: Saur, 1991).

John Horne is Senior Lecturer in Modern European History and a Fellow of Trinity College, Dublin. He has written widely on the social history of twentieth-century France, comparative labour history, and the comparative history of the First World War. His publications include *Labour at War. France and Britain, 1914–1918* (Oxford: Clarendon Press, 1991); (with H. Gough, eds.), *De Gaulle and Twentieth Century France* (London: Edward Arnold, 1994); and (with A. Kramer), *'German Atrocities', 1914: Meanings and Memory of War* (Cambridge: Cambridge University Press, forthcoming). He held fellowships at the Institute for Advanced Study, Princeton, and the Center for Historical Analysis, Rutgers University, in 1994–5.

Alan Kramer is Senior Lecturer in Modern European History and a Fellow of Trinity College, Dublin. He has published widely on the economic and social history of Germany since 1945 and on the history of the First World War. His publications include *The West German Economy, 1945–1955* (New York and Oxford: Berg, 1991); *Die britische Demontagepolitik am Beispiel Hamburgs 1945–1950* (Hamburg: Verlag Verein für Hambürgische Geschichte, 1991); and (with J. Horne), *'German Atrocities', 1914: Meanings and Memory of War* (Cambridge: Cambridge University Press, forthcoming).

Wolfgang J. Mommsen is Emeritus Professor of Modern History at the University of Düsseldorf. He is also a former director of the German Historical Institute in London, a past president of the Verband der Historiker Deutschlands (Association of German Historians), and current president of the International Commission for Historiography. He has held visiting posts and fellowships at various institutions, including the Historisches Kolleg, Munich, in 1992–3, and the Woodrow Wilson Center in Washington, DC, in 1995. He has published widely on Max Weber, German and British history in the nineteenth and twentieth centuries, European imperialism, the history of historiography, the theory of history and related subjects.

Giovanna Procacci is Professor of Contemporary History at the University of Modena. She is the author of books and articles on Italian participation in the First World War. Her current interests include typologies of industrialization and millenarianism. Her most recent study is *Soldati e prigionieri italiani nella grande guerra* (Rome: Editori Riuniti, 1993).

Jean-Louis Robert is Professor of History at the University of Orléans and directs the national research laboratory on 'Travail et travailleurs en France, 19e–20e siècles'. He has published numerous books and articles on French social history and on the history of the Paris and French labour and socialist movements in the period of the First World War. His most recent work, which forms the second part of his 1989 doctoral thesis, is *Les Ouvriers, la patrie et la révolution. Paris 1914–1919* (Besançon: Annales Littéraires de l'Université de Besançon no. 592, Série Historique no. 11, 1995).

Leonard V. Smith is Associate Professor of History at Oberlin College, Ohio. He has published widely on the social and cultural history of the French military, including *Between Mutiny and Obedience: the Case of the French Fifth Infantry Division during World War I* (Princeton: Princeton University Press, 1994), which won the 1994 Paul Birdsall prize from the American Historical Association for the best book on European military history since 1870.

Preface

This volume originated in an international conference held in Trinity College, Dublin, in June 1993, with the title 'Mobilizing for "total" war: society and state in Europe, 1914–1918'. It is, however, both less and more than the conference proceedings – less, in that it only includes half the papers delivered on that occasion, as a result both of the economics of publishing and of editorial decisions to concentrate on particular countries and themes; but more, in that nearly all the essays that follow have been revised (in some cases substantially so) to take account of the requirements of a book that seeks to examine comparatively a particular process – that of the cultural and political mobilization of European societies during the First World War. The book, in other words, represents a further stage of reflection and selection from the conference. It is a genuinely international effort, with contributions in almost equal numbers from historians working in Britain, France, Germany, Ireland, Italy and the USA. The hope is that it will take its place in a sequence of collaborative volumes published in the last ten years which have used a comparative approach in order to understand the common, or systemic, features of the Great War while measuring the particularities of national cases.

Two points need clarifying on the editorial thinking behind the book. Firstly, many fine papers delivered at the conference do not appear here simply because they did not fit the volume's tightened focus. Some have been published elsewhere. One entire session of the conference, devoted to the social and political implications of the provisioning of civilians in different countries, has appeared in French translation. It forms a special dossier on 'Nouvelles pistes de l'histoire urbaine 1914–1918', in the Parisian journal, *Guerres mondiales et conflits contemporains*, 183, October 1996, and contains essays by Thierry Bonzon on Paris, Belinda Davis on Berlin, Jonathan Manning on London, and Luigi Tomassini on Italy. Although fully part of the broader theme of the conference, the social emphasis of these contributions, raising the central question of whether the First World War generated a specific social morality or (to adopt

E. P. Thompson's celebrated term) 'moral economy', was eschewed in this volume in favour of more explicitly political and cultural modalities of wartime mobilization. Additionally, the conference paper by David Fitzpatrick on 'The logic of collective sacrifice: Ireland and the British army, 1914–1918', was published in *The Historical Journal*, 38, 4, 1995, pp. 1017–30.

Secondly, an even more obvious lacuna compared with the conference is that of Russia and the eastern front (with the exception of Mark Cornwall's essay on the Austro-Hungarian army). This does not reflect any conviction on the part of the editor that the western front and western belligerents warrant the oligopolistic status they enjoy in the current resurgence of interest in the First World War – on the contrary. But he, like others, has had to confront the disproportion in the knowledge base and state of debate between Germany and the main western belligerents on the one hand, and the countries of southern and eastern Europe on the other, including most notably Russia, where the First World War was so long obscured by the Revolution and the origins of the communist regime. The one clear exception is Italy, where a great deal of innovative work has taken place over the past fifteen years; hence the decision to abandon the attempt to incorporate a Russian dimension and to opt instead for the Italian case as one where the limited legitimacy of the pre-war regime was destroyed (amongst other things) by the imperatives of wartime mobilization – though the result, of course, was fascism not communism.

Most editors are acutely aware of those limitations to any collective volume for which they, not the individual authors, are responsible. This sense is especially acute in the case of a comparative study on an international topic. Strictly parallel investigation of a sufficiently wide range of national examples is hard to achieve; internally comparative contributions are scarce. Some obvious and important dimensions do not work out or cannot be included. In the present case, it was hoped that gender (on which a good deal of work has been done in relation to the First World War) would infuse a range of contributions, and this seemed a chance to escape from artificially delimiting the concept with a section on 'women and mobilization' or 'gender and mobilization' – though both were obvious themes. But neither women nor gender did emerge as a significant frame of reference at the conference, and in this as in more positive ways, the volume bears the mark of its genesis. In the end, any book of this kind proceeds more by suggestion, insight and hypothesis than by systematic demonstration. It is hoped that the degree of genuine cross-national comparison that emerges from the essays in each section, the thematic focus on mobilization as a cultural and political process, and above all the relevance of the latter to the broader questions of why the war turned out as it did and what it bequeathed to the post-war world, justify the volume as it stands. If the book stimulates further research and debate, it will have realized at least the editor's expectations.

The book is not the conference, but without the conference the book would not exist. It is only right, therefore, that all those who made both of them possible should be acknowledged here. The conference was jointly sponsored and financially supported by the Research Centre of the Historial de la Grande Guerre, Péronne, France, and the Department of Modern History, Trinity College, Dublin. The partnership of the two institutions was, in its small way, a model of the easy and effective international cooperation which is so vital in opening up new, trans-national approaches to historical research. Additional financial support was provided by the Faculty of Arts (Humanities) and the Trinity Trust, both of Trinity College, Dublin; by the British Council, the Goethe Institute and the Istituto Italiano di Cultura, all in Dublin; by the Cultural Service of the French Embassy in Ireland; and by the Maison des Sciences de l'Homme in Paris. Special acknowledgement must be made of the very substantial grant from the Fritz Thyssen Stiftung, Cologne, without which neither conference nor book would have happened. All the above are warmly thanked for their generosity. The smooth organization of the conference was in large measure a tribute to the skills of Mrs Gay Conroy, secretary of the Centre for European Studies, Trinity College. Thanks are also due to a number of colleagues and friends who offered help, advice and moral encouragement for both the conference and the book: Paul Corner, of the University of Siena; Patrick Fridenson, of the Ecole des Hautes Etudes en Sciences Sociales, Paris; Gerhard Hirschfeld, director of the Bibliothek für Zeitgeschichte, Stuttgart; Giovanna Procacci, of the University of Modena; Jean-Louis Robert, of the University of Orléans; and Jay Winter of Pembroke College, Cambridge. Special thanks go to Alan Kramer, of the Department of Modern History, Trinity College, Dublin, and Ioannis Sinanoglou, executive director of the Council for European Studies, Columbia University, New York. Finally, the constructive support of William Davies and Cambridge University Press in deriving the book from the conference has been appreciated at every stage.

John Horne

1 Introduction: mobilizing for 'total war', 1914–1918

John Horne

The subject of this volume is a major feature of the First World War both as an experience and as a shaping event in twentieth-century history. It is the relationship between national mobilization and 'total war'. The claim is not that this relationship determined the outcome and consequences of the war. Many other factors contributed to both. The argument, rather, is that if we think of the First World War as a trans-national or supra-national phenomenon, this relationship constitutes one of its essential dynamics which, along with others, needs to be explored comparatively across national cases, in order for the nature and significance of the war to be better understood. It is also a theme with obvious comparative relevance for the Second World War and other wars in the twentieth century. The two key terms of the relationship, 'mobilization' and 'total war', need further definition, however, before the parameters of the book can be indicated and some of the arguments which arise from it developed further.

'Mobilization' is used here in a broader sense than is customary in historical analysis of the First World War. The primary process of military mobilization, of raising mass armies from the population and delivering them to the battlefield within the cadres of a professional military establishment, is not the principal subject of investigation. Neither is the secondary process of economic mobilization, which rapidly revealed itself as no less crucial to the outcome of a war waged in the image of the industrialized societies that had generated it, and to which a good deal of attention has been devoted. Rather, the 'mobiliza-tion' explored here is that of the engagement of the different belligerent nations in their war efforts both imaginatively, through collective representations and the belief and value systems giving rise to these, and organizationally, through the state and civil society.

The nature of national mobilization so defined, both generically and in its particular manifestations, was naturally conditioned by the development of political and cultural life in pre-war society. Here, it is important to note a fundamental paradox in the broader emergence of the modern state. While bureaucratization and technology have vastly extended the state's capacity for surveillance and repression, mass involvement in the political process has made legitimacy, the consent of the ruled, an increasingly vital condition of the state's effective operation. Political mobilization as a process has acted to legitimize (or contest) the authority of regimes as well as to articulate interests within them.[1] The paradox was apparent in the half century before 1914. The state responded to a variety of threats to public order and social cohesion by expanding its repressive capacities and intensifying surveillance and control. But increased popular participation in politics provided the major internal challenge for most European states. Political regimes sought, or were forced to seek, broader acceptance, while the building or consolidation of nation-states necessitated the articulation, and even the invention, of the national 'communities' on which these were based.[2]

Political legitimacy and a sense of nationhood derived ultimately from the founding acts and embodying mythologies of regime and nation. But both gained constant reinforcement from the rituals, symbols and repeated gestures that became characteristic of national politics in this period (elections, national days, mass meetings, monuments).[3] Moreover, while legitimizing values and ideals of cultural community were promoted through the state apparatus, including national educational systems, they were expressed much more widely by a host of private and semi-private agencies, such as newspapers, political parties, pressure groups and churches. Popular legitimization of this kind and the sense of belonging to a densely defined national community were increasingly central to European politics by 1914, though with considerable differences of degree between countries.

The First World War dramatically reinforced both terms of the paradox. Exceptional wartime legislation conferred vast powers of repression on governments while millions of men were swept into the armed forces and subjected to military discipline. Yet in most cases, the war was held to involve not only the physical and territorial integrity of the national community but its distinctive values, ways of life and political institutions. The persuasive, legitimizing powers which underpinned mass politics immediately turned to generating support for the war effort. Not only the state, but the associational life of civil society, rallied behind the national cause. The conventional image of rampant jingoism greeting the outbreak of war has been modified by recent research.[4] But what replaces it is an altogether more complex picture of a process of engagement in the war by the major belligerents which galvanized pre-existing sentiments of national community and political affiliation in what was usually perceived to be a defensive national mobilization. Popular support for the war, initially at least, stemmed from persuasion, and self-persuasion, much more than from coercion. Repression, however, was available in abnormally strong measure if persuasion flagged.

National mobilization was, then, an essentially political and cultural process. Like so much else in August 1914, however, it was premissed on a short war in which (like those of the recent past) military conflict could be seen as a rational instrument for achieving political ends, a deplorable but necessary evil, or even as beneficial to cultural development.[5] The nature of combat under modern conditions was disastrously misread by general staffs, and to the extent that it entered popular consciousness did so in the form of conventional images of a war of movement replete with hand-to-hand encounters and heroic deeds – as press representations of the first few months of war in 1914 testify.[6] In reality, the full application of modern industrial and bureaucratic capacities to warfare itself, and a particular conjuncture in military technology which conferred an overwhelming advantage on the defensive, combined to plunge Europe into the novel experience of industrialized siege warfare, in which successive hopes for military breakthrough, victory and a political settlement subsided repeatedly into a grinding conflict of attrition.[7]

Did this amount to 'total war'? There is the danger, as with any large concept, that the term may distort more than it reveals. This is particularly so if we adopt a fixed point as our measure and seek to grade all other cases by reference to it. If the Second World War exemplifies 'total war', with its unprecedented inclusion of civilians as combatants and targets, its perfection of mass destruction, and its global scale, the First World War looks less than total on any of these counts. If, on the other hand, we take the waging of 'total war' to be an evolutionary process, its origins can reasonably be identified much further back in, for example, the French Revolutionary wars as the first secular ideological conflict, with the American Civil War as an early example and the capacity for nuclear annihilation its logical term. In this perspective, the First World War is merely an important stage in the growing capacity of war to mobilize and destroy societies. Alternatively, it might be objected that no social phenomenon is total, least of all one planned by leaders and elites, and that 'total war' is only important as a contemporary illusion.[8]

These arguments all have force but all risk missing the essence of the First World War which lay in a totalizing logic, or potential, of which contemporaries were acutely aware and which appeared profoundly new. This dizzying escalation occurred in different spheres. It was manifest in the trauma and casualties of trench warfare, in the sinister spiral of military technology and forms of warfare that overturned established norms of military conduct. It was apparent in the compelling but unanticipated need to reorganize the economy for war. It was equally clear, however, in the readiness to represent the war in absolute terms, as a crusade against a total (and often dehumanized) enemy in which great emphasis was placed on morale, opinion and what amounted to the ideological capacity of each nation to sustain the war effort.

The etymology of 'total war' and analogous terms is revealing in this regard. Ernst Jünger coined the term 'total mobilization' (*Die totale Mobilmachung*) in his celebrated essay of 1930 to capture the unprecedented way in which the war harnessed the energies of entire national societies – something he considered the democracies ideologically better equipped to achieve. Ludendorff, in both his war memoirs (written in 1918–19) and his significantly entitled *Der Totale Krieg* (1935), likewise described the First World War as in essence a 'total war' that relied ultimately on the 'spiritual and psychical forces of the nation'. Criticizing Clausewitz for failing to include this dimension in his notion of 'absolute war' and implicitly German politicians and the home front for failing to deliver this form of mobilization to the military leadership in 1914–18, Ludendorff (like Jünger) identified its historic source in the 'nation in arms' invented by the French Revolution and saw a remodelled, totalitarian version of this as the key to Germany's victory in a future war.[9] Less remarked on is the fact that the terms *guerre totale* and *guerre intégrale* also made their appearance in France in the last year of the war, particularly to describe a renewed political and ideological commitment to the military effort.[10] In the French case, the *levée en masse* of 1793 (with its appeal to the old men to 'stimulate the courage of the warriors and preach the unity of the Republic and the hatred of kings') indeed provided a potent and much cited precedent. It is significant, in other words, that the very term 'total war' arose from the First World War and connoted in particular the political and ideological investment of the nation in the conflict.

All this suggests that there is no simple dichotomy between national mobilization and 'total war', the former representing the innocent effusion of national sentiment that evaporated in contact with the reality of the latter. The terms and language of national mobilization and 'self-mobilization' in the principal belligerents in 1914, and the deeper processes of national formation and political participation that underlay them, were themselves a vital dimension of 'total war' without which neither the combatants' tenacity nor the duration of the conflict is readily explicable. By the same token, however, the radical heart of the First World War perhaps lay here, in the encounter between national mobilization and the industrialized killing fields of trench warfare. The latter tested the legitimacy of pre-war states and the sense of national community to the limits and it was here, arguably, that much of the battle over the meaning of the war was fought out within and between the various belligerents. The way ordinary soldiers understood industrialized siege warfare, and either rebelled or kept fighting, had a good deal to do with the varying capacity of different powers to keep mobilizing their soldiers' will to continue. So, too, did the resilience of non-combatant populations faced with mounting bereavement and economic distortions of varying degrees, accompanied by a heightened sense of social injustice. The advantage of considering 'total war' (and national mobilization as one of its elements) to be a process, or a compelling logic, in 1914–18, rather than an achieved result, is that it encourages analysis of its form and evolution but also of its constraints and limitations – and of the variants in these between different belligerents.

Investigating mobilization at this level therefore involves the plans and projects of the state, which sought to stimulate and control 'opinion' and 'morale' (civil as well as military) to a degree and in ways that were hitherto inconceivable. But it also encompasses society, many elements of which fully engaged in the mobilization process, but much of which ultimately proved indifferent or resistant to state-led forms of mobilization or sought to redirect these in more autonomous ways. The study of wartime mobilization is partly about the ideal projections of military and civilian planners; but it is also about the lived relationship of a variety of different groups (intellectuals, school teachers, children, soldiers and many more) to the war and to its meaning.

Both individually and by the comparisons they establish, the essays in this volume raise a number of ideas and hypotheses for further research. The first of these concerns the chronology of mobilization in the different societies. Britain, France and Germany appear to share a common pattern of national mobilization in which the first two years of the war were strongly characterized by persuasion rather than coercion, and by a high degree of 'self-mobilization' in civil society. This is not to deny the real increase in state power. As already argued, coercive powers were hugely enhanced, though initially not much needed, given minimal collective opposition to the war. States also framed the process of persuasion in highly directive ways, through news control, censorship and early (though limited) forays into domestic propaganda. But what stands out is the strength of the process of voluntary participation by a host of organizations and agencies both in the formal definition of 'national ideals' (and of their negative obverse, the enemy) and in the generation of a sense of national community.

Intellectuals and artists played a key role in Germany, as Wolfgang Mommsen shows, in defining the war less as a moment of suspended domestic politics than as one of cultural fusion. The nation appeared to rediscover its essence as a cultural community shaped by the spiritual values of a German *Kultur* which stood in sharp opposition to the rootless abstractions and shallow commercialism of western 'civilization', as exemplified by Britain and France. British and French academics and intellectuals responded with their own projections of the war as one of 'civilization' (variously defined) against a negative German *Kultur* of naked militarism and authoritarianism loosely wrapped in philosophies of power, dominance and nihilism. Although the intellectuals on both sides often derived their prestige from state educational institutions and academies, and cooperated with government in defining the war as a universal crusade, they willingly anticipated the state's needs and enrolled themselves in the national cause. Indeed, precisely because the war as a total struggle seemed to re-infuse existence with a sense of meaning beyond the humdrum banalities of daily life, it generated an irresistible attraction, according to Wolfgang Mommsen, even for writers and artists who could never remotely be considered propagandists.[11]

Intellectuals and artists exemplify with exceptional clarity a much broader process. All kinds of social groups and institutions mobilized themselves behind the war effort and in so doing contributed powerfully to a cultural fusion, or at least convergence, in defence of state and nation. In effect, the war triggered what Nettl calls a 'national-constitutional mobilization', in which the legitimization of state and nation were reasserted and reinforced in what was perceived as a crisis of survival.[12] Stéphane Audoin-Rouzeau shows how the primary school system in France provided a uniquely potent instrument by which the state could direct this process, given the ideology of secular republicanism with which it was invested and its centralized direction by the Ministry of Public Instruction. Even here, however, a crucial ingredient was the enrolment of the teachers as a social corps with a highly defined professional ethos and organization as the willing agents of a mobilization that extended far beyond the classroom itself.[13] It remains an open question as to whether the primary school teachers of Britain and Germany played a directly comparable role, given the more hybrid systems of compulsory primary instruction that had emerged in the half century before the war – though if they did so, despite less singular and centralized state direction, it further strengthens the evidence of 'self-mobilization'.

The resonance and variants of the languages of self-mobilization enunciated by the intellectuals went far beyond the mass education system, however, to encompass a host of pre-existing organizations as well as bodies set up with specifically wartime functions – whether to promote war aims or deal with a multitude of practical requirements, from charitable work to war loans. In France alone, there were 1,806 such organizations officially recognized by the government in 1918.[14] Perhaps the clearest indication of the centripetal power of this mobilization process comes from the response of feminist and labour organizations which on the eve of the war had been battling against the entrenched political establishments in all three countries – and which, as more recent research has insisted, supported the war not just because of the collapse of pre-war ideological paradigms but also because the national component that had been one source of their pre-war identities reshaped the affiliations of class and especially gender in response to the crisis of 1914.[15]

If 'self-mobilization' marked the first phase of the war, the corrosive effects of a long war, soaring casualties and receding prospects of victory combined to force belligerent states in the second half of the war to adopt a more directly interventionist role. This was not a simple matter of altering the balance between coercion and persuasion in favour of the former. Political legitimacy remained central to the process of national mobilization. But states were faced with the need to play a more direct role in sustaining national commitment to the war as voluntary energies waned. This in turn posed a sharp challenge to the state's own authority and its capacity to represent diverse elements of the nation – a theme to which we shall return.

Arguably, the differences in political ideology and national values between opposed belligerents such as Britain, France and Germany initially mattered less in determining the process of national mobilization than the pre-existing strength of the associative webs and mechanisms of national integration that were common to all three, in contrast to less developed polities such as Russia, Austria-Hungary and Italy. This represents a second major theme of this volume and one which is explored essentially through the Italian case.[16] The crisis of Italian intervention from August 1914 to May 1915 was self-consciously played out in relation to the process of national mobilization already taking place in the other belligerents. The conservative elites represented by the Salandra administration sought to use a short-war intervention with tangible territorial results as an alternative to the domestic processes of expanded political participation for which they had condemned Giolitti since the turn of the century.[17] Logically, this committed them to avoiding a national mobilization and relying instead on the traditional authority of the local notables. Democratic and radical interventionists, by contrast, divined in the war an opportunity to infuse Italian politics with a vaguely revolutionary idealism without, for all that, enjoying mass support.[18] Thus a limited declaration of war against Austria-Hungary alone was dangerously charged with hopes of political transformation, while lacking the persuasive mechanisms of national mobilization and 'self-mobilization' available in more developed nation-states, which could also more credibly present themselves as the victims of aggression.

The result, as Paul Corner and Giovanna Procacci show, was a strongly authoritarian wartime state, in which military authority penetrated the civilian sphere more directly and with less institutional mediation than in Britain, France and Germany. At the same time, the logic of 'total war' drew the Italian government into extending the war against Germany in 1916. As the cost and casualties of the conflict rose (nearly 600,000 war dead in all), it also induced a process of combined state and 'self-mobilization' pivoted on the primary school system which, as Andrea Fava demonstrates, took up the themes of the radical interventionists (who entered the enlarged coalition government of 1916), expanded the sense of the nation, and undermined the restricted political culture of pre-war liberal Italy. The military catastrophe of Caporetto in October 1917, which at last lent plausibility to the cry of the nation in danger, galvanized something like the 'self-mobilization' experienced by other belligerents at the outset, though at a moment when indifference or even hostility to the war were growing among much of the population – thus maximizing the divisiveness of the Italian war experience.

Although the Russian government did not enjoy the same freedom of choice over entering the war, it would appear to have shared the Italian dilemmas and difficulties, considerably magnified. The domestic role of the army intensified state authoritarianism while fear of state reform left even something as fundamental as the industrial effort largely in the hands of private initiative (in the shape of the War Industries Committees). Unable to incorporate the wider forces necessary to mount a successful war effort without threatening its own existence, the regime moved in the opposite direction by reducing its legitimacy to the person of the Tsar – just when military setbacks compounded the incoherence of the home-front administration.[19] The point of both the Italian and Russian cases is that the dynamic of national mobilization became a powerfully contentious factor in domestic politics, given the relatively fragile basis of the pre-war regimes and limited degree of national integration. Feared by conservatives, embraced by radicals and uncertain of surmounting either mass apathy or counter-mobilization against the war, the mobilization process rapidly confronted narrowly based regimes facing the imperatives of 'total war' with the limits of their own legitimacy.

A third theme to emerge from the volume concerns the forms and languages of national mobilization. This is less a matter of the latter's concrete functions – solidarity with the front, social aid, industrial organization, military recruitment – than of its inner processes. The function of national mobilization, after all, was to generate unity and a sense of inclusiveness and this happened in different ways. It meant, most obviously, a weakening of sectoral mobilization around competing interests or ideologies within the nation in favour of unity against the external enemy, with a corresponding enrolment of particular identities behind the national effort. Here, pre-existing solidarities played a crucial role. Jean-Louis Robert shows that in the case of the Parisian labour and socialist movements there was a complex tissue of micro-cultures which maintained the identification of home with fighting front during the first year of the war, in the name of diverse values. Such specific social solidarities, especially where they linked with local or national political structures, were capable of strongly underwriting the mobilization process. This was equally true of cultural identities – those of religious minorities, such as German catholicism, for example – and of regional identities. In western France, even the conservative local administrations most hostile to the Republic engaged wholeheartedly in the national defence, in part precisely because it was a question of defending nation as well as regime, but also because the republican state respected the role of the local notables.[20]

Broader languages, temporal and spiritual, also constituted a powerful vector of national mobilization. The conventional terminologies of national identity and the different political ideologies that coalesced behind the war effort naturally provided much of this. So, too, did the churches.[21] Annette Becker has recently pointed out in her study, *La Guerre et la foi*, that the war itself reinvigorated the categories of religious faith (far beyond formal religious adherence) as an essential medium, and mediator, of the experiences of mobilization, combat, death and mourning.[22] The argument can be extended, however, to include secular faiths – what Maurice Barrès in the French case termed the 'spiritual families' composing the nation.[23] The war was presented as a crusade not just for each nation's survival but for the values (variously interpreted) that it was held to embody. This imparted a chiliastic dimension to the conflict as the upheaval preceding a new world, a dimension which was not necessarily dimmed by the lengthening experience of the war. The language of sacrifice, consolation, redemption and rebirth (the fatherland triumphant, the world freed of future wars) ran through the war experience in secular as well as religious terms, presiding over the confrontation of national mobilization with mass death.

Minority identities frequently benefited from enlarged space and consideration in the process of national mobilization, especially at the beginning of the war. Yet mobilization had the capacity to achieve the reverse by a negative self-definition, internally as well as externally. The 'enemy within' was one of the essential categories of the mobilization process. Although applied most obviously to 'enemy aliens' (the British term) who in all the belligerents were rounded up, classified and incarcerated in camps (another manifestation of the totalizing tendency of the war), the notion could easily be extended to domestic elements suspected for various reasons of sympathy with the enemy – such as Alsace-Lorrainers in both France and, as Alan Kramer argues, far more starkly in Germany. As wartime tensions mounted, more systematic distrust or outright hostility towards such groups might emerge as a form of mobilization by exclusion, rather than inclusion, through the creation of domestic scapegoats. But the extent to which this happened depended (amongst other things) on the degree of pre-war national integration, the particular value systems mobilized, and the severity of the national war experience.[24]

Thus, anti-semitism remained current on the extreme right of French politics, but the Jewish community in France by and large experienced the war as a moment of powerful integration, prepared by the prior republican mobilization around this very issue during the Dreyfus affair.[25] In Germany, by contrast, as Christhard Hoffmann shows, an increasingly authoritarian military regime under Hindenburg and Ludendorff activated the anti-liberal fault lines in Germany by clumsily responding to anti-semitic sentiments and thus alienating a Jewish community which had begun the war, as in France, by reaffirming its integration into national life. None of this compares with the scale of anti-semitic pogroms that marked the chaos of rampant nationalism and nascent state-formation in eastern Europe in the wake of the war, let alone the Turkish genocide of the Armenians (a Christian minority accused of sympathy with the Russian enemy) in 1915.[26] The latter marked the most extreme and lethal mobilization against the 'enemy within' during the First World War (though falling far short of the organized extermination practised by the Nazis during the Second). But as Hoffmann and Kramer show, anti-semitism and hostility to the population of a key frontier province marked the limits of inclusive mobilization in Germany during the second half of the war – and the relevance of the example for other states (especially Russia and Austria-Hungary) merits exploration.

No belligerent, of course, could escape the mounting strain of the war. A succession of failed offensives in 1915–17 brought soldiers face to face not only with the horrors of a particular type of industrialized slaughter but also with the question of whether the strategy and tactics of their own military commands were capable of achieving the proclaimed goal of the enemy's total defeat. The official version of military operations, recounted as the successful attainment of (ever more limited) goals, contradicted the haunting perception amongst many ordinary soldiers of a 'disproportion' between sacrifice and gain, and hence of military meaninglessness.[27] Sustaining military morale while breaking the deadlock became the overriding task of all powers in the last two years of the war, while the possibility of short-circuiting the whole destructive process by a partial or negotiated peace seemed to some an enticing alternative.[28]

But the strains were no less evident on the home front. Here the war and the mobilization process itself generated a specifically wartime 'social morality' – or set of reciprocal moral judgements on the contribution of different groups to the national effort. This was potentially divisive and equally engaged the state's responsibility.[29] In part, the social morality of wartime pivoted on the relationship between soldier and civilian, front and rear. It is a truism that combat in 1914–18 was an affair between mass armies to the exclusion of civilians (apart from occupied zones and the limited effects of submarine warfare and aerial bombardment), and thus emphasized the gulf between military and civilian experience. Certainly, every army manifested this friction in the soldiers' dismissive hostility towards the 'detested rear' of 'shirkers' (or *embusqués*) and profiteers. Yet mass short-service armies were civilian forces in which the relations between men and the intimate home front of family, friends and locality remained powerful, sustained by unprecedented letter-writing and home leave, and reinforced by the influence of civilian culture.[30]

Some of the deepest cleavages in wartime morality precisely concerned the differential connection of social groups to the fighting front and the highly variable risk of the loss of loved ones and breadwinners. Industrial workers and technicians in all countries, for example, were withdrawn from the front for an industrial mobilization that was necessarily based on the division of labour and specialization of function

– and hence on the inequality of risk. Much of the hostility to 'shirkers' was disguised rural and lower-middle-class resentment against an apparently privileged working class judged by the yardstick of what the French called the 'blood-tax' of military service. Other moral antagonisms, however, assumed different social configurations. The pragmatic reliance on private enterprise and the profit motive in the war economies provided a vocabulary of working-class hostility against industrialists by reference to the presumed equality of the national effort. In another way, it generated a moral community of working- and lower-middle-class urban consumers against rural producers and urban retailers, who were accused of 'hoarding' and 'profiteering' and blamed for inflation.[31]

Thus, on the home as well as the fighting front, the war challenged the very basis of the mobilization process. It strained the assumption that the primary, military mobilization could achieve its goals and cast doubt on the supposed moral unity of the nation by resuscitating sectional divisions, though not always in pre-war terms. It became apparent, too, that the very solidarities and languages expressing national mobilization could also do the exact opposite. Class, even nation (as the Czechs, Poles, Irish and others began to show), provided powerful vocabularies of counter-mobilization either against the war or in favour of the enemy. In some ways, the key term in the mid-period of the war was that of 'sacrifice', conveying as it did both the human cost of the military effort and the sense of differential burdens distorting civilian society and the home front. Sacrifice did not in itself negate the national mobilizations of 1914–15. But in tandem with the declining 'self-mobilization' already referred to, it strained the legitimacy of state and nation and intensified the pressure on governments and military commands to arbitrate between different perceptions of inequity and to remobilize the nation for 'total war'.

One manifestation of this tension was a distinct military crisis which occurred (with variations and very different outcomes) in virtually all the belligerents in 1917–18. This constitutes a fourth theme of the volume and is examined in parallel essays by David Englander on the British army, Leonard Smith on the resolution of the French mutinies of 1917, Wilhelm Deist on the 'underground strikes' in the German army, and Mark Cornwall on the extraordinary difficulties faced by the multinational Austro-Hungarian army. The essential nature of the French 'mutinies' of May–June 1917 has long been understood as a protest against the French High Command's inability to solve the military deadlock rather than as a refusal of the political logic of a war in defence of nation and Republic.[32] It is clear, too, that morale in the Austro-

Hungarian army was undermined from mid-1917, despite the Italian collapse at Caporetto, though this was only fully revealed in the failed offensive on the Piave of June 1918. But Wilhelm Deist argues that the German army also faced a severe psychological crisis from the autumn of 1917 which was only partially overcome in order to mount the offensive of spring 1918 before precipitating a final haemorrhage of disobedience matching the French crisis of the previous year. Whether the British army might in time have been as seriously afflicted as either its ally or enemy is uncertain. But from the autumn of 1917 (coinciding with the disastrous Passchendaele offensive) there is clear evidence, according to David Englander, of falling morale and widespread peace-talk by soldiers which was only stemmed by the ultimately successful resistance against the Germans the following spring.[33] The lethal conundrum that was industrial siege warfare, in other words, posed a fundamental problem for discipline, morale and the identity and purpose of the ordinary soldier that no army could avoid, except perhaps the newly arrived Americans.

Significantly, in view of the paradoxical relationship between coercion and persuasion already noted in the modern state, a draconian strengthening of discipline does not appear to have been an option. Contrary to post-war anti-militarist legend, there was a remarkably light disciplinary hand behind the theatre of military law-enforcement following the French mutinies. The German military command found the instrument of military discipline crumbling in its grasp as the 1918 spring offensive faltered. The number of executions in the British Expeditionary Force was considerably less in 1918 than in preceding years (under half the 1917 figure), possibly indicating a shift away from disciplinary violence.[34] Military commands, confronting the limits of both discipline and traditional morale, were forced in 1917–18 to opt for more formalized persuasion by adopting some form of 'patriotic instruction' or political education, in (often grudging) recognition of the fact that mass short-service armies were bound by notions of citizenship and sacrifice to the nation. Remobilizing the national effort meant remotivating the ordinary soldier.

It is questionable whether any of these schemes had much impact (the British version had barely got going by the end of the war). But they are symptomatically important for what they reveal about the larger question of the relationship between military authority and national legitimacy. In the German case, as Wilhelm Deist makes clear, 'patriotic instruction' was doomed before it began because the issue of political and social reform, which might have provided the basis for a new national compact, was rejected by the military leadership. This left only conservative politics or the apolitical reassertion of authority for a propaganda programme. Mark Cornwall shows how the Austrian High Command faced the even more daunting task of remobilizing military motivation in the face of politicized national identities which threatened the essence of the Dual Monarchy and increasingly formed the basis of a counter-mobilization aimed against the army itself, especially in Slav units. Little as yet is known of the French army's political instruction campaign.[35] But Leonard Smith shows that French soldiers resumed the war, firstly, through a renegotiation of authority by which the disastrous offensives of the past were ended (France's position in a coalition permitting this solution) and, secondly, through the affirmation of the soldier-citizen, an identity deeply embedded in republican political culture which legitimated both the protests and the renewed defence of the nation on more acceptable terms.

In this sense, the military crises were deeply political. They formed part of the larger malaise that stimulated state remobilization of the national effort in the last two years of the war, an endeavour which marks the strengths and limitations of the mobilization process as a whole and further distinguishes between its national variants. This forms the fifth and final theme of the book, which is explored in the editor's essay on Britain and France as liberal democracies, in Richard Bessel's analysis of the militarized regime in Germany, and in Paul Corner and Giovanna Procacci's essay on Italy. As the 'self-mobilization' and idealism of the initial phase of the war declined (a process charted by many of the contributors), two dangers confronted governments and military commands – a privatized disengagement of soldiers and civilians from the war, with 'morale' and 'opinion' weakening to the point of jeopardizing military resistance, and a counter-mobilization in favour of peace or even revolution (whether on socialist or nationalist principles), which would challenge the war effort directly. The two dangers were not always clearly distinguished from each other. But if enhanced repression was a logical response to counter-mobilization, it was inappropriate to the less tangible problem of disengagement. The only effective answer to the latter, and probably the best insurance against it turning into the former, was some form of remobilization. This in turn begged the question not just of the organizational resources available to the state for such an operation but of the terms on which to conduct it and the changes it might demand.

In the resultant responses, important distinctions emerge between the types of regime concerned. In the Russian case, the corrosion of the Tsarist regime's legitimacy after 1905 left little but repression by 1916, helping to explain why remobilization for the war and counter-mobilization against it converged in the February 1917 revolution. In Germany, by contrast, the complex political structure and competing legitimacies of the Wilhelmine system split and realigned around alternative war aims and projects for remobilization in 1916–17, as the military rule of Hindenburg and Ludendorff diverged from the parliamentary coalition on which the post-war republic would be founded. The predominance of the army as the authoritarian core of the Wilhelmine system, however, accentuated the distinction between the German wartime state and those of Britain and France, as something approaching liberal democracies.

In the British and French cases, the state engaged in a major campaign of domestic propaganda in 1917–18, using ostensibly autonomous umbrella organizations, in order to counteract both disengagement from the war and pacifism (the 'enemy within' in its most politicized form). But one of the leitmotivs of the campaign in both countries was the inclusive emphasis on democracy and on a range of war aims (once the commitment to total victory was uncompromisingly accepted), including the Wilsonian rhetoric of a new democratic world order. This reciprocal remobilization of the national effort and reaffirmation (even expansion) of the legitimacy of the national regime occurred in other ways, too, not least in the emergence of a new type of democratic and resolutely civilian war leader, whose persona and oratory gained direct and popular endorsement. Clemenceau, Lloyd George and Woodrow Wilson outlined a model that Churchill and Roosevelt perfected a generation later.

In Germany, by contrast, the identity of the regime and its legitimacy splintered in the same attempt, with successive Chancellors (periodically backed by the Kaiser) promising constitutional reform which the military leadership repudiated. War aims were equally divided, with the military mortgaging their appeal for further sacrifice to achieving victory plus massive, external expansion, in order to escape domestic reform. This formulation was reversed by the opposition majority in the Reichstag which accepted much more limited expansion as the framework for a negotiated peace and reform. And the displacement of monarchic legitimacy onto the military produced the cult of Hindenburg – the silent, soldier father-figure, so very different to the democratic leaders of the Entente. In effect, the remobilization of the second half of the war confirmed the 'national constitutional' mobilization of 1914–15, in Britain and France, and in some ways reinforced its democratic specificity. In Germany, by contrast, it helped fracture the terms of the initial mobilization, accentuating the exclusive, rather than inclusive, potential of the process (as noted in relation to Alsace-Lorraine and the

German Jewish community) and rejecting many of the sectional solidarities and 'spiritual families' of the nation.

This accentuation of authoritarian tendencies, while it may not have made the military regime substantially more dependent on domestic repression than the British and French states, fundamentally compromised its capacity to respond to the tensions arising from the conflictual social morality and competing claims of sacrifice on the home front. This is perhaps less so in relation to the industrial effort, where the strength of organized labour and socialism forced major concessions as the price of cooperation in the Hindenburg programme of expanded war production.[36] But the British and French administrations were more attentive to the claims of equity as well as efficiency in supplying the civilian population with food and basic necessities, responding to the popular 'moral economy' of provisioning and incorporating some of its resonant language into the official mobilization.[37] The British and French proved significantly better at balancing civilian and military needs.[38]

These comparative distinctions need to be kept in perspective. The British and French attempts at remobilizing the national efforts in 1917–18 were by no means completely successful. Significant sections of public opinion remained disaffected or disengaged. Conversely, the western Allies (including Italy) enjoyed substantial advantages by 1917 which contributed centrally to their greater resilience, including access to the international economy and American entry into the war.[39] Nonetheless, to return to the paradox of the state with which we began, successfully mobilizing for 'total war' required far more than the expanded powers of repression conferred by emergency wartime legislation. It needed a degree of popular consent which was intimately related to the internal cohesion and legitimacy of the states and nations involved. Liberal democratic states, such as Britain and France, were able to draw on considerable reserves of legitimacy and on broader political participation in order to sustain the process of national mobilization, despite serious erosion, in 1917–18. More authoritarian states (and especially those such as Germany with a developed institutional life and public opinion) were trapped by the need to regenerate that consensus and the impossibility of doing so without engaging in a political process that would destroy authoritarian principles and the privileged role of the military.

In a way, the 'stab in the back' legend was not a uniquely German phenomenon but rather a generic expression of this dilemma. Generals naturally sought to blame subversive civilians rather than themselves for the military crises resulting from their own inability to resolve the stalemate of the trenches. This was as true of France as of Italy, Germany or Austria-Hungary (as the essays by Smith, Corner and Procacci, Deist and Cornwall all show). French generals, even Pétain, were convinced that the real weakness of the war effort lay on the home front rather than in the human cost of a military conundrum with no clear solution. But where the military exercised substantial civil power (as in Germany and Austria-Hungary), this explanation turned into a broader conspiracy theory indirectly expressing the military's deficit of political legitimacy and disguising or condoning its own weakness. And, in the German case, it was then available retrospectively to excuse the German military leadership from responsibility for defeat.

Ultimately, deeply political questions of will and consensus lay at the heart of the mobilization process. Raymond Aron once suggested that if the two world wars together constituted the civil war of 'the Republic of the Occident', the first had been more concerned with hegemony, the second with ideology. The formulation is too neat. Both were about both, but if there was a shift of emphasis from hegemony to ideology, it partly occurred through, and as a result of, the process of national mobilization (and its limitations) during the First World War.[40]

This suggests a coda to the arguments arising from the volume which is touched on, especially in the Italian case, but which has wider relevance. The legacy of the wartime process of national mobilization (as analysed here) was diverse but substantial. In the case of Britain and France, the apparently successful model of the First World War served as the basis of the comparable process in 1939–40, albeit in quite different circumstances. In Soviet Russia, however, the Bolshevik military effort during the Civil War sketched out a new synthesis in which politics was strongly militarized while the military mobilization (under Trotsky) was infused by the political persuasion (as well as coercion) which the Tsarist army so obviously lacked. Italian fascism and National Socialism in Germany were likewise marked by the mobilization process of the First World War. The myth of the trench elite and the image of a militarized society unified against an external enemy were powerful influences on fascist politics. The latter, however, promised to supply the renewed legitimization of state and nation which had been so critically absent from the more authoritarian forms of mobilization during the First World War – whether as a peacetime surrogate or as a new model for national mobilization in a future war.[41]

I

National ideals

2 German artists, writers and intellectuals and the meaning of war, 1914–1918

Wolfgang J. Mommsen

Well before 1914, the coming of a major European war was widely anticipated among the international cultural community. This was certainly so in Germany. The last decade before 1914 witnessed the spread of a fatalistic expectation that sooner or later a major war was bound to occur and that it made little sense to try to stem the tide.[1] Even so, it is surprising to find just how widespread was the feeling among writers, artists and intellectuals that war, or a warlike cataclysm, was in the offing. Some, like Friedrich von Bernhardi, even championed preventative war by 1912 in order to defend imperial Germany's position in the world against rival powers and in order to secure a propitious future for German culture in a world that seemed likely to be dominated by just a few empires. In order to maintain the position of German culture in the future, it was argued, Germany needed to become a world power as well.

Many other writers welcomed the idea of war as a way of providing relief from the boredom and sterility of bourgeois materialist culture. George Heym's well-known poem 'Der Krieg', written in 1912, is perhaps the best-known expression of this feeling. Privately Heym conceded that 'if only a war would come, then I would be healthy again . . . everything is so boring'.[2] In 1913 Stefan George, who was by no means a warmonger, envisaged that war might come about as a purge for the decaying civilization around him and wrote that 'ten thousand must die in this Holy War'.[3] Much more outspoken was his follower Friedrich Gundolf who proclaimed that 'universal, passive peace is an ideal of tired old men. Wherever youth, change, and creation are possible or needed, there war is needed; it is a fundamental form of human activity, like country walking, love, prayer or poetry: civilization may do without them.'[4]

Likewise, the theme of war was a recurrent one among contemporary painters. There was nothing in Germany directly comparable to Marinetti's famous Futurist Manifesto which hailed war as a creative force of the highest order. The enthusiasm of the Italian Futurists for war as a means of revitalizing art and of creating an entirely new cultural order had only a limited impact on the German cultural scene.[5] Nonetheless, many works of art in Germany depicted war with a sort of involuntary fascination. There is a well-established continuity in the artistic treatment of war – mostly allegorical – which extends from von Stuck (1894) and Böcklin (1896) to Klinger (1911), Klee and Kandinsky.[6] The message of these artists did not convey any enthusiasm for war but was characterized for the most part by a sort of heroic fatalism. The pre-war work of Ludwig Meidner, for example, was full of grim depictions of wholesale violence, destruction, war and catastrophe to which the individual is helplessly exposed. Here we find an anticipation, however indirect and blurred, of the bloody slaughter that some years later engulfed most of the western world and eventually destroyed the old European order.

The universal dissatisfaction with the old order of things expressed by the cultural elites was certainly shared by many German, and indeed European, writers and artists. It may be noted in passing that in November 1911 Oswald Spengler first conceived of the idea of writing what later became his momentous book *The Decline of the West* under the assumption that a European war was imminent – as indeed it was. A great European war, he assumed, would trigger change of world historical dimensions. As the first stage of the decline of traditional European culture, the age of charismatic dictatorship envisaged in *The Decline of the West* would commence with eventual German military triumph in this momentous conflict. Although none of these works supported the idea of war, they tended to weaken the arguments for preserving peace, if only because the fatalistic mood that they transmitted to the public reduced the latter's willingness to resist this trend of affairs.

Among historians, geographers, social scientists and philosophers we do not find quite the same pattern of anticipation of war. However, the assumption that war would be an ideal, and perhaps unavoidable, means of revitalizing a national culture that had grown stagnant was widespread, even among more liberal thinkers. The fatalistic feeling that a European war would come sooner or later hardened into a self-fulfilling prophecy which contributed to bringing about what it predicted. Besides, few people worried about war as such. Technical studies abounded on themes like 'War and public finance' or 'War and socialism' (Sombart), even though their authors seldom pleaded seriously for war.

In view of these findings, it is not surprising that the German cultural community, with few exceptions, initially welcomed the war almost to a man when it eventually broke out in July–August 1914. Indeed, among the German intellectual classes, artists and writers included, the sudden surge of national enthusiasm that erupted in August 1914 was almost universal. Only a very small minority remained immune from this populist eruption of nationalism. It is a matter of controversy among historians whether the famous spirit of 'August 1914' actually encompassed the whole of the German population, as was almost unanimously claimed at the time.[7] The bulk of the working classes and in particular the peasant population, farmers and labourers alike, were certainly far less enthusiastic than the urban middle classes. A well-known drawing by Max Beckmann entitled *Die Mobilmachung* ('Mobilization') indeed catches the mood of anxiety and despair prevailing among the people rather than enthusiasm for the nation's war effort. Yet though the 'spirit of August 1914' may to some extent have been a myth, its impact on the intellectual climate was undoubtedly strong. The apparent unity of the German nation on the outbreak of war was seen by the German intelligentsia as an indication that a new, more unified, and perhaps more popular culture was in sight.

It is perhaps more surprising that few of those writers and artists who later became ardent opponents of the war stood aside. Even if they did, the momentous events stirred their imagination. One of these was Ludwig Meidner. In early August 1914 he scribbled in his notebook: 'instead I sat at my painting board, depressed and strained, with my teeth pressed together, and only distorted faces emerged from my pen, and smashed corpses came from my fingers like Satan's saliva'.[8] Hans Richter, who later became one of the co-founders of Dada, stayed away from the beginning, and agreed with his friends to meet again in two years' time in a Swiss café in order to discuss what could be done against the war. But this was not so with his co-fighter Hugo Ball, who by 1916 had become one of the most determined literary opponents of the war. Indeed, most of the artists and writers jubilantly volunteered for military service.

Most conspicuous was the case of Richard Dehmel who volunteered even though he was already fifty-one years of age. This act was intended to be a public manifestation of support for the German war effort. On his way to the front he was hailed by large crowds for his patriotism. Franz Marc and August Macke immediately enlisted. Marc became a successful officer, proud of his men and conscientious in his duties, and held in high esteem both by his superiors and those under his command. Both men paid for their war enthusiasm with their lives, Macke in October 1914, Marc in February 1916 at Verdun. Falkenhayn had deliberately intended to turn the Verdun offensive into a 'blood-mill' to break the demographic base of the French nation, but it became a bloody disaster for the Germans as well. Max Slevogt was eager to serve, if only to see the conduct of war from close quarters. He went to great lengths to be accepted as a volunteer and was eventually sent to the front in October 1914. Max Beckmann sought service in a medical unit while Otto Dix opted for field service as late as autumn 1915, and he served throughout the war with distinction in command of a machine-gun unit. Among writers the situation was similar. Even Hermann Hesse, who soon became one of the few outright opponents of the war, volunteered in the early days from his residence in Switzerland for military service in Germany. Fortunately, his request was refused.[9] Later he served as a kind of liaison officer with German soldiers detained by the Swiss for various reasons. Another case in question is Ernst Toller, who volunteered at once for military service because he believed the war to be just and necessary in order to defend German national culture, only later becoming one of its most ardent opponents.

Many of those artists who initially sought service in the army were soon bitterly disillusioned, and many of them proved unable to bear the extreme mental strain of combat and the experience of intense suffering on the battlefield. Some were dismissed, others employed in hospitals or in various bureaucratic functions in the rear, sometimes at the behest of influential followers. Schmidt-Rottluff, for instance, was given a job at the Supreme Command in the East in order not to have him exposed to the dangers of combat, thanks to the influence in high military quarters of an aristocratic lady admirer of his work.

For the most part, those who stayed behind supported the war with the artistic or literary means at their disposal. There was a desire to serve the country with the pen or the brush wherever physical shape or age prevented active service. It is somewhat difficult to understand why there was such a strong initial rush to the colours by artists and writers, and why they almost unreservedly responded in precisely the same way as the rest of the German intellectual community. In part, this was because they were swept by the same wave of emotional national solidarity. But other factors came into play as well. For one, it was hoped that the joint effort of all, artists included, would help to close the gap between the artist and the community at large which had emerged since the 1890s. Additionally, it was believed that aesthetic creativity itself would receive a strong stimulus from the war.

The great majority of artists and writers assumed that the war would bury for good the shallow pre-war culture in which all creative activities had supposedly been impaired by the materialist mentality of bourgeois society and by a state of intellectual saturation. They presumed that the war would clear the way for a more genuine cultural life and lead to an intensification of artistic creativity. In his *Gedanken im Kriege* ('Thoughts in Wartime'), published early in 1915, Thomas Mann answered Romain Rolland's plea that the German intellectuals should dissociate themselves from the deeds of Prussian militarism: 'Why should the artist, the artist as soldier, not have praised God for the collapse of a peaceful world with which he was fed up, so fed up? War. It was a holy purification, a redemption which we felt, and an enormous hope.'[10]

Most telling in this respect, perhaps, is the case of Franz Marc who sincerely believed that the war would bring about a sublime purification of culture. 'The world wants to become pure again, it wants the war', he wrote, and he argued further that 'this great war is a European civil war directed against the inner invisible enemy of the European spirit'.[11] Among the drawings in his 'Field Sketchbook' of 1915 is one entitled *Arsenal for a Creation*.[12] Marc saw the destruction around him as a first step towards the creation of a rejuvenated European culture. For Ernst Barlach, the war brought about a new, intimate sense of togetherness among the German people of an almost religious quality. Wishing to be part of it, he welcomed the war unreservedly. His *Avenging Angel* bears witness to this frame of mind; it represents the symbiosis of national and religious feelings which served as an inner guide for his work during the early part of the war.[13] The sociologist Georg Simmel also welcomed the war as a means of overcoming a stagnant pre-war culture which had been deteriorating into a seemingly meaningless multiplicity of aesthetic creations and individual modes of life, devoid of substantial meaning. According to Simmel, the war presented the opportunity to create a new, genuinely cultural order in line with the real needs and the true feelings of the people.[14]

These were certainly rather optimistic assumptions, and as time brought the enormous cruelty of the war home to everybody, they lost all plausibility. But in the early stages, views such as these were shared by most members of the cultural community. The intellectuals, artists and writers were invited to close ranks. Karl Scheffler, the editor-in-chief of *Kunst und Künstler*, the leading journal in the visual arts, hailed the coming of the war as beneficial for German culture because it would lead to a revival of idealism.[15] Scheffler urged the various artistic movements in Germany to give up their infighting: 'We urgently require a united German art, not a multitude of artistic movements fighting each other tooth and nail.'[16] He considered this a precondition of the Germans taking over the leadership of the world in artistic matters as well as others. 'We must become a master race not just in politics, but also in the spiritual realm.'[17]

To some degree, the common war effort did have a unifying effect upon the cultural scene. The Secessionists, who had hitherto been denied any official support and found themselves socially marginalized, were now given full recognition by society and government alike for their artistic contribution to German culture and to the war effort. In 1917 Liebermann was decorated by Wilhelm II who declared that he now accepted all sections of German art in the same manner.[18] Many Secessionists contributed to a new patriotic art review, *Die Kriegszeit*, edited by the renowned art publisher and patron Paul Cassirer.[19] Lovis Corinth was especially adamant in his defence of the German case; he argued that it was time to prove to the world that 'today German art is marching at the front in the world'.[20] On the whole, the war led to the social acceptance of the avant-garde even though many of its representative figures had been ousted before the war from official art patronage because of their alleged leanings towards pacifism and non-German art. Conventional academic art that had been favoured in high circles now irretrievably lost its predominant position while the genre of historical paintings (*Historienmalerei*) vanished almost completely.

Even artists like Max Beckmann, Otto Dix and Ernst Ludwig Kirchner shared something of this initial absorption into the mood of national support for the war, albeit to a lesser degree. It is true that works such as Beckmann's famous painting *Die Granate* brought home to the public from the very beginning the horrors of war, such as the panic-stricken reactions of the soldiers, the feelings of extreme fear – even utter despair – or the distressing atmosphere in military hospitals, the suffering of the wounded or disfigured, and the anxiety of those who stayed at home. Even so, their work did not contain any direct anti-war message, but presented war as an extreme condition of life that brings out the best and the shallowest features of humankind. In due course nature was supposed to restore the wounded earth to normality.

Artists were also motivated by other, non-political reasons which help explain the spontaneously positive response of the artistic community to the war. Many artists considered the war a natural event of momentous dimensions which appeared to offer them fundamentally new life experiences and hence new openings for artistic creativity. Max Beckmann confessed in May 1915, soon after he had been called up for service on the western front, that 'the point is that I (myself) am getting used to this thing which is, as it were, a mode of life just like illness, love or desire. And just as I pursue phenomena of desire, love and hatred to their most extreme expression, so I now try to do this with war. Everywhere there is life, miraculously manifold and rich in new ideas. Everywhere I see deep lines of beauty in living up to and bearing this frightful destiny.'[21] War was seen by Beckmann as an extreme form of human life which had to be studied and dealt with regardless of its brutality and meaningless suffering. Otto Dix was even more outspoken on this point: 'I must see everything. All the baseness of life I must experience myself.'[22] And in his war diary which he began in 1915 he noted down, among many sketches of combat scenes and soldier's graves: 'Inter alia the war must be seen as a natural law.'[23] It was this sort of mental detachment, associated with intense emotional engagement, that determined Dix's attitude to the war at this stage rather than any pacifism. Many of his paintings and drawings express his view that war, with all its cruelty, had to be considered first and foremost as an element of nature. Again and again he depicted soldiers' graves, grenade holes or ditches overgrown with flowers, symbolizing the eventual victory of nature over human misery and brutality. Retrospectively Dix put it this way: 'The war was abominable, yet none the less it was something colossal. I simply could not miss out on it. If one wishes to know anything about mankind, one has to have seen human beings surviving in this extraordinary state in which all restraints on behaviour fall away. One must see for oneself the full baseness of life; that's why I went to war, and why I volunteered for military service.'[24]

Certainly, there were other artists who did not share these views. Most conspicuous is Kirchner who soon came to express the conviction that in reality war and militarism were incompatible with artistic creativity. His famous self-portrait in 1915, depicting him as a soldier with a bleeding stump where the right hand had been cut off, is telling enough. Others like Schmidt-Rottluff, after their first encounters with the military machine and military service, sought to avoid any direct artistic confrontation with the war.

Among other strata of the cultural elites the initial reaction to war was not all that different. In September 1914 Rainer Maria Rilke wrote his famous 'Fünf Gesänge' ('Five Songs') which praised war as the creator of a new order of things. Hugo von Hoffmannsthal adopted a similar stance. Later they both retreated to a detached position, and fell more or less silent. Gerhart Hauptmann contributed a violently anti-British poem to the public campaign against Great Britain that was certainly below his usual standards and which he later regretted, but which at the time received considerable praise. Only Stefan George reacted in a rather more cautious manner. Unlike his followers, such as Friedrich Gundolf and Ernst Bertram, who were swept away by the strong current of nationalist opinion, George voiced his views about the war in a more serene manner which steered clear of shallow nationalism. His poem 'Der Krieg' ('The War') avoided the trivial idealization of the war which featured in thousands of poems by lesser authors. George warned: 'The old God of battles is no more'. In his view the war had come as a sort of penitence for the cultural decadence of the previous decades: 'Accumulated wrongdoings seen by all as the work of destiny and fortune, the deterioration of man to larva . . . What does it mean for him the murder of hundreds of thousands if set against the murder of life itself? He cannot join in the populist emotions about German righteousness and Gallic nastiness.'[25]

On the whole, the academic community sanctioned Germany's war effort with even greater enthusiasm than the artists and writers. Unlike the artists who, for the most part, held a rather detached position *vis-à-vis* the Wilhelmine state, the professoriate was closely linked to the state and often maintained intimate connections with the ruling circles and administrative elites. With but few exceptions they were prepared, and even eager, to support the German war effort with their intellectual capabilities, and in so doing they harboured almost no critical reservations at all. They found little difficulty from the outset in justifying the war as an effort to defend German 'culture' against the threat of what was considered western materialist, formalistic 'civilization'.

Friedrich Meinecke for one, a leading German historian and editor of the *Historische Zeitschrift*, presented the German war effort in 1914 as the final stage of a long historical process. The national upsurge of August 1914 was, in his view, the last of four great German national 'Erhebungen' (uprisings), the precursors of which had been the War of Liberation in 1813 against Napoleon I, the German Revolution of 1848–9, directed against the traditional monarchical order and striving for national unity, and the 'German war' against France in 1870–1, which had completed the unification of the German people and established the Reich. Hence he placed the German war effort in the perspective of German national emancipation and linked it with the traditions of German idealism. The war, in consequence, was not only about defending imperial Germany's political and military status against Tsarist Russia and her western allies, in what was generally considered a defensive, and therefore justified war, but also about the status of German and, indeed, of central European national culture.[26] Admittedly, Meinecke admonished his readers that they ought not to become preposterous in this respect. He pleaded for German culture to remain open to the other great world cultures and maintain its international orientation, rather than getting entangled in trivial, narrow-minded jingoism.

This, however, is exactly how things developed. The emergence of an extreme nationalist approach to cultural affairs was accelerated in part by the famous controversy between German academics and their French and English colleagues, which was triggered late in September 1914 when a group of prominent British and French academics mounted an impassioned attack on the German intelligentsia for not dissociating itself from the barbarous acts of Prussian militarism in Belgium (especially the destruction of Louvain) and for failing to work toward reconciliation and peace.[27] The 'Appeal to the World of Culture' ('Aufruf an die Kulturwelt') of 4 October 1914, signed by ninety-three leading representatives of German cultural life, was the first of many similar declarations with a common theme, namely the solidarity of the German intellectual and cultural elites with official policies and, above all, with Prussian militarism which, it was claimed, had proved to be the sole defender of German culture against the onslaught of Russian barbarism and western materialist 'civilization'. In a declaration of 16 October 1914, signed by various German academics, it was claimed bluntly that the future not only of German, but also of European, culture was at stake in the war. The survival of both depended directly on the fortunes of Germany's armies in the field: 'We believe that the culture of all Europe depends upon the victory that German "militarism" will bring about.'[28]

These declarations were foolish and even naive. Eduard Meyer, for one, confided privately that the official statements on these matters ought not to be taken unreservedly as true without further investigation. Nonetheless, in public he stuck to his previous declarations. The controversy became a launching-pad for a campaign that set out to prove that the war was in effect a cultural war, a war fought in order to preserve German – or more precisely central European – culture against Anglo-Saxon materialism and French formalist rationalism. It was a defensive campaign in its origins, with an underlying universal-historical sentiment that the tide of events was leading relentlessly toward western formal and rational industrial civilization rather than towards German *Gemeinschaft* (or cultural community), as the sociologist Tönnies formulated it. But the argument was often given an aggressive, even imperialist, note as, for instance, in a speech given by Rudolf Borchardt on 5 December 1915, at Heidelberg. 'Culture is a purely German notion', he declared; 'it is not translatable into any other European language. As truly as God lives our victory must finish off this "civilization", this "European civilization", once and for all.'[29]

The climax of this cultural war campaign was reached in 1915. In a small booklet published early that year, the social scientist Johann Plenge coined the catchphrase 'the ideas of 1914' in order to prove that the German political system and the political and cultural traditions associated with it were essentially superior to those of the West. Indeed, the 'ideas of 1914' were supposed to be diametrically opposed to the 'ideas of 1789', that is, to the democratic tradition which originated in the Enlightenment and the French Revolution. The German variety of 'freedom', so it was argued, had nothing in common with the extreme individualism and egalitarianism of the French Revolution. Instead, it was said to represent a happy balance between individual freedom and obedience. Only a political order in which the citizens practised voluntary self-restraint by paying due respect to the authority of the government could flourish and solve the serious social problems that had developed with the rise of industrial society. It was held to be far better suited to mastering the problems of the twentieth century than were individualistic western democracies, which were thought to give too much leeway to individual selfishness. The 'German idea of freedom' was considered to be much more attuned to the German cultural tradition than western democracy. It was felt that English democracy, by contrast, rested upon materialist foundations and gave free reign to the acquisitive instincts of the individual at the expense of the great communal traditions of European culture.

The allegedly 'false' individualism of western democracy, in which egotism and a philosophy of reckless self-enrichment were supposed to be dominant, was contrasted with the so-called genuine individualism of the German political system based upon the voluntary subordination of individuals to the common good. These ideas found their most spectacular expression in Werner Sombart's book *Händler und Helden* ('Heroes and Merchants') also published in 1915. In Sombart's view the German nation represented the Faustian ideal of man who does not care for economic gain or enjoyment but strives instead for the universal unfolding of all his human capabilities, with a corresponding readiness for personal sacrifice. British society was represented by the ideal-type of the 'merchant' who is merely interested in material gain whereas German society was still dominated by 'heroic ideals'. The war, Sombart argued, was being waged in order to defend these German cultural ideals against the encroachment of the narrow-minded mercantile mentality of the English. He did not hesitate to express this message in exceedingly crude terms. 'This war will bring the heroic view of the world to its high point of historical realization. It is absolutely necessary to protect it from falling prey to the powers of evil, to the meanness of the merchant.'[30]

Admittedly, Sombart's book was above all a piece of war propaganda, with huge exaggerations and excessive generalizations. But more fundamental issues were at stake. Sombart wished to defend and, more importantly, to legitimize the German path of development toward modernity, while keeping clear of the western parliamentary model because of its supposedly egalitarian consequences. Accordingly, he pointed to the advantages of bureaucratic organization and authoritarian rule by an enlightened class of civil servants in a modern industrial society, especially with regard to social policies. As late as mid-1917 Friedrich Naumann who, unlike the great majority of his contemporaries, had become an adherent of parliamentary government, could still praise the Germans as 'the first great revolution-free people of the organized living-space' which was destined to play a leading role in the reconstruction of post-war Europe and to solve the massive social problems lying ahead.[31]

These ideas, and others like them, which gave Germany a missionary role in the cultural sphere, were based on a quite unrealistic assessment of Germany's real power in the world. Nonetheless, the strand of thinking which fundamentally opposed the intellectual traditions of the Enlightenment and Anglo-Saxon pragmatism ran deep. Max Scheler proclaimed it as one of the essential objectives of the war to overcome the individualistic rationalism of the Enlightenment for good. 'The first and fundamental precondition for a deeper understanding of the cultural values embodied by the state, by the law, and by poetry and religion alike' would have to be, in his opinion, 'the rediscovery of the concept of the objective spirit' vis-à-vis the relativism and subjectivity of Anglo-Saxon utilitarianism.[32] The great traditions of German culture were mobilized in order to underpin a specifically German notion of political domination, with particular attention being given to Goethe, Fichte, Schopenhauer and especially to Nietzsche. They were to provide the ideological justification of German imperialist objectives during the war. Scheler assumed that the conflict would end with a far-reaching reconstruction of Europe under German leadership, both politically and culturally. He envisaged the emergence of a continental bloc directed primarily against the East which would guarantee Germany's intellectual world leadership for a long time to come and create, in the footsteps of classical Mediterranean culture, a new and even grander culture of Teutonic and Roman spirituality which would be politically supported and defended against potential rivals by Germany and Austria.[33] All this was tantamount to suggesting that a cultural 'Mitteleuropa' should parallel the political and economic 'Mitteleuropa' which the central powers sought to bring about.

An influential minority of academics and writers strongly objected to this sort of nationalist rhetoric which sought to eradicate all western political ideas from German intellectual discourse and insulate it against the supposedly pernicious influence of the Enlightenment and the French Revolution. Ernst Troeltsch and Friedrich Meinecke among historians and Max Weber and Leopold von Wiese among social scientists objected to the ideological message of the 'ideas of 1914'. Ernst Troeltsch in particular tried hard to convince his readers that German culture did not stand in sharp contrast to Anglo-Saxon culture and must not be seen to be so, but was rather part of a common European heritage by no means disrupted by the war. Yet his pleas had little effect. Max Weber was adamant that the *Literatenideen* of 1914 were absurd but he was concerned at their destructive impact on German political culture. In his view they served only one objective, that of perpetuating the current state of affairs in Germany in which irresponsible government by bureaucrats failed to fulfil its duties to the nation and to history.

The argument that the existing semi-constitutional system was ideally adapted to the traditions of German culture received additional support from the literary profession. Romain Rolland's famous 'Open Letter' addressed to Gerhart Hauptmann and Thomas Mann appealing to the German cultural elites to dissociate themselves from the Prussian authoritarian system and from the spirit of militarism and imperialism embodied in the German war machine, produced the opposite effect to the one intended. Likewise Hermann Hesse's and Heinrich Mann's attempts to win the German intellectual elite to a more discretionary position on the war and to keeping aloof from nationalist propaganda had little effect. Instead they induced Thomas Mann to argue all over again that the war was being fought to defend German 'culture' (or the intellectual tradition symbolized by Fichte, Schopenhauer, Hegel, Wagner and Nietzsche) against the stupefying consequences of the supposedly shallow ideas of western 'civilization', in respect of what was considered to be French egalitarian rationalism. Mann's *Betrachtungen eines Unpolitischen* ('Reflections of an Unpolitical Man'), published early in 1919 in the hour of German defeat but written during the war, are a telling example of this trend of German social-conservative thought. Similar views were dominant in intellectual circles whereas the alternative views of the moderate left did not get very far.

By the fall of 1916, however, a gradual shift of opinion was perceptible among the German intelligentsia, and even more among artists and writers. The initial assumption that the war would revitalize cultural activities had been proved wrong and, if anything, the opposite was true. Furthermore the reality of warfare did not match the grand ideals which the intelligentsia had invested in it. Rather the war appeared to have gone completely off course and to have lost whatever rationality it may have had. The intellectual debate had become more acrimonious. Many scholars and writers were beginning to have second thoughts about the conduct of the war and its likely consequences. The battlecry that German culture in its unique character must be defended against Anglo-Saxon materialist pragmatism and French soulless rationalism did not disappear. But the debate was somewhat toned down and it lost the self-righteousness that had prevailed during the first years of the war. The moderates who argued that the international dimensions of cultural life must not be completely sacrificed on the altar of war now gained a hearing. Late in 1916, Walter Goetz admonished his audience: 'No people can hope to impose its national culture on others. The nation is always the foundation of culture, but only its international features may have an impact upon the rest of the world. Because German culture is so rich in international elements, it is capable of spreading its ideas to the world. Why should we now reduce its range with violent means when the chances of extending its sway abroad are improving by the day?'[34] Goetz chose to turn the nationalist argument, which emphasized the uniqueness of German culture, on its head. In this way he tried to justify a more balanced evaluation of German culture which in due course, and in conjunction with a negotiated peace, might make reconciliation between the various national cultures once again conceivable.

Up to mid-1916, literary or artistic journals voicing moderate or even pacifist views had a very difficult time. They fought continuously for survival, not only financially but also politically against the permanent danger of reprisals by the censorship authorities. It was not possible to attack the war and war policies directly, or even indirectly to challenge mainstream public opinion on the issue of culture and the war. Heinrich Mann was forced to discontinue the serial publication of his famous trilogy on 'imperial Germany' in which he had been attacking Wilhelmine society tooth and nail in the tradition of French naturalist writers. In the field of art it was only Franz Pfempfert's *Die Aktion* which, in spite of constant trouble with the censors and repeated suppression, had been consistently taking a pacifist course. Here Ludwig Meidner published many of his exceedingly critical drawings in which he depicted the war as an apocalyptic event with dehumanizing effects. Man was shown to be helplessly exposed to the destructive violence of war, which was itself portrayed as a sort of cosmic force. Likewise René Schickele managed to keep the *Weiße Blätter* afloat, although its anti-war campaign was conducted indirectly rather than openly.

After October 1916, with the relaxation of official censorship, it was no longer possible to suppress pacifist and anti-war views to the same extent as before. By and large, the cultural community now split apart into various factions. The extreme right wing among the intellectual elites was still strong, and in 1917 it received additional support from the newly founded Vaterlandspartei. But on the whole, it was in retreat. In May 1917 the publisher Eugen Diederichs attempted to rally the representatives of cultural life once again around a national programme. He arranged a series of conferences at Lauenstein castle in Thuringia in conjunction with the Dürerbund, the Comenius-Gesellschaft and the Vaterländische Gesellschaft für Thüringen. Things came to a head at the second of these conferences, which took place on 30 May and 1 June 1917. About sixty well-known figures from various sections of the German cultural community, among them Richard Dehmel, Max Maurenbrecher, Max and Alfred Weber, Friedrich Meinecke and the young Theodor Heuß, assembled at Lauenstein for two days of intensive talks. By now, it was agreed that the 'ideas of 1914' would no longer suffice as the sole basis of a new cultural consensus that might provide the backbone for a new German identity. Once again, the alleged superiority of Germanness over the western notion of 'civilization' was invoked, along with the German tradition of a strong state as the core of a well-ordered community in contrast to western materialist individualism. But this time, these arguments no longer passed without strong opposition. The 'new Germandom' to be created by the cultural elite and then extended to the people at large, so Diederichs fervently hoped, would instil a new sense of purpose in the German nation and restore the people's morale. Yet this message never got off the ground. Instead, the attempt to invoke it brought the deep cultural and intellectual divisions fully into the open. Diederichs arranged yet another Lauenstein conference in the spring of 1918, but it no longer had an appreciable impact upon the German cultural scene. Such well-intentioned but inept efforts could not preserve the German cultural elite, however superficial its unity at the beginning of the war, from further tearing itself apart.[35]

This diversification of views was strongest in the visual arts. Most of those artists who initially had taken a positive, or at any rate a neutral, position on the war now became increasingly critical. Many retreated into private life and, if serving in the army, sought wherever possible to leave it. Paul Cassirer discontinued the journal *Kriegszeit* and instead published a new, far more critical art journal, *Der Bildermann*. Its critical treatment of war issues incensed the authorities, and eventually they prevented its further publication. Indeed, in the fall of 1916, a circle of writers and artists with decidedly liberal and radical views gathered around Herward Walden and Paul Cassirer. It became the core of artistic opposition to the continuation of the war. Some artists and writers now avoided themes related to the war altogether, at least in any direct sense, such as Schmidt-Rottluff or Rainer Maria Rilke. Others depicted the war and its suffering in a far more drastic manner, and sometimes openly criticized military combat as devoid of any meaning whatsoever. Oskar Kokoschka is a case in point. His drawing, *Soldiers fighting each other with crucifixes* (*Soldaten, sich mit Kruzifixen bekämpfend,* 1917), symbolized the view that by now the war had become utterly meaningless, and even grotesque.[36]

A far more radical line was pursued by the group of artists who founded Dada early in 1916. Their work at first sight showed no direct relationship to the bloody events around them. But Dadaism was born out of radical opposition to the war and it was meant to challenge the very foundations of the society which (in this view) had made the war – and, indeed, all wars and violence – possible and even inevitable. In retrospect, Hans Arp, one of the leading Dadaists, confirmed that the driving motive of the group had been their dismay at the 'mass slaughter of the First World War'. He defined the artistic objectives of Dada as follows: 'We looked for an elementary art which might cure man from the craziness of the age, and searched for a new order of things which would restore the balance between heaven and hell.'[37] Hugo Ball's *Death Dance*, smuggled into Germany and illegally circulated there, was the most effective single war critique of this sort.

In its early stages Dadaism had only a limited impact upon the artistic scene in imperial Germany. Very few artists were prepared to follow Dada's radical path which sought to create an entirely new art form, declaring all previous artistic production to be arbitrary and therefore meaningless – just as meaningless as social reality itself. The Dadaist position could well be described as aesthetic anarchism. Yet its message encouraged other artists, such as Oskar Kokoschka, Otto Dix and George Grosz, to express their views on war, warfare, destruction and human deprivation in ever more radical ways. Indeed, close though indirect connections developed between Dadaism and Expressionism, in literature and modern music as well as in the visual arts. Arnold Schönberg frequently attended Dadaist meetings at the famous Dadaist Café Voltaire in Zurich, and these visits had a direct impact upon his work.

The shift towards a radical anti-war stance associated with the left was particularly marked among Expressionist writers. The career of Ernest Toller, an Expressionist author of some distinction, was typical of this trend. Initially, Toller had volunteered for military service, motivated by a deeply felt emotional nationalism. In doing so he felt himself united with his fellow countrymen in the service of the fatherland. His military service was distinguished and he was dismissed in 1916 because of physical disability due to war injuries. But by then, Toller had become totally disillusioned with the war. He found a new allegiance in socialism, though his socialism had little in common with the Marxist message. It was largely based on an emotional devotion to the common people who were undergoing unimaginable suffering, whether in the trenches or toiling to utter exhaustion in the armaments factories. Toller's views were, if anything, anarchist rather than socialist though, like others, he joined the Independent Socialists. He believed that only a socialist upheaval could put an end to the senseless bloodshed and utter destruction of the war. Significantly, at Lauenstein, Ernst Toller passionately attacked not only the representatives of the right but also moderates like Max Weber who pleaded for 'Durchhalten' (staying the course). In Toller's opinion this was wrong on both factual and moral grounds. The war had speedily to be brought to an end, and by a socialist revolution if need be.

By 1917, the cultural community was more divided over the war effort than ever. Whereas a substantial group of writers and intellectuals, the most prominent among them being Thomas Mann, essentially maintained their positive attitude toward the national war effort on the assumption that the survival of German culture, as they saw it, was at stake, the bulk of artists and writers drifted increasingly towards criticism of the war and of German war policy. Before the First World War, the avant-garde had by and large been critical of bourgeois materialist culture and emergent industrialism. Now their views hardened into a socialist perspective which was nonetheless not identical with social democracy, let alone with the Independent Socialists or the Spartacists. Many younger Expressionist writers, like Walter Hasenclever, Georg Kaiser, and Reinhard Goering, now embraced the idea of socialism as an alternative to the slaughter which they saw around them. These views only superficially matched the ideologies of the political left. Their notions of socialism had strong humanitarian, pacifist and even anarchist connotations and they chose the working-class movement largely because it seemed the only plausible way to bring the bloodshed to an end. Their great vision was the birth of a new human being and a peaceful world which would supplant the butchery of war. Kaiser's play, The Citizens of Calais, which was performed in Frankfurt late in 1917 for the first (and during the war the only) time, sought to demystify the war. Its message culminated in the emergence of a society in which everybody refrained from the use of violence.

Most of the Expressionist authors, however, were themselves in two minds as to whether such a state of affairs could ever be brought about.

For the majority of them, like Reinhard Goering or Berthold Brecht, a socialist revolution would not necessarily result in a society free of violence. Their pessimistic world view induced them to seek redemption in the privacy of a secluded personal life. The first version of Brecht's *Drums in the Night* ends with the hero's retreat from participation in the revolutionary struggle into the intimacy of the erotic relationship with his former girlfriend, even though she, as Brecht put it, had not remained 'undamaged' during the war years. Even so, the impact of revolutionary ideas was substantial. It is indicated by the development of Käthe Kollwitz's views about the war. She had been greatly impressed by the October Revolution in Russia and while she was never associated with socialism in any concrete sense, she became a convinced opponent of the war and a determined pacifist. Even so, the dominant theme of her work remained remembrance and bereavement rather than a direct critique of war and its endless bloodshed.

In a way, this was true of the artists in general. Only a few of them, like George Grosz, became outright opponents of the war in retrospect. Beckmann concentrated on religious themes, notably his famous *Resurrection*. It contained an apocalyptic message: a black sun symbolized the fact that the world had been turned upside down and that its end might be approaching.[38] It is significant that Beckmann was never able to finish this work, in which all his war experience found sublime expression. Others, like Oskar Kokoschka, pleaded for a retreat into the artistic sphere: 'Please bring the war to an end', he remarked, 'I wish to work.'[39] Yet it would be wrong to backdate the pacifist convictions that dominated the work of many of the Expressionist artists in the 1920s to their work during the war. In reality, few of them actively opposed the war. At the time it was seen as a superhuman cataclysm about which nothing could be done and which had to be endured and mastered by aesthetic means.

The initial expectation that the war might revitalize German culture and heal the sharp divisions among the cultural and intellectual elites turned out to be a chimera. Instead, the rifts within the German cultural community widened at accelerated speed as the end of the war approached. Indeed, the bitter infighting between the different camps in the 1920s which eventually sealed the fate of the Weimar Republic originated in the artistic and intellectual divisions of the war. The right considered the defeat of the central powers a severe setback for German culture, as Thomas Mann's diary indicates. Mann feared that with the imposition of western democracy upon Germany by the victorious powers (which he believed to be imminent), the German culture which he associated with the great names of Goethe, Nietzsche, Luther and

Frederick the Great could not long survive.[40] He felt that the specificity of German culture could only have grown within a social order in which the cultural elites were freed from the necessity of paying attention to political affairs. These views received additional support from the new-Germany ideologists who had been gathering under the aegis of Eugen Diederichs' publishing house. By 1918, the message of the 'New Conservatism' was ready. Oswald Spengler emerged as one of its mouth-pieces and the George Circle was its secret intellectual power-base.

The avant-garde, on the other hand, felt at home in the new democratic republic, only to find that it came under immediate attack from the right and from substantial sections of the bourgeois classes. The old charge that their work was 'un-German' and 'degenerate art' was thrown at them once again. Eventually, the National Socialists were able to exploit these rifts within the German cultural community to their own political advantage, by pandering to the aesthetic taste of the petty-bourgeoisie and by fostering a new style in architecture and the visual arts which pretended to revitalize the grandeur of imperial Germany. The 'Conservative Revolution' and the artistic avant-garde were thrown to the wolves. They were not allowed to continue their work, let alone show it to the public in the new German Reich. They survived largely thanks to the interest and assistance of the West, where most of these artists and writers had to emigrate in order to maintain their artistic identity.

3 Children and the primary schools of France, 1914–1918

Stéphane Audoin-Rouzeau

From 1914 to 1918, the concept of a 'war for children' was continuously preached by the adult world. Presented to children as a war to protect their safety, the conflict was also portrayed as a war to build the future – their future. In such circumstances, the pressure exerted on children from the outset was extremely heavy.

Schools as a mobilizing force

These adult demands on childhood during the war were particularly evident in the world of education. In effect, the war added an additional burden to the classic aims of the school system and reinforced the traditional mechanisms for imposing responsibility on childhood. The soldier's duty on the battlefield was a beacon of inspiration that was referred to regularly and constantly emphasized in defining the duty to work in the classroom. The traditional demands of the republican schoolroom drew fresh moral sustenance from the war. At the beginning of the new school year in September 1914, the headmaster of a Paris school wrote a brief injunction in his pupils' notebooks which, significantly, linked schoolwork and patriotic duty. 'At this time each of us must perform his duty to the utmost. The duty of schoolchildren is to be obedient, hardworking, to prepare a sound future for themselves . . . This is how they can serve the nation for which their elders are fighting with such heroism.'[1] The teachers' professional journal, the *Revue de l'enseignement primaire*, compared schoolwork even more straightforwardly to action on the battlefield: 'To work, young friends! – or rather, to battle, for you too are already engaged in the struggle.'[2] One school inspector found a striking phrase in 1915, as he urged: 'Come on, children, your weapon is your penholder.'[3]

Directly in the tradition of civic instruction that had been central to French state primary school education since the 1880s, numerous directives delivered the same message and established a comparable role for education in wartime. Jean Guirbal wrote in the introduction to his school textbook, *La Grande Guerre en compositions françaises* ('The Great War in French Composition'): 'Now more than ever, children in our schools must be associated with the depth of thinking and the great nature of action at the present time and, more than ever, every intellectual effort which is asked of them must therefore be concerned to *exalt patriotic feeling*.'[4] The military dimension of education was nothing new. In the 1880s, there had been the *bataillons scolaires* (military training formations attached to schools), which were replaced at the end of the century by clubs for physical education and military preparation, and also by the school shooting groups which proliferated down to 1914.[5] The 'little friendship associations' created in state primary schools from the 1890s at the instigation of the Ligue de l'Enseignement Primaire, and initially intended to provide leisure activity as well as civic and moral instruction, had acquired a marked paramilitary connotation by the time war broke out, particularly in Paris.[6] The republican tradition dated back to the revolutionary Convention which in October 1793 prescribed 'military exercises' for children, and by its decree of 17 November of the same year emphasized military-style physical exercises in school. In 1794, the Convention formed 'youth battalions' and created the Ecole de Mars in Paris (this last being intended for sixteen to eighteen year olds rather than children in the true sense).[7]

Essentially, the war of 1914 followed this Jacobin tradition. Once more it was a matter of making use of the war to *transform* the children of the war period into a generation of outstanding adults, by 'exalting in our children, for the benefit of current events, courage, boldness, the spirit of sacrifice, by working at turning them into manly beings'.[8] This was what a teacher at the front demanded of his former pupils when he urged them to 'continue . . . the task begun by your elders, the task for which so many brave men die every day'.[9] Preparation for future military service was in fact one of the central tasks assigned to children in wartime. For the beginning of the school year in October 1914 the Minister for Public Instruction, Albert Sarraut, requested head teachers that they should 'quickly organize the recruitment of purposeful and intelligent individuals among the younger generation who will immediately begin to fill the gaps in the ranks of the sons of the victorious nation'.[10]

Teaching war

The demands and expectations which the adults' war imposed on children resulted in a specific 'war culture' within the schools whose central objective was morally and intellectually to mobilize childhood.

The Ministry of Public Instruction was quick to formulate the revised orientation of republican teaching in wartime. By 7 August 1914 a circular from Albert Sarraut to school inspectors, chiefly concerned with support for children deprived of tutelage when the head of the family was summoned to the army, concluded with the need to provide day facilities for the most advanced pupils in holiday periods with readings 'designed to make children understand present events and to encourage the patriotic beliefs in their hearts'.[11] A circular followed quickly at the beginning of the school year. Although drawn up in the context of a war which it was still hoped on all sides would be short, it sketched out the broad lines of a 'war education' by telling schools of their new obligations. These primarily consisted of creating a unique start to the school year, which was transformed into a commemorative ceremony for the numerous soldiers already killed in battle:

It is my wish that on the opening day of the school term, in every town and in every class, the teacher's very first words should raise up all hearts to the nation, and that the very first lesson should honour the sacred struggle in which our forces are engaged. Throughout the land, all at the same moment, France's sons will venerate the spirit of their nation and will salute the heroism of those who are pouring out their blood for liberty, for justice, for human rights. The lesson will be simple and powerful. It must be suited to the age of its listeners, some of them children and others adolescents. Every one of our schools has sent soldiers into the line of fire – teachers or pupils – and every one, I know well, already bears the proud grief of its deaths: the words of the teacher within the classroom will evoke first and foremost the honoured memory of these dead men, to praise their example and to engrave it in the minds of the children.

Once homage had been paid, it was a matter of teaching the war and giving it meaning. This meaning was to persist virtually unchanged until 1918: 'Next, in broad lines, soberly and clearly, [the lesson] will explain the causes of the war, the groundless attack which unleashed it and how, before the civilized world, France, the eternal champion of progress and of right, has had to stand up once more, with her brave allies, to repulse the barbarians' assault.' With the significance of the war thus described – a war for civilization, of worldwide dimensions, combined with a superior concept of humanity – the Minister sketched out the beginnings of the educational orientation of wartime teaching. 'Every day in this ferocious struggle which is leading us inexorably towards victory adds a thousand heroic deeds to the glory of our soldiers, and provides the schoolmaster with the best part of his instruction. Rather than the empty emphasis of words he will stir young emotions with these supreme models of action.' With this proposal to give full credit to examples of heroism in the front line, Albert Sarraut established the first targets of an educational process which was to make the war – or, more precisely, the tales of the war available in the press – the bedrock of teaching. Further, this was not limited to the period of war itself, which was still expected to be short, but was to assist in the long-term strengthening of the patriotic basis of the nation. Sarraut concluded that: 'From this very first classroom period, a powerful memory must be indelibly imprinted on the mind of the pupil, tomorrow's citizen. The teacher who has achieved this will be worthy of the Republic's full confidence.'[12]

The educational policies which the national government adopted promptly in 1914 were strengthened for the start of the school year in September 1915. The demand now was for teaching directed in depth towards the events of the day and built around them. This amounted to nothing less than a full-scale revolution of the content and methods of learning adopted by teachers, particularly those in charge of the four and a half million pupils in public primary schools. The Minister announced:

If there is one teacher whose existence I cannot for a moment imagine, it would be the Frenchman in our schools who ignores the war, who could carry on his life with the same school registers, the same exercise books, the same lessons and the same homework, and who would merely address his pupils, in these crucial hours, in the same words as before.[13]

Ministerial messages for these first two new school years of the war merely suggested a generalized outline of how to incorporate the war into the teaching programme. Nonetheless, they illustrate the direction taken by the Republic's schools at the outbreak of war, in which the conflict was used as the foundation of an ethos that aimed at a complete change in both the content and methods of teaching. The ministry, moreover, was not content merely to give a few broad indications. Circulars, always extremely precise in their prescriptions, initiated the pattern of 'patriotic days' in schools: for 1915 alone, four such documents were drawn up to ensure the success of the 'Day of the 75' (or French light field gun, on 23 January), the 'Serbian Day' (6 March), the 'Day for War Victims' (2 October), and the 'National Defence Loan Day' (13 November).[14] Events of major significance also became a focus for educational initiatives imposed on the schools.

This activity at the highest levels of the public education system had powerful results. The inspectors were the true keystone in the development of wartime teaching and their demanding and critical reports illustrate their decisive role in the educational direction imposed on all teachers. Proof of this comes from the irritation – fairly unusual – of an inspector in the department of the Finistère who commented, on finishing his school visits at the end of 1914:

I have said it often enough this time, I think, for everyone to understand what they should be concerned with, for everyone to understand his duty. This duty consists of two main obligations. The first, which concerns teaching in all its aspects, is to render the war of 1914 our 'centre of interest'. The second, which concerns certain sections of teaching more closely, such as ethics, history and geography, is to make the provision that it deserves in our planning, our use of time, for the new topic of education which is provided by this war, or rather which [the war] imposes on us. Indeed we must make use of the passionate interest with which our pupils, of all ages, approach the events of the war, and make this serve our education.[15]

This report, which is directly in line with official instructions, is highly revealing. Not only is the war a fresh item on the syllabus, it now lies at the very heart of *all* teaching. From now on, teaching is expected to proceed directly from current events. Subjects suggested as examples also leave no room for doubt, with dictation and essay topics such as 'The regiment departs', the 'Letter from an unknown big brother who is fighting for us', 'Arrival of a trainload of wounded men'. The history syllabus was turned into a history of the war; geography proceeded from a map of the theatre of operations designed for daily up-dating; instruction in ethics was based on quotations from soldiers on the orders of the day. It was still a matter of 'teaching the war', of teaching on the basis of the war.[16] Those best qualified for this task were, naturally, none other than wounded teachers who returned to work in their schools. At the beginning of 1917 an inspector used one of them as an example, forcing him to take lessons in his lieutenant's uniform, his leg stretched out on a stool: 'How can one think of educational methods in the face of this admirable sight?' commented the inspector; 'the lessons which he gave in this way will be engraved on the heart of the most heedless schoolchild'.[17]

Although the inspectors' role in providing an orientation and a framework was certainly decisive, it would be quite wrong to assume that the new direction taken by schools from 1914 was only the result of constraints placed on the teaching world. If there was a new direction, it was first and foremost a voluntary one. And yet the world of primary school teachers in the early 1900s had developed some considerable way towards pacifist and socialist-leaning positions – to the point where, before the war, it stood for a patriotism of reason, often complex, ambiguous, but stripped bare of the jingoistic excesses of the 1880s. In 1904, the Ligue de l'Enseignement Primaire (the principal pressure group supporting universal state primary education, which was strongly backed by teachers themselves) renounced its motto, 'For the Nation, by the book and by the sword'. In fact, although only a small minority of the teaching body spoke out in favour of formal pacifism before 1914, it is beyond dispute that the state primary school teachers of the second generation, at the turn of the century, had abandoned all warlike patriotism. By the end of the nineteenth century, 'education was losing its bellicose attitude', writes Antoine Prost, while recalling that it nonetheless remained 'massively patriotic' until 1914.[18] Jacques and Mona Ozouf have also shown that the second wave of republican primary manuals, from the 1890s, saw concepts of nation and war as separate henceforward, rejecting all forms of jingoistic aggression in favour of a 'thoughtful patriotism' and seeing a defensive war as the only just war.[19]

Educational journals, however, held a central place in establishing the 'war school'. The case of the *Revue de l'enseignement primaire et primaire supérieur* is the most significant. Founded in 1890, socialist and pacifist in its orientation (Jean Jaurès, Albert Thomas, Marcel Sembat and also Gustave Hervé were among its principal editors), and violently anti-clerical, it had a circulation of 14,000 on the eve of the war, a substantial figure for a total body of 120,000 state primary school teachers.[20] The *Revue de l'enseignement primaire et primaire supérieur* did not appear again after the outbreak of war until 3 October 1915, and reading it provides a means of measuring the distance covered by teachers' changing attitudes. Although it still maintained a purely theoretical pacifism, and strong opposition to the *bourrage de crâne* (or propaganda 'brain-washing'), it can now be seen to have transformed itself into a patriotic firebrand, its tone sometimes breathless and violently anti-German. Pragmatic, distilling in its 'academic review' section the topics of essays, exercises, school records and practical information, the *Revue* supplied substantial amounts of information, if not on the teaching that actually went on in the classroom (which is virtually impossible to ascertain with certainty), at least on what was *attempted* in terms of 'teaching the war'. The evidence is conclusive: before the end of 1916, when a certain normalization prevailed, the *Revue de l'enseignement primaire* unhesitat-ingly adopted the war as a 'focus of interest' and based its educational section on official instructions which, indeed, it sometimes appeared to exceed.[21]

The new educational tools forged during the war made up another branch of propaganda, this time in direct contact with pupils. The most important school book of the war, remarkably neglected today in view of the fame of its author, was published in 1916 by the author of the *Tour de la France par deux enfants*, G. Bruno (pseudonym of Augustine Fouillée). This was the *Tour de l'Europe pendant la guerre. Livre de lecture courante. Cours moyen,* which remained the school book best able to explain, in its preface, the theoretical and ethical need for teaching the war.[22]

It seemed to us that the gravity of the present moment has created a new obligation towards the children in our schools. No French citizen should be ignorant of the causes of the barbarous war that we are suffering; no French citizen should disregard them. It is never too early for our children to learn about them in school. They must therefore be brought within their grasp as early as possible; we do not think that oral lessons are adequate . . . little remains, 44 years on, of what happened in 1870 . . . If, as our young readers read this little book, they experience the emotions which we felt in writing it, we can be assured that it will leave a deep mark in their hearts: the nation will mean more to them, and their adult life will become the greater for it.[23]

Based on the earlier work, which was first published in 1877 and met with immense success before 1914, the *Tour de l'Europe* places its 'action' in La Grand' Lande, where the *Tour de la France* ended. This time the heroes are not the two little Lorraine children, Julien and André; this role has passed to Jean, son of the former and nephew of the latter. Aged 21 in 1914, the wounded second lieutenant returns home to convalesce, the Military Medal on his chest: this model teacher already has an exemplary military career and is engaged to Josette, herself a future teacher who, but for the war – we are told – would have been a head teacher. The plot of the book consists of a three-week-long dialogue between Jean and the inhabitants of La Grand' Lande, with children appearing as privileged interlocutors.

To school books was added a mass of new educational tools, also linked to current events, such as illustrated slips for mental arithmetic offering encouragement to subscribe to war loans with exercises on the topic; pictures conjugating the verb 'to subscribe' in all its tenses, praising the Allies or indicating the 'Ten Commandments of Victory' ('Think before acting and do not let yourself be fooled by the Boche'); and good marks of a new type blending explanation of the meaning of the war with a call to patriotic subscriptions ('to liberate humanity', 'to liberate Serbia', 'to liberate our compatriots', 'to liberate the oppressed', etc.).[24] Even prize certificates were modified: Delagrave's version published in 1916 shows a soldier surrounded by children of all ages (including two from Alsace), their eyes turned towards a patriotic inscription: 'France is our Nation: *Vive la France'*.[25]

The new educational framework was matched by new topics of study. The general themes of the October–December 1915 issues of the *Revue de l'enseignement primaire*, when it began to appear once more, provide an excellent gauge of the extent to which the war had affected teaching: 'gold', 'the soldier', 'All Saints Day and death', 'fear', 'war far from home', 'the future', 'honesty', 'wartime winter', 'egotism', 'the *poilu*', 'wartime Christmas'. Directly or otherwise, the 'school review' section is almost exclusively focused on the events of the day.

No part of primary education was allowed to escape from this pressure of the present, but 'academic' subjects were the most strongly affected. Thus history was henceforward based entirely on the history of the war. To this end, in 1915 the *Revue de l'enseignement primaire* offered highly detailed analyses of the beginnings of the war, the setbacks on the frontiers, the invasion, the battle of the Marne, the race to the sea, the beginnings of the static trench war. For the end of 1915, the first exercise dealt with the following subject: 'Who wanted the war?' And in 1916 again, virtually all history topics, with supporting details, were related to the current conflict: 'Cities under bombardment – Rheims', 'Serbia and Austria', 'The Russian front', 'Blockade', 'Naval war', 'Communiqués', 'Conquest of the German colonies', etc. History teaching was almost wholly taken up with contemporary history, or systematically connected to it and henceforward dependent on current events. Reading the official communiqué each morning also became the rule in many schools.

Geography, though somewhat less affected, did not escape this general trend. For the year 1915, the *Revue de l'enseignement primaire* offered as topics of study 'the Ardennes', 'Belgium', 'Alsace', 'The Rhine', 'Germania', 'The German people', 'Maritime and colonial Germany', etc., as well as the Danube, the Vistula and Poland, Russia and the Balkans. Geography became the geography of the front (with illustrations, maps of the various combat zones and studies of the actual areas of confrontation), or at the very least turned into the geopolitical study of France's allies and enemies in the war.[26]

Ethics and civic instruction, in their turn, could not ignore the new concerns. In this area, the general inspectorate particularly appreciated timetable alterations which matched the realities of the day while still maintaining a traditional content. 'The child and the family', for example, became 'New duties which the war imposes on children'; 'The child at school' could be turned into 'How the school has prepared men capable of defending it'; 'Duties to oneself' became 'The courage of soldiers in the trenches' and the study of 'The nation' became that of the '*Union sacrée*'.[27] Henceforward, 'the War of 1914–1915 . . . was an ample source of all civic and even moral instruction'.[28] By the end of 1915, the *Revue de l'enseignement primaire* offered this striking topic: 'You have just seen your little brother lying to your mother. You take him aside and say to him: "Do you want to be like the Boches?" Confession of the little boy, who promises always to tell the truth to be worthy of his nation, for Frenchmen never tell lies!'[29]

French, the fundamental subject of the primary school curriculum, was even more profoundly marked by the imprint of war. To judge by the contents of the educational journals, all aspects of its teaching were affected. The topics suggested at the opening of the school year 1915 by the *Revue de l'enseignement primaire* are typical: the preparatory course suggested only a simple lullaby ('You don't yet know that over there your fathers are cold') and two essay subjects unconnected with the war. But from the elementary level, the material to be learned by heart concerned 'the little refugee sister', and the dictation was on 'the mother's courage'. The four essay subjects suggested were as follows: 'The five reasons why you love the little refugee children', the signs by which 'you have seen how brave your mother is since the war began', the way in which a pupil 'will be worthy of the soldier', and 'what you will do in school this year, to show yourself worthy of your soldier father'.[30]

Many more examples could be offered from the vast number available. Even mathematics suffered from the influence of the war. The very serious *Revue pédagogique* had no hesitation in suggesting in 1915 the following exercise: 'A cruiser is chasing a liner. At 10 in the morning, it is 14 kilometres away from it. The cruiser is going at 15 knots and the liner 346 metres per minute. After an hour of pursuit, the cruiser increases its speed by 4 km/h. Find out at what time the cruiser fires its first shell on the liner, assuming that it opens fire at a distance of 1,800 metres.'[31]

It is of course open to question whether teaching of this type was really carried out in the classroom. Methodologically, it is very difficult to break into the privileged world of daily relationships between teacher and pupil between 1914 and 1918 in order to find out. Yet where schoolchildren's exercise books and the teachers' preparation books have survived, they provide a convincing survey, despite their no doubt restricted and haphazard nature, which tends to confirm in general terms the genuine depth of this new, wartime approach to teaching.[32] The extent to which the latter penetrated the classroom was undoubtedly very uneven, and varied according to educational level, age, sex and subject. It was above all the learning of French (writing, dictation, essay writing) which appears to have been most profoundly affected by the war, particularly in boys' classes and at the middle and senior levels.

Inspection of topics in the *certificat d'études* examination shows relative resistance to this type of teaching, despite its growing intensity. But the final session of the war (July 1918) provides another fine harvest of dictations on the men killed in action, the need to endure the difficulties of daily life, children's patriotism, ruined villages, unknown heroes, Alsatians' attachment to France, etc. Essay topics also show at least partial support, until the end of the war, for the new school demands on childhood: 'A soldier on leave. Describe him. Recount his arrival, his visit, his departure'; 'A parcel has been prepared by the pupils of your class, to be sent to a young twenty-year-old soldier who has just received a decoration. You are instructed to announce the despatch of the parcel and to address everyone's congratulations to the young hero'; 'A soldier's tomb. Describe it. Say what passes through your mind. Does it strengthen your determination always to do your duty?'; and 'In a family that you know, a letter is received, after several days of waiting and anxiety, from their son who is fighting in a sector under severe attack. Describe the scene. Say what thoughts it inspires in you.'[33] It is true that the *certificat d'études* examination had a particular, symbolic importance. This explains why, until the very end, it had to be subordinated to the educational directives elaborated at the beginning of the war.

Schools thus attempted to teach the war until the very end; at first, indeed, they wished to teach nothing else. It would appear that at least for the beginning of the war, the following school inspector's opinion in 1915 accurately represented what had happened to schools after the culture shock of August 1914: 'In all our schools the war has certainly become the principal focus of interest; it is more than an echo of the war which has reached into our classrooms, it is a concept of it that is always present, almost an obsession.'[34] And an inquiry into Paris primary schools carried out by Madame Hollebecque was no doubt correct in its observation of the fundamental modification in wartime of the 'status' of schoolchildren: 'The child who until yesterday was deprived of all initiative, is now bidden to action. He is instantly required to know, to judge, and to give his opinion . . . Thus, during the year 1914–1915, the child has acquired a position in society that is never assigned to him in normal times.'[35]

Attrition

Unable to resist turning the war into an everyday matter, propaganda aimed at children nonetheless failed to maintain the initial tension over four and a half years. This relative wearing down of the framework of childhood in wartime was very noticeable in the school setting.[36] Careful examination of the *Revue de l'enseignement primaire* shows, for example, that if the 'presence' of the war remained powerful in the topics suggested, the tone altered significantly after the beginning of the new school year in September 1916, notably with the emergence of a theme hitherto left in the background – paternal absence. By the 1916–17 school year, the link between education and the war was becoming weaker and the war obsession was diminishing in a manner all the more noticeable as the school year neared its end. Among the topics suggested by the journal for this particular school year, only nine (out of a total of thirty-four) were related to the continuing conflict. From 1917 on, the war tended to become a 'side issue' and the journal turned back to wider and more traditional preoccupations. During 1917–18, the wheel turned full circle: the 'focus of interest' selected for the new school year was 'being a pupil' and the war, although not wholly ousted, was reduced to a minor element.[37] Further, the end of the war was not greeted with any fresh surge of patriotism.

Naturally, criticism of school propaganda aimed at children did not wait until the second half of the war before making an appearance. As early as 31 October 1914, the journal *L'Ecole*, which took over from *L'Ecole émancipée*, founded in 1910, and which in September 1915 adopted the title *L'Ecole de la fédération des syndicats d'institutrices et d'instituteurs publics*, adopted in its first issue a tone which was completely at variance with that of the other teachers' professional journals. Even at the outbreak of the conflict, the war and the nation were entirely absent from this far-left journal which was completely impervious to the current cultural climate. Its attitudes represented only a small minority in the educational world. Its first article connected with the war did not appear until 30 January 1915, in its fourteenth issue: once more this was an essay theme on the arrival of a trainload of wounded men, with a suggested plan more concerned with realism than the heroic style. With a few exceptions, the items in the school section of the review superbly ignored the war during 1914–15. For the new school year in September 1915, it openly took the side of Romain Rolland, announced its opposition to the *bourrage de crâne* and refused to evoke the war in the exercises it suggested for pupils. From 1917, the magazine moved from a socialist and relatively moderate pacifism to frankly anti-government attitudes, continuing to ignore the war or offering only negative views that were occasionally censored. The educational school culture was thus not wholly homogeneous.

Investigation of the *content* of the dominant discourse is even more interesting. From 1916, which certainly marked the turning-point, a school inspector corrected certain initial options for teachers in the Basses-Alpes.[38] 'The school must continue to give a proper place to events. However', he continued, 'I think I should warn you against certain dangers: it is important not to neglect the essential lessons in the syllabus, nor to abandon the timetable under the guise of keeping children informed of events relating to the war.' It was no longer a matter of using the war as the basis for all lessons, nor of systematically integrating current events into them, except for major happenings. It was even necessary to 'be on guard against distorting certain subjects, history for example, by systematically denigrating certain enemy nations'. It was also important 'to take care not to upset the feelings of pupils by too-often repeated tales of terrible events'.[39] This development turned away from the initial recommendations, a change very lucidly assessed in 1917 by another general primary inspector:

In the first year of the war there was only one topic in schools relating to the war. The teachers were told, and the teachers repeated, that 'the war must be taught. The war should be the centre of attention from which all lessons radiate outwards.' Since the struggle has lasted for more than two years, a second school of thought has developed which claims attention on the basis of very reasonable arguments . . . a return to normality.[40]

Wisely, the writer argued for a median position which appears to have won the day in most cases.

None the less, teaching in 1918 was very far removed from that of 1914–15. By 1917, moreover, the record of the 'wartime school' drawn up by the enquiry *Nos enfants et la guerre* ('Our Children and the War') was not optimistic: based on questionnaires on the effects of the war on pupils, returned by teachers in twenty-two schools, the survey concluded that 'evil was winning over good'. It added: 'Good elements have doubtless improved, but poorer ones are currently worse, and as numerous.' The survey concluded that there was 'a lowering in the level of children's instruction' connected with material difficulties and also with 'disturbed behaviour'.[41] Education had in fact largely failed in its attempt at intellectual and moral instruction and the 'mobilization' of childhood. Once the exceptional tensions of the beginning of the war were over, the initial plan had to be abandoned. Its most resounding setback – and a highly revealing one – was the matter of the 'school garden plots', launched officially in 1917. The original objective, which initially envisaged 1,500 hectares established through public education institutions and cultivated by school pupils to mitigate the agricultural crisis, was never attained. The *Revue pédagogique*, in its first report drawn up in June 1917 and then in a second in March 1918, observed that in addition to unforeseen material difficulties, a long list of factors – abandonment by pupils, parental irritation at a project suspected of depriving children of education, jeers from the peasant population, and the refusal of more than half the country's communes to offer any support at all – had made the operation a total failure.[42]

Structuring childhood in wartime came up against a major contradiction, both social and cultural, that was impossible to resolve. To succeed, it required the mesh of the net that surrounded the world of childhood in normal times to be drawn tighter.[43] However, the circumstances of total war made large snags in this net and weakened, instead of strengthening, the traditional socializing structures of childhood. Each of the manifold demands of the war (school buildings requisitioned, absence of teachers, the need to keep children at home more often for farm work, urban work attracting children from the age of twelve through a tight labour market, the return on leave of members of the family, etc.) represented an obstacle to the efforts of republican education, the very force which since the 1880s had been concerned with regularity of school attendance. From the outbreak of the war, and increasingly so towards the end of the war as material conditions deteriorated, school inspectors sounded the alarm. The situation was obviously particularly serious in the areas that were directly exposed behind the front line, as in Rheims where, in a heroic gesture, classes took place in cellars during bombardments before the children had eventually to be evacuated, or in Nancy, also shelled in 1917. The Somme once again offers a typical example. The school year 1914–15 was less disturbed than might have been expected, despite the disruption occasioned by fighting and the arrival of vast numbers of troops; absenteeism was not spectacularly high in comparison with pre-war levels, to the rather surprised satisfaction of the school authorities. But matters deteriorated during the following school years, with increasing labour shortages. The reasons most frequently indicated for absence from school at the beginning of 1916 were connected with the need to keep children at home for farm work, often from the age of nine or ten. From 1916 to 1917 other factors were added: the shelling of Amiens, the use of children to collect family food and heating supplies or to look after brothers and sisters. Children also took up small-scale trade with the constant flow of passing troops; and finally mourning, as well as the arrival of fathers or brothers on leave, took up a large number of school days, even though work in the fields remained the chief cause of absence. The educational determination of the teachers was no doubt largely responsible for preventing the complete collapse of the school system; in the Somme, school attendance for the year 1916–17 was recorded as nil, bad or poor for 75 schools for which records are available, fairly good for 51, and good or very good for 103. The year 1917–18, the time of the final enemy offensives, was much worse, to the extent of eliminating all statistics.[44] Absenteeism in the Seine-et-Oise, which had run at 13 per cent in 1913–14, exceeded 25 per cent during the war and even 50 per cent in some institutions.[45]

Additional sources of educational disruption, particularly significant in areas behind the front line, were also relevant, albeit to a lesser extent. On 1 October 1917 a ministerial circular noted that 'the application of our pupils has never been so seriously affected', though it had no proposals for improving matters.[46] While the facts and the causes of the phenomenon remain difficult to assess with precision, it appears that an increase in juvenile delinquency was a clear sign of the social breakdown provoked by the war.[47] Circulars from the Ministry of Public Instruction were reduced to urging the repression of 'vagrancy among children of school age' and to recommending their return to school by the police.[48]

Overall, there seems little doubt that the youngest citizens, whom the Republic's primary schools had sought so strenuously to mobilize, had increased rather than diminished their independence with the help of the war. Here lies the heart of the paradox. The school system wished to mobilize childhood intellectually and morally just as children were moving to a significant degree beyond its reach.

4 War, 'national education' and the Italian primary school, 1915–1918

Andrea Fava

The historical context

The question of the role played by Italian primary schools and their teachers in the mobilization of Italian society during the Great War involves two important contextual questions. The first is that of the relationship between the war and fascism and hence of the war's place in longer-term Italian history, a question that has been the subject of lively historical debate (continuity versus rupture, turning-point versus acceleration, etc.).[1] Certainly, the fact that wartime mobilization was quickly followed by the fascist takeover of the Italian political system cannot be ignored, though neither can it be assumed that the connection is purely chronological. The wartime history of primary schooling has failed so far to arouse the interest of education historians.[2] Yet poised mid-way between the institution of 'primary education for the people' by the liberal state in 1911 and the fascist proclamation of the 'nationalization' of primary schools in November 1923, the wartime experience of the school system poses with exceptional clarity the question of whether the war should be seen as rupture or continuity.[3]

The war undoubtedly provoked a crisis in the primary system. It drastically reduced financial resources, both as a result of the general tightening of wartime budgets and through the cancellation of the special funds earmarked for primary education in 1911. In 1917, only 1.2 per cent of the entire state budget was allocated to education and culture, the lowest level since Italian unification.[4] Yet this material impoverishment occurred at just the moment when the school system was undergoing a major readjustment in the content of the curriculum and in teaching methods. Primary schooling was irreversibly orientated towards the promotion of national values under the impetus of a war effort which demanded moral resistance from the home front. The schools were harnessed to this resistance by the introduction of an improvised but widespread system of 'war education' with a new, 'patriotic' representation of childhood. Since the government proved unwilling to coordinate in any coherent way the enrolment of the schools in the national effort, the responsibility for achieving this fell largely to the primary school teachers themselves and to their professional associations.

This raises the second important contextual question – that of the process of civilian mobilization during the First World War. Was the mobilization of society behind the national war effort directed by the government and state apparatus from above, or was it based on voluntary activity 'from below' and on the spontaneous adoption of national ideals by substantial segments of the population? There was, doubtless, a complex interchange between these two levels of mobilization, which were far from mutually exclusive.[5] This was especially likely to be so since voluntary 'self-mobilization' operated through a framework of inducements and restrictions determined by the state and because the state enjoyed abnormal power in wartime to select and promote various agencies in civil society. In the Italian case, which has been characterized by contemporary accusations and historical controversy over the interventionist ruling class's alleged inability to organize effective mass war propaganda, it might be suggested that the state sought to resolve the thorny problem of a weak and contested consensus on intervention in the war by discreetly promoting the 'self-mobilization' of patriotic energies on the home front.[6] The educational system provides an ideal field for testing such a hypothesis about the process of mobilizing Italian society for the Great War, especially through an analysis of the role of the teachers' professional bodies and the tasks which the school was expected to perform.

Wartime teachers' organizations

Italian teachers, especially those in the primary school system, were professionally well organized by the outbreak of the war, and their diverse associations and connections with the world of politics provided one of the key connections between state and voluntary mobilization during the conflict. An important manifestation of this linkage was the attribution of ministerial roles in the field of propaganda to politicians such as Senator Vittorio Scialoja and Deputy Ubaldo Comandini. Both men derived part of their wartime political influence from their contacts with the primary school teachers' associations – notably the Unione Generale degli Insegnanti Italiani per la Guerra Nazionale (UGII – General Union of Italian Teachers for the National War), the Unione Magistrale Nazionale (UMN – National Teachers' Union) and the Opere Federate di Assistenza e Propaganda Nazionale (Federated

Society for Assistance and National Propaganda) – as well as from their influence with the educational bureaucracy.[7] This connection is significant in its own right, since the primary school system played an important part when the lengthening of the war compelled the government to introduce new emergency functions on the home front in 1916. But it also sheds light on the typically didactic approach of home front propaganda in wartime Italy. The primary school system came to be seen as vital in helping the whole population to pass the supreme historical test that trial by combat was held to constitute for the fatherland. Nor was this role restricted to the aims and needs of war; it was extended to overcoming the 'backwardness' of Italian consciousness and forging national identity.

In effect, the various primary school teachers' organizations mediated and filtered government actions and transmitted directives from above while seeming to act as spontaneous associations. Their very existence suggested an exemplary readiness for self-mobilization by schools and school teachers whose innate patriotism they seemed to demonstrate. In fact, research in the archives of the Ministry of Public Instruction on the mobilization of teachers and the penetration of patriotic propaganda into the daily life of the primary school suggests that reality lagged a long way behind appearance, as portrayed by the UGII, the UMN and the Federated Society. Yet it would be a serious mistake, when judging their autonomy and spontaneity, to consider these school teachers' associations as simple, private bodies, for this they only in part were.[8]

The UGII was born in the spring of 1915 out of a proposal that had originated within an elite body of professional educators, the National Association of University Teachers.[9] On the basis of a moderate programme of civilian preparation for war, all the associations connected with education, from university to nursery school, very soon joined the new organization, with Senator Scialoja becoming president on the eve of Italy's entry into the war. The decision to create this overarching teachers' association was part of a broader process instigated by prominent local personalities in the liberal ruling class in the winter and spring of 1915 which led to the setting-up of Committees for Civil Preparation in about thirty Italian cities (beginning with Milan, Padua, Bologna and Turin).[10] These aimed to equip the country for its eventual participation in the European conflict by harnessing the self-discipline and voluntary organization of the citizens, thereby increasing the freedom of action of the central state.

With intervention, these model organizations fed into the larger movement of Committees for Civilian Assistance, set up and promoted by the government in every municipality. On 29 May 1915, five days after the Italian declaration of war on Austria-Hungary, Prime Minister Salandra made a stirring call to parliament and the country as a whole to carry out 'the *leva in massa* [*levée en masse*] of national charity', and it was in line with this that the UGII defined its wartime aims.[11] In essence this meant harnessing the strengths of the schools so that they would be ready to provide voluntary wartime social assistance (starting with the children and families of soldiers), whether directly through school associations or through the individual participation of teachers in the Civilian Committees for Social Assistance. It also entailed keeping an eye on the 'civilian army of teachers' and bringing the latter into line with government directives, while supplying illustrated material on the 'the reasons and ideals of the war' and coordinating the professional activities of teachers.

By the end of 1917, the UGII numbered more than 6,000 branches and by the last year of the war it had become one of the main producers of propaganda material.[12] It showed that it could expand by attracting voluntary, qualified members but its swelling enrolment also benefited on several occasions from the indirect pressure of the Ministry of Public Instruction. The value of its programme and its initiatives was praised in various ministerial circulars (notably those of 1 July 1915, 13 April 1916, 31 December 1917 and 15 January 1918). Peripheral school authorities were encouraged to make use of its activities and to support its expansion by bringing it to the attention of staff as a model to be emulated. December 1916 also saw the granting of its request to have published in the Ministry's *Bollettino Ufficiale* lists of teachers who had distinguished themselves in coming to the aid of the wartime needy. This enabled a large number of those on the teaching and administrative staff of primary schools (well over 10,000) to see themselves singled out by their superiors for their patriotic qualities and for their extensive contribution to the wartime social institutions (nursery schools, recreational facilities, childminding, summer camps) which helped minister to the 'tender children of the warriors'.[13]

Additionally, a government decree of February 1917 granted the UGII the legal status of a 'moral entity', thus enabling it to be included by law the following July among the four national societies officially designated to care for war orphans.[14] During the course of the school year 1917–18, moreover, the UGII was given the task of organizing a special course of 'war lessons' which, according to a ministerial decree of 31 December 1917, was to be carried out regularly in all secondary schools and to consist of a series of weekly conferences known as the 'patriotic hour'. Finally, the fact that from June 1916, the president of the UGII also held the position of minister without portfolio in Boselli's cabinet and that in the following November he took on the task of coordinating war propaganda both at home and abroad, demonstrates how difficult it is to draw a clear line between state and civil agencies in the educational sphere.[15]

The UMN (National Teachers' Union) was a very different story. This was the most important association of primary school teachers and had already been in existence for a number of years.[16] It had some of the features of a trade union in terms of dealing with the training and conditions of teachers as well as pursuing the expansion and democratic reform of primary education. In 1915 its president was the socialist deputy Giuseppe Soglia, who, after Italy's entry into the war, seized the opportunity to set aside trade union battles in order to ensure that the teaching body provided a strong 'philanthropic' commitment to the children as well as material and moral assistance to the soldiers and the civilian population. The UMN as a body also joined the UGII. But from the autumn of 1915 it came under violent attack from the nationalist and interventionist press, with Soglia increasingly accused of 'defeatism', leading to his resignation and the calling of an extraordinary general meeting.

The upshot of this internal crisis of the UMN in April 1916 was the return in an unopposed election of the former president, the republican deputy Comandini. To the world at large, this move seemed to guarantee a balanced administration of the union and the preservation of continuity with its pre-war politics. Appearances notwithstanding, however, the outcome of the crisis in the UMN in fact expressed the unequivocal position adopted by Italian school teachers in matters of nationalism and patriotism as a consequence of the war. This reality was underlined by the 'chauvinistic' backing which Comandini's candidacy received from senior figures in Italian freemasonry. In a letter to Comandini of 9 March 1916, the Grand Master of Italian freemasons, Ettore Ferrari, underlined the importance of ensuring for the UMN 'a presidency which would lead and impel Italian school teachers, condemn the direction taken by the outgoing leadership, and affirm their patriotic and interventionist sentiments'.[17] Two months later, Comandini, like Scialoja of the UGII, entered the Boselli government as a minister without portfolio – in charge of coordinating the task of civilian wartime assistance. The parallel activities that the two teachers' leaders were therefore able to carry out in government, even though they occupied irregular and precarious posts by normal standards, inevitably influenced the teaching body as a whole.

It should be added that in July 1917, when the UGII strengthened its authority by assuming the legal role of protecting war orphans, Minister

Comandini expanded his own powers by taking over responsibility for home front propaganda from Scialoja. This balanced exchange of tasks between the UGII and the UMN was underpinned by a new 'spontaneous' grouping of patriotic associations in the summer of 1917, in the form of the Federated Society for Assistance and National Propaganda. Its very title suggests the essential function of this body which, until its disbanding in spring 1919, became the main instrument for coordinating civilian mobilization and internal propaganda. Comandini remained its president throughout. The UGII belonged to it, along with nine other founding associations, all of which, though 'private' institutions, were characterized both by a spirit of 'sacred union' in serving the nation and by their full collaboration with the government's political directives.[18] And through the nomination of over 4,000 minor officials to this branch of the government on the home front, Comandini was able to make ample use of his wide influence with the staff of schools. A good half of the local commissioners of the Federated Society in the various provinces consisted of male and female primary school teachers, school inspectors and educational directors.[19]

Apart from the strictly propagandistic functions which characterized the ideological adhesion of this more politicized group of teachers, what were the fields of intervention and the cultural content which activated the patriotism of so many others? What were the themes and the activities capable of involving primary school teachers, and even pupils, which achieved the successful functioning of the hybrid form of mobilization which has already been identified as a mixture of instigation from above and the self-organization of intermediary elements behind the war effort?

Social assistance and the wartime primary school

One of the most important wartime problems attracting teachers was the need for social assistance. This was not merely a question of stimulating their humanitarian qualities in keeping with the traditional and slightly romantic aura of philanthropic vocation which still surrounded the image of the teacher. This last was certainly used to involve primary school teachers in the civilian mobilization. But the role of assistance gained specific importance in wartime for two reasons. First, social assistance, especially for children and adolescents, was a constant refrain of official appeals to primary school staff for voluntary mobilization. The circulars from the Ministry of Public Instruction never asked teachers for their direct involvement in propaganda and only at a few difficult moments of the war appealed openly for the intensification of patriotic values in teaching. But, right from the start, they stressed that the spontaneous participation of teachers in activities of civilian assistance, even outside school hours and the school curriculum, was essential for the moral well-being of the nation.

These ministerial directives warrant a brief comment, precisely because they did not constitute a direct order to mobilize. Taking it for granted that such a command would be unnecessary, they assumed as of right that teachers could be expected to redouble their voluntary efforts obediently and automatically, out of a genuine spirit of patriotism, in the face of the exceptional historical test faced by the whole country. They gave little clear indication of what was to be done or the resources to be used. They therefore replaced normal administrative clarity with a kind of implied ideological complicity, and finished by formally endorsing the notion that patriotism was a prerequisite for any school teacher, a basic premiss of his educational mission. At the same time, however, fulfilling this prerequisite now went beyond teaching as such, and could no longer be measured purely within the classroom. The dual values of philanthropy and patriotism were turned outward, and a commitment to social assistance dictated by patriotic sentiments now became the clearest proof a teacher worthy of the name could offer of the ideal qualities of his profession.

There was a good deal of rhetoric and false consciousness in the logic of these appeals. But from the moment that such activity was requested by those at the top of the hierarchy and was answered with varying degrees of improvisation by voluntary structures for providing help and assistance, it became increasingly difficult for any teacher who did not feel his duty to lie with the war effort to justify his position, ideologically or morally. This in turn led to a progressive change of emphasis in the scale of professional ethics of the teacher body. In the exceptional situation of a society at war, those involved in teaching were called upon to give proof of their duty by promoting a militant version of national values in the schools – implying their own full-scale mobilization for the service of their country.

The significance of this mobilization around the theme of social assistance is further confirmed by the specific activities requested of schools for children and adolescents. In particular, teachers were asked to play a leading part in the substantial increase in childcare suddenly made necessary by the violent upheaval in family life occasioned by the war – supervision after school hours and during holidays, recreational activities, summer camps and pre-school crèches. None of these structures existed in substantial form before the war, but they became indispensable with the mass military conscription of men, increased work outside the home by women, and the social crisis resulting from the declining living conditions of poor families.

It should be added that neither the state nor the educational system in Italy was even minimally equipped to cope with such problems, whose scale far exceeded the traditional corollary of compulsory schooling, in the shape of subsidies and other forms of assistance. This was a totally new social demand. Its scale and urgency encompassed the basic needs of a new section of the child population, those of pre-school age, as well as the extension of the care of school pupils through supervision, meals and even education outside normal school hours and terms. Action on behalf of children formed one of the main areas of social assistance during the war. It was provided almost entirely by patriotic volunteers, first and foremost amongst whom were school teachers. In every Italian city the Committees for Civilian Assistance, the public authorities, the patriotic associations, the press (including the organ of the UMN), endlessly promoted this type of emergency aid for children, with repeated calls for subscriptions, volunteers and additional premises which could serve as crèches and places of recreation and supervision.[20]

There are no precise figures to quantify this phenomenon, but there is no doubt that it spread to even the smallest urban centres, revealing a huge amount of activity.[21] It will suffice, by way of example, to outline one aspect of these 'spontaneous' institutions which lay mid-way between social service, patriotic philanthropy and education. The voluntary activities referred to above created 'para-educational' places of care which had no definite school programme but which, by their nature and by the type of supervision they provided, transmitted the themes and values of wartime patriotism to the many children who attended them. Children were read the daily military bulletins, followed the 'geography of the front', and listened to anecdotal and edifying versions of Italian history. The moral example of the soldiers and the sacrifice of those who had died was held up to them, while through patriotic songs and small daily activities they were shown that even young boys and girls could contribute to the winning of the war.[22] Thus a 'war education' was born which invaded the regular classrooms and timetables of primary schools. Associations such as the UGII and the Federated Society were in the front line of this movement, providing teachers with standardized patriotic texts through which everyday school lessons were aligned with the demands of a society at war.

Finally, children's assistance illustrates a broader phenomenon of great importance that went beyond schools (while completely involving them) – the social representation of childhood. Mass war brought the condition of children to the attention of the public, social institutions and the state in a completely new way. These were now 'the precious children of those who in this supreme moment are serving their country in the armed forces', and therefore every help that could be afforded them became an act of solicitude toward the soldiers and a symbol of the nation's gratitude towards their brothers at war. Moreover, assistance for children became the precondition for another indispensable contribution to the war effort, that of freeing mothers to work in industry and agriculture. Ultimately, the ability of the new patriotic institutions for civilian aid to take care of children became an instrument of national resistance when signs of food shortages and social crisis increased on the home front. The provision of school meals, which increased significantly in 1918 (though no longer as a means of combating absenteeism), illustrates this changing reality. In effect, school meals became part of the official programme of 'wartime food provisioning' instituted in the summer of 1917 by the Ministry of the Interior. A circular of 15 January 1918 mobilized the school authorities in an unprecedented manner behind this effort, through the local sections of both the UMN and the UGII. It specified that 'particularly during the winter months it is desirable that school meals should be provided in the largest possible number of schools for the benefit of the neediest pupils', and insisted that 'it is imperative that this benefit be made available to the children of soldiers in the army'.[23]

All of these factors conferred a distinct patriotic value on the process of making children's welfare part of the national interest 'while the country was in the trenches'. As with the ministerial circulars mentioned above, there was a certain gap between the tangible results achieved by these social measures and the cultural categories or symbols which were used to initiate and control them. Yet these rhetorical symbols put into circulation new and lasting images of the very young which systematically linked their identities and destinies to the life, strength and hopes of the nation. Thus, the protection of children for the duration of the war became a subject of propaganda which was already projected into the post-war future – as in the case of the war orphans, the compensation of whose loss was declared to be the inescapable duty of the whole nation. Children were pushed centre stage by the war effort and entrusted to the care of social institutions as both real and symbolic 'children of the fatherland'. As such, they came to be seen as a 'sacred reserve' of strength which alone had the power to make up for the biological loss of those who had died for their country. It was as if the inescapable social duty of consoling and compensating children for their wartime bereavement was counteracted by this representation of children as willing bearers of their own sacrifice and as a living symbol of the 'continuity of the fatherland'.

Wartime representations of childhood

Childhood was portrayed publicly in two basic but complementary tones – the poignant and the heroic. The sad figure of the infant victim of war (orphans, refugees from front-line areas, impoverished children of conscripts) alternated with the proud figure of the child possessed of a precocious but solid national consciousness. Both were in evidence on occasions where children participated in large numbers at collective national ceremonies – such as the schoolchildren's 'guard of honour' at the funerals of fallen soldiers, the processions of schoolboys and schoolgirls in town squares during patriotic ceremonies, the presence of school representatives at the decoration of soldiers, groups of children visiting the mutilated and wounded in hospitals, individual primary classes joining the Italian Red Cross, the collection of 'gold for the fatherland', contributions to the war effort, and even the collective 'swearing of oaths to the fatherland' by young children who joined the new Young Italy movement which spread throughout primary and secondary schools in 1918. This double image confirmed the indissoluble link between the figure of the child and the patriotic ideal exemplified by the soldier as war hero and the duty of defending the homeland.

The portrayal of childhood through pathos is especially clear in the numerous photographs that appeared in the press (from mass circulation dailies to the professional teachers' journals) showing the children of soldiers receiving public assistance in the 'refuges of the fatherland', images which were often reproduced as postcards for soldiers or to raise funds 'for infants'. The converse, heroic, portrayal of childhood is most obvious in the 'guards of honour', while the two tones were combined effectively in the impressive patriotic ceremony that took place in Rome on 2 November 1917. A large procession wound through the streets of the city and converged on the Piazza Venezia, where wreaths were placed on the Altar of the Fatherland (the monument to King Victor Emmanuel II) in honour of the fallen soldiers. A squad of little war orphans brought up the rear and laid the largest wreath of all, made of laurel leaves interwoven with white ribbons and bearing the inscription in letters of gold: 'From the orphans of Italy to their fathers who fell while fighting for the ideal.' Even more significant for the regimentation of childhood was the declared aim of the founder of Young Italy of 'turning every child into a "sentinel of the Fatherland" within the family, where he may keep watch, give a good example, exhort and admonish. Children, even tiny infants, understand their duty fully and carry it out with touching insistence.' According to the directives of this association, the teachers who joined were to 'turn [Young Italy's] oath of allegiance into the essence of their teaching' so that 'all the children know how to become part of this great new militia and are enthused with everything that calls on their powers of love and arouses their imagination (oaths, bravery, badges, pride in being mobilized)'. The teachers were also to ensure that 'while [the children] are still open to faith with all their senses, [they] absorb the education which will give them the awareness of being fully Italian'.[24]

What were the repercussions of this patriotic representation of childhood on the schools themselves and on the very concept of a national school system? As already observed, the war made only too plain the gap between the enlarged needs of children in a time of social upheaval and the inadequacy of a school system whose state support was diminishing. Symbolically investing childhood with patriotism was a rhetorical response which had more to do with propaganda than reality. Yet as far as the social elites were concerned, this rhetoric appeared to reduce the worrying and dangerous gap between real needs and institutional response. And it was natural that the schools' own contribution to this 'symbolic transferral' should in some measure radicalize their ordinary teaching programme. This now became redefined in terms of current events, with the true teachers seen as being the Italians in uniform – the combatants.

An equally fundamental, if less obvious, change also requires analysis. The young pupils were no longer simply the 'recipients' of the patriotic content of teaching programmes designed to safeguard their future as adults. They were now also active witnesses and symbolic bearers of the idea of nationalism. Displaying this patriotic identity was part of the war effort on the home front. By guaranteeing the ritual mass presence of children at the numerous collective ceremonies which publicly celebrated the nation's faith in victory, both the primary schools and the institutions for children's assistance performed the reassuring task of showing what a precious 'well' of new, strong patriotism the mobilized children represented. Additionally, the primary schools used pupils as instruments of patriotic propaganda in the home. This was achieved both by supplying children with openly propagandistic material and, more importantly, by the patriotic cast given to schoolwork, especially essay writing, reading and dictation.

Thus, the periodical, *I Diritti della Scuola* ('The Rights of the School'), created a special column entitled 'From the school to the trenches' and even more explicitly, 'Echoes of war in the classroom'. The same weekly openly urged the use of the schools for propaganda following the disaster of Caporetto, with suitable examples widely disseminated through its supplement, *La scuola in azione* ('The School in Action'). The latter's editorial of 20 November 1917 pointed out that 'with school exercises we can continuously speak to the families through the children'. In order to facilitate the 'supreme duty of school teachers at the present time', patriotic catechisms were published 'in order to refute popular prejudices against the war', along with readings on the value of sacrifice and heroism (to which were to be added 'the death notice of a fallen soldier related to one of the children'). Little speeches were issued on the value of the wartime institutions of public assistance and on the courage of the soldiers, together with patriotic posters to be put up 'in the classrooms, corridors, and halls of every school'. Patriotic litanies were circulated for group recital, in the form of a rosary. In Rome, the Lazio branch of the UGII published a patriotic fortnightly magazine for children and teachers, from February 1917 to April 1919, called *Il Piccolissimo* ('The Smallest One'), which was financed by Comandini and conceived for use both in the classroom and for reading at home. Overall, a host of texts were published by teachers and educational administrators with the same basic titles – 'school and the fatherland' or 'school and the war' – making the twinning of the terms a commonplace. And the numerous public subscriptions raised by primary schools in support of wartime social assistance and various patriotic works provide unequivocal (albeit less spontaneous) evidence of the 'propagandistic' function of schoolchildren with regard to their own families.

Even within the normal scholastic sphere, teaching became more markedly patriotic, especially in subjects such as history, geography and Italian. Equally important were various 'manual activities' for boys and 'domestic tasks' for girls. In effect, the war radically changed the aims of education from the promotion of literacy to nationalist indoctrination. This tendency was reinforced by a more general offensive which confirmed the educational superiority of the concrete historical values of nationalism over the abstract universalism of humanitarian principles and pacifistic optimism, positions which seemed to have been confounded by events. The school system could not ignore the overwhelming presence of the war and it was widely accepted by teachers that even the most humdrum aspects of school life must acknowledge a reality that shaped the very existence of their pupils. Inevitably, such an understanding of the school's role profoundly undermined the humanist approach to education that had prevailed before the war and provoked a crisis in the 'progressivist' ethos of many school teachers. But apart from the lively debate surrounding the change of political direction of the UMN in April 1916, it seems that the weight of wartime events silenced any arguments for a pacifistic education. And even in the case of the UMN, the controversy over Soglia's presidency did not concern the state's tightened control on pedagogy but rather the perception (whipped up by the nationalist press) that it was unacceptable for a neutralist to run the leading teachers' union while the country was at war. The socialist minority of the UMN merely claimed that pursuing its own ideals was compatible with a formal patriotic loyalty and urged that primary schooling should be maintained apart, its aims and resources kept intact, until the 'folly of the war' had passed. Works of social assistance and the promotion of basic patriotism in the classroom were not seen as being at variance with this line, nor were they particularly felt to run the danger of importing overt nationalism into the school syllabus.[25]

From liberalism to fascism: 'national education' and the war

From the outset, the cult of patriotism and its traditional presence in the primary schools offered a solid basis for an interpretation of the war in terms of the Risorgimento, as the last stage of the struggle for independence against the historic enemy, Austria. By itself, however, this theme was not enough to produce the definitive turn towards the promotion of national values. The formula, and the myth, of 'national education', which was to triumph in the period following the war, was in fact definitively shaped by two turning-points of Italy's wartime experience.

The first turning-point was the emergence of the idea of the 'Great War' as a clash of civilizations, which only occurred in 1916 during the political debate preceding the declaration of war on Germany in August. This expanded definition of national ideals was accompanied by a rising flood of criticism of Prime Minister Salandra, and the narrow formula of *sacro egoismo* which he used to justify both neutrality in 1914–15 and the declaration of war solely against Austria in May 1915. Faced with an unprecedented war effort (as for all the powers involved), the meaning of the war that this slogan expressed seemed too limited and impoverished, even by reference to the Risorgimento. Particularly important in this ideological contest – to the point of provoking the fall of the government in June 1916 – was the current of democratic interventionist opinion, which had been especially active in the civil mobilization but which until now had not been directly represented in the cabinet. Its struggle to impose new and more 'democratic' war aims led to the government of 'sacred union' and to a more aggressive interpretation of traditional patriotic values. The idea was relaunched of a 'civilizing mission' for the Italian nation, which meant a struggle against the militarism of the central powers in order to achieve the triumph of the nationality principle, including the conquest of territories demanded by Italian irredentism. The appeal to democratic principles signalled the desire to complete the Risorgimento internally, with the full integration of the people into the apparatus of the nation. This was to be achieved by means of patriotic mobilization and a more energetic conduct of the war on the home as well as the fighting front, hence the typically didactic vision of Italian home-front propaganda, which sought not merely to popularize war aims but also to educate the people in the idea of the fatherland. From this perspective, the war became a national 'trial of arms' and was justified as a prerequisite for the birth of Italy as a great power.

This development had considerable consequences for the school system, even if the latter had not yet taken on a directly propagandistic role. Foremost among the key advocates of this enlargement of national goals in the spring and summer of 1916, were the groups who secured the change of line and leadership of the UMN, and who shared the common commitment to mounting a 'total war'. The campaign over the proper role for school teachers, although initiated by the nationalist right, was fully backed by major daily papers like *Il Secolo* of Milan and *Il Messaggero* of Rome, which were the mouthpiece of liberal democratic opinion in parliament – the republicans, radicals and social reformists. The new orientation of these groups (already vital in the evolution of the UMN) created a political split on the left throughout 1916 which isolated the socialists and fractured the 'progressivist' alliances which had tended to control the most important bodies promoting popular and primary school education – the UIEP (Unione Italiana per l'Educazione Popolare), the Università Popolari (Popular University) and the Società Umanitaria (Humanitarian Society).[26] This explains the solid base for the recruitment of primary school teachers as patriotic propagandists (and also the bitter recriminations accompanying the process) between the summer of 1916 and that of 1917. However, the government of 'sacred union' never managed completely to overcome the dualism between state and private efforts in the mobilization of the home front which was Salandra's legacy. It was precisely in this period that the extra-curricular educational activity of the teachers and their 'spontaneous' production of propaganda material was more and more openly praised and supported 'from above'.

The second turning-point of the war which shaped the definition of 'national education' was the crisis of Caporetto. This galvanized the propaganda drive to mobilize the home front and marked the apogee of the blatant use of primary education as an instrument of propaganda. The shock of the military disaster and the invasion of the Venetian provinces swept away any residual caution over the bellicist content of primary school teaching. A series of circulars from the new Minister of Public Instruction in the Orlando government, the social reformist, Agostino Berenini, translated this orientation into practice by officially requesting the maximum contribution of the school system in all its aspects to the moral and military resistance of the nation, until victory was achieved.

However, a fuller and more critical rethinking of the function of primary school teaching also began to occur. This came from a moralistic understanding of the defeat at Caporetto as the military equivalent of a strike, which had been fomented by the pacifist poison of the 'enemy within' but caused above all by the moral deficiency of the country and the chronic fragility of national identity. The immediate fear of an even bigger enemy invasion had no sooner been overcome, in the few weeks after the defeat, than this corrosive attitude called into question the school system itself. A major article appeared in Italy's most respected daily, the *Corriere della Sera*, with the provocative title 'Has the school failed in its duty?' The answer was a severe (and false) accusation: 'perhaps the kindest judgement that can be made on the Italian school system is that it was absent when the generation that is now fighting was being formed'.[27] The unforgivable offence was held to be the failure to instil in the people an understanding of the fatherland as something sacred. History teaching was given as an irrefutable example. This was seen to have been reduced to uninspired pedantry, filled with rote learning, 'abstractions', and lists of words to be memorized. It was considered to have been deprived of the coherence and passion needed in order to provide 'the consciousness of our country's reasons for being' and the sense that Italy's position 'in the concert of nations' was a matter of intimate concern to the young. It was on these grounds that the article measured the backwardness of the Italian school system against those of the other great powers, which were seen as having succeeded in 'implanting in their young generations the consciousness of [their nation's] mission in the world'. Not only France, Britain and Germany but even Austria – the living negation of the nationality principle – had been able to utilize the teaching of history in order to turn the 'memories of the past' into an 'idealistic cement' among its peoples and subjects that sustained 'a belief in the now vanished mission of the Danubian monarchy'.

The Giolittian school system thus found itself placed on trial by a kind of 'examination of conscience' which all 'educators of youth' were invited to undertake. Its supposed prevailing tendencies – the under-valuing of the spiritual in character-formation, the harmful influence of a tired positivism, a misplaced faith in economic and social progress through knowledge and teaching, and a belief in the peaceful evolution of relations between peoples – were condemned *en bloc*. Much of this portrayal of the pre-war school system was a caricature which suggested that the real target of the polemic was Giolitti himself – symbol of the old ruling class and of 'neutralism'. But it also accredited the idea that the whole school system required radical change because its pedagogical baggage – so arid, 'faithless' and irrelevant to the life and interests of the nation – would be useless in the schools of the 'new Italy'.[28]

In the opening stages of this debate, under the impact of Caporetto, the school teachers themselves did not escape criticism. But their contribution was too precious to be attacked heedlessly, and their involvement in the movement of national resistance from the end of 1917 was so massive that it silenced all direct accusations relating to their past. Whereas the old school system and ruling classes were condemned totally, it became widely accepted that future improvements in the career conditions and social status of the teaching profession were premissed on the patriotic merits that it displayed on the home front during the war. This frame of mind was encouraged by the Minister of Public Instruction who stimulated the voluntary ardour of the teachers by promising future recognition of their patriotism through enhanced institutional power in new school arrangements.

In this way, the duality of Italian wartime mobilization in which spontaneous activism coexisted with institutional coercion, was pro-jected into the political crisis of the post-war years. While fierce controversy continued unabated over the achievements and defeats of the school system in building national identity, the teachers' disillusion-ment, as promised reforms failed to materialize, turned into exasperated social protest in 1919. But the implicit root of the discontent remained the demand that the maturity and patriotism that they had displayed during the war in defence of the national ideal should now be recompensed. This revealed clearly the price paid by wartime govern-ments for the use they made of the teachers' extra-curricular functions and professional bodies to sustain and direct the civil mobilization. The apparent spontaneity of the teachers' role had bred the proud but 'false consciousness' of a 'self-mobilization' whose generous action 'from below' had substituted for the inertia of the authorities.

From this point of view, the resentment of the primary school teachers at the authorities' inaction was merely one element in the profound tension which the attempt to mobilize for a total war bequeathed to post-war Italy. The elites of the liberal state were de-legitimized in the eyes of many of the key components of the wartime patriotic mobilization, and loyalty to the pre-war regime was broken. Without entering into a discussion of the post-war crisis and of the school system under fascism, it is clear that the twin turning-points of the Italian war experience discussed above consolidated the idea that the nation was the only reliable instrument by which a people might accomplish its 'civilizing mission' and the only worthy spiritual horizon for school programmes. Especially in the last year of the war, the definition of a crudely propagandistic 'national education' went hand in hand with an onslaught on the greatest alleged failing of the pre-war primary school – the submission to abstract, humanist values which prevented teachers from carrying out their basic duty of forming the patriotic awareness of the young.

II

Solidarities and minorities

5   Mobilizing labour and socialist militants in Paris during the Great War

Jean-Louis Robert

Introduction

Wartime mobilization, which is taken here to mean that of the home front, was an essentially ambiguous process. Mobilization could be conceived of as undertaken by the dominant forces in society, by different elements of the state including what used to be known as the ideological apparatus (a term that has too readily gone out of fashion). There is much evidence for such a view – including most obviously at the ideological level, the discourse of propaganda. Nonetheless, if the idea of a social contract is accepted as having validity in the French case, the state must to some extent be seen as reflecting general opinion, even if it also forms the latter. The same point can be made about the press, which is often the subject of a dual and ambiguous interpretation. Historians alternate between seeing it as an instrument of propaganda and as a reflection of its own readership, without always clarifying the reciprocal status and interplay of these two views. The press can indeed be seen as a mobilizing agent by virtue of its propaganda while at the same time reflecting the self-mobilization of its own readership. Are strident headlines or nationalist, xenophobic cartoons urging the war to be fought to the bitter end best considered as a simple means of indoctrinating opinion or as the expression of the thoughts and expectations of the readers? These uncertainties are added to in wartime by the effects of censorship and self-censorship (in itself a complex phenomenon), and such difficulties become an argument for taking another path, though one which is not without its own problems.

The approach adopted here is the analysis of the concrete mobilization of one particular group: the trade unions and local socialist organizations of Paris and its suburbs. 'Concrete' mobilization is not taken to include all the actions of these groups; battles over wages and conditions, political campaigns, pro-war or pacifist speeches do not fall within the ambit of this study, which is not that of a classic history of

73

attitudes to the war. Only tangible actions which were part of a civil mobilization will be considered here, such as group solidarities, relations between soldiers and their families, actions concerned with wartime economic and social conditions, etc. But studying concrete manifestations of this kind immediately raises the question of the goals of civil mobilization. Should the forms of solidarity displayed by organizations with such different political attitudes to the war – some premature pacifists, others hostile to peace for the duration (there was no overtly defeatist current) – be lumped together? Did supporting the soldiers at the front mean the same thing to revolutionary syndicalist building labourers as to the patriotic socialists of Belleville? A definitive answer cannot be given at this point but will be returned to in the conclusion.

A further question posed by the approach adopted in this essay comes from social and cultural history. Does the degree of vitality of the different mobilizations really stem from the initial strength of the groups concerned, from their existence as a real culture in the sense that Lévi-Strauss defined the word? If so, the weakness of a mobilization might well have more to do with questions of the decomposition and recomposition of the group in question than with a lukewarm relationship to the war. The answers to these questions necessarily entail a socio-cultural consideration of the actors involved, which in turn centres on the question of their identity. Did mobilization occur for the group and/or for the nation?

As far as the social actors are concerned, a fuller study can be found in the author's thesis which deals comprehensively with the subject of the Paris labour and socialist movement during and immediately following the war, and which contains the main bibliographical references.[1] The intention here is to examine the question of concrete mobilizations during the war as near as possible to the base of the chosen organizations, which is also the best vantage-point for identifying the phenomenon of self-mobilization. Rather than taking the Union des Syndicats de la Seine and the Fédération Socialiste de la Seine (the department which contained Paris in 1914), whose mobilizing activity in large part occurred through the Comité d'Action, organized by the Socialist Party, the Confédération Générale du Travail (CGT – General Confederation of Labour) and the cooperative movement – and which has already been thoroughly studied by John Horne – it is the local trade unions and socialist sections (i.e., local organizations) which will be analysed here.[2] For the sake of clarity, the trade unions will be considered first, followed by the socialist organizations.

Trade union mobilization

As far as the trade unions were concerned, the concrete action discussed here consisted essentially of various forms of social solidarity towards mobilized members and their families. But it is also important to remember that the Union des Syndicats de la Seine (the trade union grouping of the Paris region) was active over a number of broader economic questions (the cost of living, the revival of economic activity following the outbreak of war, etc.).

In studying systematically the meetings held by unions in different trades and industries in Paris during the war, it becomes clear that the building unions were much the most active in organizing solidarity with mobilized members and their families. Two-thirds of their meetings involved this kind of work for the 'family' of a sector which stood in the vanguard of Paris labour militancy prior to 1914. This contrasts with a third of the meetings for printing unions, 30 per cent for the railway unions, and 18 per cent for clothing workers' unions which were devoted to similar questions. Very rich data survives for two Paris building unions, the *terrassiers* (building labourers) and the so-called Bâtiment et Maçons d'Art (in fact, the cement workers and masons who did not work in stone).[3] In the culture and practice of these unions, solidarity with serving soldiers was partly a pre-war tradition, that of the *sou du soldat* (soldier's penny), by which five francs a month were granted from union funds to young members during their military service, provided that they stayed in touch with their organization. From August 1914, this sum of five francs was extended to all mobilized members who remained in contact with the union. The figures show that only a small minority of about 150 to 200 building labourers received these sums, whereas the number of mobilized members was perhaps 5,000.

The two unions made greater efforts on behalf of the wives of mobilized members. A joint solidarity fund was established together with the Syndicat des Travailleurs des Industries Electriques (electrical workers) which was fed by a weekly solidarity stamp. In addition to their normal union subscription, non-mobilized members were asked to pay a further sum of twenty-five centimes a week for this purpose. But it remained voluntary. The monies collected were distributed as meal tickets for the 'communist soups', or communal meals, set up by labour organizations and above all by the socialist sections (to which we shall return) or were allocated in small sums (of three to five francs) to the women who came to 'family' meetings organized by these three unions – which had an exclusively male membership. Until the end of 1915, the sums gathered in this way were quite substantial, allowing up to 4,200 meals a week to be funded. If help with funerals and subsidies for various labour orphanages are added, a total of 100,000 francs was raised in eighteen months – which is remarkable given that French trade unions did not customarily handle sums of this order.

It is all the more important, therefore, to note that these two trade unions were clearly and from early on located on the pacifist wing of the labour movement. The building labourers' union had opposed the war from August 1914 (being the first to do so in the Paris region) while the Syndicat du Bâtiment et Maçons d'Art went over to the pacifist minority from the beginning of 1915. Both unions, moreover, were on the hard-line wing of the pacifist tendency, maintaining a markedly revolutionary line. Conversely, the Syndicat des Maçons-Pierre (union of stone masons), firmly on the pro-war majority side, showed no such zeal for solidarity. It waited until the end of February 1915 before instituting the solidarity stamp and the results were indifferent, since only 2,500 francs were disbursed in 1915.[4] Significantly, the figure who most urged this kind of solidarity in the stone masons was Péricat, one of the leading figures in the Paris pacifist movement, who constantly insisted that municipal subventions to the union be spent on relief work.[5]

Another particularity of the building workers was the extent to which the unions succeeded in maintaining some degree of contact with their mobilized members. Letters from the front – sometimes as many as thirty – were regularly read out during building union meetings, and in this way news of comrades was passed on. Mobilized members home on leave (especially those in leadership positions) attended and even spoke at meetings. The unions also regularly sent letters and newspapers in the reverse direction.

Overall, one has the distinct impression of witnessing a form of solidarity that was simply a sign of the continued liveliness of the revolutionary syndicalism of the Paris building trade, whose moral dimension is familiar in other contexts. It thus seems hard to talk about a civil mobilization in this case; indeed, it could be seen instead as an early form of counter-mobilization in a form, however, which did nothing to disturb the national mobilization.

Two other sectors also established very strong solidarity with their mobilized members or their families – printing and the railways. The Paris unions of these two industries were distinctive in that both were reformist before the war (with the exception of the two stations of the state railway network), and both belonged to the national pro-war majority of the CGT at least at the beginning of the war (a strong minority pacifist current developed among the railway unionists from 1917).

In the printing trade, where there had been a massive haemorrhage of workers to the army and where employment was fragmented between numerous small businesses, trade unionism had been strong before the war. The Fédération du Livre (federation of printing workers) had deep and long-existing roots in the tradition of mutualist self-help. It is not surprising that its Paris branches redirected this activity towards their mobilized members and their families in 1914. At the end of 1914, the Paris typographers' organization, the most important of the printing unions, established a very high compulsory 'war tax' on its non-mobilized members, amounting to between 5 and 15 per cent of their income.[6] This 'war tax' was kept up until the demobilization in a powerful gesture of solidarity with mobilized union members and their families which was also a manifestation of the living tradition of social assistance that was so characteristic of the 'brotherhood' of the printing trade. Here, solidarity, craft culture and civil mobilization merged.

The situation was different among the railway workers, since they were largely exempt from mobilization for the front and worked for powerful companies. Railway unionization was still mediocre, especially since the national strike of 1910. The companies instituted an official system of social aid to their mobilized workers and their wives and companions. The unions' action was therefore directed to getting the companies to improve these allowances or to supporting the railway workers' own, complementary institutions of social aid – the principal one of which was the National Orphanage for the Children of Railwaymen, run by the union affiliated to the CGT. Nearly all railway workers' meetings in Paris provided an opportunity to take a collection, vote a subvention, or organize a fete for the orphanage, whatever the railway network concerned. 'To no longer pay one's [union] subscription is to reduce six hundred orphans to misery, to refuse them bread', declared the union of the Paris-Nord network in January 1915.[7] And it was not without pride that an activist could declare at a fete of trade unionists on the eastern region, in February 1918, that 'only the railwaymen succeeded through their sense of solidarity in setting up an orphanage'.[8] The other particularity of the railwaymen's unions (though it was most apparent at the national level with few traces in the rank and file) was the participation in the Union Nationale des Cheminots (national union of railwaymen), a body whose function was to collect and disburse the social solidarity funds of all the railwaymen's associations. The role played by the CGT-affiliated national union in this body was very important, as the recent thesis of A. Fukasawa has shown.[9] The culture of the railway workers went beyond wage questions, and the railway unions' sense of solidarity was part of a more general, economic activity, though this was most in evidence at the leadership levels.

It is nonetheless striking to see how little news circulated among either printers or railway workers concerning the situation of their mobilized members. It is as if the soldiers were absent from the discourse of trade unionists in both sectors. To be sure, the labour press gave some information, such as the tragic lists of those who had died in battle. But no letters were read out from mobilized members, nor did the latter ever make a personal appearance. They seem to have been passed over in a deliberate silence which is difficult to interpret. In both sectors, there was clearly a civil mobilization that linked group identity with the broader mobilization of the home front from which the soldier seemed excluded – whether by conscious censorship or unconscious self-censorship.

On 3 April 1916, the delegates of the unions belonging to the Union de la Seine refused by a considerable majority to support a motion in favour of devoting 50 per cent of the municipal subsidies received by the unions for works of solidarity with the mobilized soldiers.[10] This decision was highly significant because it indicated a more general trend. Everywhere, the feeling of solidarity with the front was on the wane. The mobilized men's wives were the first affected in the building trade. The solidarity fund of the two craft unions and of the labourers was wound up at the beginning of 1916. The big meetings open to women at which the unions distributed the five-francs allowance were discontinued. Meal tickets and funeral subsidies were also ended in the same period.

Material solidarity with the mobilized men themselves, which as we have seen was less expensive, lasted longer but at a slightly diminished level. The public reading of letters or news of the mobilized men gradually faded out of union meetings (fifty meetings in 1915, twenty-nine in 1916, six in 1917, none in 1918). This was mirrored by the totality of the sectors being considered here (250 for 1915; 173 for 1916; 95 for 1917; 45 for 1918).

What caused this weakening of solidarity with the men at the front, which spared only the printing workers with their compulsory contributions? From July 1915, union activists complained about insufficient payments of the voluntary stamp for solidarity purposes, denouncing a 'lack of urgency' or sense of 'indifference'.[11] The same reaction became general throughout Paris in 1917. This doubtless reflected the surfeit of demands for financial contributions to which the home-front population had been subjected by this stage of the war. But the turning-point in the building workers' organizations also coincides with their decision to reorient their action to questions of wages and conditions. A tract of January 1916 declared: 'This, comrades, is the balance sheet of your trade unions, which have been reduced to a skeleton at the end of seventeen months of war; following the solidarity [with members in the army] that we imposed on ourselves, we now have a moral duty to expand our trade union ranks.'[12] Some trade unionists insisted that action or the reconstitution of a strike fund were now the top priorities, like Toularastel of the Métro workers, in February 1918.[13] An anarchist in the metalworkers' federation, Le Meillour, considered that funds should go first and foremost to the victims of repression, and in 1917 many unions indeed gave support for imprisoned activists precedence over that for mobilized members.[14] Other trade unionists felt that such unequal manifestations of solidarity made for division, discontent and bitterness.[15] A pacifist style of opposition was also apparent in the case of an activist in the postal service who considered that solidarity with members at the front meant giving 'money just so [our comrades] can get themselves smashed up'.[16] When two leaders of the aviation and automobile workers' union, Leclerc and Becker, suggested establishing a solidarity fund for mobilized members sent back to the front following the Mourier law, the idea was met with cries of 'it's up to the bourgeois to pay our pals who get themselves smashed up for them'.[17] These reactions, mainly from the union rank and file, clearly indicate a certain demobilization of the home front – but the question remains, which home front?

The initial activist mobilization of the building workers' unions, with their revolutionary syndicalist tradition, expressed first and foremost the vitality of this particular organization and its culture rather than a civil mobilization in tandem with the military mobilization. In practice, however, there was little to distinguish it from other civil mobilizations, such as that of the national charitable council, the Secours National, or of the Union Nationale des Cheminots of the railway unions, and in strengthening the links between front and rear and supporting both the soldiers and their wives, the building unions in fact contributed to the morale of both home and fighting fronts. The weakening of this response from 1916 to 1917, as trade union membership began expanding, was not simply due to financial difficulties but also reflected a reorientation of resources and activity towards new concerns, as well as a certain indifference on the part of the rank and file. In effect, this amounted to a kind of demobilization (except in certain sectors, such as printing) and a disruption of the sense of connection between trade unionists in the rear and those at the front.

Socialist mobilization

In a letter addressed to its mobilized members, the executive commission of the socialist Fédération de la Seine pointed proudly to the fact that two-thirds of the communal meals (*soupes communistes*) provided in the department had been the work of bodies established by the local socialist organizations.[18] In October 1914, for example, Paris socialism provided 1,223,800 meals (in seventy-five establishments) out of a total of 1,808,000.[19] Furthermore, many of the remaining one-third of the meals were provided by socialist town halls in the suburbs or by municipal administrations which were not themselves socialist but received local socialist support.

These figures demonstrate the scale of activity at the beginning of the war which marked an undeniable success for Paris socialism. Paris socialists were the motor of a formidable effort of social provision for the poorer sections of the capital's population during both the military mobilization and the serious unemployment crisis which followed it in late 1914 and 1915.

Two contextual points, however, are essential in explaining the nature and dynamism of this socialist action. First, military mobilization affected socialist organizations less severely than the trade unions.[20] The leadership of the socialist federation reckoned its membership to have dropped by one-third in December 1914.[21] Even adding movement of members to the provinces or those who disappeared, the federation kept at least half of its pre-war strength, and its activity, which had fallen to 40 per cent of the pre-war level in September 1914, rose to 50 per cent by the end of the year.[22] In the upheaval of Paris life during the late summer and autumn of 1914, the socialist organizations – and especially the most important among them – were an element of stability in the social life of the capital.

The second contextual point is the changing demographic balance within the city's districts (or *arrondissements*) and suburban communes in September 1914 by comparison with the eve of the war.[23] Where the population of the bourgeois *arrondissements* or of the wealthy suburb of Neuilly fled in the face of the German advance, the working-class population by and large stayed put. Paris in this second half of 1914 was thus a popular Paris, something the socialist sections were fully aware of. 'As the German armies rolled irresistibly towards the Ourcq and the Marne, as Senlis was burned, and as the terrified inhabitants of the outer suburbs fell back on the capital . . . the best informed elements of the bourgeoisie had already deserted Paris . . . Their fast cars raced after each other along the departmental roads, thus avoiding the anguished wait [of others], day and night, around the overcrowded railway stations.'[24] The solidity of the socialist structures of the city and this strong working-class presence explain in large measure the essential role played by Paris socialism at the beginning of the war.

In order to study the activity of the capital's socialists, we shall rely above all on the case of the twelfth section (the socialist organization in the corresponding twelfth *arrondissement*) because of the existence of a particularly interesting document. But it was in no way exceptional, its social activity being very similar to that of the other Paris sections. As early as 9 August 1914, the twelfth section set up a Socialist Wartime Aid Committee (Comité Socialiste d'Aide et de Sauvegarde pour la Durée de la Guerre) with the purpose of organizing works of solidarity: 'United and grouped together, socialist families will be sheltered from a demoralizing isolation.'[25] On 11 August 1914, the Socialist Aid Committee decided to organize communal meals and on 15 August it launched an appeal which made it quite clear what kind of effort was envisaged:

On the great occasions of history when the defence of Right and Liberty have required sacrifice, the French proletariat has never been found wanting. The worker in reality only possesses two things: his Life and his Home . . It is the duty of the Nation, of those whose fortune was bestowed on them in the cradle, to ensure the security of [the worker's] home in these grievous times. We cordially and urgently appeal [for support] from those who have understood the grandeur of the effort made by the working class, in all its united and resolute immediacy.[26]

The socialist family and the private family – these were the two domains favoured by this socialist action. Ensuring the 'security' and the existence of both was seen as essential to preserving the morale of the absent soldier. It was also necessary to prevent the hunger 'which destroys energy and demoralizes the mind'.[27] Thus 'the workers, having read our little war communiqués against wretchedness and unemployment will have firmer hearts and more manly courage'.[28] In order to underline this dimension of socialist action, it was suggested that the women companions of the mobilized men should send them 'letters which will tell them that the socialists have not forgotten their families or their children during their absence'.[29] Indeed, the section of the twelfth *arrondissement* itself sent a letter to the mobilized men telling them of its activities.[30]

The example of the eighteenth section of the socialist federation is identical. It announced on 9 August 1914 that it was setting up a communal meal programme for the families of party comrades and on 15 August it established an Aid Committee for the families of all soldiers. From 27 August 1914, it served 1,200 meals a day in two locations.[31]

We have seen just how extensive was the free or subsidized provision of these meals by the local socialist organizations. They were variously financed, but the national relief organization, the Secours National, largely funded the three establishments organized by the twelfth section.[32] The latter also received 'the help . . . of supportive bourgeois circles which may even have sympathized with socialism', among them Bercy wine merchants who supplied their wares free of charge, furniture manufacturers and local residents.[33] The local authorities also contributed to this socialist activity. The Prefect of the Seine provided potatoes and the Director of Social Assistance made a financial contribution.

Thus, even in a section which early on was to become a particularly reluctant supporter of the 'sacred union' (Bourderon, one of the leaders of the French anti-war socialist minority who went to the Zimmerwald conference in September 1915, was a key figure in the twelfth section), a whole network of relationships developed between socialists, the Paris bourgeoisie and the local representatives of the state.

Alongside communal meals, the socialist groups or sections instituted a whole series of wartime activities. Information services were opened for the womenfolk of mobilized men and for Parisians generally on questions such as wartime separation allowances or rent controls.[34] The twelfth section set up a Soldiers' Clothing Service (Vestiaire du Soldat) which sent packages to men in the trenches.[35] It also established a shelter for refugees and evacuees 'who, disoriented and missing their homes, might have been suddenly demoralized', which bore the name of the 'Fraternal Welcome' (*Accueil Fraternel*).[36]

Other sections had their 'workrooms' (*ouvroirs*) for giving work to women. The socialist groups of the Goutte d'Or and the Chapelle, in northern Paris, set up a workshop making sacks on the rue Ordener which employed up to 400 women.[37] At Montreuil, the socialist workroom produced trousers. Initially established in the local offices of the justices of the peace, it was given premises by Klein et Frères, one of the biggest piano manufacturers in the Paris region.[38] At Pantin, the sewing workshop employed ninety women.[39] It was much rarer, however, to see the socialist sections undertaking delivery of coal.[40]

In the suburbs, the situation was often very little different. When the town hall was socialist run, the local section of the party tended to leave this kind of social action to the municipality. At Pavillons-sous-Bois, which served as a model socialist town hall, it was the latter which organized the communal meals (in October 1914), a municipal food provisioning service, a municipal ambulance (in October 1914), an apprenticeship workshop for youths between thirteen and sixteen years of age (in October 1914), and a military equipment workshop which employed up to 600 women (set up in January 1915). The municipality also ensured that contact was maintained with the front by sending letters to the 1,000 mobilized men from the commune.[41] The municipalities of Pré-Saint-Gervais and Saint-Denis did the same.[42] At Saint-Denis, the socialist town hall served 2,600 free meals to the children of mobilized and unemployed men and set up a network of communal dining-rooms which assured up to 10,000 meals a day.

In the non-socialist town halls, the situation was more diverse. Sometimes the socialists managed to get the local authorities to set up communal meals which they helped administer.[43] But often conflicts broke out. At Boulogne, the socialist section created its own communal meal service because 'the reactionary municipality sought to use the commune's activity for its own ends'.[44] At Clamart, a 'bourgeois commune', the socialist section denounced the inactivity of the authorities who only served a thin soup without meat to the unemployed, provided no monetary aid and had very little by way of coal stocks.[45] At Pantin, the socialist section stressed the fact that from the outset the municipality showed no interest in works of social assistance.[46] At Villemonble, the socialists condemned the municipal authorities for refusing to make premises available where they could organize a communal dining-room and for waiting five months before setting up an unemployment commission.[47]

Nonetheless, the general tendency remained clear, even if it was stronger in the city than in the suburbs. There was a new cooperation between the socialists and their pre-war opponents. Beyond any doubt, solidarity, social action and civil mobilization were widespread within Parisian socialism. One consequence of this phenomenon was that the 'sacred union', which sprang naturally from support for the defence of the nation, was translated into networks of a rank-and-file socialist activity in defence of workers and socialists in their homes and localities. This same impulse also found institutional expression in the Paris Municipal Council and the Conseil Général of the department of the Seine. The wartime history of the latter is at the margin of our concerns here, but it is impossible not to refer to it in passing.

From the outset in August 1914, socialists offered to collaborate with the mayors of the Paris *arrondissements*. At a meeting on 7 August, the secretaries of the sections of the socialist Fédération de la Seine went even further and decided to 'put the collective organizational strength of our party at the service of the administrative authorities', especially for provisioning, services, urgent construction works, and even 'public order measures'.[48] 'The bureau [of the fifth section] offered the mayor of the fifth *arrondissement* the devoted collaboration of [its] members.'[49] On 1 August, even before the declaration of war, the eleventh section had made contact with the town hall of its *arrondissement*, via its elected representatives, in order to provide social aid. Little by little it established common activities to such a point that it could declare that 'socialist activities supplement perfectly the work of the municipality'.[50] Unemployment relief and military separation allowances were even disbursed at the headquarters of the socialist groups so as to free up the town hall of the eleventh *arrondissement*.[51] In the thirteenth *arrondissement*, the socialist section placed itself 'at the disposal of the municipal authorities'.[52] In the sixteenth *arrondissement*, delegates from the socialist section sat on the municipal commission which distributed unemployment relief.[53] Admittedly, certain town halls prompted criticism, as in the twentieth *arrondissement*, where Loyau attacked the 'functionaries, [all of them] insolent [and] haughty, [who] take arbitrary measures'.[54] But overall, the result was without question seen as positive.[55]

At the level of the department of the Seine (which is not our concern here), the logical outcome of this action was the election of a socialist as president of the Conseil Général in 1915, in the person of Paris, the socialist councillor for La Villette and a former wheelwright. Moreover, another leading socialist and civil servant, Henri Sellier, was made responsible for presenting the budget, a highly sensitive and responsible task. On the Municipal Council of Paris, two socialists were introduced to the executive, Deslandres, as vice-president and Reisz as secretary. For nearly four years, the elected representatives of Parisian socialism were to play an absolutely decisive role in these two councils. From March 1915, Fiancette persuaded the Municipal Council to withdraw its subsidy from the Free Trades Council (Bourse Libre du Travail), which was in the hands of a 'yellow' (or strike-breaking) union.[56] Above all, Henri Sellier got the Conseil Général to establish the Office Départemental de Placement et de Statistique du Travail de la Seine, or departmental labour exchange, which was to become an important mechanism for regulating the labour market in the inter-war period.

But the development of the 'sacred union' in the municipal government of the capital was to lead the socialist representatives into a class collaboration whose foundations and logic went beyond the temporary circumstances of national defence. The war provided the occasion for rediscovering the national community as something at least as vital as the community of class. This reorientation is perfectly captured by the speech of Henri Sellier to the Conseil Général of the Seine on 23 June 1915:

Both [the employers and the working class] have too often forgotten that beyond the obvious opposition stemming from the phenomenon of class conflict, which it would be foolish to deny or ignore and which can raise difficulties between them in a variety of circumstances, they have an equally clear community of economic interest when it comes to the improved organization of the labour market, the perfecting of plant and equipment, and the industrial prosperity on which they depend.[57]

This basic analysis, which virtually constituted a new war socialism, was strengthened by the perception of a broad community of class support for the national defence. 'Industrialists, shopkeepers, workers . . . are defending the interests of France.'[58] Sometimes, the most hostile tone was reserved for the popular classes. Henri Sellier attacked 'irregular workers' and the 'professionally unemployed', an unflattering portrait which could not have been more opposed to the proud self-image of the independent Parisian artisan.[59] For Lauche, the parliamentary deputy of the Seine, the increase in munitions prices was due to the workers in the arsenals who 'slumber over their work and demand high wages . . . these workers are the most to blame'.[60] Vendrin, the mayor of Levallois, criticized passengers on public transport who got away without paying due to the small number of conductors.[61] He did not hesitate to write an article entitled 'The situation of the poor: they should only ask for aid if they really need it.'[62]

Thus, for most elected socialist representatives in Paris, the 'party truce' which was an essential requirement for the national defence also contributed to a longer-term re-evaluation of French society and its forms of social and political regulation.[63] But although this change of view, marking a real break with the past, was related to a similar practice on the part of the local socialist sections in late 1914 and early 1915, it was to become increasingly separated from a reality which evolved in a different direction.

The exhaustive, computerized examination of the 18,000 motions passed by meetings of the Paris socialist sections during the war allows reasonably confident conclusions to be drawn about their orientation and practice (table 5.1). The importance of the kinds of social action undertaken by the local socialist groups at the beginning of the war shows up very clearly in the table. Organizing the home front would seem to be the fundamental meaning of this new departure for Paris socialism. The longer-term evolution of expressions and acts of solidarity with the mobilized soldiers indicates that they declined from the middle of 1915, and that by 1917 they had virtually disappeared – and there can hardly have been any self-censorship on subjects like these that might have affected the pattern seen here. The fundamental

Table 5.1 *Agendas of Paris socialist meetings on selected themes, 1914–1919*

Theme*	b1914	e1914	1915	1916	1917	1918	b1919
Solidarity	0	98	96	29	4	4	0
National days	0	0	4	17	1	0	0
Mobilized men	0	41	125	82	16	6	1
Provisioning	0	3	3	44	17	3	0
Communal meals	0	61	44	20	10	1	2
Local action	7	3	5	24	5	2	4
Cost of living	0	1	36	34	29	1	6
Other	1	8	5	1	2	3	1
Total (1)	8	215	318	251	84	20	14
Total (all agendas) (2)	744	450	1,904	2,174	1,586	1,549	1,164
% (1)/(2)	1.1	47.8	16.7	11.5	5.3	1.3	1.2

* b = beginning of; e = end of

conclusion must therefore be that the network of social activity instituted by Parisian socialism at the beginning of the war progressively unravelled, and this coincided with an overall decline in socialist activity, which from May 1917 to October 1918 sank into deep lethargy.

In late 1915 and early 1916, the socialist organizations of the Seine tried to extend their control over the local economy. This was no longer a question purely of social solidarity, as it had been with the communal meals of 1914, but meant taking responsibility for food provisioning, countering the increased cost of living, initiating municipal policies on domestic gas and coal supplies, etc. But here, too, as table 5.1 shows, this new socialist practice collapsed in 1917 (essentially from May to June) and only revived to a very limited degree after the Armistice, mainly for electoral reasons. There can be no question of distortion due to self-censorship here either, since these were not controversial issues in relation to the national defence. Thus, there was a profound demobilization within the ranks of Parisian socialism from the winter of 1916–17.

In relation to the theme of this chapter, it can be concluded that Paris socialists, like Paris trade unionists, experienced a powerful reflex of social solidarity at the onset of the war. The socialist mobilization, like that of the trade unions, aimed first and foremost to safeguard the activist 'family', as a social network, but it also went further and approached a total civil mobilization of the rear, something which was never as clearly envisaged by the trade unionists and which was even experienced as a counter-mobilization by the building workers. The strength of the economic and social activities undertaken by the socialists is the most powerful testament to this socialist self-mobilization behind the war. The collapse of this mobilization, however, was even more dramatic than in the case of trade unionism. The practice of social solidarity and the attempt to impose a degree of control over the local economy completely disappeared during 1917. The dual phenomenon of the rise and decline of this new orientation expressed not only the abandonment by rank-and-file Paris socialism of its civil mobilization but also the wider disintegration of its identity and culture in a long-term perspective, a phenomenon that has been demonstrated in many other ways in our thesis. This explains the sharp tension between the base of the movement and its elected representatives, who sought to sustain this form of mobilization throughout the war on the Paris Municipal Council and the Conseil Général of the Seine.

The overall result is thus clear. Chronologically, there was a first phase, fairly widespread in the Paris labour movement, that was characterized by a powerful surge of social solidarity – which was all the stronger where vibrant pre-war cultures of militancy existed (the building trade, Belleville, etc.). The presence or absence of these currents of solidarity does not easily match the division between pacifist and pro-war feeling, or between revolutionaries and reformists. Rather, they expressed (in whatever form) the natural self-defence of a family of 'militants'. But they also assumed the form of a civil mobilization at the leadership level of the Paris labour movement (the Union des Syndicats and the Fédération Socialiste), in most of the big local organizations of Paris socialism, and in certain trade unions whose reduced support with military call-up was for a while counteracted by activities to alleviate wartime economic and social conditions. There was, therefore, a real self-mobilization by sections of rank-and-file Paris labour in 1914–16. However, in the case of certain trade union organizations (such as those in the building industry), the solidarity thus expressed was in reality a precocious counter-mobilization for the preservation of the organization and its members against the effects of the war. The constant evocation of the absent soldiers at building workers' meetings can thus be seen as a discourse of latent pacifism.

It can also be concluded that this self-mobilization by labour militants disintegrated in 1917 (with the exception of some trade unions, like those of the printing workers), and that this collapse was paralleled by weariness, personal withdrawal from labour activism, the disruption of the pre-war social networks of the Paris labour movement, and a reshaping of the culture of labour activism. Paris workers remained generally committed to the national defence, as is shown by their defensive reflex in 1918 during the German spring offensive. But this could not reverse the underlying tendency, and the patriotic upsurge of

1918 was not accompanied by any of the forms of social and labour solidarity that have been discussed here. If there was still a mobilization of the home front, it did not take place through the channels of labour militancy.

6 Between integration and rejection: the Jewish community in Germany, 1914–1918

Christhard Hoffmann

History shows that wartime treats minorities and marginalized social groups in a paradoxical way. War often creates opportunities for integration where few had previously existed. But it can lead to even greater discrimination and alienation from the majority society. The necessity in modern wars to mobilize all social forces in the battle against the external enemy encourages a tendency towards internal cohesion, equalization of the population and 'democratization' of the polity. It can lead, at least temporarily, to pacification of social conflict and the inclusion of marginal groups. Minorities gain an opportunity to prove their membership in the majority society through unconditional patriotism, creating conditions for the repeal of discriminatory measures, and the fostering of integration and equal rights. On the other hand, there is the growing danger during wartime that minorities will be blamed if the war takes a negative course. Shortages on the home front often result in the persecution and exclusion of minority members from the majority society.

The form taken by the majority society's reaction to minority groups largely depends on the direction taken by the war. However, it is also affected by the previous level of integration of the minority in question, the tradition and strength of discrimination, and the extent to which the majority society is able and willing to integrate minorities. Comparative research on the situation of minorities during wartime has not yet been systematically developed. Panikos Panayi's recent work, however, provides an excellent starting-point. Panayi identifies three ways that majorities have treated minorities during wartime: first, as 'representatives of the enemy who have lived within the country at war with their land of origin for a prolonged period' or 'members of a group which has traditionally received hostile attention from the dominant society'; second, as 'members of a hostile group following the invasion of their land by the enemy' such as the Jews in France or the Netherlands during the Second World War; and third, as 'a "friendly" or "neutral" minority to the dominant society', such as African Americans in both World Wars.[1]

The attempt to classify the relations between Jewish minorities and their majority societies in pre-First World War Europe according to Panayi's typology reveals a very diverse situation. In Russia, which had a long tradition of state-sponsored discrimination and had denied the rights of citizenship to all but a very small number of Jews, the Jewish minority was largely seen as a 'hostile group' by the government and public opinion. Considered a 'security risk' in the borderlands, Jews there were subjected to numerous forms of persecution (pogroms, deportations, etc.).[2] In contrast to Russia, Jews in France, Britain and Germany were largely considered to be 'friendly' or 'neutral' minorities. Though the process of emancipation in these countries had permitted Jews to become loyal citizens, their acceptance by the majority societies varied in each case. Traditions of rejection and exclusion which had survived, or were reshaped by the anti-semitic movement, further frustrated the Jews' desire for complete integration. The war now offered them a unique opportunity to prove their unconditional patriotism and achieve more complete integration into the majority societies. For this reason we find among Jews in almost all European countries a particularly high degree of self-mobilization for the war. In this respect, the German Jews were no different from those in France or England. However, despite their contributions to the 'national cause', German Jews' hopes for greater integration and reduced discrimination were not fulfilled. In France, the position of Jews in French society became more secure as a result of the war. In Germany, Jews found themselves confronted with anti-semitic government measures and increasing stigmatization as the 'internal enemy'. Public attacks against Jews during the war also took place in France and especially in Great Britain, where the supposed lack of loyalty on the part of Russian Jewish immigrants was at issue. But compared to Germany these attacks were minimal, and in general they did not damage the reputation of the native Jews in the eyes of British and French Gentiles.[3] The deeply ambivalent reaction of German society *vis-à-vis* the Jews makes the German case especially troubling. This essay examines the situation of the Jews in Germany during the First World War. It argues that far from uniting German society, in the end the mobilization efforts created an even deeper rift. For the German Jews, the war experience thus marked a turning-point in their self-perception.

On the eve of the war, the Jewish community in Germany consisted of some 600,000 members, or approximately 1 per cent of the overall population. It was hardly a homogeneous group. In contrast to the situation in Great Britain and France, which had centralized rabbinical institutions, the German Jews had no religious or political representatives who spoke for the community as a whole. They can be divided into three main groups, based on how they defined themselves politically or religiously.

The large majority of German Jews were represented by the Central Association of German Citizens of Jewish Faith (Centralverein deutscher Staatsbürger jüdischen Glaubens), or CV.[4] Its very name showed the organization's programme to be Jewishness as a purely denominational, not a national, category. According to this form of self-definition, Jews in Germany were just as German as their Protestant or Catholic compatriots; they did not form a national minority with special interests. Thus the CV did not consider as 'Jewish lobbying' its efforts to fight anti-semitism and discrimination, which had continued even after formal equality had been achieved in 1871, and included the almost complete denial of state positions in the judiciary, civil service, education and military to non-baptized Jews. Instead, the CV considered its anti-discrimination efforts to be part of a general, universally beneficial political struggle to implement the constitutional principles of the liberal *Rechtsstaat*. This aim led to a close political alliance with left liberal political forces.[5] The CV was convinced that anti-semitism was a curable social ill. German Jews, it held, could assist in the 'cure' by fulfilling their civic responsibilities, demonstrating a love of fatherland and showing a willingness to make 'necessary' sacrifices. The CV thus attempted to ensure the integration of Jews into German culture by promoting 'German attitudes'. With nearly 36,000 individual members in 1919, the CV can be described as the most important organization representing German Jews.

The second largest Jewish grouping in Germany was the Zionist Organization for Germany (Zionistische Vereinigung für Deutschland), or ZVD.[6] Following the programme established at the First Zionist Congress in Basel in 1897, it called for the 'creation of a legally secured homeland in Palestine for the Jewish people'.[7] Until the early 1910s, the ZVD was too numerically insignificant to contest the CV's leading position among German Jewry. With barely 10,000 members in 1914, it clearly represented a minority position. At first, there were even some attempts at cooperation as, for example, in the Association of German Jews (Verband der deutschen Juden), or VDJ, which was founded in 1904 as a body to represent Jews in dealings with political institutions and the authorities. However, because of its organizational structure and lack of independence, this body remained a clumsy and largely ineffective tool. In the years leading up to the First World War, open conflict broke out between the CV and the ZVD as younger, more radical elements assumed leadership of the latter and Zionist ideas began to gain popularity with the non-Jewish public. The Zionist position that all Jews in the world belonged to a common nation and remained permanent aliens in their 'host countries' directly contradicted the CV's most basic principle – that a synthesis of Germanness and Jewishness was both desirable and possible. The CV demanded 'the application of German attitudes to bourgeois life' as a condition of membership, causing many Zionists to leave the Association.[8] Polarization and mutual polemics between the two groups did not abate before the outbreak of war.

The Orthodox and neo-Orthodox, finally, represented a very different milieu.[9] Orthodoxy had emerged in the mid-nineteenth century in response to liberal reform Judaism. It aimed to gather together traditional Jews in order to preserve obedience to religious law in the modern world. Organizationally, the Orthodox were not a unified group – they were divided among various subgroups (*Austritts* Orthodox, community Orthodox and the Zionist *Mizrachi*). Common to all, however, was the effort to preserve a degree of autonomy in religious and educational matters. Acculturation to the non-Jewish environment, which took place even among the Orthodox in cultural and scientific areas, was limited by the normatively conceived religious tradition. The complete integration into the Gentile majority society desired by the CV was necessarily rejected by the Orthodox, for whom the Jewish religion was an expression of national identity.

Despite these internal differences and, in some areas, growing tensions, the positive reaction of German Jews to the outbreak of the war was nearly unanimous. All groups were convinced of the justice of the German cause, and called upon their members to fulfil their patriotic duties unstintingly. Their justifications, however, revealed important differences. To the CV, the war offered German Jews the opportunity 'to prove themselves genuine Germans', and thus, as in the wars of 1813–15 and 1870–71, to reduce discrimination and achieve greater integration into the majority society. The CV therefore called on German Jews 'to devote their energies to the fatherland above and beyond the call of duty'.[10] The proclamation of the *Burgfrieden* (or suspension of politics in favour of national unity) by Wilhelm II was received with enthusiasm, and the war was lauded as a great domestic 'peacemaker' and 'unifier of the nation' (*Volksgenossen*).[11] The CV's aims at the start of war were described as follows by the association's attorney, Ludwig Holländer, in November 1914: 'First the German Fatherland, first its well-being; only then our own interests. They take not second place, but fifth and sixth place, and first of all Germany, Germany above all [*Deutschland, Deutschland über alles*]!'[12] With an eye to the German public, the CV exhorted its members to 'enthusiastic participation' in the war and 'simplicity, naturalness and economy' in their personal behaviour, putting aside their own 'special interests'. It wished at all costs to prevent its members from 'expressing any sort of oversensitivity that could easily erase the impression of the fact that for us, in times of danger to the Fatherland, only those things are important that unite all Germans'.[13] One hears here the clear desire of a minority eager to integrate, but still restricted and subject to discriminatory scrutiny. Their wish was to become invisible as a group by merging completely with the national community. The tension between the wish to belong and the rejection experienced until then led to a high degree of self-mobilization for the sake of the 'common cause'.

This degree of self-divestment could not be expected from the Zionist and Orthodox proclamations at the outbreak of war. The ZVD in particular, as a member of the World Zionist Organization, had difficulty explaining why Jews, who formed one people despite their differing citizenships, should now shoot at each other. Thus it emphasized that the war also involved specifically Jewish interests, in particular the liberation of eastern European Jews from Tzarist rule. The *Jüdische Rundschau*, the central Zionist press organ in Germany, wrote on 21 August 1914: 'They [the Russians] will be taught a lesson that will rob them of their lust to pogrom even the powerless in their own country. And when our Zionist youth enthusiastically volunteers to serve under the German flag to protect Germany's freedom and honour from the heroes of crime, in their hearts burns another, particular fury: Revenge for Kishinev!'[14] Kishinev, of course, had been the site of an infamous anti-Jewish pogrom in 1903. Similarly, articles in Orthodox press organs underlined the significance of the war as a 'Jewish war' aimed at liberating eastern European Jews.[15]

All in all, German Jews allowed themselves to be swept up just as much as their Christian countrymen in the national enthusiasm at the outbreak of war, in the common experience of August 1914, and in the vague but highly charged hopes of a 'true' and 'united' Germany.[16] Their collective commitment and willingness to mobilize may, in fact, have been even stronger, as a way of compensating for their own marginality by 'overfulfilling' their duties. In retrospect, sociologist Franz Oppenheimer described the motives and mood of Jewish volunteers in August 1914 as follows: 'Now we'll fight our way out of quarter-citizenship, the hated *Metökentum*, to full citizenship. Now we can and will show that we love our Fatherland no less passionately than anyone else; now we will prove that we possess no less strength, courage and willingness to sacrifice.'[17] Kurt Alexander, the editor of the liberal

Jewish *K. C. Blätter* expressed the same attitude when he wrote in September 1914: 'We have to endure the sad experience that even though a great period of time has elapsed, people still minimize our deeds and our work and still will not observe us for what we are. Therefore it is our holy duty to do more than anyone else. Each Jew must attempt to become a hero, whether it is in battle or in his occupation is unimportant. The deeds of each Jew must be so worthy that they are written into the history of the German people with golden letters.'[18]

These calls were not mere rhetoric. It is nearly impossible to quantify Jewish participation in the war; since Jewish organizations were officially forbidden from keeping wartime statistics, and the data collected as a result of the 'Jewish census' in the German military on 1 November 1916 – insofar as they were published – are unreliable.[19] However, more careful post-war statistics that take into account the particular demographic structure of the German Jews suggest that Jewish participation in military service was at least comparable to that of the non-Jewish population.[20] And non-military sacrifice must also be considered – for example, the Jews' large financial contribution to the war effort through subscriptions to war bonds, and the prominent involvement of numerous members of the Jewish economic elite, such as Walter Rathenau, in the organization of the German war economy.

Jewish expectations of greater integration seemed justified at the outset of the war. During the initial months, a number of events indicated a change in policy towards the Jewish minority. Because of the *Burgfrieden*, the anti-semitic press softened its polemics against the Jewish minority, or was forced to do so by the military censor – at least in cases of major disturbances of domestic peace. In individual cases, anti-semitic writers were even forbidden to publish or to speak in public. Thus, for the first time, the fight against anti-semitism did not fall solely to the Jews, but was taken officially in hand by the state. Elsewhere, the restrictions responsible for the fact that not a single Jewish applicant had been accepted into the German officers' corps (with the exception of Bavaria) since 1885 – not even as a reserve officer – were lifted.[21] As a result of increased demand for personnel during the war, Jews were once again promoted to the rank of officer (with captain as the highest rank), although their numbers were few and began to diminish as early as 1915. Jewish military chaplains were offered the same privileges as their Christian counterparts.[22] On the home front, Jewish experts were called upon as advisors in various capacities by national and military authorities, and entrusted with official responsibilities. Numerous Jewish bankers and commercial experts were appointed to high positions in the

German war economy, for example in the war societies (*Kriegsge-sellschaften*). Walter Rathenau's creation of the War Raw Materials Department in the Ministry of War is only the most spectacular example of the Jewish economic elite's extensive participation in the war effort.[23]

Finally, on such foreign policy issues as the future of eastern European Jews in a newly created east–central Europe dominated by Germany, German Jewish experts were invited to give their views. In some cases, after these regions were conquered, they were even granted administrative powers. The various aid committees founded by German Jews to support their eastern European co-religionists, such as the Komitee für den Osten or, later, the Deutsche Vereinigung für die Interessen der osteuro-päischen Juden, worked closely with the German military administration and attempted (though generally unsuccessfully) to influence German policies in the occupied areas in the direction of their own aims.[24]

At least during the first months of the war, the experience of Jewish soldiers seemed to confirm hopes that greater integration would occur. In September 1914, a Jewish volunteer wrote from the battlefields: 'I am convinced now, as I have always been, that at least in war we are all equal.' Three months later, another soldier reported, that 'in the fields there are no Catholics, no Protestants, no Jews, no Centrists, no Social Democrats . . . but only Germans, as our Kaiser has already pro-claimed'.[25]

As the war claimed ever more victims and sacrifices, however, the fragile *Burgfrieden* began to show signs of fracture, posing an increasing threat to the position of the Jewish minority. This was largely the result of the propagandistic activities of anti-semitic organizations, which the censors restricted less and less. The anti-semitic movement had been losing ground continually since the 1890s as a contender in party politics due to internal splintering. However, it had undergone organizational reform following the Reichstag elections of 1912, in which the Social Democrats became the strongest party, and new anti-semitic associa-tions were founded, including the Verband gegen die Uberhebung des Judentums and the Reichshammerbund. In addition to the already anti-semitically-oriented trade associations, such as the Bund der Landwirte and the Deutschnationaler Handlungsgehilfenverband, anti-semitic views began to dominate nationalist organizations like the chauvinist Pan-German League (Alldeutscher Verband).[26]

The ideology of anti-semitism combined anti-capitalism, anti-socialism, anti-modernism and *völkisch* nationalism, and considered the 'Jewish question' to be the key to all political, social and cultural ills. By the early years of the twentieth century, however, the ideology had moved farther and farther away from confronting the actual conflicts between Jews and non-Jews. It had become instead a comprehensive world view, a political shibboleth for the anti-liberal, reactionary camp.[27] It served as a means of integrating traditional conservatives and the more radical *völkisch* elements in the right-wing spectrum, which felt themselves to be increasingly on the defensive, given the electoral victory of the democratic parties. In the radical anti-semites' pessimistic world view, distinguished by expectations of harm and decadence, the 'Jewish elections' of 1912 spelled danger. They were prepared to go as far as a *putsch* to further their 'defensive struggle' against alleged 'Jewish subversion of the Fatherland' and 'enemies of the Reich'. This is indicated by plans drafted by leading pan-Germanists like Class and von Gebsattel, which would have installed a military dictatorship to eliminate parliamentarianism and Jewish civil rights, and eventually expel the Jewish population.[28] From this point of view, Germany's 'salvation' could only be found in the exclusion of the Jews from public life. It was hoped that a future war would foster a new racial consciousness among the German people and permanently separate 'Germanness' and 'Jewishness'.[29]

Given this attitude, it is not surprising that a *Burgfrieden* encompassing Jews, Social Democrats and Liberals was rejected by the 'national opposition' from the beginning.[30] Only in exceptional cases did anti-semitic ideologues acknowledge the German Jews' wartime efforts. Houston Stewart Chamberlain, who had made racial anti-semitism popular among the German *Bildungsbürgertum* (educated middle class), was one example. In 1914, he wrote: 'Germany has ten times as many Jews [as England], and where are they now? It is as though they were wiped out by the violent revolt, no longer discernible as "Jews", for they are doing their duty as Germans, facing the enemy or on the home front.'[31] Such general observations clearly contradicted the anti-semites' own world view, so that their propaganda strategy after the outbreak of war consisted of making the 'Jews' once again visible. Already in August 1914, the anti-semitic Reichshammerbund encouraged its members to make 'war enquiries' regarding the Jews.[32] The anti-semitic propaganda aimed to segregate the Jews on the pretence of being 'un-German', and to denounce them as 'harmful' and 'dangerous' to the polity. For example, the notorious anti-semite Theodor Fritsch wrote in October 1914: 'A *Burgfrieden* is impossible as long as one group of the population which is bound by separate laws continues to seek its own particular advantage and place its own interests maliciously above those of the totality.'[33] In consideration of the censors, the attacks were at first aimed at Jews from Germany living in enemy territory; later they were directed against the German Jews themselves.

Four basic accusations were used to encourage renewed segregation of the latter. Firstly, it was claimed that 'the Jews' in the war societies (*Kriegsgesellschaften*) were making money from the war (as 'profiteers'), keeping food artificially scarce so as to increase their profits. Highly visible prominent persons such as Rathenau, Ballin and Melchior were offered as 'evidence' of the 'judaization' (*Verjudung*) of the war societies. In effect, Jews were blamed for the poor supply situation and other economic ills in wartime Germany.[34] Secondly, 'the Jews' were held to be 'shirking' service at the front and to be disproportionately represented behind the lines and on the home front ('their grinning faces were everywhere but in the trenches!').[35] Thirdly, 'the Jews' were accused of assisting mass emigration by their eastern European co-religionists to Germany ('six million inferior, Mongolized people').[36] These were deemed to be a great threat.[37] Fourthly, the 'Jewish press' (which meant, for example, large liberal dailies like the *Berliner Tageblatt* or the *Frankfurter Zeitung*) spread the 'poison' of democratic ideas, thus 'subverting' the German people's political and moral resistance.[38]

The anti-semites spread this propaganda in numerous petitions, complaints and memoranda to the authorities, as well as in newspapers and pamphlets. This had not been much different before the war, when the propaganda had enjoyed little success with those in power. However, war weariness and a growing general sense of dissatisfaction created a need for scapegoats, and anti-semitic agitation found sympathetic ears. In addition, anti-Jewish attitudes – in a seemingly more 'moderate' form – had become widespread, not only among the conservative nobility but also among the academically educated bourgeoisie. Most of the elite in the administration and the military were likely to harbour anti-Jewish sentiment. During the war, a *rapprochement* between moderate and radical (the so-called *Radau,* or 'rough') anti-semitism came about.[39] In addition, 'patriotic' bureaucrats, teachers, ministers and party function-aries – many of whom already had anti-semitic leanings – found new avenues of influence beginning in 1916, with the government's attempt to mobilize the 'spiritual and moral home-front forces'.[40] This had the effect – whether it was intended by the government or not – of renewing the tendency to exclude Jews.

A new opportunity for the political instrumentalization of anti-semitism arose with the growing polarization of public opinion con-cerning submarine warfare, electoral reform and war aims. Bethmann Hollweg, for example, was called the 'chancellor of Jewry' and 'servant of the Jews' in right-wing extremist propaganda.[41] Negotiated peace was denounced as a 'Jewish peace'.[42] In this way, anti-semitism functioned as an integral part of the political self-image and rhetoric of the 'national opposition', which opposed Bethmann Hollweg's policies and any democratic 'new orientation' whatsoever. For the German public, the 'Jewish question' was thus linked inextricably to the central wartime debates on domestic and foreign politics, regardless of the actions that Jews did or did not take.[43] As these controversies became more bitter, the 'Jewish question' grew disproportionately significant. In the end, even government authorities began introducing various anti-semitic measures – such as the *Judenzählung*, or Jewish census, in the German military on 1 November 1916, the simultaneously planned, but unimplemented, census of Jews in the *Kriegsgesellschaften*, and the imposition of a 'closed border' exclusively against Polish Jews in April 1918.[44]

On 11 October 1916, Prussian War Minister Adolf Wild von Hohenborn issued an order to all military commands to carry out a census of Jews serving in the military who were subject to military duty, as well as those who had not yet been drafted, released from armed service, or found temporarily or permanently unfit for duty.[45] The motives and political background of the order cannot be completely explained based on existing sources. However, it may be assumed that the decision was connected to the mobilization of all available forces demanded by the Third Supreme Army Command, under Hindenburg and Ludendorff. Because of the anti-semitic campaign, numerous complaints of Jewish 'shirking' had been received by the War Ministry. In addition, Wild von Hohenborn was under pressure as a result of the Supreme Army Command's demand that all men eligible for active duty be called up. Thus, unlike his deputy Franz Gustav von Wandel, who had been slow to handle such complaints, Wild von Hohenborn may have deemed it advisable to investigate the anti-Jewish accusations by way of an official census. It is hardly likely that he took into account the fact that such a discriminatory measure against a single group was unlikely to contribute to the desired mobilization of *all* forces, since the morale of the German Jews was certain to be considerably affected by this humiliation. The long tradition of anti-semitic prejudice and disparaging behaviour towards Jews in the Prussian military continued to operate. Although the War Ministry probably did not intend to strengthen radical anti-semitic forces through the *Judenzählung* order, it had precisely that effect. The Jews as a special group were once again made visible and suspected collectively of representing a harmful element.

To Jews, the psychological effect of the order was devastating. In the field, the rift between Christians and Jews, which had seemed at least partially healed, was opened once again. 'The Jew feels himself a marked man', an army rabbi remarked. Harmony and authority had been undermined 'because every company secretary received the "secret order", misunderstood it and had to misunderstand it to mean that he, the company secretary, was authorized, even required, to investigate his Jewish comrades for shirking'.[46] In individual cases, the order was even understood as a demand that Jewish soldiers behind the lines be sent to the front. The War Ministry was forced to check such unauthorized behaviour in a second order on 11 November 1916.[47]

The official Jewish response to the discriminatory War Ministry order remained entirely within the scope of the *Honoratiorenpolitik* (policy towards the notables) that generally characterized Jewish reactions to anti-semitism under the empire. After a Reichstag debate on 4 November, in which the measure first became public knowledge, and in which Social Democratic and Liberal deputies questioned the War Ministry's insistence that the census was not motivated by anti-semitism, the third chairman of the VDJ, Oscar Cassel, attempted to convince the government to make a declaration restoring the honour of Jewish soldiers.[48] After several petitions and an informal conversation with the new War Minister, General Hermann von Stein, Cassel was able to achieve only a personal clarification by Stein 'that the behaviour of Jewish soldiers and fellow citizens during the war gave no cause for the order by my predecessor, and thus cannot be connected with it'.[49] However, there was no public acknowledgement of the Jewish contribution to the war. This alone might have eased the humiliation of the *Judenzählung*.

Yet the functionaries of the VDJ and the CV accepted this state of affairs. They preferred neither to risk wartime gains nor to give the anti-semites a pretext for accusations of disloyalty. They felt an offensive campaign had little chance of success, though it might indeed have been possible, given the great bitterness the order had created in the Jewish community. For these reasons, they continued to keep a low profile until the end of the war, publicly emphasizing the patriotism of the German Jews. As late as 2 November 1918, the CV called a membership meeting to emphasize its 'firm commitment to our Fatherland and our religious community'.[50] It accentuated its unbroken loyalty to the government and military leadership, and announced its willingness to 'forget' all repressive measures experienced by Jews during the war in the course of future reconstruction. The official CV policy, which today appears obsequious and – given the rapidly growing anti-semitism at the end of the war – extremely unrealistic, was probably also a result of the increasingly ideological nature of the internal conflict between the CV's integrationist concept and the Zionists. The CV had placed all its hopes on the *Burgfrieden*, and continued to cling to it long after it had been proved a fiction.[51]

However, there were also many Jews who rejected the CV functionaries' restrained strategy, demanding a clearer protest against the *Judenzählung* and growing anti-semitism. The Hamburg banker Max Warburg, whose opinion carried considerable weight with the Foreign Office due to his good relations with the USA (at the time still a neutral power), sent a memorandum and letters of protest to various government offices expressing German Jewish dissatisfaction.[52] He even threatened that the *Judenzählung* could negatively affect subscriptions to new war bond issues. Although Warburg received sympathy and support from the Foreign Ministry and the Reich Chancellor, the extreme tensions between the civilian and military hierarchies made it impossible to persuade the War Minister to issue a formal apology to Jewish soldiers.[53]

Warburg's assessment of the negative atmosphere among much of German Jewry after the *Judenzählung* was not exaggerated. This is revealed in a letter from the police chief of Frankfurt-am-Main to Arnold von Wahnschaffe, under-secretary in the Reich Chancellery, on 16 January 1917, in which he described the agitation among Frankfurt's Jews – even 'sensible' and financially sound ones: 'The Jews here . . . are now intimidated, and they respond with reserve to my appeals for national contributions and the like. Even very calm people have been gripped by the agitation. In view of the forthcoming issue of new war bonds, I do not consider the situation harmless. Not that I expect opposition; but I am afraid they will not respond with enthusiasm, as in the past, but instead will watch with arms folded.'[54]

There is not enough precise data to determine whether and to what extent this fear became reality – whether the Jews' willingness to sacrifice did in fact decrease perceptibly with the anti-semitic census. There is much evidence that they continued to do their duty, but that the high degree of self-mobilization, sparked by hopes of complete integration at the start of the war, abated. However, the recognizable effect of the *Judenzählung* lay less in a change in the external political behaviour of the Jewish minority than in the intensified internal debate on its own self-definition.[55] Insecurity and disillusionment were particularly widespread among acculturated Jews who had sought a synthesis of Jewishness and Germanness. They began to come to the painful realization that anti-semitism could in no way be influenced by the positive or negative behaviour of Jews. In an article published in the CV newspaper in October 1917, this disillusionment came to the fore: 'A war after the war stands before us [the German Jews]. When the weapons are laid to rest, the war's storm will not have ended for us . . . The Reichstag accepts a peace resolution which the Pan-Germans do not like: it is a Jewish resolution; the Reichstag is not lucky enough to be in favour of the anti-semites in its entirety: it is a Jewish Reichstag . . . A negotiated peace works against them – it is a Jewish peace.'[56] Walther Rathenau, who made his position in the war materials division available as early as 1915 because of anti-semitic agitation, gave up hope of a fair assessment of the Jewish contribution to the war even before the 'Jewish census' took place.[57] Resigned to the situation, he wrote to his sister in August 1916: 'The more Jews that die in this war, the more persistently their opponents will prove that they all sat behind the front in order to profiteer from it. The hatred will double and triple.'[58]

As early as a few months after the war started, many Jewish soldiers already experienced a renewed sense of exclusion in spite of all their efforts to the contrary. In October 1914, Julius Marx wrote: 'For a while now it has become palpable to me that I am looked down upon as a Jew. Every prejudice seemed to have disappeared when the war began; there were only Germans. Now one hears the old, despicable expressions again. And suddenly one is all alone surrounded by comrades whose plight one shares, to whom one has taken a liking, with whom one marches for the common goal.'[59]

The feelings of alienation and exclusion were not solely the result of direct or indirect anti-semitic attacks. Many Jews at the front experienced the cultural gap between them and their Gentile peers as something much deeper than they had expected. At the start of the war, army Rabbi Salzberger optimistically predicted that the war would result in a better understanding between Jews and Christians: 'This close life together [in war] results in a very precise process of acquaintance: each man acts as he is. We Jews can only rejoice at this: when they get to know us, they will also learn to understand and respect us.'[60] The reality was otherwise, as army Rabbi Lewin discovered: 'The process of mutual acquaintance, with its unheard-of intimacy, seldom taught kinship: it uncovered differences.'[61] It was on the battlefield that Rabbi Lewin, like many Jews, first noticed the extent to which he had lived in a ghetto, the extent to which the world of his non-Jewish comrades was alien to him. Alienation was felt particularly in the company of others, during the crude soldierly rituals, the drinking bouts and the sexual jokes in the officers' club. But the feeling of not belonging was also experienced alone, when the Jewish holidays had to be spent on the battlefield.[62]

The majority of the Jews were also psychologically far removed from the nationalist pathos and religious fervour of *Kriegserlebnis und Heldentod* (war experience and heroic death), which were propagated in innumerable sermons, poems and pamphlets, and which became the basis for the myth of the front-line soldier after the war. The internal distance had less to do with the fact that this national myth was permanently bound to Christian conceptions of martyrdom and salvation than with the fact that the Enlightenment ideals of cosmopolitanism and liberalism remained meaningful aspirations for the Jewish bourgeoisie long after they had ceased to be so for its Protestant counterpart.[63] The religious tradition of non-violence and pacifism, the belief that a pious Jew could be 'a good soldier, but never a good militarist', and not least the vague notion that a common bond connected Jews across the fronts, all help explain why the Jewish elites saw through the illusions of the German war leadership earlier than others, and why they agreed to a quick negotiated peace.[64]

The alienation and sense of setback that many Jews experienced on the battlefield led to a new sentiment of Jewish solidarity and togetherness. For many assimilated 'western Jews', their encounter with the Jewish communities in eastern Europe, which they felt to be 'authentic' and 'powerful', was decisive.[65] Others drew a logical conclusion from the 'Jewish census' and became Zionists. Ernst Simon described his conversion experience especially forcefully: 'All this [the cleft between Germans and Jews brought about by the 'Jewish census'] now hit us with the full force of a terrible awakening . . . Our whole life force . . . threatened to shatter . . . if the second great living community had not opened, from which we originated and to which we returned: if Judaism had not lovingly opened it arms . . . Now we were ready to experience Judaism as something positive . . . With opened souls we enjoyed the happiness of life together with our fellow Jews . . . Here was the community we had sought our entire lives . . . At this moment we were Zionists, at first without desiring or even knowing it.'[66]

Of course individual reactions cannot easily be reduced to a common denominator. They ranged from a shift to Zionism to a religious reorientation, from defiant insistence upon the goal of German–Jewish synthesis to defection to the radical pacifist and socialist camp. For the younger generation of German Jews in particular, the experience of setbacks during the world war sparked a new awareness which, for many, led to greater emphasis on the Jewish aspect of their identity. Their negative experiences during the war also made it easier for most German Jews to accept the new democratic republic, in which they were no longer subjected to discriminatory restrictions administered by the state. But anti-semitism in society at large had by no means been overcome. The tension between integration and rejection remained characteristic of the Jewish situation in Germany long after the war, in ever more acute form. The propagandistic link between the 'Jewish question' and domestic political power struggles continued in a fatal fashion during the Weimar Republic. The year 1916 thus marked a clear turning-point in the history of the German Jews.

In conclusion, the Jewish experience in Germany during the First World War abruptly illuminated the limits of the ability to mobilize within an internally divided, largely politically paralysed society. The concept of the *Burgfrieden*, which required all citizens to unite in combating the external enemy – thus including minorities and previously disadvantaged classes – appeared to promote the model of a liberal, integrationist nation-state. It was therefore welcomed by liberal forces, above all by Jews. However, since the founding of the Reich in 1871, an alternative had developed in the form of a more narrow definition of national identity. It aimed to create *unity through exclusion*, defining the 'German nature' in opposition to all kinds of 'enemies'. This 'self-definition by branding the enemy' only rarely went as far as the irrational, *völkisch*, racist world view of the radical anti-semites.[67] But the four exclusionary campaigns of the 1870s and 1880s (against Catholics, Social Democrats, Poles and Jews) had firmly established the 'internal enemy' as a constitutive element of this form of nationalism. It became typical of the right-wing, German nationalist camp.[68] From their point of view, the *Burgfrieden* was a mistake from the beginning. It offered the 'enemies of the Reich' greater opportunities for influence, necessarily harming the 'national cause'. 'Inner unity' could only be achieved by fighting and eliminating the 'internal enemy'. Thus it is probably no accident that the anti-semitic campaigns reached their first peak in the summer and autumn of 1916, just as German society was experiencing total mobilization for war. In the end, radical racist forces had no qualms about quite explicitly blaming the Jews for the German defeat. In October 1918, the deputy head of the Pan-German League, Heinrich Class, called on his members in case of an unfavourable – that is, in his view, democratic – development in post-war Germany, to return to the 'Jewish question' for propaganda purposes and to 'use the Jews as lightning rods for all that has wronged us'.[69]

Objectively, this right-wing extremist propaganda against an illusory 'internal enemy' helped to torpedo the *Burgfrieden*, while also contributing to internal destabilization and interfering with German mobilization. That the government did not succeed in the long run in keeping these destructive anti-semitic forces at bay and effectively defending its own concept of national unity was due, in the end, to the decisive resistance of reactionary social classes, who feared that the spirit of the *Burgfrieden* would lead to democratization and their own loss of privilege. In this ambiguous situation, the German Jews had little behavioural leeway. In accordance with their own self-definition, the majority hoped to overcome the social barriers that had so far prevented their social integration by an increased willingness to make sacrifices and by enthusiastic participation in the war. When these expectations were called into question as a result of growing popular and official anti-semitism, German Jews (or at least the official policy of their most important organization) continued to cling to protestations of solidarity with the government and to the fiction of the *Burgfrieden*. Perhaps, as a minority subject to discriminatory scrutiny, they had no realistic alternative to this behaviour in time of war. However, it effected an internal change in perception which would lead to the beginnings of a new form of Jewish self-awareness during the Weimar Republic.

7   *Wackes* at war: Alsace-Lorraine and the failure of German national mobilization, 1914–1918

Alan Kramer

Introduction

In Alsace-Lorraine, a largely German-speaking region annexed from France in 1871, the mobilization process of 1914–18 was a failure that transcended the general failure of mobilization in Germany. This chapter aims to show how the military leadership proved unable to realize the military potential of its Alsace-Lorraine troops, and how the attitude of Alsace-Lorrainers towards the Reich was transformed by the war from acquiescence into hostility. The argument is thus about the breakdown not only of military, but also of political and cultural mobilization.

Before 1914, a strong regional identity was still alive, based not only on anti-Prussian resentment, but also on the ideas of parliamentary democracy under the influence of French republicanism and the legacy of 1789.[1] After the granting of the constitution in 1911 the parliamentary representatives of Alsace-Lorraine campaigned for a degree of autonomy equal to that enjoyed by the other *Länder*.[2] Its citizens continued to resent discrimination, such as the perceived lack of French language instruction and the prohibition of speaking the Alsatian dialect in schools, even in private conversation.[3] Above all they felt humiliated by the treatment of Alsace-Lorraine civilians and recruits as untrustworthy *Wackes* by the German military, as in the Zabern affair of 1913.[4]

In view of such discriminatory treatment and mutual distrust, the argument that Alsace-Lorraine hardly differed from other German regions with strong federalist tendencies, such as Bavaria, and was on the road to full integration into the Reich, is not convincing.[5] Wehler's argument, at the other extreme, that only the coming of war prevented the outbreak of new, more violent conflict between the people and the Reich authorities is unfounded speculation.[6] Almost certainly, what the people of Alsace-Lorraine preferred was republican autonomy, impossible to realize under German rule.[7] Violent confrontation was not inevitable. In a situation of so many imponderables the contingency of

105

history should be stressed. Alsace-Lorraine's rejection of confrontation by not voting for the autonomists in 1911–12 reflected both a unique identity and a conscious desire not to be the *casus belli*.

In the years after 1905, the rediscovery or re-invention of Alsace-Lorraine culture contributed to the formation of regional identity. Newspapers and weeklies in French or Alsatian dialect were founded, the concept of a unique 'dual culture' was popularized, and Alsace-Lorraine was seen a 'bridge' between France and Germany.[8] Increasingly, discontent with German rule was expressed: in 1912 the number of men who evaded military service rose for the first time since 1874.[9] This ambivalence of Alsace-Lorraine opinion towards the Reich presented a major challenge for the political and cultural mobilization of German society for war. In effect, it posed the question of whether a strong regional identity displaying apparent affinities with what was now an enemy state could be successfully incorporated into that process. Germany's ruling elites indeed saw the war as an opportunity to 'germanize Alsace-Lorraine once and for all' (Bethmann Hollweg) and 'teach the *Wackes* a good lesson' (former General Staff member Lieutenant-Colonel von Gleich).[10]

The failure of German policy towards Alsace-Lorraine was not preordained. Military mobilization appeared to be successful: during the war 380,000 men from Alsace and Lorraine served in the armed forces.[11] From the start, however, Alsatian soldiers felt alienated in the army, and the army treated both recruits and civilians from Alsace-Lorraine as unreliable, potentially treacherous elements (*Reichsfeinde*). As in other border regions, an 'intensified state of war' was applied to Alsace-Lorraine, in which executive power passed to the military commanders and most civil liberties were suspended.[12] Unlike other regions, Alsace-Lorraine was regarded virtually as enemy territory and its soldiers as the 'enemy within'. The residual hostility to the authoritarian German nation-state and the consciousness of an alternative model of political culture meant that the inhabitants of Alsace-Lorraine soon began to correspond to the negative stereotype imagined by the military.

The 'August 1914 experience' in Alsace-Lorraine

The 'ideas of August 1914' – expressed in the military, political and cultural mobilizations – were the touchstone of national unity, to which German elites returned again and again in the Great War.[13] Alsace-Lorraine proved to be an uncomfortable irritant in this. There was a concerted campaign to talk up the success of military mobilization by pro-German Alsace-Lorrainers and most German newspapers. The author Friedrich Lienhard, a *deutschgesinnter* (German-thinking) Alsatian, wrote that there were 'exceptionally numerous' volunteers in Alsace in the first weeks of war, and many had won the Iron Cross.[14] The Alsace-Lorraine press carried extravagant claims of a 'revival of German national consciousness'.[15] Gratitude was expressed by generals Deimling, Mudra and Below to the people for the smooth mobilization in the areas of the 15th, 16th and 21st Army Corps.[16] The *Statthalter* (governor) of Alsace-Lorraine, von Dallwitz, sent a telegram to the Chancellor on 4 August reporting on the 'perfect mood' of the population and their enthusiastic cheering to send off the troops.[17] But this, like the newspaper articles praising the patriotic enthusiasm of the people, was no more than an attempt to construct the special Alsace-Lorraine façade of the *Burgfrieden*.

There were some discordant notes. The right-wing *Deutsche Tageszeitung* of 19 August claimed there were several cases of treason by civilians in Gebweiler and Mulhouse; in Metz Germans were fired upon from two houses.[18] The usually pro-government *Kölnische Zeitung* of 25 August 1914 accused the inhabitants of Saarburg of treason, greeting the French warmly, and aiding them in plundering the houses of the absent Germans.[19] Assuming the reports of pro-German patriotism were not entirely fabricated, we can deduce that opinion in Alsace-Lorraine at the start of the war was polarized between pro-French and pro-German national sentiment, while the expression of ambivalent attitudes such as Alsatian regionalism was temporarily muted.

The complexity of reactions to the war can be explained by Alsace-Lorraine's social history. The widely reported enthusiasm in Strasbourg was no doubt connected with the fact that one-third of its population was *altdeutsch* (or German settlers since 1870).[20] Lower Alsace was more likely to be germanophile, for it was taken over by France fifty years later than Upper Alsace, which had come under the French crown in 1648. Lorraine had been largely under French influence since the fourteenth century. In Alsace and Lorraine the French Revolution had had a profound influence – the *Marseillaise* was composed in Strasbourg – while the movement to unite Germany had passed them by untouched. The 'notables', especially the industrialists and large landowners, tended to be francophile in language and culture, even if their business connections were with Germany. The industrial workers of Alsace, although germanophone, either followed their employers in their francophilia, or had democratic, republican, pacifist and socialist political sympathies.[21]

One way of assessing the success of mobilization is to examine the number of volunteers in the army. Despite newspaper claims of 100,000 to 150,000 volunteers, an army survey calculated there were only 8,000.[22] Of the 12,361 men who volunteered for service in the 15th Army Corps (one of the main army corps which recruited Alsace-Lorraine men) from August 1914 to June 1915, only 3,153 (25.5 per cent) were Alsace-Lorrainers; the rest were from Prussia (40.9 per cent) and other federal states.[23]

The records of the 'extraordinary war courts' reveal that patriotism and war enthusiasm were not the only sentiments expressed in Alsace-Lorraine: anti-militarism, and even outright hostility to the Reich were openly given expression. At the beginning of the war there were many cases of 'uttering incitements to rebel' (paragraph 9c of the state of siege law of 1851). For example, on 17 August a steel worker was sentenced by Diedenhofen (Thionville) court to six months in prison for shouting 'Down with the war, down with Prussia! . . . *Vive la France, merde la Prusse.*' He also allegedly insulted policemen with the epithet '*Stinkpreußen*'.[24]

In August 1914 an awakening of Alsace had been expected, but none had come, to the great disappointment of Prussia and the Reich.[25] As General von Falkenhausen, commander of the three army corps in Lower Alsace and Lorraine, wrote in his war memoirs, the appearance of mass enthusiasm in August 1914 in Alsace-Lorraine was deceptive.[26] There was near consensus among senior commanders that Alsatian loyalty was no more than an invention of government propaganda,[27] and that the population in Lorraine and Upper Alsace had been 'hostile towards the troops'.[28] The failure to mobilize volunteers and the many accounts of hostility to the German military show that the 'August 1914 experience' in Alsace-Lorraine was a chimera.

Germanophobia: an invention of the military?

German soldiers entered Alsace-Lorraine predisposed to believe that the civilian population was at best uncooperative and unpatriotic, at worst liable to help the enemy, even engage in armed resistance. As early as 3 August a large number of rumours about Alsace-Lorraine were circulating – spies had been caught, mayors executed, and francophile priests and the mayor of Zabern locked up.[29] In fact, the arrest of about 400 Alsace-Lorraine citizens at the start of mobilization, including many notables, twenty Catholic priests from the Metz diocese and several autonomist members of the Landtag, demonstrates that Alsace-Lorraine was regarded as a real threat.[30] By contrast, no Social Democrats, those great *Reichsfeinde*, were arrested at this stage of the war. The events at Burzweiler, Dalheim, Dornach and St Moritz, incidents in which civilians were accused of firing on German troops, coupled with tendentious press reports, assisted the growth of distrust and prejudice. At Burzweiler six civilians were shot in a dawn execution on 14 August.[31] In St Moritz near Schlettstadt (Sélestat), in the night of 18–19 August, after there was allegedly shooting at the German troops from the houses, the people were ordered out into the street with their hands up, and several were killed.[32]

Even everyday encounters with the Alsace-Lorraine population made the German soldiers assume widespread hostility. The initial impression given to German soldiers was that the local population refused to cooperate with the war effort. Lieutenant-Colonel von Gleich, commander of the 25th Dragoon regiment, noted in his diary on 4 August 1914 that the people in Saaraltdorf (Lorraine) were hostile to Germany. Indeed, he said, the *Wackes* were all untrustworthy: not only did they show no enthusiasm, but they also put up passive resistance at every step. They complained they were being impoverished by the high number of German soldiers billeted on them, and claimed to have run out of oats, but officers soon found six hundredweight of oats at the house of the mayor, who allegedly had been a *franc-tireur* in the Franco-Prussian war.[33]

At the declaration of hostilities French troops captured the south-western corner of Upper Alsace, and kept it until the end of the war. They also occupied for a few days Mulhouse, Sennheim, Gebweiler, the western outskirts of Colmar, the middle Vosges, and a strip of Lorraine. The French invasion of Mulhouse on 8 August was greeted by the local people who allegedly joined the troops in singing the *Marseillaise* and danced in the streets. This first French visit was ended by the German advance the next day.[34] The reception given to the French on their second visit to Mulhouse, 19 to 24 August, was more reserved, because the people had in the meantime been subjected to interrogation and threats by the German army.[35] The Mulhouse area was regarded with special suspicion by the German troops, not only because of the brief French invasion, but also because of the collective memories of the Franco-Prussian war and the fear of *franc-tireur* and proletarian resistance.[36]

In reality, opposition to Germany was expressed only by individuals, and left traces only when they came into conflict with the state. Only a small proportion of anti-German incidents therefore came before the courts, but the absolute number is high, given that courts could only try persons who were overheard and denounced. By the end of the war there had been at least 2,389 prosecutions for 'showing an anti-German attitude' (paragraph 9b, state of siege law, 1851), about 80 per cent of them successful.[37] Army Department B collected numerous examples of anti-German remarks made by people in the Weiler, Breusch and Leber valleys, which, it said, were representative of all of Alsace-Lorraine: deriding German bulletins, doubting news of victories, spreading stories of atrocities committed by German soldiers, singing about liberating Alsace from the 'barbarians', singing the *Marseillaise* in the presence of German soldiers, boycotting and refusing to speak to 'German-minded' Alsatians, and desecrating the graves of fallen German soldiers with words like 'Here rest fifteen Bavarian swines.'[38]

Another expression of opposition was 'provocative use of French'.[39] This form of cultural francophilia was more important than has hitherto been assumed. French had great symbolic value even for germano-phones, who made up 1.6 million out of Alsace-Lorraine's total population of 1.8 million.[40] While pre-war German policy on the French language was a 'reasonable achievement' that had taken some account of the needs of the French-speaking minority, in contrast with language policy towards the Danish and Polish minorities and with French policy after 1918, the hostility of the military towards the French language in wartime rapidly destroyed any remaining good-will.[41] Using French in public was a cultural demonstration of hostility to the military or of anti-Reich sentiment, and for this reason in autumn 1914 the military government issued proclamations which contradicted the relatively enlightened language policy pursued hitherto. The language conflict was most intense in Lorraine, where one-quarter of the population were francophone.[42] The army prohibited the speaking of French in the street or in taverns under pain of arrest.[43] Firms had to cease using French in their business correspondence.[44] All French signs had to be removed within forty-eight hours from houses, shops and other premises, and the use of French on printed forms, invoices, etc., was prohibited.[45] General von Falkenhausen ordered the 'germanization' of several thousand French place-names in Lower Alsace and Lorraine.[46]

Anti-Reich sentiment in Alsace-Lorraine, although it was not part of a political programme and there was no organized demonstration of opposition, was thus not merely a reaction to German suspicions: it was an underlying mentality, rejuvenated by the experience of military rule and wartime mobilization.

Alsace-Lorrainers in the army

The degree of loyalty of many young men to the German state can be seen in the fact that of the 16,000 Alsace-Lorraine men living abroad who had received their mobilization papers in March 1914, only 4,000 returned. In addition, at the start of the war at least 7,000 court martial cases for desertion were pending. During the war 17,650 men from Alsace-Lorraine served in the French army (*engagés volontaires*).[47] Once war began, men liable for conscription evaded military service by fleeing across the borders. There were stories of groups of from 20 to 150 men, even of the entire male population of military age of some villages, crossing the border to France in the early days of the war.[48] At least 3,000 young men escaped to France to avoid the call-up.[49] From the neutral zone, bordering Switzerland, there was a continual haemorrhage of men. But proximity to the border was only one factor. The army commanders in Upper Alsace were in no doubt that the population were 'lukewarm in their patriotism', 'shirking' was common, and that military service was seen to be a punishment. Village mayors tried to sabotage the call-up.[50] Significant numbers of men evaded military service; e.g. in Markirch, Upper Alsace, out of a population of 11,800, no fewer than 811 men evaded military service.[51] By June 1917, out of 427 men liable for service in the border zone, 213 had fled into Switzerland.[52] Thereafter conscripts were informed only a few hours before their departure and guarded by soldiers until then. In Lorraine and Lower Alsace, too, a 'very high number' of men evaded military service.[53]

Paradoxically, as if to reinforce the idea that military service was punishment, the army resorted to mobilization as a means of repression. In August 1915 the army called up almost the entire adult male population of a part of Alsace, expressly for political reasons. The extreme limits of the definition of 'fitness for military or labour service' were to be applied.[54] The result of such measures was not improved mobilization, but increased discontent. The call-up was unpopular from an early stage in all parts of Alsace-Lorraine.[55] Towards the end of the war, an increasing number of civilians called on men to desert.[56]

Once in the army, Alsace-Lorraine men employed various stratagems to defend themselves against the widespread discrimination: group solidarity with fellow-countrymen; refusal to obey dangerous orders; the open expression of hostility to Germany; desertion; and even mutiny. Above all, it was desertion which prompted the military authorities to react, for desertion not only had the potential to demoralize the remaining men, but also brought the danger of the betrayal of military secrets. But although desertion statistics have to be viewed with caution, since armies are not always able to distinguish between men taken prisoner in a battle and those taking advantage of obscure circumstances to desert, there is much subjective evidence of a high rate of desertion. The Quartermaster-General calculated that up to July 1917 more than 1,000 Alsace-Lorraine soldiers had deserted to the enemy, or 80 men per 10,000. The comparable figure for other German men was one deserter per 10,000 soldiers.[57] At least another 530 men deserted from December 1917 to September 1918.[58]

The response was repression and increased discrimination. The first measure was to have Alsace-Lorrainers regarded as 'unreliable' transferred to the eastern front. As from October 1914 several army corps on the western front began to demand the removal of their Alsace-Lorraine troops.[59] In December 1914 some men were transferred east, and rumours soon began to circulate that this was not for merely operational reasons, but because Alsace-Lorrainers were regarded as potential traitors. By March 1915 there was a systematic policy to remove those Alsace-Lorraine soldiers whose unreliability presented a danger, and send them to the eastern front.[60]

For some time, the level of desertions abated. Transfer to the eastern front had the desired effect.[61] However, there were several unintended consequences. It created or worsened a sense among the Alsace-Lorraine troops that the Reich rejected them, and produced unreliability where there was previously loyalty. Loyal Alsace-Lorraine troops transferred to the east resented the humiliation of being regarded as potential traitors. An Alsatian soldier, Dominik Richert, recorded in his memoirs the disastrous effect on morale. In early March 1915 Richert, by nature a pacifist who had thought of desertion as early as September 1914, travelled to Freiburg in the company of Alsatians who cursed the Prussians and used expressions which 'did not sound very patriotic'.[62] In his new unit, Replacement Battalion 112, the mood of the Alsatians due to be transported to the eastern front was grim.[63] General Eberhard, who had commanded several Prussian regiments in which Alsace-Lorraine men performed well, confirmed that the order to transfer all Alsace-Lorraine soldiers to the east had a devastating effect on morale.[64]

But even before discrimination had transformed the morale of Alsace-Lorrainers, they had a separate identity. One element of this was the divergent attitude to humanity in warfare implied by Richert. He recounts how a Baden soldier wanted to kill a wounded Frenchman on 9 August 1914, but Richert and an Alsatian comrade managed to stop 'the monster' from carrying out his intention.[65] On the day of the notorious order issued by Major-General Stenger not to take prisoners, 26 August 1914, having seen an NCO kill a wounded Frenchman, Richert prevented him from killing a second wounded soldier: he parried the NCO's bayonet thrust and shouted, 'If you touch him I'll kill you!' Richert bandaged the wounded Frenchman, who wept and thanked him. Since Richert could not speak French, he pointed to himself and said: 'Alsacien Kamerad!'[66] Clearly, Richert expected a Frenchman to understand that an Alsatian was a different kind of German.[67]

The demoralizing effect of the imputation of collective guilt is well illustrated by Richert's account. On 1 January 1917 he and all the other Alsace-Lorrainers were taken out of the division to which his 44th Regiment belonged. The division was to be transferred to the western front, while the Alsace-Lorraine men had to stay on the Russian front. Although the Alsace-Lorraine men knew that conditions on the western front were far more dangerous, they felt the discrimination intensely. Next day the several hundred Alsace-Lorraine soldiers of the division set out on their march to the north. The swift change in mood was amply evident, as the men muttered audible imprecations, and also shouts of 'Epinal!', 'Vive la France!' and 'Vive l'Alsace!' An anti-German song in Alsatian dialect was heard, and when the commanding officer gave the order to sing a marching song the men refused, and sang instead the Alsace song, 'O Straßburg, o Straßburg, du wunderschöne Stadt!'[68] This sense of a regional identity, reinforced by collective humiliation, was the common experience of Alsace-Lorraine troops.[69] It indicates the existence of a more complex set of mentalities than a dichotomous model of 'patriotism/defeatism', or 'pro/anti-German', and shows that under different circumstances, the German state could have successfully mobilized the men from Alsace and Lorraine.

The remaining long-serving and apparently 'reliable' Alsace-Lorrainers on the western front were subjected to continued harassment and the suspicion of treachery, above all in relation to the battle of Verdun.[70] This may have been the reason for the continued measures of security imposed by the army, which the Alsace-Lorraine men *and* their German comrades could easily interpret as discrimination. Thus, as from autumn 1917, Alsace-Lorraine soldiers were deployed only in mixed units and not on advance patrols from which they might desert.[71] However, mixing Alsace-Lorraine soldiers with 'reliable' troops created the risk of 'contamination'. Alsace-Lorrainers who were previously regarded as reliable and had been awarded the Iron Cross were identified as the main influence in the increased number of desertions of soldiers irrespective of regional background in summer 1917.[72] In August 1917 the Second Quartermaster-General, Hahndorff, circulated a secret memorandum which claimed that the prosecution of the war had suffered serious losses because of the treasonable activities of Alsace-Lorraine soldiers and civilians.[73]

Again the response was to intensify repression, and the Ministry of War instructed all area commands to publish warnings that deserters were mistaken in thinking that they would be pardoned after the war.[74]

The number of deserters was such that in January 1917 the previous practice of publishing lists of deserters was deemed undesirable, for it could 'only have a harmful effect abroad'.[75] Before transfer back to the western front, 'unreliable' elements were weeded out and left in the east.[76] But it proved to be very difficult to distinguish between 'reliable' and 'unreliable' men,[77] for most men were careful not to let suspicions arise, and were thus usually 'reliable' soldiers. In December 1917 one regiment called the Alsace-Lorraine soldier the 'enemy in our own ranks', and demanded a thorough purge of all Alsace-Lorrainers, 'for the morale of the troops is seriously endangered by the justified distrust and growing hatred they have for the *Reichsländer*' (i.e. Alsace-Lorrainers).[78]

At the end of December 1917 Army Group Duke Albrecht, which was soon to become responsible within the army for collecting all material on Alsace-Lorraine, exasperated by the desertion of Alsace-Lorraine men who had served loyally for a long time, recommended abandoning the policy of mixing Alsace-Lorrainers with 'reliable' units. Any further redistribution would mean that soon not one division could be completely relied on, and the plans of the German army would no longer be safe from betrayal anywhere. The Alsace-Lorrainers could only be prevented from deserting by stern measures of repression. The Army Group demanded an imperial proclamation that all deserters would be punished with the death penalty.[79] By the end of 1917 the Chief of General Staff decreed a ban on the wholesale transfer of Alsace-Lorrainers to the east.[80] On 12 January 1918 the Ministry of War cancelled the decree of May 1917 which regulated the transfer of Alsace-Lorraine troops from the western front because the 'changed situation on the eastern front' would mean that the 'unreliability of Alsace-Lorrainers would be rewarded' by not having to face the dangers and difficulties of the fighting on the western front.[81]

Meanwhile, the discrimination against Alsace-Lorraine soldiers had begun to worry the Ministry of War. In August 1917 the minister wrote to the Army Group Duke Albrecht, admitting that Alsace-Lorraine men were frequently treated in an unfair and offensive manner. The minister asked the commanders to instruct all army units to ensure unprejudiced treatment.[82]

Constitutional reform and the failure of remobilization, 1917–1918

In 1917 there was a concerted effort by government and publicists to win back the support of Alsace-Lorraine. In late 1914, despite press censorship, news had emerged of the plans to dismember Alsace-

Lorraine: Alsace was to be given to Bavaria, and Lorraine to Prussia as a penalty for their disloyalty. The debate on the plans produced three years of uncertainty and a feeling of damage done to the right of self-determination.[83] As a secret service agent reported in October 1917, there was a widespread impression among the people of Alsace-Lorraine that Germany would lose the war, and Alsace-Lorraine would be repartitioned, or even that Germany would have to renounce control of the territory.[84] The Minister of the Interior, Wallraf, admitted in a long memorandum of 29 December 1917 that the people of Alsace-Lorraine had been repelled by harsh military rule, and that the people's real mood was reflected in the anti-German conduct and opinions collected in Hahndorff's memorandum.[85]

In June 1917 a conference was held at the invitation of the Oberste Heeresleitung (OHL – the supreme command) in Bingen, at which the Second Quartermaster-General, Hahndorff, senior officials from the Alsace-Lorraine government and Berlin ministries, and important military figures were present. Just as the government capitulated that spring to the OHL's radical programme of war aims, including extensive annexations in Europe and a colonial empire, it agreed, at the bidding of the OHL, to force the germanization of Alsace-Lorraine, above all by liquidating French ownership of property and settling German farmers in Lorraine.[86]

Erzberger, the influential Centre Party politician who had been an extreme annexationist and had favoured the plan to repartition Alsace-Lorraine, changed his policies in July 1917 and accepted that only by granting full autonomy within the Reich could the wishes of the people of Alsace-Lorraine be met and the basis laid for peace negotiations with France.[87] This became the demand of the Reichstag majority parties as from July 1917, but it proved impossible to overcome the resistance of the military and successive governments. Nevertheless, it unleashed a major debate in Germany on the future of Alsace-Lorraine. For example, Dietrich Schäfer, who published a memorandum in 1917 at the request of the Pan-German League, was in no doubt 'that an autonomous Alsace-Lorraine will strive away from the Reich', while Kautsky published a study that lent implicit support to the idea of autonomy.[88] The gulf separating the two sides in German politics is illustrated by the Kaiser's marginal comments on a memorandum by Foreign Minister von Kühlmann. On Kühlmann's rejection of the plan to repartition Alsace-Lorraine because of the unfavourable international repercussions, Wilhelm wrote: 'That's exactly what I intend! None of the enemies' business!' On Kühlmann's proposal to grant autonomy, he wrote: 'So that the French can enter as quickly as possible! Never!'

Wilhelm commented at the end: 'I have known and studied the Alsace-Lorrainers for thirty years and can only say . . . that Herr von Kühlmann has no idea at all of real conditions there. Autonomy is absolutely *impossible*. I will never grant it.'[89] There was deadlock, and the question was left unresolved until October 1918.

Coinciding with the attempt by the OHL to remobilize German opinion for the spring offensive of 1918, the campaign to remobilize Alsace-Lorraine soldiers was intensified, involving a mixture of threats and promises. On 1 February 1918 Ludendorff demanded a propaganda campaign, using wall posters to reach every civilian.[90] The effect of the campaign must have been somewhat diminished by Ludendorff's unreasonable insistence that the high level of desertions of Alsace-Lorrainers was not caused by dissatisfaction with their conditions of service. The Richert memoirs and the many letters intercepted by postal control in 1918 bear eloquent witness to the contrary.[91] In a seven-week period from mid-February to early April 1918, the Field Post Inspection Department for a small area, Mulhouse and its immediate vicinity, uncovered fifty-three letters from soldiers indicating their intention to desert or refuse to go to the front, some simply adducing war-weariness, but many displaying an anti-German attitude.[92] Many referred obliquely to the remobilization campaign. One wrote:

Yesterday I read another piece in the newspaper about Alsace. At the start of the war we were *Wackes* and Frenchheads and spies, and now the Alsatians are heroes and brave soldiers. But I don't want to be any of that. The main thing is to return home in good health.[93]

Clearly, Ludendorff did not have much confidence in his own measures. The campaign was combined with an effort to shield the soldiers from the deleterious effects of exposure to the home front by restricting their leave entitlement. A directive from Ludendorff of 28 February cancelled home leave for Alsace-Lorraine soldiers in all but exceptional cases.[94] In fact, Ludendorff's assessment that soldiers who had just returned from home leave were often prone to desert was correct.[95] Several divisions reported in summer 1918 that even reliable men deserted after returning from home leave in Alsace-Lorraine.[96]

In the early days of the offensive the Army Group Duke Albrecht, while recognizing that the treatment of Alsace-Lorraine conscripts was in principle an insoluble problem, recommended a policy of attempting to rekindle the patriotism of the Alsace-Lorrainers by selecting for praise the loyal men whose reliability had been exemplary. The Army Group conceded that 'every soldier from Alsace-Lorraine is regarded as a dubious element – with full justification'. But postal control had revealed

that many Alsace-Lorrainers with a 'good German attitude' were
suffering badly from the mistrust they encountered. By distributing the
absolutely reliable men among Alsace-Lorraine replacement troops it
was hoped to achieve a good 'educational influence'.[97]

The policy did not work. The increasing number of desertions,
frequently of experienced, reliable and decorated men, acted as an
example to the inexperienced recruits.[98] One division, from which an
Alsatian deserted just before the spring offensive, took all Alsace-
Lorraine men out of the front, although it was aware that tactical
necessities ran counter to political considerations.[99] Perhaps the
problems faced by the German state in mobilizing its people were in
general insoluble, because of the nature of the authoritarian nation-state.
The alternative policy suggested in a newspaper article published in
autumn 1917 by General von Deimling, commander of the 15th Army
Corps, was predicated on non-discrimination, recognition of Alsace-
Lorraine particularism, trust rather than suspicion, tolerance rather than
repression. He spoke out against the collective condemnation of Alsace-
Lorraine soldiers, and praised the bravery and loyalty of the Alsatians
who had fought willingly against the French for three years.[100]
Deimling's turn to pacifism as a result of his war experience and his
career as a democrat in the Weimar Republic show that the alternative
course would have been diametrically opposed to the essence of the
authoritarian nation-state. In his reply to Hindenburg's letter criticizing
the newspaper article, Deimling outlined what such a policy might have
looked like. He was positive about the Alsatians in his corps, and he had
many Alsatian officers who knew how to treat their fellow-countrymen;
he ensured that the Alsatians were not treated with mistrust and
prejudice, and that they collectively were not held to blame for the
misdemeanours of individuals. The sense of alienation caused by
collective penalties had not been restricted to the Alsatian soldiers, but
had spread to the population. Moreover, the 'mean and bureaucratic'
treatment of the home leave applications of the Alsatians had increased
their bitterness. Deimling claimed that before the war the majority of the
people, especially the rural population, had been pro-German. The
reason for the shift in attitude lay in the mistakes 'which we have made
in wartime in our treatment of the Alsatians'.[101]

Although the evidence presented here suggests strongly that most
Alsace-Lorraine soldiers were hostile to the Reich by 1917, a survey
conducted by the Army Group Duke Albrecht in summer 1918 found
that many divisions still regarded the men from Alsace-Lorraine as
reliable. But the officers who wrote the reports were looking for active
disloyalty, such as desertion. They were not looking at the results of

postal control or other sources of evidence of mentalities. Many of the reports contained *de facto* admissions of the failure of German mobilization.[102] While the 46th Landwehr Division reported that with very few exceptions all its Alsace-Lorraine troops had proved themselves to be good soldiers who demonstrated their patriotism by signing war loans and contributing donations to the Ludendorff appeal, this was in fact an exception: the Alsace-Lorraine soldiers had only been with this division since mid-July, hardly an adequate time for assessment.[103] The 106th Division, which had a large number of Alsace-Lorrainers, divided them into two categories: the reliable, dutiful soldiers, and the 'taciturn or dishonest' men who could not be trusted. But even reliable men who had served in the division for months or years had sometimes deserted.[104] The Army Group Crown Prince Rupprecht (of Bavaria) reported that treatment of Alsace-Lorraine soldiers varied widely; if treated correctly, they were good, reliable soldiers.[105] The 4th Army confirmed this, but recognized that a considerable proportion were unreliable, because of the 'failings of the German administration over the past nearly fifty years', and military responses which had had a deleterious effect.[106] The 34th Infantry Division could 'not pass a favourable judgement on the Alsace-Lorrainers'.[107]

Acquiescence to military discipline despite alienation undoubtedly characterized the conduct of most Alsace-Lorraine recruits until the end of 1917, but not their underlying mentalities. The attempted remobilization of late 1917–early 1918 was dissolved by a deluge of anti-Reich sentiment among the Alsace-Lorraine soldiers starting in the spring of 1918, amounting to a process of mental demobilization. In Infantry Regiment 353 there was a case of mass insubordination in March, when the seventy Alsace-Lorraine soldiers were placed under arrest and armed guard: while in detention they caused a disturbance, sang 'our national anthem' – the *Marseillaise* – talked back to the regiment's commander who tried to reawaken their patriotism, announced they would refuse to go to the front, and threatened to desert. 'After such treatment . . . we cannot feel ourselves to be German any longer', they said.[108]

Given the heightened tension in spring 1918 it is hardly surprising that there was eventually a mutiny of Alsatian soldiers, on 12 May 1918 at Beverloo training camp, Belgium. News of the Beverloo mutiny reached the enemy, and British and French newspapers alleged that 10,000 Alsatian troops were involved. According to German reports, only twenty-four men attempted to escape; they were given relatively lenient sentences by the court martial. Nevertheless, at least several hundred men were involved in the discussion of plans for a mass breakout.[109] According to one witness the camp contained 8,000

Alsatian soldiers, 'a large number' of whom intended deserting to Holland, using force if necessary. From then on the Alsatians were kept under armed guard at all times, and when men were transported to the front there were 'innumerable guards at the station'.[110] Having learnt from the Beverloo mutiny, the authorities managed to prevent a later mutiny by withholding the men's ammunition and removing a spring from the rifles. There were at least three further near mutinies of Alsace-Lorrainers in August–September 1918.[111]

The military commanders, informed by postal control and other means, were well aware of the landslide in public opinion. In June 1918 the Ministry of War realized that the restrictive treatment of home leave applications was causing hardship. The Ministry conceded that the purpose of the restrictions – to shield the men from the anti-German influence of the home environment – could no longer be met by maintaining them, and therefore lifted the restrictions, except for the war zone. Switching policy towards conciliation, the Ministry was prepared to put up with some 'disagreeable incidents', in the hope that the people of Alsace-Lorraine would not be 'permanently alienated from the Fatherland by over-harsh measures'.[112] This was an irrational expectation. In any case, in September 1918 troops were still not being granted home leave, despite a reminder sent by Ludendorff, and they complained bitterly about this in their letters.[113] By mid-September 1918 the Army Group Duke Albrecht finally recognized the game was up: the people of Alsace-Lorraine could not be held to Germanness any longer. But it still insisted for reasons of prestige on maintaining the ban on soldiers using French in their letters home.[114]

A few weeks later the Army Group Duke Albrecht sent two reports to the OHL. The first amounted to a condemnation of German military policies in Alsace-Lorraine. The Army Group chief of staff now criticized the measures of postal control, censorship and the 'inept' regulations against the use of the French language for exacerbating the ill feeling. The Alsace-Lorraine people, who did not possess the 'sense of sacrifice' other Germans had, and thus did not see the necessity of special measures in wartime, especially resented discrimination and their sense of honour had suffered irreparably. The most that could be expected of a propaganda campaign was that the population of Alsace-Lorraine might vote for independence, rather than French rule. 'German-national' propaganda would be useless, since it would be met with derision and be counter-productive. The Army Group therefore recommended using the Elsässer Bund (Alsatian League) which it had set up in order to carry out propaganda (there was no equivalent organization in the more 'difficult' territory of Lorraine). The policy of concessions, which the Army Group claimed to have tried, had had no success. The results of the years of war were ineradicable:

The Alsace-Lorrainer, inordinately embittered, sees Germandom as the embodiment of all measures of compulsion, all the pressure, and all the hardship which war has brought upon him, while Frenchdom appears to him as the symbol of liberty, goodness, and peace . . . The Alsace-Lorrainer sees in France only advantages, or at least such great advantages that they outweigh any disadvantages which might result from separation from Germany.[115]

Any propaganda campaign was, the Army Group argued, doomed to failure. Only the constitutional reform now promised by the new Chancellor, autonomy and the introduction of full parliamentary government to Alsace-Lorraine, offered any hope, although it was probably too late.[116] The second report reiterated that the mood in Alsace-Lorraine was 'as unfavourable as can be imagined', and recommended that a propaganda campaign, ostensibly not German-financed, of 'Alsace-Lorraine for the Alsace-Lorrainers' should be encouraged.[117]

Conclusion

Much as the German leadership wanted to merge Alsace-Lorrainers into the Reich and imbue them with Germanness, its actions during the war achieved the opposite of its intentions. *Statthalter* Dallwitz recognized the failure of German national mobilization in February 1918 when he conceded that 'Germany cannot risk holding a referendum [on the future of Alsace-Lorraine]'.[118] Implicit in the subversive nature of Alsace-Lorraine particularism was the refusal to behave according to the racial definition of nation. Although they were 'by descent German to the core', sharing a common Rhineland culture, their choice of nation did not follow their 'race'.[119] Choosing France was not merely an indication of the Alsatians' sense of expediency. It was evidence that after half a century under the Reich the German nation-state was rejected, and the French version of the nation-state, a political community of citizens, was preferred. The realization of autonomy would have burst the iron cage of the authoritarian Wilhelmine state, for the political aspirations of the people could not have been attained within the existing state structure. *Statthalter* Dallwitz recognized this clearly: 'If autonomy is introduced, then a suitable Regent will have to be named. This is important, otherwise the idea of a republic will gain ground.'[120] In the war the German military leadership was caught in a dilemma: it needed the full mobilization of Alsace-Lorraine, but the more complete the mobilization, the greater the subversive risk to the German army, and the more rapid the alienation of Alsace-Lorraine. The desperate oscillation between repressive and conciliatory policies, neither of which succeeded, showed how national mobilization in the authoritarian state of the Wilhelmine empire proved to be self-destructive.

III

Army and nation

8 Discipline and morale in the British army, 1917–1918

David Englander

'The whole art of making war may be summed up in three words – courage, action, determination.' So wrote the chief of the Imperial General Staff, Sir William Robertson, in November 1916.[1] Robertson's extreme voluntarism, a reaction to the advent of modern firepower, was fully representative of thinking within the British military elite. The possibilities of modern weapons systems, though not denied, disturbed the ethos and values of an officer corps that gave primacy to human agency in the conduct of war. Machine-guns, mortars, automatic rifles and high-powered artillery were disliked, distrusted and undervalued. Assigned a subsidiary role, they were incorporated, grudgingly and clumsily, into the dominant soldier-centred framework of contemporary military analysis. Never was the tendency to hold fast to nurse more pronounced than among the Camberley cohort that reached seniority in the years that separated the South African War from the Great War. The revolution in firepower and the tactical–operational problems arising therefrom, far from provoking a fundamental reappraisal of practice and performance, served to emphasize the superiority of tradition over technology, character over intellect, manpower over machines, will-power over weaponry and the offensive over the defensive.[2] Industrialized mass warfare had, if anything, rendered traditional conceptions of the human-oriented battlefield more rather than less useful. Intelligence, initiative and élan were never more relevant and the scope for personal valour was wider than ever. Napoleonic dicta on the ratio of the moral to the material were, indeed, in need of revision – but upwards, not downwards. 'During the last three quarters of the twentieth century', General Sir Ian Hamilton predicted, 'the moral factor will transcend the physical, not as three to one but as four to one.'[3]

The upward adjustment reflected an acute awareness of the devastating effects of concentrated firepower on the mind and body of the troops. Heavy casualties, far in excess of those to which the British people were accustomed, were taken to be inevitable. How, then, could soldiers be persuaded to endure the unendurable and advance to

125

victory? The solution, it was generally agreed, lay with improved morale and sterner discipline. The soldierly spirit, properly cultivated, would enable the man in uniform to cope with the requirements of the new technological battlefields. That spirit found its truest expression in patriotism and self-sacrifice. 'Character' constituted its core component. The organizing concept of contemporary social theory, the formation of the higher character, was deemed to be an essential condition of victory. Courage, devotion to duty and unselfishness were its outward expression. Character was held to be the source of great deeds and character-training, the means by which the soldier acquired the moral strength to withstand the stresses of modern warfare. Apart from military training, the army sought to build up character through religious influences and through the provision of rational recreation and leisure pursuits. The moral contribution of organized sports was considerable.[4]

The primacy accorded the moral factor derived in part from a strategically specific vision of the modern battlefield. Crossing the fireswept zone, it was thought, required an army steeled, disciplined and inspired by the idea of the attack. Active patrolling and trench raiding parties were more often concerned with the assertion and re-affirmation of British moral predominance than with securing information on the condition of the enemy. 'The whole value of the trench raid to the battalion commander', wrote Lieutenant-Colonel Sandilands, historian of the 23rd Division, 'lies in the effect it has in maintaining the morale of his men. Underlying the keenness of the officers and men who carried out these raids was . . . a definite wish to be given the opportunity of proving, above all to themselves, that they were as anxious as ever to meet the Boche face to face, and as confident of the result of the encounter.'[5]

The offensive spirit, however, was more than a matter of strategy. It also expressed the military's self-image as the vanguard of a virile, manly, martial and racially effective nation. Professionally, socially and politically senior officers were ill-prepared for the enlistment of the citizen-soldier. Pessimist in outlook, corporative in spirit, with an exalted respect for hierarchy and the elevation of obedience into the supreme virtue, the regular officer, drawn from the privileged classes, viewed the town-bred individualist working-class recruit with less than enthusiasm. The perfect soldier, according to this way of thinking, was the long- service professional for whom the regiment was his home, the flag his symbol of the faith, and military honour his religion. 'The merit of the old soldier', wrote one right-thinking critic, 'was that his government could trust him. He was not the kind of man who was likely to be found sitting on a soldiers' and workmen's soviet.'

Industrialized mass warfare, it was feared, had changed all that. The New Armies, recruited from the mainstream rather than the marginal elements of the population, seemed confident, assertive and altogether more resistant to the culture and ethos of the fighting services. Citizen-soldiers, though they might be made into efficient troops, remained suspect. As a contemporary put it, such men 'cannot be endowed with the military character. They are no class by themselves; they have not the same tribal loyalty. The people from which they have just been drawn, and to which they soon will return, is not alien to them. Its feelings are theirs.'[6]

The New Armies were to be fashioned in the image of the Old. Nothing innovatory in respect of morale and discipline was anticipated. The old methods had lost none of their relevance. 'Discipline', wrote Sir Douglas Haig, 'has never had such a vindication in any war as in the present one, and it is their discipline which most distinguishes our New Armies from all similarly created armies of the past.'[7] Haig and his commanders were equally traditional in respect of morale management. Their corporative approach was narrowly professional in scope and character. The principal concern of the Old Army was to cultivate the regimental spirit, to encourage in the men a pride in the battalion, its history and record of bravery, its colours and battle honours. The focus was upon action rather than ideas, upon the defeat of the enemy rather than the purpose of victory. In these respects, though, British generals were not unlike their continental compeers. In other respects, too, they were remarkably similar. In their responses to signs of division and disaffection – the surveillance of adverse movements of opinion followed by interventions to restore morale – they were doing what those of comparable rank did elsewhere. In timing, as well, there existed a broad correspondence in policies and programmes. The traditional methods of morale management which had been operative in the first three years of the war were by 1917–18 widely recognized as needing revision and supplementation. Adjustments to the coercive and corporative character of military authority, with a shift from domination to motivation, found advocates in enemy and allied camps alike. The Central Powers were, indeed, the first to create and deliver new schemes of patriotic instruction for the ideological remobilization of their armies. The British who, like the Austrians, had hoped to get by on traditional methods boosted by the contribution of the padres, introduced compar-able measures shortly afterwards.[8] The context of these changes as they relate to British military participation is discussed below. The aim of this chapter is to describe how morale and discipline were understood and monitored, to consider changes in styles of command and man-

management, and to assess their significance in respect of the organizing themes of this volume.

Morale

The nature of morale was largely taken as understood. Its sources, though, are readily identifiable. The morale theories available to Haig's command were empirical in character, based on knowledge acquired in previous campaigns and on such space as was reserved for systematic study in the Camberley curriculum. Du Pique's *Etudes sur le combat* and Colin's *Les Transformations de la guerre,* presented to students in English translation, served to familiarize the British military with the most substantial writings on the place of morale within an offensive-minded strategy. Morale emerged from such sources as an action-based, group-centred concept that summarized the relative combat willingness of individuals and units. The focus was upon the problem of unit cohesion and group solidarity – that is, upon the subordination of self and the formation of a loyalty that outweighed all personal considerations.

Definitional difficulties were compounded by the slippery nature of the concept. Its variable spelling – with and without the 'e' – was indicative of a certain elusiveness. Morale considered as a psychological condition was not tangible, measurable or localizable.[9] Indirect measures, some ocular, some quantifiable, were in consequence employed to identify its possible variations. Traditional indicators of troop morale embraced dress and demeanour, attitude and expression, as well as health, hygiene and conduct. Troops were constantly inspected and their turnout and bearing carefully scrutinized in order to assess the state of morale. The smart soldier, erect, alert and with a ready salute, gave satisfaction; the slovenly soldier, shambling, untidy and apathetic, gave cause for concern and was punished. Appearance, gesture, gait and body language were kept under constant review by officers searching for reassurance in the movement of the men, in their carriage, comportment and conduct as well as in what they said and how they said it.

Morale assessment, however, took place within the context of an offensive framework that was as much psychological as strategic. The maxim, drummed into new recruits during officer training, that 'fighting patrols are the finest stiffeners of morale', was reinforced by various tract-like publications issued by the General Staff which directed subalterns towards a self-critical interrogation of attitudes and practices.[10] Aggression in the line was regarded as proof conclusive of the British soldier's imagined desire to close with the enemy and kill him. Hand-to-hand combat was often valued less for its fighting efficiency than for its symbolic importance as an indicator of morale. In the words of the General Staff: 'Bayonet fighting produces lust for blood.'[11] Willingness to undertake such assignments was widely regarded as a measure of morale and also served to establish the enlisted man's bona fides as a reliable soldier. Never to have volunteered marked a man down as an inferior soldier, wanting in character and commitment. Men of this stamp who fell foul of the military justice system might pay for their indifference with their lives.[12]

Morale-raising measures also embraced styles of command. Soldiers, as members of an institution in which information was still principally imparted by word of mouth, were from time to time assembled to receive messages of congratulations from army, corps and divisional commanders and to listen to accounts of gallantry and heroism in citations for exemplary conduct. Medals awarded for exceptional performance were likewise part of the traditional means of morale management.

Senior officers, aware of the effects of distance in modern mass armies, also took steps to project themselves and their ideas more effectively to the rank and file. Some cultivated eccentricities or acquired engaging affectations. 'Dicky' Fanshawe, commander of the 48th Division, for example, tried to create a persona around soldier comforts rather like his junior, Bernard Montgomery, was to do around badges and hats in World War II. General Fanshawe was known affectionately as 'the Chocolate Soldier' for his distribution of slabs of chocolate to front-line troops during inspections. Army commanders, like Sir Charles Monro (3rd Army) or Sir Hubert Gough (5th Army) directed divisional commanders to relay their ideas to units and formations they could not personally visit. The former upheld a vision of empire as the basis of the British war effort. The latter, in his attempts to boost morale, addressed the men as citizens and soldiers. Appeals were pitched at their patience, patriotism and endurance and the imminence of enemy collapse. Troops were also reminded of their responsibilities as opinion-forming agents for the civilian population and of the great cause – our Homes, our Honour and Peace – that had been entrusted to them.[13]

Adjustment was not confined to the higher ranks. Regimental officers learned that their authority, though in theory non-negotiable, was in practice conditional upon the development of appropriate man-management skills. Inefficiency and incompetence were not easily concealed from men who rapidly became keen judges of officer performance. Expressions of censure and grievance were readily voiced by the victims of poorly trained or inadequate superiors. Commanders who were deficient in orientation skills or unable to sit upon a horse, or who were inconsistent and offensive to the men's sense of fairness, provoked truculent murmuring, insubordinate remarks, surliness and ridicule.[14] Discipline, officer cadets were informed, supplied a necessary but not sufficient basis for effective command. The respect of the rank and file and the authority it conferred were not to be taken for granted. Apart from the mastery of arms, officers were required to exercise a benevolent paternalism, to be attentive to the men's needs, solicitous on their behalf and personable without ever becoming familiar. The efficiency with which these duties were discharged was critical. In the language of the training schools: 'The fighting spirit of the platoon is derived from its commander.'[15]

Morale, in short, was deemed to be a function of leadership. Its scope was vast. The military authorities had gone to war with few ideas on behavioural issues, on problems of motivation in mass armies and the sorts of measures that might be required for their sustenance and elevation. That compulsion allied with an unreflective patriotism might prove insufficient as a basis for authority and endurance had not been anticipated and no special provision was made to satisfy the socio-psychological needs of the citizen in uniform. Questions of morale and welfare were left to local and voluntary initiative. The latter, it must be said, was not negligible. The philanthropic and benevolent cast of the Old Army, with its emphasis upon manliness and sportsmanship and the cultivation of a tireless activism, set an example in the initiation, finance and administration of popular leisure and recreational facilities that diffused rapidly through the New Armies. Place was reserved for the participation of civilian organizations, with provision widened and deepened by the contribution of the YMCA and the Church Army.[16]

Army sport and recreational pursuits, though available all the year round, came into their own at the close of the autumn when large-scale military operations ceased. Apart from the strengthening of unit loyalties, these were designed as an effective counter-attraction to the 'crime and unrest' to which troops in desolated regions might otherwise have succumbed.[17] Equally important was the carnival atmosphere which leisure provision sometimes engendered. Equestrian events in which officer participants were rudely unhorsed, boxing matches in which they were soundly beaten, or football competitions in which they were thrashed all provided situations in which anger might be discharged and criticisms of authority voiced without invoking the sanctions of the military justice system. Concert parties in which officers were parodied and risqué remarks passed on their conduct served a similar purpose.[18]

A different kind of spectacle came with the organized visits of royalty and other celebrities. For the military authorities the monarchy had both practical and symbolic importance. Royalty was viewed as the protector of the professional spirit of the military against civilian interference in army affairs. The crown, as the focus of loyalty and fount of all military honours, also served as a useful source for the integration of a more socially diverse army. Visits from the King and members of the royal family were widely considered to have exerted a positive effect on troop morale.[19] Royal processions were valued not only in themselves but also as an indicator of morale. Troop response in the form of spontaneous cheering was taken as faithful evidence of the soldierly spirit. Politicians and reliable labour leaders, entertainers and men of letters, were also invited to cheer, amuse, lecture and encourage the troops.

Discipline

Morale, it was understood, was separate from the influences that produced or sustained it. Chief among these was discipline. Its primary function was to enable the soldier to conquer fear and do his duty in spite of it. Drill supported by punishment and fear was traditionally the means by which it was developed. Discipline focused on the physical and instinctive, it was claimed, had been superseded by a discipline that appealed to the spiritual and the intellectual. The mechanical obedience produced by the former was quite unsuited to the conditions created by the extended firing line and isolating effects of the new technological battlefield.[20] Discipline, secured by consent rather than constraint, was to be based upon a soldier-centred style of command, in which the authority of the officer was exalted by the force of example, and through the cultivation of an *esprit de corps* and a high level of camaraderie so that troops persisted even when personal contact with the officer had been lost. Such statements, and there were many of them, represent an aspiration rather than a description of military practice. The wars of swift movement and wide extension which prompted the recasting of discipline in the decade before 1914 were rendered nugatory by the realities of trench warfare. Class fears and the failure to integrate men and machines meant that traditional methods were intensified rather than abandoned. As Ian Hamilton confessed: 'The British Army . . . retained almost as firm a grip upon the essentials of the old discipline as those central European powers who had held on to it all the time.'[21] The concept of the intelligent and responsible soldier, capable of individual initiative and rational corporate action, remained an ideal, advanced by tactical reformers like Ivor Maxse, rather than an achievement.

The lash had gone but not its rationale. Many, including the commander-in-chief himself, seemed scarcely reconciled to its abolition.

Its absence, he felt, made the retention of brutal, degrading and, for the most part, highly visible field punishments essential. 'I am quite certain', he wrote, 'that it would not have been possible to maintain the high standard of discipline in the British Army in France if Field Punishment No. I had been non-existent.'[22] Summary punishments, however, were not the only source of contention. The greater severity of the military justice system has rightly been the focus of much critical attention. In relative and absolute terms the British soldier was more severely dealt with than either his German or French counterparts.[23] The judicial system has been criticized on grounds of morality, irregularity, inefficiency, even irrationality.[24] The last of these charges, though, is unfounded. The military justice system existed within a rational bureaucracy that was as much preoccupied with problems of motivation and morale as with the enforcement of discipline. Its character has received less attention than its importance merits.

The modern mass army, Weber observed, was a bureaucratic army in which the pen, if not mightier than the sword, was of equal importance.[25] Weber's is an army in which the rational management of violence is just as concerned with organizational and administrative questions as with the more heroic conceptions of service. Technological developments in warfare, combined with the rapid expansion of the military establishment and the widening of its social base, created new skill and knowledge needs and a dawning awareness among some military professionals that manipulation might be as important as domination in sustaining combat efficiency. Generalship itself was becoming less a matter of leading from the front than of supervising a large communications network through which flowed enormous quantities of information. Data evaluation was a prime task. The bureaucratization of violence and the separation of the soldier from the means of destruction meant that army commanders and their staffs spent their time writing rather than fighting.

Their writings, though poorly preserved, are sufficient to indicate just how well informed the authorities were in respect of morale and discipline in the British Expeditionary Force (BEF). Responsibility for the gathering, collation and circulation of information in matters respecting welfare and troop morale fell to the adjutant's office. Included with the weekly notes circulated to army corps and divisional commanders was a summary of the state of crime and indiscipline arranged by corps and with a comparison of the previous week's progress. More detailed monthly returns, prepared by the Provost Marshall's office, monitored the extent and nature of indiscipline. Information presented in tabular form displayed the progress of court-martial cases (not persons) through the military justice system. Separate tables showed the classification and distribution of offences by corps, division, brigade, regiment and battalion.

Returns were carefully scrutinized. Attention was directed at formations and units with eye-catching figures. Commanders assessed their own performance and sense of identity against these measures. Senior officers, anxious lest their own competence be called into question, came under pressure to secure reductions by the imposition of more stringent discipline or other measures. Special circumstances were taken into account. Returns inflated by the inclusion of troublesome Australian divisions received sympathetic consideration at GHQ.[26] Commanders without comparable sources of mitigation may well have been more ready to authorize exemplary punishments as much to satisfy their superiors as to impress the soldiery. Whatever the motive, it is clear that the material existed on which rational decisions could, in theory, be taken. Confirmation of the death sentence imposed by field courts-martial was determined by the character of the offender and the state of discipline in the unit or formation from which he was drawn. Such decisions were unlikely to have been based on a precise mathematical formula, if only because experienced officers were aware that the figures were not a simple register of criminality or an adequate representation of their concerns. Not only were they capable of multiple meanings, the courts-martial summaries were but one of several measures which demanded consideration.

The close connection between leadership and fighting efficiency meant that courts-martial statistics were regarded as more than a simple indicator of officer quality. Troop morale, too, was read into the figures. Increases in reported offences might indicate accumulating sources of disintegration or, worse, suggest an imminent breakdown in operational capabilities. Alas, much of the relevant documentation is not readily locatable.[27] Returns for the 5th Army for the eleven months preceding the German offensive of March 1918, have, however, been preserved. These are summarized in table 8.1.

It will be seen that the absolute number of court-martial cases received each month at 5th Army headquarters was small and that, on average, 90 per cent of trials resulted in convictions. The 5th Army formations, it should be noted, included the Canadian Cavalry Brigade, the South African Brigade and the Australian 4th Division. The latter attracted many more convictions than either the Canadians or South Africans. Even so, the overall level of indiscipline does not seem unduly high. Contemporaries, looking at the incidence of cases (convictions and acquittals) per 1,000 men between April 1917 and February 1918,

Table 8.1 *5th Army, summary of courts-martial, 1917–1918*

	April	May	June	July	Aug.	Sept.	Oct.	Nov.	Dec.	Jan.	Feb.
Total army strength	230,515	212,456	212,074	540,964	508,607	389,137	310,137	213,260	140,336	200,269	274,615
Cases received	352	323	195	521	514	453	259	114	150	310	327
Cases convicted	293	291	175	374	465	394	233	106	133	262	280
Cases acquitted	47	27	20	45	39	46	26	7	16	39	45
Cases quashed	8	4	–	3	9	6	–	1	1	4	1
Cases not continued	4	1	–	3	1	7	–	–	–	5	1
Incidence per 1,000 men	1.47	1.49	0.91	0.77	0.99	1.13	0.83	0.52	1.06	1.50	1.18

Source: PRO WO 95/524–5, Monthly summaries of courts-martial, 5th Army war diaries.

would not have seen any obvious upward movement or discerned any clear pattern that gave more than usual cause for concern. The nature of the offences that were tried by courts-martial are displayed in table 8.2.

Most prevalent was absence without leave which, it will be noted, accounted for nearly a third of convictions. Drunkenness came next (17 per cent of convictions) followed by insubordination and violence to superiors (12 per cent), desertion (8 per cent), disobedience (7 per cent) and self-inflicted wounds (6 per cent). The incidence of desertion, the most serious of offences, however, showed no tendency to rise and remained well below 1 per cent per 1,000 men. Precise comparisons are difficult, but there seems little in these figures to indicate any imminent collapse or breakdown.[28]

The 5th Army's courts-martial statistics are particularly valuable, given its controversial record in the spring offensive. The German breakthrough, which brought the British to within a hair's breadth of defeat, has been the subject of extensive investigation. The failure of the 5th Army has been described as a moral collapse brought about by exceptionally high casualties sustained in the heavy fighting in the previous year. Much of the blame fell upon the allegedly poor preparatory work by its commander, General Sir Hubert Gough, who was relieved of his command and sent home in disgrace.[29] It is to be emphasized that the figures above do not undermine or necessarily conflict with current orthodoxies. More needs to be known about generals as decision-takers, and about how the information that was available to them was organized, read and understood, before sound judgements can be reached.

Illness and indiscipline were closely connected. The assumption, deeply engrained within the military, that enlisted personnel would

Table 8.2 *5th Army, classification of convictions, 1917–1918*

	April	May	June	July	Aug.	Sept.	Oct.	Nov.	Dec.	Jan.	Feb.	Total
Cowardice	3	–	1	6	3	2	3	–	–	–	–	18
Leaving guard or post	2	1	2	4	3	3	1	–	1	2	5	24
Sentry sleeping on or leaving post or guard	3	2	4	6	–	1	1	–	–	2	3	22
Violence to superior	11	6	12	27	24	13	12	6	3	12	4	130
Wilful defiance and insubordinate language or conduct	21	14	26	35	50	46	20	13	11	22	23	281
Disobedience	21	19	12	49	60	30	19	7	4	13	16	250
Desertion	23	38	11	34	50	39	19	11	26	26	18	295
Absence	120	128	46	137	130	115	78	39	46	91	97	1,027
Malingering, intentional self-maiming etc.	–	1	1	2	1	2	–	–	–	–	–	7
Theft, fraud or embezzlement	6	4	2	9	18	7	13	2	1	8	13	83
Offences against inhabitants	2	4	2	4	1	7	7	2	1	–	3	33
Drunkenness	51	34	36	130	70	65	52	17	24	58	48	585
Self-inflicted wounds	15	26	11	30	30	30	15	5	6	17	30	215
Miscellaneous	50	44	40	113	30	79	36	13	18	47	37	507

Source: PRO WO/ 95/524–5, monthly summaries of courts-martial, 5th Army war diaries.

invent disorders of the body and the mind to escape combat, gave the medical officer a significant role in the military justice system. Medical officers were required to pronounce upon the men's fitness for active service and upon their mental condition in respect of alleged crimes and misdemeanours. They were also consulted in suspected cases of self-mutilation, malingering and other contrived ailments and required to certify that convicted offenders were fit to undergo field punishments.

Standards of healthcare were also compromised by the pressure to minimize sick wastage rates. The military, having pioneered the collection and analysis of medical statistics, was apprehensive lest losses due to ill-health deplete the ranks, depress morale and lower combat efficiency. Sick returns for weekly circulation not only covered battle casualties, but also included comparative statistics on 'trench foot' and the incidence of venereal disease. Senior officers could see at a glance the relative health of their command. But, as with the returns on indiscipline, more was read into the figures than that which was classified as either criminal or sick. Statistics on illness, like indiscipline, provided a surrogate measure of morale. The length of the sick queue set a standard which regimental clinicians could not ignore. Their

Table 8.3 *Sick wastage in the British armies in France, 1918*

(a) Admitted to field ambulance (%)

	5 Jan	12 Jan	19 Jan	26 Jan	2 Feb	9 Feb	16 Feb	23 Feb	2 Mar	9 Mar
1st Army	0.84	0.91	0.98	0.91	0.70	0.84	0.84	0.84	0.84	0.77
2nd Army	–	–	–	–	–	–	–	–	–	1.12
3rd Army	1.61	1.75	2.03	1.47	1.26	1.40	1.33	1.19	1.26	1.26
4th Army	1.45	1.43	1.45	1.42	1.11	1.21	1.15	1.24	1.16	–
5th Army	1.75	1.68	1.63	1.21	1.17	1.21	1.17	1.12	1.05	1.09

(b) Evacuated to base (%)

	5 Jan	12 Jan	19 Jan	26 Jan	2 Feb	9 Feb	16 Feb	23 Feb	2 Mar	9 Mar
1st Army	0.56	0.63	0.63	0.70	0.49	0.49	0.49	0.56	0.42	0.56
2nd Army	–	–	–	–	–	–	–	–	–	0.58
3rd Army	0.97	0.99	1.41	1.16	0.57	0.77	0.66	0.72	0.73	0.91
4th Army	0.85	0.67	0.85	0.70	0.50	0.46	0.51	0.56	0.51	–
5th Army	0.99	0.85	0.64	0.62	0.54	0.20	0.44	0.36	0.69	0.53

Source: PRO WO 95/527, 5th Army notes on directors' services, January–March 1918.

autonomy to admit and treat patients was curtailed by forceful commanding officers whose priorities were fixed by the gaze of their superiors and the need to maintain the effective strength of their battalion at the highest possible level. From this perspective, there are few signs in the 5th Army at the opening of 1918 of the disaster that would soon overtake it. Sick wastage for all armies in France is shown in table 8.3. It will be seen that wastage in the 5th Army compares favourably with conditions in the 3rd and 4th Armies. Indeed, the weekly sick percentage return is consistently lower in the Fifth Army. It would, however, be wrong to conclude that the failure of the 5th Army was more of a military defeat due primarily to enemy superiority in manpower and firepower than a moral collapse due to fatigue and depression. The evidence, from postal surveillance, should it ever be located, may well present a different story.

Postal control and military intelligence

Statistics of health and indiscipline were not the sole quantitative measures of morale collected by the military authorities. Additional measures, for example, developed from the campaign to strengthen patriotic feeling in connection with the sale of war bonds and savings certificates. British generals, like their counterparts in both Allied and enemy armies, viewed the promotion of war savings as a useful source of instruction in sound ideas. Care was taken to monitor the outcome. Particulars on the volume and distribution of purchases were gathered for the information of senior officers who might also be called upon to comment on variations in take-up or untoward departures from the mean.[30] Not all information was supplied at source. Military intelligence, which expanded enormously during 1917 in anticipation of a deepening crisis of legitimacy, provided General Headquarters with significant additional data. Some of this came from reports of agents in the field, much of it from press reports and the retailing of gossip and a great deal more from the reading of letters to and from the front. The knowledge-base of Haig's command was, indeed, very considerably extended through the contribution of the military postal censorship.

British postal surveillance, like its French counterpart, grew from a narrow concern with security issues into a powerful instrument of social research and remedial action. Regular reports brought under review the nature of morale, the interaction of soldiers and civilians, the enormous variation in conditions along the front and the ways in which shifts in locale acted as stimulant or depressant to the troops. No formal definition of morale was included. The 'spirit of the men, their conception of duty, their moral', or, more specifically, confidence in the superiority of British arms, supplied the focus of an analysis that was punctuated by much pithy quotation.[31] The structures and strategies adopted in these reports, however, left morale as a residual category that was largely determined by the varying combination of the influences upon it. Prominent among them was religion. The disclosure of a widespread religious feeling among the troops recalled the example of the New Model Army to underscore the connection between religion and morale. Religion was here conceived both as an opiate and source of ideological uplift. Measures to strengthen religious feeling were deemed desirable on secular rather than spiritual grounds.[32]

Of equal importance was the question of leave. For front-line troops it was *the* priority. Leave, though, was more than just a respite for war-weary troops; it was also a chance to reaffirm their humanity, to express their identities as members of families and coherent communities. Always a source of tension, the leave issue became particularly fraught during the spring and summer of 1917, as heavy fighting in France combined with outbreaks of measles at home led to denials and deferrals and questions in the House of Commons.[33] British, like French, censors found that leave was the most common topic of correspondence and the single most important determinant of morale.[34] More than anything else, it was the likelihood of leave which sustained the men at the front.[35]

The Green Envelope system (i.e. the privileged system whereby service correspondence was selected for censorship at base rather than in the sender's unit) was monitored both as a source of intelligence and as an independent influence upon troop morale. Indeed, the cathartic effect of such communication was considered an important morale-raising measure in itself. 'A supply of Green Envelopes in many cases comes next to the prospect of leave in maintaining good spirits.'[36] Food, clothing, billets and 'minor matters', a euphemism for lice, also engaged the censors' attention. The first was considered the most important. Half the letters examined by postal control in May 1917, for example, addressed the issue but it was hoped that complaints would prove self-cancelling.[37] Apart from the improved training of regimental cooks, no exceptional measures were suggested on the assumption that the rotation of troops and the enormous variety of billets and facilities would dilute criticism and prevent its build-up into a dangerous source of grievance.

Political influences, by contrast, resisted definition as resource management issues that were capable of remedial action. Politics, indeed, had no place in the reports submitted by postal control. Politics and military service were in theory incompatible. The military considered politics dangerous and divisive, a threat to the discipline of the forces and the integrity of the state. In practice, however, the authorities were concerned with the exclusion of those forms of politics that were perceived as socially and militarily subversive. Politics in the army was subject to a dual standard comparable with that applied to women in civilian society. The considerable freedom of expression allowed to officers was a punishable offence when exercised by the men. Officers might entertain a critical independence of outlook, not the men. The commitment of the former was taken as axiomatic whereas the loyalty of the latter was generally deemed problematic.

Political discussion, prohibited by King's Regulations, left a void to be filled by a selfless and noble patriotism. The cultivation of such sentiment was one of the priorities of military training. The very absence of politics from service correspondence was, indeed, upheld as proof of the efficiency of these methods. 'Peace', the heading under which political opinion was gathered, became the vehicle for the conveyance of displaced fears about stability and social hierarchy. 'In reading letters on this subject', wrote a 3rd Army censor, 'one cannot help feeling impressed by the fact that the British Army – a heterogeneous collection of men who before the war had the wide freedom of thought, speech and action that are their national birthright – should submit without a murmur to guidance and authority, and be prepared simply to "carry on" without comment or discussion.' Surprised and relieved, he found an explanation in national character. British compliance was voluntary and personal whereas German submission was imposed.[38]

The weakness of that explanation was quickly exposed. American and German peace proposals at the beginning of 1917 triggered the reassertion of a suppressed civilian identity which gave rise to considerable apprehension.[39] The peace issue, the same censor readily appreciated, was more than the expression of a simple or non-doctrinal war-weariness. Peace was a radicalizing and mind-enlarging issue which entailed a precise statement of war aims and also directed attention to social reconstruction and the rewards that the returning troops might reasonably expect to receive. 'In this respect, in its apparent readiness to discuss Peace as a branch of politics, the Army shows an entire change from its attitude of a year ago', wrote the censor in November 1917. 'A year ago men seemed to be sublimely unconscious of political considerations. They were out simply to "do their bit". They rarely mentioned and never discussed political questions . . . Now, they are ceasing to some extent to possess their corporate personality and to reassert individuality of opinion.'[40] The situation, he advised, required a propaganda campaign to check the despondency emanating from the army and a successful military campaign to raise morale at the front.[41]

Political education

Three years of inconclusive fighting, of fear and discomfort, and of death and mutilation, had taken its toll of even the stoutest constitutions. Depression was deepened by the disbandment of the broken battalions and under-strength formations that were finally withdrawn after the heavy fighting of 1917. The decision, taken at the close of the year, to reduce divisions to nine infantry battalions and brigades to three, caused universal gloom. The subsequent reorganization, with a loss of 175 battalions, seemed to many officers to be the very negation of all that had been said and done to promote group solidarity.[42]

The disturbance caused by rapid reconstruction was aggravated by manpower shortages and concerns about the quality of reinforcements. The volunteers, for all their alien ways, seemed unquestionably committed to the defeat of Germany. Their successors, by contrast, were suspect.[43] New drafts sent from home seemed restless and resistant and altogether less reliable. Discipline was tightened. Monthly executions on the western front peaked in September 1917 when one-fifth of the 100 unfortunates who faced the threat of the firing squad that year were shot.[44] The military intelligence organization set up shortly afterwards to monitor industrial and political unrest in home commands also found evidence that gave cause for concern.[45] Its findings contributed to the growing body of military opinion favouring new initiatives to restore troop morale.

Indications of a slump in morale, supplied by postal control and military intelligence, found concrete expression in acts of collective defiance among troops at home and overseas from the autumn of 1917 onwards. The formation of workers' and soldiers' councils in one or two units at home and in the Army Service Corps in France, the mutiny at the Etaples base, and the political subversion which, according to General Gough, brought about the collapse of the 16th Division in March 1918, seemed symptomatic of a loss of élan and will to win.[46] Similar perceptions, found among German troops, underscored the recognition that discipline and morale were not enough, and that, in the absence of a decisive breakthrough, some form of political education was necessary to sustain the men and maintain their fighting efficiency. The Germans, indeed, were first to introduce special measures for the ideological mobilization of the armed forces.[47]

The British were moving in the same direction. The corporate cast of military thinking left the generals ill at ease with a self-regarding army that appeared to be driven by private and personal concerns rather than the public service ethic exemplified in the officer corps. Previous responses to morale crises, as in 1915, had been localized and limited in scope. Then, the commander-in-chief, Sir John French, had recommended a series of organized talks and addresses, led by junior officers, which combined the cultivation of the regimental spirit with an explanation of British participation in the fighting.[48] Haig, his successor, seems to have thought that the task of patriotic instruction should be shared with the military chaplains. Encouraged by their superiors, and cheerfully compliant, the padres assumed a commissar function among the men, monitoring their moods and combining spiritual guidance and comfort with assurances as to the necessity and justice of the allied cause. Haig in retrospect thought that the chaplains had played a major role in sustaining troop morale. 'As the result of their teaching', he wrote, 'all ranks came to know and more fully understand the great and noble objects for which they were fighting.'[49] In 1917, however, he was less confident that their unaided efforts were sufficient. The YMCA, which included lectures and classes with the provision of comforts and welfare, was also encouraged to extend its educational activities to become the agent of General Headquarters for these purposes in the lines of communication and base areas in all theatres of war.[50]

The road to normality, so long debarred by the impossibility of an honourable settlement, was reopened at the beginning of 1917 by President Wilson's peace note. Peace talk at once brought together a number of strands which the generals would have preferred to have remained separate. It focused upon reasons for fighting and, more importantly, for not fighting, and raised horizons narrowed by the conditions of trench warfare towards a consideration of the post-war world and the soldiers' place within it. General Rawlinson, commander of the 3rd Army, who was alarmed by the 'peace without victory' formula that issued from the White House, arranged for the printing and circulation of 30,000 copies of Balfour's reply. 'It is right that all soldiers should know and appreciate the cause for which they are fighting. Balfour's letter will raise the morale of the army as a whole, and I shall send it specially to all our schools. No better statement of the objects for which we are striving could have been written.'[51] By the autumn of 1917, however, the longing for peace among British troops in France was well nigh universal. By that time, too, localized interventions had given way to an army-wide campaign, directed by military intelligence, against pacifism, socialism and labour unrest, while preparations proceeded for the delivery of a systematic programme of political education.[52] The resumption of the war of movement after the German offensive of 1918 had spent itself, however, meant that victory was secured with minimal exposure to the proposed courses in citizen training. Had the fighting continued into 1919, as Haig and his commanders expected, things might have been different. The soldiers of the First World War rather than their successors of the Second World War would then have been the first recipients of an ABCA-style educational programme.[53]

Conclusion

It had been a close run thing. How close is still a matter for speculation. Whether there was a mutiny in the making which, but for the March offensive, would have issued in a spectacular conflagration comparable with those in the other allied armies, is an intriguing possibility. The British army, like others, became deeply depressed during 1917–18. Evidence of stress, fatigue, division and dissidence, gathered by postal surveillance and military intelligence, raised disturbing questions about the cohesion and commitment of the forces. Traditional methods of morale management seemed to operate with diminishing efficiency. Signs, symbols, speech and statistics had become less meaningful and more problematic. What positive feelings about king and country could be divined from front-line troops who were ordered to cheer on the appearance of the sovereign or pressured into the purchase of war loan bonds? Pep talks from generals and stirring addresses from visiting dignitaries were scarcely more revealing. Was the absence of political interests, noted by civilian leaders, an expression of censure or a form of inertia? Even the offensive spirit, so carefully cultivated, seemed less reassuring than formerly. Bullishness in the line, once taken as a sign of moral superiority and confidence, was viewed increasingly as a source of recklessness which needlessly sacrificed the bravest and the best and generally deprived the troops of rest and training.[54]

Both the latter were desperately needed. Neither was secured. The fear of men out of control with time for rumination and reflection meant that periods out of the line were not, as expected, given over to mental relaxation and physical refreshment but to 'recreational training'. The discovery that ' "rest periods" were a snare and a delusion' did little to relieve the sense of gloom in the lower ranks or of unease in the higher.[55] The connection between declining enthusiasm and deficient leadership, a connection made unavoidable by contemporary thinking about morale, may well have influenced the resurgent interest in improved training in the last eighteen months of the war.

The training regime initiated by Ivor Maxse and Charles Bonham Carter encompassed innovations in infantry tactics and a re-statement of the principles of command. Premature retirement in action and indiscipline and want of good order in the ranks were all attributed to ill-trained holders of the king's commission. 'Duds' and mediocrities were to be purged and junior officers properly instructed in the art of man-management.[56] The restoration of leadership, however, was not simply a matter of imposition. A measure of consent was necessary. The sanctions of the disciplinary code were not a substitute for the acquisition of appropriate manipulative skills and methods of control. Respect, officers were told, was difficult to earn and easily forfeit. Once secured, it required constant maintenance. Line officers in their everyday encounters learned quickly that subordinates were neither silent nor submissive and that grousing was a fluid form of social interaction by which officers and other ranks defined and re-defined their relationship within the rigid and otherwise unworkable framework created by King's Regulations. Grousing, baldly summarized, was the principal means by which soldiers conveyed their views, verbally or visually, to a commanding officer who could, without loss of authority, choose to ignore them, to penalize them as insubordinate, or to accept them as valid criticism and modify his conduct accordingly. Such adjustments were an expression of an on-going process of negotiation which probably constituted the single most important means by which troop morale was maintained.

The idea, popular among certain social scientists, that cohesion and commitment were simply a function of primary group loyalties is, in many respects, an extension of the top-down morale theories developed by du Pique and his successors. By 1917–18 the authorities thought otherwise. The corporate ideal, potent though it remained, was no longer considered sufficient. The rank and file, it was feared, had acquired independent, or at least non-approved, thoughts. Implicit in the information-gathering process was a mechanistic conception of morale in which there existed scope for certain forms of social engineering. The military authorities, though not free agents, did have it within their power to influence the willingness of the men to fight and endure. The organization of human and material resources, even within the constraints imposed by the enemy and the environment, could just as easily constitute a negative as a positive influence on troop morale. Manpower and man-management policies, food distribution and im-proved measures for the de-lousing and laundering of clothing, were identified by postal control as areas of concern where action might be possible. Leave, a major source of discontent, received sympathetic consideration.[57] Political education, a more radical departure, also came within the scope of army intervention. The military authorities, having at first mobilized the padres and the YMCA for this purpose, assumed direct responsibility in both management and provision from the spring of 1918.

In character, though not in application, the proposed education programme was comparable with the remobilization that was in progress in the civilian sphere. Soldiers, it was conceded, were in need of a new set of ideals and a new vision to sustain them in the advance to victory. But however conceived and delivered, education and citizen training required more time than was available to register a positive influence upon troop morale and combat performance. In this sphere, as in so many others, the German army again proved itself a formidable source of disruption. Its unforeseen collapse in the summer of 1918 meant that Britain's most ambitious attempt to manufacture morale was denied a proper testing.

9 Remobilizing the citizen-soldier through the French army mutinies of 1917

Leonard V. Smith

With incidents of open resistance to military authority occurring in units of nearly one-half of the divisions in the French army, the mutinies of May and June 1917 constituted the most significant internal challenge to the prosecution of World War I in any of the victorious powers. In the terminology of this volume, the mutinies constituted dramatic acts of defiance of state mobilization at its most explicit level – that of formal military authority. Most commonly, a mutiny in a given unit involved an explicit refusal at embarkation points to take up positions in the front lines. The discontented soldiers would then hold some form of demonstration in which they would air all manner of grievances. Sometimes they protested about particular situations and commanders. More often, however, soldiers expressed a highly embittered disengagement from 'the war' writ large. Yet no less striking than soldiers' anger and even their despair was their restraint. Nearly everywhere, officers (the most immediate instruments of state authority) were treated with respect, even when they were openly disobeyed. Most importantly, soldiers did not cross the line into violent resistance, which could well have turned the mutinies into another French Revolution. Without the actual use of force on the part of the command structure, soldiers ultimately accepted remobilization into the war, and into a complex symbolic economy both of repression and of reforms in the way the war was carried out. Reconciling the virulence of the mutinies with their outcome becomes the key interpretive task in explaining the remobilization of the French citizen-soldier in the spring of 1917.

Historians have tended to explain the mutinies in terms of ineffective state mobilization, whether at the governmental or military level. Early interpretations were 'political' in that they faulted the civilian authorities for allowing defeatism and pacifism from the interior to infect the army.[1] But after the publication in 1967 of Guy Pedroncini's landmark study *Les Mutineries de 1917*, the first to be based on the archival record, historians have agreed that the mutinies were essentially 'military'.[2] The French High Command nearly ruined the army through its blind devotion to its doctrine of the offensive, which reached its nadir along the Chemin des Dames. The new French supreme commander, General Philippe Pétain, repaired the damage through a cautious but effective combination of repression and reform. The mutinies thus became a solved historical puzzle. 'We do not, therefore', John Keegan observed as recently as 1994, 'really need an elaborate conceptualization to explain the mutinies of 1917.'[3]

The problem with this historiography, I would argue, lies in its nearly exclusive concern with state mobilization, whether political or military. It leaves out what this volume calls 'self-mobilization', or in this particular situation, 'self-remobilization'. Consequently, historians have accorded a curiously marginal role to the central protagonists – the discontented soldiers themselves. I will take 'self-remobilization' to mean the soldiers' struggle to figure out just what it meant during the mutinies to be a citizen-soldier of France. I will argue that state and self-mobilization played complementary roles in remobilizing citizen-soldiers through the mutinies of 1917. Understanding these two forms of remobilization revolves around understanding two interconnected aspects of the power relationship between soldiers and their commanders. The first involves military authority as conventionally conceived, an aspect of the power relationship that only partly explains the outcome of the mutinies. The second involves republican citizenship, which showed that the most effective means of remobilizing French soldiers already existed in themselves, in their most basic conceptions of who they were as political entities. Democratic citizenship, I will conclude, both authorized soldiers to question military authority and in the end compelled them to obey it.

Military authority and the limits of state mobilization

Military authority is a vestige of paternal, absolute power theorized most thoroughly in the early modern period. Like early modern sovereigns, those who exercise military authority are not directly accountable to those over whom their authority is exercised. Military society, particularly in wartime, operates according to highly precise rules of conduct enforced by separate disciplinary and juridical apparatuses. Military authority has been justified in practical terms – on the principle that absolute power is necessary to compel men to accept the physical perils of war, including the certainty that a number of them will suffer disfigurement and death on the battlefield. The theory of military authority was brought into the modern age by Carl von Clausewitz.[4] Clausewitz argued that war is simply that form of state administration that uses violence. His successors have concluded that even in a democracy, an army serves as a mechanistic and 'apolitical' instrument of state, and individual soldiers serve simply as that instrument's tiniest parts.

This was precisely the conceptualization of military authority overthrown by the mutinies. From the moment soldiers successfully refused to obey orders, the mutinies became 'political'. They involved open defiance of an essential institution of state, as soldiers reclaimed citizens' rights of dissent and opposition. For this reason, the command structure found the demonstrations confusing, difficult at first even to name. The term 'mutiny' appears to have been used only rarely in the rivers of paper that flowed up and down the command structure at the time, perhaps because it implied a hostility toward the officers on site that did not exist.[5] More common were such terms as 'acts of collective indiscipline', 'pacifist demonstrations', the 'movement of disorder' or simply 'the movement'.

By whatever name, the mutinies dramatically illustrated that military authority had ceased to function in conventional ways. For once presented with explicit disobedience by substantial numbers of soldiers, commanders' options proved few indeed. Personal engagement on the part of a particular officer could carry considerable risk. A brigade commander in the 41st Division intervened in a demonstration involving some 2,000 soldiers, only to find himself surrounded and roughed up, his regimental lanyard torn away. Division commander General Mignot prevented worse only by promising that the two regiments involved would not have to take up positions in the front lines right away, and to transmit the soldiers' grievances to his superiors.[6] In another division, an intrepid company commander from the 109th Regiment (a lawyer and local politician in civilian life) issued a stern warning to his superiors:

If the command structure takes care to look deeply into the soul of the French soldier, it will see that the best of our men will never consent to fight against their fellow citizens. And this must be well understood, for if these events were to grow worse and the command structure were to cede to conceptions that no longer correspond to the general mentality, conceptions that would lead it to believe that it could take certain extreme measures, there would be grave miscalculations.

Many officers will never, never, never consent to order their men to attack French soldiers. And our soldiers would refuse to execute such an order if it were given to them.[7]

Even if violent repression had been desired, an overwhelming display of force was simply not available. As Pedroncini has shown, only the cavalry were deemed certain to fire on their countrymen, and they were never sufficiently numerous to prevail had words passed to deeds.[8] Even here, the situation may have been more ambiguous than it seemed. General Féraud of the 1st Cavalry Corps reported in an actual meeting between his men and the demonstrators that the latter 'looked at the cavalrymen in silence, but without rendering the exterior marks of respect to the officers marching at the head of the columns, even the generals'.[9] Féraud reported that some of infantry asked the cavalry: 'You're not going to shoot at us?', but did not record the cavalrymen's response. In the event, the cavalry was not ordered to arrest the demonstrators, because 'it would have meant arresting entire units'. To be sure the cavalrymen reporting these incidents showed 'surprise and sadness, but not one the least sentiment of hesitation'. For his part, Féraud opposed using cavalry as 'simple police', and particularly if this involved dispersing them, lest they suffer 'contamination' by the disciplinary disease affecting the infantry.

The only practical command response involved a high-risk bluff. For example, on 1 June, the second battalion of the 308th Regiment refused to take up positions in the front lines because the soldiers believed they would be ordered to attack in order to retake trenches lost by another regiment.[10] Sometime later, General Taufflieb, commander of the 37th Corps, appeared before some 250 armed soldiers. He listened to their explanations, but responded simply that they would be given sufficient time to rejoin their units. In the meantime, he had posted cavalry and gendarmes around the demonstrators. Taufflieb had made ready trucks to carry away the 'leaders', to be determined by each company commander naming the five most undisciplined men in his unit. He interrogated each of these men personally, and swore to the regiment that more severe measures would follow should this prove insufficient. The show of force was symbolic but powerful, as Taufflieb presented the soldiers with a straightforward choice between obedience and violence. In the event, resistance wilted, and the 308th Regiment took up its positions without further incident. In a memo to army group and army commanders, Pétain praised Taufflieb's actions as exemplary: 'This line of conduct must be followed by all leaders at the different levels of the hierarchy.'[11] Taufflieb's gamble had paid off, though if it had not it is hard to see how his forces could have prevailed had violence erupted. Exactly why soldiers throughout the army understood the situation the way generals expected them to, and consequently did not call this sort of bluff, will be the subject of the next section.

But once soldiers had returned to the trenches, the idea of absolute military authority faced a certain problem of appearances. For the mutinies effected real if limited changes in the ways the French army carried out the war. Pétain had endeavoured to blunt some of the edges of daily suffering in the trenches by reforming leave policy and food distribution. Most importantly, he had made clear that no further efforts on the scale of the Chemin des Dames offensive would be attempted until time, tanks and the Americans gave the Allies a decisive military edge. As 2nd Army commander General Marie Louis Guillaumat put the problem:

Wrongly or rightly, the good soldier as well as the bad is not far from thinking that the regrettable mutinies were not without usefulness and that because of them soldiers have received certain concessions, or at least certain promises.[12]

Paradoxically, the most historically visible forms of remobilized military authority took place after the mutinies were over. In a sense, remobilizing military authority involved carrying forward the bluff of using force, through multi-faceted forms of insistence on the part of the command structure that the concept of military authority had never really been disrupted in the first place.

The first and most obvious way to present such an image involved the juridical identification of a group of men to take responsibility for the mutinies. Too many soldiers were involved in one form of disobedience or another for them all to be prosecuted. But prosecuting a select group suited a broader command narrative of the mutinies, according to which normally obedient soldiers were led astray by 'leaders', who in turn were under the sway of subversion from the interior. Absolute military authority could be applied to its limit against the alleged 'instigators' through courts-martial, long terms in prison or a labour camp, and executions.

Pedroncini effectively debunked the myth of savage repression of the mutinies, and showed that Pétain maintained regular court-martial procedures despite protests from key subordinates like Army Group North commander Louis Franchet d'Esperey. Pedroncini arrived at a figure of 554 death sentences, of which only 49 were actually carried out.[13] Even Pétain's foes, contemporaries and historians, have agreed that his moderation saved the army and perhaps the nation. The point is well taken, as far as it goes. But, in a sense, how many death sentences were commuted is not exactly the point. The objective of the courts-martial after the mutinies was to display military authority at its most intense. As a vestige of a form of power in which the sovereign literally has the power of life or death over the subject, military justice has an element of arbitrariness built into it. With the mutinies barely concluded, the command structure badly needed to show its strength, at least over someone. Displaying that its power could be absolute mattered more than the number of individuals over whom that power was exercised. The courts-martial thus provided a way out of the dilemma identified by Guillaumat, and so contributed to the narrative of uninterrupted, one-directional command authority, able dramatically to strike down at least a few of those who had dared defy it.

Courts-martial were used to define 'leaders', not just to punish them. Orders from Pétain dated 8 June complained that 'certain officers and non-coms have hidden behind the fact that since the movements have a collective character, they have found it difficult to unmask the leaders'.[14] He maintained that a collective act could always be rendered individual: 'It suffices to give a few men (beginning with the unmanageable ones) an order to execute.' Those failing to obey an individual command were to be designated 'leaders', whatever their actual conduct in the demonstrations. In the 74th and 274th Regiments, four privates were chosen simply because of 'their poor spirit and their usual manner of service', and two others because they were 'intelligent and well-instructed'.[15] Estimates of the percentage of soldiers who took part in the demonstrations and were subsequently tried are just that, given the fluidity of the mutinies and the probable imprecision of reports from the field describing them. Among common soldiers in the two regiments I studied closely, the figure could vary among companies by over 20 percentage points, from 4.4 per cent to 24.3 per cent.[16]

The issue of just who among those tried was sentenced to death and who was actually shot deserves more historical attention. Pedroncini maintained that the sentencing rather than actual execution was the most important disciplinary act, in that it demonstrated the seriousness of the command structure.[17] But he never questioned that 'leaders' existed (though many soldiers at the time did), and never questioned the wisdom of Pétain or anyone else in selecting them. In the 74th and 274th Regiments, the hundred soldiers tried admitted taking part in the demonstrations, though they denied leading them or even knowing who led them.[18] When asked why they took part, they responded nearly to a man: '*J'ai suivi les camarades* [I followed my comrades].' The one soldier actually executed came from the 274th Regiment, in which the mutiny was so fleeting that its participants had returned to their units even before the regimental commander finished writing his report of the incident. His case was essentially indistinguishable from those of his comrades, who even if given sentences in prison or a labour camp were released by 1922 at the latest.

Officers were themselves the object of remobilized command authority, through both criticism and encouragement. In his telegram of 8 June to key subordinates, Pétain lamented that 'certain officers have hidden from their superiors the poor spirit that has been reigning in their regiments', and warned that 'inertia equals complicity'.[19] The officers of the 5th Division, who diffused some of the most difficult demonstrations in the French army without loss of life, received a barrage of thankless criticism.[20] The 2nd Army commander, Guillaumat, observed that 'there was nothing but empty chatter between officers of all grades and the soldiers, chatter such that certain of the latter ended up wondering if the officers were not at heart on their side'. Pétain likewise criticized the officers of the 5th Division for responding to the demonstrators 'naively, as mere strikers, whom words would certainly restore to a better way of thinking'.

At the same time, however, Pétain encouraged officers to follow his own example of severity tempered with an enhanced concern for the daily lives of soldiers. Just a few days after he assumed supreme command, Pétain wrote: 'The benevolent attitude of the commander conforms to the most noble traditions of the French army. In no way does it exclude firmness.'[21] This attitude was to replicate itself all the way down the command structure. 'The qualities the soldiers appreciate in their commanders', a member of Pétain's staff observed in July 1917, 'is that they "don't pester them", that they show toward them a certain *bonhomie* and a certain familiarity of tone. Affectionately referring to them as *tu* touches them.'[22] To be sure, there is nothing necessarily sinister about officers treating their subordinates kindly. But gentleness could have its disciplinary intent as well as firmness. Pétain sought to demonstrate that reforms came from benevolent but strict fathers, rather than as concessions won by citizen-soldiers who had changed the operation of a war waged in their name.

The senior command sought to purge the military sphere of civilian influence. Most generals blamed the mutinies on civilian subversion, some obsessively so.[23] Army Group East commander Edouard de Castelnau cited 'secret organizations from the interior, whose decisions are transmitted by soldiers returning from leave'.[24] Army Group North commander Franchet d'Esperey considered the threat from the interior serious enough to request the expulsion of all civilian workers from the Zone of the Armies.[25] Pétain, though more moderate than most, agreed that 'the movement, in sum, has deep roots in the interior'.[26] Accusations of massive civilian subversion were never proved, at the time or subsequently. In any event, soldiers hardly needed civilians to tell them that something had gone wrong with the way France had been conducting the war. But generals found in civilian defeatism a useful tacit indictment of the government and the politicians, who failed to protect the military sphere from civilian 'politics' of the most unsavoury kind. Generals could also sidestep their own responsibility for military circumstances of much more immediate relevance.

The answer to protecting soldiers from subversion in the future lay in strictly controlling the information they received from the civilian press. As much as possible, citizen-soldiers were to be isolated from 'politics' insofar as it touched on the state institution they served. After extensive consultation with his senior subordinates, Pétain explained to War Minister Paul Painlevé in August 1917 how this should be done.[27] Under the category 'subjects to avoid', Pétain listed all military legislation before the National Assembly, lest such discussion give rise 'to hopes that are unrealizable in practice'. Also to be avoided were questions such as the demobilization of older soldiers, 'social projects' to be put into effect after the war, and controversies about the level of military discipline necessary when soldiers were resting behind the lines. Especially to be eschewed was criticism of the command structure, which, he observed, 'is carefully registered and commented upon by hotheads and the leaders of indiscipline', evidently still present even after the juridical repression of the mutinies.

For a variety of reasons, remobilized military authority does not adequately explain the outcome of the mutinies. The command structure drew the line between mutiny and revolution, but did not have enough physical force at its disposition to make sure that soldiers would decline to cross it. And the civilian and military spheres were too intertwined for the command structure to hope for much in separating them to its advantage. Indeed, generals themselves sometimes admitted as much. Pétain pleaded to Painlevé on 29 May that a civilian crackdown on dissent in the interior was essential 'because of the leave policy, which moreover, can in no way be changed'.[28] Likewise, Franchet d'Esperey lamented that: 'we must not forget that in effect, nearly a fifth of the army is always in the interior, on leave or convalescing. There is thus a floating and idle mass, available to all suggestions and bringing with it each incessant and inevitable exchange of ideas between the country and the army'.[29] State mobilization in the form of remobilized military authority set the basic parameters and choices for the discontented soldiers, but it did not determine the outcome. Thus, it is necessary to look at means of internal suasion, that is, the processes of the 'self-remobilization' of the French citizen-soldier.

Discipline within resistance: the political identity of the French citizen-soldier

In his 1963 study of the mutinies, Richard M. Watt observed: 'Any army is but a flicker away from becoming an armed gang. The only thing that prevents this is military discipline, which is actually an incredibly flimsy institution, if its subjects but knew it.'[30] But the evidence suggests that the discontented soldiers knew the fragility of formal discipline very well, yet behaved quite otherwise. It has long been known that incidents did not occur in the front lines, where formal authority was weakest. Mutineers behaved at times with a calm resolution senior commanders found most unsettling. When 37th Corps commander General Taufflieb went to speak to 250 mutineers from the 81st Division, he discovered to his surprise that:

As soon as I arrived, everyone stood up, and by their behaviour showed complete respect. But I considered this a deliberate and concerted gesture, of a disconcerting character for troops that had just committed one of the most grave acts of indiscipline.[31]

'No better proof of the guarded secret [of a plot organized in the interior]', observed 6th Army commander, General Maistre, 'than the uniform attitude of the men toward the remonstrances of their officers, the somewhat affected respect toward them to which they testified, the nearly complete absence of overexcitement and drunkenness'.[32] The key to understanding the internal discipline of the mutineers lies in understanding the constructed political identity of the French citizen-soldier. Disentangling the resistance and the internal suasive capacity that coexisted within this identity makes it possible to explain self-remobilization through the mutinies.

The mutinies took place against the backdrop of the oldest tension within French democracy – between representative government and direct democracy.[33] This tension was built into identities of both citizen and soldier, which from the time of the French Revolution constructed each other. During the Revolution, as Isser Woloch put it, 'conscription constituted the ultimate frontier of state building, of the articulation of the administrative state projected by the Revolution'.[34] And as Richard Challener put it, conscript service for the Frenchman constituted 'both the badge and moral consequence of citizenship'.[35] Citizens served the army as a representation of the state, and the state as a representation of the sovereign people. Military service thus carried to its conclusion Jean-Jacques Rousseau's logic of the social contract, in that obedience to military authority made the citizen-soldier as free as before, in the sense that he obeyed a source of authority originating in himself and his compatriots.

But also present in the identity of the citizen-soldier was the powerful political mysticism of the general will, which legitimized the exercise, from time to time, of direct democracy. The theory, not to say the theology, of the general will authorized the sovereign people directly to challenge representative institutions and in some way to rule directly. Once discontented soldiers successfully flouted military authority, the mutinies became an exercise in direct democracy. Joseph Jolinon, who defended soldiers before courts-martial following the mutinies, wrote rather romantically of a new Commune, 'a democratic republic on a war footing'.[36] More often, the mutinies have been represented as some form of military strike. I have generally resisted this comparison, on the principle that military service is not 'work' in an economic sense, and war is not production – quite the reverse. But there are similarities, particularly if we consider strikes of the late-nineteenth century – the strikes of the mutineers' fathers. As Michelle Perrot has pointed out, labour unrest during this period was considerably more spontaneous than the choreographed confrontations of later periods between unions and management.[37] Violent language contrasted with great caution in behaviour. The mutinies perhaps most resembled these strikes in that they served as dramatic and often poignant demonstrations of a simple and collective human need to be heard without mediation by societal organization, the essence of direct democracy. 'We marched not to bring about a revolution', wrote a soldier from the 36th Regiment, 'rather to attract the attention of the government in making them understand that we are men, and not beasts to be led to the *abattoir* to be slaughtered.'[38]

But direct democracy is seldom a tidy affair, whether on the Champs de Mars in 1792 or on talk radio in the United States today. Military authority had made the soldiers' relationship to the war relatively straightforward. At a certain level, they supported the war because they were commanded to do so. But once that external authority was removed, citizen-soldiers had to re-examine their whole relationship to the war, suddenly, brutally and directly. The result is a fascinating, if frequently baffling, array of emotions and interpretations of their situation, and some poignantly naive solutions.

Many soldiers had shared General Robert Nivelle's frenzied, indeed desperate, confidence that the Chemin des Dames offensive would break the stalemate on the western front. As officers' reports stressed again and again, soldiers were bitterly disappointed by the results. 'The Plateau of Craonne [on the Chemin des Dames] can't be taken. They persist in attacking it. We aren't commanded anymore.'[39] Soldiers felt abandoned, not just by Nivelle and the senior command, but by France. As Captain Jean of the 109th Regiment conveyed his soldiers' words:

We've had enough. Here we are, after three years of getting our bodies broken without result. The last offensive gave us nothing. We've been screwed over. There are too many shirkers. Make them come here. We want peace. The Germans also want peace. The people don't want to fight anymore. *Yes*, we will have peace in refusing to march.[40]

In their most idealistic moments, soldiers believed that the war of the trenches had created some sort of new identity across the lines beyond national identity. Front-line soldiers, French and German, would establish peace on their own through the exercise of direct democracy. As soldiers from the 36th and 129th Regiments put it: 'When we go into the trenches, we will plant a white flag on the parapet. The Germans will do the same, and we will not fight until the peace is signed.'[41]

Paradoxically, soldiers asserting themselves as citizens involved them pressing a sometimes confused array of 'private' demands, and asserted precisely those connections to the interior that their commanders were trying to regulate. Leaves, the most important regular form of connection between the civilian and military spheres, had come to be perceived as capriciously administered. Soldiers demanded a reformed leave policy as often and as vociferously as they demanded an immediate end to the war, even though the latter would presumably have rendered any leave policy irrelevant. Some soldiers found inspiration in the strikes conducted by female textile workers in Paris and other large cities: 'We're going to win. Honour to the *midinettes*. They are taking up our defence.'[42] But soldiers were no less concerned with asserting more traditional gender roles as protectors. 'We don't want the blacks in Paris and in other regions mistreating out wives', wrote a soldier from the 36th Regiment, referring to widespread but untrue rumours that colonial troops had been used to repress women's strikes.[43] Soldiers from the 77th Regiment (the would-be Communards portrayed by Jolinon) even saw the Americans as a threat, as another source of foreign labour that would release yet more Frenchmen to be killed in the front lines.[44] In a letter to his fiancée, a soldier from the 5th Division imagined the mutinies as a panacea:

I am one of the most persistent in spreading propaganda. I know that I am risking my hide, but by this means I might save it. My darling, say with me, 'Down with the war that separates us, and long live the Revolution that in bringing peace will reunite us.' I love you, and I don't want to die.[45]

Of course, the tension between direct and representative democracy was not definitively resolved in 1917 – any more than in 1792, 1848,

1871 or 1968. In the event, soldiers had to find a way out of their particular discursive tangle. What they held on to during the mutinies as essential aspects of their public identity proved even more important than what they rejected. Most significantly, soldiers never let go of a very individualized sense of responsibility that stemmed from membership in the Republic of France. This sense of responsibility led to self-remobilization through a series of choices leading back to obedience to military authority.

Soldiers actually emphasized their links to representative government through the Chamber of Deputies, though frequently in hostile tones. 'We see well, Monsieur', a soldier from the 129th Regiment wrote to a member of the Chamber of Deputies, 'that you are "far from the front", otherwise you would not take so lightly the suffering of others by the war. But know well that you are under surveillance everywhere by a resolute group and that an "accident" could be quickly arranged.'[46] A soldier from the 274th Regiment wrote to a deputy:

The minister of war declares that the concern of our commanding general [Pétain] is to spare French blood. That won't be enough. Do not forget that we hold in our hands the fate of the country. If you reach next winter without having shown your intention to negotiate [with the Germans] we will give ground.[47]

To be sure, these soldiers proposed an untenable mix of direct democracy and representative government. One posited disciplinary surveillance of politicians with an implicit threat of violence, the other threatened a grass-roots military takeover of French military and foreign policy. But to these soldiers and many others, the deputies remained the focal point of the demonstrations. This in itself, I would suggest, had great significance in revealing the internalized republican identity of the discontented soldiers.

Soldiers also never let go of what the war meant to France militarily. This is demonstrated most clearly by the lack of demonstrations in the front lines. But even soldiers unambiguously in rebellion never fully disengaged from the war. On 31 May, a group of about a hundred soldiers from three divisions met to debate what to do next.[48] The significance of such a meeting was lost on no one, for it suggested the possibility of collaboration among mutinous units. But a majority of the participants concluded that they would agree to hold a sector, but not to attack. The soldier from the 274th Regiment, mentioned above, proposed remaining on the defensive and asking the Germans for their intentions. Thereafter, he stated, 'if the Boches do not want to accept a peace corresponding to the sacrifices we have made and satisfying our honour, we will push them out ourselves'. A police investigator sent to infiltrate the mutinies of the 36th and 129th Regiments reported a quixotic set of peace aims: 'They demand Alsace, Lorraine, and the maintenance of the status quo (no indemnity, no annexations).'[49] Recovering the 'lost provinces' of 1870–71 presumably did not qualify as annexations because the soldiers considered that they had never ceased to be French. The soldiers added, in the language of Verdun, that if the Germans took advantage of the mutinies to attack, '*Les Boches ne passeront pas.*'

The mutinies ended when the internal suasion of citizenship joined forces with the external suasion of remobilized military authority. The moment of decision in the 129th Regiment came at 3.00 a.m. on the morning of 30 May.[50] The regiment was ordered to get into trucks for transport further behind the lines – an order that ostensibly granted the mutineers' demand that they should not advance into the front lines. Cavalry were discreetly in evidence at the transit point. The issue could scarcely have been put more clearly. The time had come for soldiers either to obey or to attack the cavalry, the designated instrument of state power and the French Republic. One company commander described an anxious but clear choice of behaviour as a choice of who soldiers were as military and political entities:

Getting the men up was painful. For the first time, I made my men face reality. I said to them that there was still time for them to regain control of themselves, and if they did not obey, they would cause the shedding of French blood. My efforts and those of my officers were finally crowned with success. My men decided to take up their packs and get into the trucks.

Their choice made, the end of the mutinies in the 129th became a ritual of reasserted military authority, the beginning of a series of rituals that continued with courts-martial and executions. The men were taken to a train station, where the three battalions were ordered bound for different directions. The 5th Division Infantry commander, Colonel Martenet, described men who had very much regained control of 'themselves', in ways military authority found recognizable. Martenet was struck by 'the way they rendered the honours with dignity and by the way the men saluted me from the cars as I watched the trains leave'. The drama of the ritual did not fail to touch the officers, whom Martenet described as 'absolutely heartbroken . . . Many had trouble hiding their tears when the time came to bid farewell.'

But the strategic game of mobilizing and remobilizing the citizen-soldier could have more than one kind of outcome. This is suggested by a fleeting incident in the 298th Regiment, as refracted through a report by 2nd Army commander, General Guillaumat.[51] On 26 June, with the mutinies essentially over and juridical repression operating at full throttle, seven company commanders in the 298th Regiment found themselves presented with a petition of remarkable audacity:

We the undersigned sergeants, corporals, and soldiers ask you to indicate to the colonel of the 298th Regiment their very determined intention not to return any more to the trenches in the event that you receive instructions obliging you to do so. We are all in solidarity with each other, because we understand that the continuation of the war, which has already made flow the blood of thousands of victims, is nothing more than a useless hoax for France, and less than that for those who are actually carrying out the war, and we hope that by our attitude, which is not ours alone, we will carry our leaders with us, while there is still time to make an honourable peace.

The petition was signed by no fewer than 884 men, close to half the men in the regiment. An inquest launched into the affair by 63rd Division commander General Andlauer revealed that this was not an isolated incident. When the regiment had been posted to a camp behind the lines, a meeting was held in which a soldier was allowed to speak, ostensibly 'to shore up the morale of his comrades and to preach calm'. In fact, the meeting had revolved around a collective observation that the French army had completed its task, and that the American army had to be required to relieve it within three months. Several anti-war demonstrations took place in the regiment between 24 June and 26 June, reports of which somehow never quite made their way up the command structure.

Nor was this the end of leniency toward the soldiers of the 298th Regiment. Only eighteen soldiers were tried, thirteen of whom were accorded attenuating circumstances. No soldier was given more than five years in prison, and the soldier responsible for circulating the petition was given a sentence of only two years. Only two of the fifty or so corporals signing the petition were tried, and only a third of those who signed even lost their rank, 'because of the great number of those guilty and of the lack of men suitable for replacing them'. The regimental colonel himself had to be given fifteen days of disciplinary arrest for reinstating leaves, which Guillaumat had ordered suspended at the opening of the inquest. Guillaumat himself was plainly perplexed. He admitted that 'discipline is not solidly established; they've been discussing terms with the troops. The word of order seems to be to avoid trouble at any price, and to prevent word of it getting around if it does occur.' Yet he also understood that his own options were limited. He ordered loss of rank for all the corporals involved, yet admitted that many kept their stripes *de facto* because of the difficulty in replacing them. Most puzzling of all for Guillaumat, the lack of severity seemed to have had no bearing on military performance. Despite the petition (or perhaps indirectly because of it), the regiment took up its position in the front lines without incident. Indeed, two companies involved in the episode 'conducted themselves most bravely' in taking back a salient in their sector. Guillaumat concluded, almost reluctantly, that 'we can thus estimate that the incident is closed and than we can once again count on the 298th Regiment'. Military authority and the citizen-soldier, it turned out, could work out a variety of arrangements in resolving the crisis of mobilization within the French army.

Mobilization and political identity

Even as they appeared at loggerheads, it has been argued here, state mobilization and self-mobilization worked together to resolve the mutinies as part of a complex, indeterminate game of power relations. State mobilization, institutionalized as formal military authority, set the behavioural boundaries. Soldiers were given what proved a straightforward choice between obedience and directly attacking state authority and the Republic that lay behind it. The command structure drew the line between dissent and revolution, but had no way of determining that soldiers would decline to cross it. Indeed, the most apparent forms of state remobilization occurred after the mutinies were over – the designation and repression of the 'leaders' and the reshaping of the story of the mutinies to make it appear as though formal authority had never really been disrupted at all.

Soldiers, for their part, decided to play the game as set up by their commanders, when no external use of power could have compelled them to do so. Nothing about the mutinies is more striking than the contrast between the depth of soldiers' anger at what the war had wrought and their continued adherence to what were essentially their commanders' war aims. Soldiers' self-remobilization was inextricably linked to their sense of who they were politically. The mutinies resurrected one of the oldest tensions within French democratic identity – direct democracy versus representative government. Direct democracy led soldiers to express an array of anguished grievances as citizens rather than as soldiers; representative government led them to express these grievances to their deputies, and in the end to obey their commanders, the instruments of state power authorized by that government. As Frenchmen, they found unacceptable a scenario in which France would lose the war – certainly what would have happened had they failed to return to the trenches. The resulting internalized suasion proved more powerful in determining soldiers' choices than any measure taken by the command structure.

But it would be a mistake to see the choices of the discontented soldiers of 1917 in terms of complete ethical freedom, or the political 'self' being remobilized as autonomous. The citizen-soldiers of 1917 were the product of more than forty years of Republican schooling, in which the army itself played no small part. Indeed, nowhere more than France was the concept of citizenship itself so closely linked to military service and its external means of suasion. In a sense, the identity of the citizen-soldier was captive to republican ideology. For, if Rousseau was to be believed, obeying external authority *was* obeying oneself. Internalized suasion could even mean Terror, if that term can be taken to mean internal surveillance of the political self.

But it is necessary in the end to view the identity of the citizen-soldier as a dynamic process rather than as a fixed state of political being. The haunting outcome of the next crisis of state and self-mobilization in France suggested that nothing was fixed about political identity there. The choice soldiers rejected in 1917 was imposed on them in 1940 – a lost war and France without the Third Republic. Over sixty years of internalized republican citizenship shattered in 1940, following a colossal failure of state mobilization, as witnessed by the widespread initial approval of the Vichy regime and the slow growth of the Resistance. The durability of republican citizenship during France's 'total' war of 1914–18 contrasted sharply with the vulnerability of that identity during the war of 1939–40, which in France never became total. Internalized suasion could be directed against the Republic itself. Philippe Pétain, who in 1917 had guided the state remobilization of his countrymen in uniform under the heading of 'apolitical' military authority in the service of the French state, would with equal vigour and equal effectiveness play the leading role in the remobilization of the French after 1940 under the very 'political' heading of *patrie, famille, travail* (fatherland, family, work).

10 The German army, the authoritarian nation-state and total war

Wilhelm Deist

On the morning of 9 November 1918, Ludendorff's successor as Senior Quartermaster-General of the German field army, Lieutenant-General Wilhelm Groener, faced his supreme warlord and stated drily: 'The Army will return in good order to its home bases, under the orders of its commanders and commanding generals, but not under Your Majesty's orders, for it no longer backs Your Majesty.'[1] Groener's statement concisely expressed the collapse of the entire former system of government, as a result of military defeat. The army refused to follow the monarch, thereby touching the very core of how the imperial German state and society perceived themselves. This is not the place to analyse the manifold reasons for the downfall of the German empire. What interests us is whether, and to what extent, the German High Command's response to the changing nature of warfare contributed to this collapse. It may seem doubtful whether the First World War can really be called a 'total war', or whether the term 'total combat' is not nearer to the reality of 1914–18.[2] What seems certain, however, is that warfare required a hitherto unheard-of mobilization of all resources of both state and society. The question is to what extent the armed forces, the core element of the authoritarian nation-state, managed to cope with the consequences of this mobilization.[3] This chapter attempts a preliminary answer to that question.

In the Prussian-dominated Germany of the late nineteenth century, the military had a double role – to provide national defence and to protect the established social order. Both functions had become much more difficult to perform since Bismarck's dismissal in 1890. The development of the Schlieffen Plan can be regarded as a symbol of the increasing difficulty of defending Germany's nearly hegemonic power position in a two-front war, without even taking into account the political and military consequences of Tirpitz's naval building programme.[4] On the other hand, the army had been given the task of keeping the Social Democrat organizations and their leaders under surveillance, and its powers for fighting the 'internal enemy of the fatherland' were constantly being extended and improved.[5] It was clear that in the case of war the divided military leadership would have to act under the burden of manifold and very intricate problems.

The treatment of the Zabern affair of 1913–14 by all those concerned (with the exception of the social democrats) showed clearly that the army, and in particular its officer corps, was still seen as the obvious protector of the established political and social order, even if criticism of its actions was sometimes quite harsh.[6] This was particularly important since the individual elements of the constitutional structure and the various forces tended to obstruct each other. The 'nearly ungovernable [political] structure' was faced with the Kaiser's command authority and the extra-constitutional position of the army.[7] Basically, the military was an unquestioned organization, and this was to have serious consequences particularly in the field of armament policies.[8] The armed forces, both the army and the navy, managed to have their armaments demands fulfilled to an extent which no other government project enjoyed. Military policy became a driving factor. Certainly no one could call this aspect of imperial policy stagnant. In spite of all resistance and all drawbacks this is true both of the army's armament bills and of Tirpitz's fleet programme.

The mobilization of national resources in peacetime, however, fairly soon met with limitations deriving from within the military itself. This applied particularly to its function in internal politics. From Verdy du Vernois through to Falkenhayn, the military's armaments policy was beset by the question of to what extent a larger recruitment of conscripts was compatible with the army's reliability when facing the Social Democrats, who were seen to be threatening the ruling order. The Army Bill of 1913, which was to expand the army even further, pushed beyond all previous limits in this respect. The Bill had been initiated and forced through by the General Staff against the War Ministry's resistance in order to counterbalance the numerical superiority of the combined Russian and French armies.[9] The newly-appointed Prussian Minister of War, von Falkenhayn, was willing to exploit the supply of conscripts even further. Simultaneously, the army was to be better protected against 'propaganda hostile to the forces' and the 'steeling of the young' was to be encouraged in all possible ways.[10] The authoritarian nation-state was preparing to complete the universal militarization of society. It was only due to the outbreak of war that the consequences which this turnaround in armaments policy might have had for the army's internal structure were never able to be judged.

The so-called 'August experience' of 1914, the image of a German nation enthusiastically united in all its classes in defence of the fatherland, has been questioned by recent research which shows that such enthusiasm was somewhat limited.[11] Nevertheless, it is the undeniable proof that the mobilization of the nation, as well as its organizational exploitation for the purposes of national defence, had succeeded, even though the military organization found it difficult to cope with the sheer numbers of volunteers.[12] This success was due not least to political decisions. Chancellor von Bethmann Hollweg succeeded in reducing the complex escalating political and military situation of the last days of July 1914 to a question of preparation against aggressive Russian designs, thus greatly reinforcing the already dominant trend toward national unity. However, the precondition for the success of this policy was the cancellation of the detailed measures against the Social Democrats and the trade unions which had been planned for the outbreak of war. The Minister of War, von Falkenhayn, urged by the Chancellor and the Secretary of the Interior, agreed to this as early as 25 July.[13] The commanding generals in the districts were instructed to act very cautiously in the event of a mobilization *vis-à-vis* the Social Democrats, the trade unions and the national minorities. This readiness to integrate the entire nation soon turned out to be very limited. Still, it was an important political turning-point, and the Chancellor, the Prussian Minister of War, and the chief of the field army General Staff repeatedly called it a wartime necessity.[14] This remarkable change in the official attitude towards the Social Democrats raised many hopes for further reform, for a 'reorientation' of internal policy. And the army, in concentrating on the nation's defence, could be seen as an instrument bringing about national unity. But these hopes were soon disappointed.

The successful political and military mobilization of the nation was adequately and symbolically expressed in the Kaiser's declaration that from now on he recognized 'only Germans'.[15] Thus the opening of the war was so successful that millions of soldiers willingly accepted the High Command's extreme demands, in particular in astonishing marching performances, during the first months of the war.[16] These demands were in keeping with the official doctrine of a short war but they eventually overtaxed the troops.[17] This doctrine of a short war called for the mobilization and deployment of all available forces within as short a time as possible, in the hope of finishing the campaign by a series of swift and decisive victories. The battle of the Marne and the subsequent battles in Flanders put an end to all such illusions of a short war, and the troops' exhaustion reached a peak.[18] Now the question became paramount of whether, and to what extent, the beginning of the war had unleashed tendencies in the High Command and the officer corps at large which valued national unity more highly than the army's hierarchical structure. Would there be forces prepared to accept that the imperial army was developing into a people's army?

No doubt there were a number of cases where this challenge was met, both in the front lines and on the barrack square at home. One example is the correspondence between the commandant of Altona and a leading social democrat official from Schleswig-Holstein, who were both prepared to compromise in order to achieve the common goal of a universal, classless military preparation of the young.[19] But, alas, this was not the general trend, for most military leaders simply expected all Germans, regardless of social class or political affiliation, to do their patriotic duty. This attitude found clear expression in a telegram from the Prussian Minister of War to his Bavarian colleague, dated 31 July 1914: the Social Democrats, von Falkenhayn wrote, could be expected to behave 'as befits any German under the present circumstances'.[20] Even more illuminating is a quotation from a letter of Wild von Hohenborn, later to be Prussian Minister of War himself, dated 8 October 1914: 'The [Social Democrat] leaders remain scoundrels. The "commies" at the front are irreproachable. In the army, there are no "commies"! just brave soldiers! Social Democracy can pack up and go home. The lads who stormed the hills of Craonne [south-east of Laon] will never attend a Social Democrat meeting again!'[21] Wild von Hohenborn was obviously convinced that the national mobilization would overcome the internal political rifts in favour of the traditional order headed by the military. His attitude was paralleled by that of the Conservative Party leader, Emst von Heydebrand und der Lasa, who expected that the war would lead to a 'strengthening of the patriarchal order and spirit'.[22] It was not a search for new ways of communicating with each other within a necessarily hierarchical army structure which dominated the situation both at home and at the front. Rather, the conviction that the traditional structure had proved itself gained ground and the Kaiser's slogan that he knew 'only Germans' was interpreted accordingly. The military class structure dominated the barrack square, and it even affected the relationship between staffs and the front line.[23] On a political level, the system of military governors prevented any attempt at a unified policy within the Reich.[24] This included a possible new orientation of domestic politics which was discussed during these months between the Chancellor and his Interior Secretary, Clemens von Delbruck.[25] The war aims movement which began to be formed worked for a continuation and extension of the existing order, not for its reform.[26] But the precondition for the existing order's preservation – decisive victory in the field – did not materialize, in spite of Tannenberg.

Seen in this light, it is a telling fact that the battle of the Marne's negative outcome was concealed from the German public.[27]

Influenced by the unsuccessful second offensive in Flanders, General von Falkenhayn, who had succeeded the younger Moltke as chief of the General Staff, explained to the Chancellor on 18 November 1914 that 'the attacking power of the Army was still there', but that it had become impossible for it to regain the initiative from the enemy. Soon after that he called the army 'a shattered tool'.[28] As with the consequences of the battle of the Marne this statement could have been used by the Chancellor against the extremist war aims movement, but he did not seize the chance.

Falkenhayn was not noted for his pessimism – quite the contrary. He had good reason for his dismal assessment of the situation. He had attempted to override the negative outcome of the battle of the Marne by two successive offensives in Flanders, and had failed. Taken in by the illusion of a short war, a swift decision had been sought no matter what the cost. The losses incurred during the first four months of the war, however, were enormous (657,974, of whom 76,541 were dead).[29] Due to the continuous offensives, losses were particularly high among the officers, a fact which could not fail to affect the units' combat readiness.[30]

The degree to which the army had changed since August became obvious not only in Falkenhayn's situation report, but also during the undeclared Christmas 1914 truce on the German–British front from Messines to Neuve Chapelle.[31] However bizarre, moving and paradoxical this truce was in itself, it clearly reflected a general weariness. There were absolutely no signs of serious mutiny either on the British or the German side, but the motivation to continue a fight to the death had obviously reached its nadir. This became even more obvious when in some sectors the truce was silently continued into the early days of 1915. There is a marked contrast between this and the high degree of mobilization achieved in July and August 1914, which had obviously been eroded in the meantime.[32] How did the military authorities react to this situation?

As part of industrialized warfare, mobile warfare changed step by step into battles of attrition. The western, eastern and south-eastern fronts were affected in very different ways. Similarly, it took the military leaderships on all sides some learning time to understand the changing nature of warfare, and its evolving demands.[33] Quite apart from the universal tactical changes, stationary warfare with vast armies caused problems of supplying and generally caring for the troops. Above all, the question was how the nation's material and manpower resources could be made optimally available for warfare.[34] The crucial, and recurring, point was how the available national manpower should be distributed between military and industrial production. Since industrialized warfare made the military command dependent on industrial output, it was forced to consider the condition of production, and that inevitably meant the labour question.[35] The General Staff officers, more than others, were faced with a multitude of new problems, mainly concerned with the war economy, which could not be solved by recourse to precedent or to mere orders.

Mobilization meant in the first place a strengthening of the people's motivation, a psychological problem which – if at all – could only be solved by political means. Considering how power was distributed within the Kaiserreich in wartime it is no surprise that this mobilization was largely expected to be brought about by the military, in particular the military command authorities. The political institutions and powers mutually obstructed each other; the civilian authorities lost their prestige when faced with the military's command structure under the state of emergency and the necessity to handle the general shortages, particularly the lack of food for the population at large.[36] All this taken together seemed to justify the expectation that the military would seize the initiative. However, this mobilization could only succeed if it were based on a motivation which encompassed and convinced the entire nation. Certainly, the initial conviction that this was a war of national defence had not lost its force with a majority of the population at home as well as of the soldiers at the front.[37] But doubts were beginning to grow.[38] The war aims debate, increasingly being waged in public, was dominated by extreme demands, and it was apt to shatter the illusion of a defensive war.[39] The military authorities at home well recognized that the public 'mood' had worsened dangerously during the autumn and winter 1915, but their suggestions to the authorities and social organizations as well as their own measures were aimed solely at reinforcing what they called 'stamina'.[40] However, the scarce food supply in some regions at home and the demoralizing effect which the battles of attrition on the western front had on the troops limited the results of any propaganda to sustain the will to 'hold on'.[41]

In both Britain and France, charismatic leaders knew how to bring about the necessary mobilization, and their political programmes set positive targets. In Germany things were different. Neither the Kaiser nor the Chancellor exuded any charisma. Only the victor of the battle of Tannenberg, Field Marshal von Hindenburg, who had been made head of the army High Command in August 1916, was put in a comparable position by the general confidence he enjoyed. However, so far there was no political programme which set any positive aims beyond merely 'holding on'. The mobilization of manpower and material resources was attempted and initiated merely by organizational means without any motivating incentives.[42] The High Command's original concept of the Auxiliary Labour Law, substantially revised by the Reichstag, may stand as an example of this.[43]

During the years 1916–17, which were to prove crucial for the outcome of the war and the future of the German Kaiserreich, there was at least the theoretical option of a programme of internal reform, which might have provided convincing motivation for the necessary mobilization. Bethmann Hollweg had announced such a programme of 'new orientation' for the post-war period, which aimed at cautiously integrating the Social Democrats and the trade unions into the political structure of imperial Germany.[44] This was in keeping with the conviction which he had already voiced during the July crisis of 1914 that 'whichever way the war ends, it will bring about a revolution of everything that exists'.[45] But the social classes which represented the ruling order fiercely resisted any substantial concessions to the Social Democrats, depriving Bethmann Hollweg of any real opportunity to initiate a reform of the existing structure, even if he had pressed for it more vigorously.[46] The officer corps and its leaders must be counted among the opponents of any reform from the very beginning. Still, it has to be noted that there were a few dissenting voices even among the military. The Bavarian Minister of War, Kreß von Kressenstein, declared in October 1916 to his cabinet colleagues that the people had a right to demand 'certain preconditions' before even more sacrifices could be demanded from them.[47] Foremost among these preconditions, he believed, must be unwavering justice in handling the shortages. The 'community of dearth and duty' had to be equalled by an 'equal right to state welfare'. The head of the newly founded War Authority, Lieutenant-General Groener, simply explained to the representatives of the Bundesrat that this war could not be won 'against the workers'.[48]

On the day before the Tsar abdicated, in the spring of 1917, Bethmann Hollweg, impressed both by developments in Russia and the situation in Germany (characterized by the 'turnip winter' of 1916–17) publicly announced a reform of the Prussian voting system as a core element of his reform policy. In the Reichstag, reform ideas found increasing support. In this situation, it was the army High Command which contributed substantially to the failure of such attempts.[49] The High Command regarded every step on the path of reform as a sign of weakness towards domestic and foreign enemies. The Prussian-minded senior officer corps, of which Hindenburg and Ludendorff were representatives, evidently found it difficult to cope with the military consequences of industrialized warfare, and if they did not refuse to face the political consequences altogether, they nonetheless found them strange and hard to understand. This officer corps, the self-assured first estate of imperial Germany, was a class-conscious means of controlling a mass army, and proved unable to deal with the political – i.e. social and psychological – component of modern warfare.

Again, it was Bavarian officers who were professional enough to overcome the limits of this specifically Prussian class ideology. The Bavarian Minister of War, von Hellingrath, declared to his Prime Minister early in April 1917 that in his opinion the 'decisive battle' could only be won if a 'wise, timely exploitation of the psychological imponderables' gave 'a new [and] mighty impulse and strengthening' to the thoughts and feelings of the 'marvellously proven' people.[50] From this point of view, the resistance to reform of the Prussian voting system seemed to him extremely counterproductive. And in his notes on the July crisis of 1917, a Bavarian officer in the army High Command, Colonel Mertz von Quirnheim, underlined the position of outstanding political power enjoyed by the High Command, and the opportunities this might afford.[51] 'How marvellous it would be if the Field Marshal and Ludendorff cooperated with Bethmann Hollweg to take charge of our destinies. The objection that this is "not possible" is based on prejudice.' And he gave an example of possible cooperation which illustrates the scope and revolutionary power which imaginative alternatives to the High Command's actual political course might have had:

It would create a really gigantic impression if General Ludendorff declared (through the voice of Hindenburg), 'Yes the High Command is also in favour of universal suffrage, for it gives to our Prussian soldiers what they thoroughly deserve.' I am sure Ludendorff would be carried through the streets, any danger of strikes etc. would vanish, the impression abroad would be enormous. How marvellously such a demonstration could be doctored! But Ludendorff lacks any understanding of how to exploit political ideas for the conduct of war. He believes the people can be kept going with pithy phrases.

Mertz von Quirnheim and some other officers realized that the basis for the successful mobilization of all national resources which the military situation required had to be internal political reform. Hindenburg and Ludendorff, together with most of the senior officers, opted against any reform. This was to lead directly to military defeat and to the collapse of the established ruling order of which they were the most powerful representatives and which they were determined to preserve at any cost.

In July 1917 the Chancellor took a further initiative for the reform of the Prussian voting system, and a majority of the Reichstag seemed to favour a compromise peace. At this point, Hindenburg and Ludendorff believed the time had come to influence political decision-making decisively.[52] Their first and foremost aim was the downfall of Bethmann Hollweg, who had become for them the symbol of a policy of weakness towards both foreign and internal enemies of the established order. Their unprecedented cabal was eventually successful, and Bethmann Hollweg resigned on 13 July. The two generals' actions had been guided by the purely negative aim of toppling the Chancellor, as was made plain by the farcical search for a successor.[53] The so-called Peace Resolution passed by the Reichstag on 19 July did not suit the High Command's intentions either, but it had only limited power to influence this body. Instead, the High Command tried to neutralize the resolution's effect through the civilian executive, in particular the new Chancellor, Michaelis, who declared himself to be in favour of the Peace Resolution 'as I conceive it'.[54] Above all, however, the High Command reacted by ordering on 29 July, ten days after the Peace Resolution had been passed by the Reichstag, the institution of 'patriotic instruction' (*Vaterländischer Untericht*) within the army.[55] It believed that this would be the instrument to mobilize first the army and then the population at large.

From the beginning of 1916, both the civilian and the military authorities had made every attempt to counterbalance the noticeably worsening 'mood' at home; in a modified way the same went for the front-line command authorities.[56] At home, attempts were made to tie in as many social organizations as possible, including the clergy and the local authorities. They were to 'inform' by describing the war situation from a point of view dictated by 'stamina' and thus assist with 'keeping up the spirit'. In order to eliminate the growing 'social grievances' among the troops, the officer corps were repeatedly urged to live up to their duty of caring for the subordinate soldiers in every possible way, in the hope that this would improve the situation at the front.[57] It was in keeping with this kind of propaganda that all political topics were to be carefully avoided. Any discussion about a 'new orientation' of the internal political system, all debates about territorial war aims were left to the political parties and pressure groups. It soon became obvious that the High Command would be content with neither the organizational structure nor the political content of this kind of propaganda. Still, under the impact of the Russian February revolution as well as of anti-monarchist propaganda at home, they initiated a propaganda organization to be set up first in Germany itself, by the regional military commands. Towards the end of July, the entire 'information organization' at home and at the front was put under the centralized control and guidance of the relevant army High Command department.

The High Command had started a political offensive as an instrument to mobilize the psychological and the moral resources of the nation. The name of 'patriotic instruction' was only designed to sustain the impression of an apolitical 'information activity'.[58] The guidelines had been carefully worded; even so, they gave away this aim. The soldiers were to be influenced so that they would want to 'continue fighting until our enemies' destructive will has been broken, and until our economic growth can continue safely'. Another principle suggested for this propaganda was even blunter: 'Necessity and importance of leadership in all walks of life (military, government, administration, industry and commerce). Deduce from this need for authority on the one hand, and subordination on the other.'[59]

The army High Command now took a definite stand on all major fields of politics, and even if it tried to camouflage the fact, it was quite aggressive in voicing its opinion. The effect on military propaganda activities was reinforced by the foundation of the Vaterlandspartei (Fatherland Party) in September 1917, headed by Admiral von Tirpitz. As a political party it did not enjoy the undivided support of the military, but its demand for extensive territorial war aims met with general approval in military circles.[60] The aim of all these measures was to achieve the spiritual and moral mobilization of all manpower resources which military expertise had shown to be necessary. As the institution of 'patriotic instruction' demonstrates, the High Command had come to realize that this mobilization could only be made effective by political means. However, the contents of this political offensive stayed well on the right of the political spectrum. Both the army High Command and the Vaterlandspartei nevertheless had to realize fairly soon that a mere appeal to patriotic feelings no longer penetrated to those social classes which now counted. On an organizational level, the 'patriotic instruction' was certainly working, but it failed to close the widening gap between officers and men, between front-line and rear echelons of the army.[61] In the field of political propaganda, which was to have been its domain, it remained ineffective. At home, it had to be admitted during the summer of 1918 that the propaganda effort had not got through to industrial labour.[62]

The 'euphoric atmosphere' on the western front just before the March offensive, and the swift collapse of the strikes in January 1918, may have had the effect of covering up the reality that communication between high and low, between those who supported and waged the war and those who suffered it, had collapsed. The High Command's political offensive, aided by the officer corps, and aiming at a spiritual and moral mobilization of the nation, had finally failed.

The 'euphoric atmosphere' and its further development are especially revealing. The German offensive was unleashed on 21 March 1918. The German armies achieved what the Allies had failed to bring about in three years, with an enormous mass of material and manpower. They overwhelmed the allied positions and gained bases for warfare on an operational level. The March attacks pushed more than 35 miles into the allied hinterland. Some of the subsequent offensives were also spectacularly successful, but the decisive aim, operational breakthrough, was not achieved.[63] A number of reasons have been advanced for the German failure; they range from the mistaken coordination of the various offensives to the uninviting terrain of the March attack, from the lack of mobility to Ludendorff's style of leadership in the follow-up offensives. I should like to draw attention to one aspect which the military authorities preferred to overlook: the psychological state of the army.

The army had undergone profound transformations since the days of August 1914. The soldier in the battles of attrition around Verdun and on the Somme did not fight out of national enthusiasm; he was tied into the universal principle of command and obedience, entirely dependent on a group for his existence, with autonomous action as the great exception. A widening gap separated the front-line military man, whether soldier or officer, from the rear echelons. The 'social grievances' could not be overcome, and they further reduced the fighting motivation of individuals and groups.[64] It comes as no surprise that, by the end of 1917, the weariness of the troops was giving cause for concern. There is no indication that the army High Command, and Ludendorff in particular, took this into account during their operational planning. However, what could not be overlooked was the problem of moving the units from east to west, with up to 10 per cent of the men deserting from the transports.[65] As elsewhere, the futility of the 'patriotic instruction' had become patently obvious. Even so, the military leadership managed to instil a spirit of confidence in the troops by intensively and impressively preparing the offensive to the last detail. As a consequence, the better equipped 'mobile' divisions which had been specially selected for the offensive were in a highly confident mood – but this derived from the universal expectation that this final heave would bring about an end to the cursed war. A young cadet coined the significant phrase: 'Target: Peace!'[66] When the spring offensive of 1918 ground to a halt towards the end of March, this hope turned out to be illusory, and the consequences for troop morale were far-reaching. A few days after the beginning of the second offensive in Flanders, the chief of the 6th Army's General Staff was compelled to report a truly shocking fact: 'The troops do not attack, in spite of orders.'[67] Within a few weeks, the negative mood of the end of March, worsened by untenable conditions in the new front line and by the lack of food and ammunition, had developed into a clear refusal to obey orders. This was the beginning of a development which was also caused by horrendous losses, general fatigue and the hopelessness of the military situation, and which came to be known as an 'undercover military strike' (*verdeckter Militärstreik*).[68] Hundreds of thousands attempted to survive the summer and the autumn as 'dodgers', and the military authorities found no ways of dealing with this – in contrast to their coping with the Christmas truce of 1914. As Ludwig Beck, then a major in the General Staff of the Army Group of the Crown Prince put it, only a 'cobweb of fighters' protected the army from the incalculable consequences of an allied breakthrough.[69] Total military defeat began to loom over the horizon and when, at the end of September, Ludendorff called for an armistice, this was but the logical consequence of the military situation that had resulted from the failed German offensives. Military defeat was to be followed by political collapse which found its terse expression in Groener's statement *vis-à-vis* Wilhelm II on 9 November 1918.

In retrospect, it has to be stated that industrialized total warfare confronted the army and its core, the officers and the High Command, with demands which it was structurally incapable of mastering. In the widespread expectation of a short war, the military command, in conjunction with the political leadership, had managed to mobilize the nation's manpower and psychological resources to a high degree. Once this phase of the war had failed, and during the development towards an industrialized total war, gaps began to open up which the High Command under Hindenburg and Ludendorff felt it had to bridge. After the experience of Verdun and the Somme, a new attempt was made to mobilize all remaining manpower and material resources. This task was highly political, and it proved beyond the High Command's capabilities. The latter's attempt to conduct a public debate over war aims divided the nation further instead of reuniting it.[70] Calling for a cautious reform of the Prussian political system, and thus rallying major sections of the population behind the necessary mobilization, would have been at least an imaginable alternative, but it was never even considered. The 'patriotic instruction' did not reach those social classes whose support both at home and in the front line was desperately needed to continue the war in the manner demanded by the High Command. The fundamental change in the nature of warfare overtaxed the guarantors of the authoritarian nation-state. And in the end the military offensive and its effects on the army eventually destroyed their power base.[71] The guarantor became the gravedigger of the ruling system when it attempted to live up to the challenge of total war.

Bethmann Hollweg had at least realized the connection between total warfare and the system of government. In a memorandum dated December 1915 he demanded that 'the unity of the entire nation must not fail because of respect for traditional circumstances, however beneficial they may have been in former times'.[72] Ludendorff, on the other hand, remained unconvinced; as late as 1935, in his book *Total War*, he drew his conclusions from his experiences in the First World War. As a precondition for future warfare he developed the concept of a militarized racist nationhood (*Volksgemeinschaft*) from which he excluded Jews, the Catholic church and the socialists.[73] Future warfare became reality only four years later.

11 Morale and patriotism in the Austro-Hungarian army, 1914–1918

Mark Cornwall

Looking back on the final years of Austria-Hungary, Field Marshal Conrad von Hötzendorf wrote bleakly in December 1924 that the empire should have followed Franz Josef to the grave in November 1916 instead of struggling on for a further two years. Neither the Monarchy nor its last Emperor, Karl, had been permitted a dignified exit from the European stage.[1] Conrad might have added that this applied also to himself. He remained notoriously embittered that in February 1917 Karl had replaced him as chief of the General Staff, dispatched him to command Habsburg forces in the Tyrol, and then made him the scapegoat for the failed offensive of June 1918. Yet Conrad's frustration under Karl's 'new regime' was not purely personal. He resented perhaps even more the weakened status of the Austro-Hungarian military. This had begun months before Franz Josef's death when, with the creation of a joint High Command for the central powers in the aftermath of the disastrous Brusilov offensive, the Austrian High Command (AOK) had been made subordinate to the German military leadership. Conrad spoke caustically at the time of the beginning of a 'Ludendorff era'. This affront was then compounded by the Habsburg military's growing weakness within the Monarchy itself. From August 1914 the AOK had tried to run a military dictatorship in the Austrian half of the empire, but their effectiveness outside the immediate war zones had been successfully restricted by Count Stürgkh, the Austrian Prime Minister (supported by his Hungarian counterpart, István Tisza, who blocked any military imposition on the kingdom of Hungary). By the summer of 1916 the war's social and economic strains were ever clearer in 'Austria' and the need for some 'secondary mobilization' of the population behind the continued war effort was equally apparent. As Count Herberstein, the general adjutant of Archduke Friedrich (commander-in-chief), observed, 'the Monarchy has perhaps never been in such a serious situation as it is today, and even now we lack a strong-arm policy which might unify everything at home'.[2]

The AOK, and senior Habsburg officers such as Archduke Eugen, reacted to this challenge by pressing Franz Josef again for a military solution: a Prime Minister should be chosen from their ranks or at least there should be an enhanced militarization of the whole empire in order to coordinate its food supplies. The old Emperor accepted neither proposal. And Karl's response, on ascending the throne, was equally damning. On the one hand, he wished to play the role of Emperor–King far more actively than his great-uncle, particularly as far as military policy was concerned; on the other hand, his decision in 1917 to restore some form of constitutional rule in Austria effectively eliminated many of the emergency powers previously exercised by the military. Some observers – for example the German ambassador – had vainly hoped that Karl's accession might boost enthusiasm for Austria-Hungary's war.[3] In fact, as we will see, the necessary secondary mobilization of the population on behalf of the Habsburg cause never took place. Instead, in 1917–18, in an environment which was laxer politically but grimmer economically, the mobilization which occurred in many parts of the Monarchy assumed the form of nationalist agitation: a mobilization of the population on behalf of radical anti-Habsburg movements. Watching this steady domestic disintegration, the 'second AOK' of Arz von Straussenburg and his military commanders at the front never tired of complaining about the poisonous effect of the hinterland upon the army's morale and discipline. It was the hinterland, the area where the military had been disempowered, which could be blamed for most evils: for insufficient censorship, for weakening patriotism, for inadequate food supplies. By early 1918 after widespread strikes in the interior, the military were still moaning about the need for a 'strong-arm policy'.[4] Some, including Karl himself, flirted briefly with the idea of a 'ministry of generals' for Austria. But the nettle was never grasped. Arz and the War Minister Stöger-Steiner were among those who shied away from such a bold step, even though Arz by this time seems to have become convinced that Austria-Hungary's war would not end on the battlefield but by a collapse in the rear.[5]

Immediately upon his appointment to succeed Conrad as chief of the General Staff in February 1917, Arz had ordered the army commands to send in detailed reports about the morale and physical state of the troops. It was surprisingly uncommon for such reports to be requested or submitted – usually only on the eve of battle or after some disaster had occurred in a particular division – and as a result descriptions of troop morale are not plentiful in the documents which have survived. According to Arz's memoirs, on this particular occasion the replies received were generally favourable, with the commanders singling out German, Magyar and Croat regiments for special commendation. Yet, at the same time, Arz was greatly alarmed at the food crisis now afflicting the Monarchy, and at the quality of the troops who were coming into the war zones: they were not only increasingly undernourished, but – as his memoirs hint – they were liable to be tainted by the insufficient moral fortitude of the hinterland.[6] Their poor quality, however, was only partially due to domestic factors. The fact that the army had to call up these men owed much to its own failure to win a speedy victory on the battlefield and to the decimation of the old army in the first months of the war. In the first confused campaign against Serbia, in stifling heat and hostile terrain, the armed forces had lost 600 officers and 22,000 men (dead, wounded or taken prisoner). By the end of 1914 the number lost on all Austro-Hungarian fronts totalled over a million, a figure then compounded by the devastating Carpathian campaign of early 1915; in freezing temperatures one Croat regiment, for example, lost twenty-eight officers and 1,800 men through spending one night in the snow.[7] Although these losses could be matched by those from, for instance, the French army in the first weeks of the war, the results for the Monarchy were more devastating because of the army's multi-national composition. The manpower shortages resulting from the decimation of the 20–42 age group would never be recovered. In April 1915, Landsturm duty was duly extended to those aged 18–20; from January 1916, those up to 55 were theoretically liable for war service. But, by this time, with a monthly loss at the front of 224,000 men, the march formations which every month carried reserves to the war zone were no longer covering gaps in the manpower. It meant increased burdens upon existing troops in the front line and a degree of restricted leave which inevitably damaged morale. This was then exacerbated by the encroaching nationality issue: namely, that there were insufficient officers of, for example, Croat nationality to command predominantly Croat regiments. Moreover, increasingly those who were called up or were promoted into supposedly reliable positions were ex-civilians, some of whom had strong nationalist sympathies or only a shaky allegiance to the Habsburg cause. The result was that the armed forces were slowly becoming infected by nationalism, or at least by a substantial degree of apathy towards the war effort. If they were to survive a four-year war, the army urgently required some programme of 'Habsburg re-education'; but to be effective it would need to be backed up by a similar programme in the hinterland.

At the start of the war the Habsburg military leadership already viewed its forces in a somewhat stereotypical fashion. Soldiers of Serb or Ruthene nationality were quickly suspect because of the degree of Serb and Ruthene civilian collaboration with the enemy in Bosnia and eastern

Galicia respectively. In the latter case, the army was so paranoid about Ruthene civilians' links to the enemy that it speedily transported thousands of them westwards into the hinterland. In eastern Galicia, as in Bosnia, the gallows were often erected too hastily.[8] Yet from the spring of 1915 it was always Czech soldiers who had the worst reputation. Although the mobilization of Czech troops had been faultless, on 3 April when attacked by the Russians, the Czech infantry regiment (IR) no. 28 laid down its arms and surrendered *en masse*.[9] The subsequent investigation revealed the damaging interaction of front and hinterland and the regiment was dissolved and dispersed among more reliable units. Arz was to write later that the causes of Czech indiscipline were not to be found in the hardships of life at the front, but 'lay deeper' in that 'the men were nationally contaminated'.[10] Yet the military solutions to this problem, certainly in mid-1915, were rather limited: firstly, to tighten discipline in the war zone; and secondly, to try to persuade Franz Josef and the Austrian government to place a general in control of Bohemia.[11] Both, of course, were defensive solutions which would not tackle the underlying Czech apathy or hostility to the war effort. Both, moreover, were likely to backfire on the military when the manpower crisis increased and damaged the national composition of units, and when (from 1917) the military's power was weakened and its dictatorial record of 1914–16 was subjected to popular scrutiny.

Yet the incident of IR 28 was still highly unusual at this stage of the war. Against it, one can always set descriptions of troops whose performance left little to be desired. Such units would survive until the end of the war. But in the East by 1916 their reputation was slowly becoming besmirched by a growing incidence of insubordination within Czech, Ruthene or Serb formations. If the AOK would soon add the Romanians to its list of unreliable nationalities, the cloud of suspicion had already fallen upon the Monarchy's Italian troops due to the same sin of irredentism. At the beginning of the Italian war, 75,000 civilians from the Tyrol had – like the Ruthenes – been evacuated into the interior and interned.[12] The AOK did not expect that these elements could ever be mobilized for the war effort. Their fears were soon confirmed when it was Italians, along with Czechs, who formed the main trickle of deserters to the Italian enemy. Early on, therefore, the AOK resolved that the Monarchy's Italian troops should be stationed only on the eastern or Balkan fronts, while Croat or Slovene soldiers were expected (correctly) to perform with more enthusiasm against the Italian enemy on their own doorstep. Such thinking shows clearly the complex number of factors which the Habsburg military had to juggle when weighing up the threats to troop morale: apart from the fundamental dangers of war-weariness and material hardships, the AOK could never escape the implications of commanding an army of different nationalities against different enemies. New opponents abroad might well boost the morale of some troops, but would depress the mood of others; and paradoxically, when an enemy was knocked out – Serbia, Romania or Russia – the effect was not always beneficial, for certain troops began to question their role or the purpose of the war and to look forward even more to a speedy peace.

It seems accurate to suggest that the Austro-Hungarian army in the East could not have continued beyond 1916 without German support – the German troops acting, in Rauchensteiner's vivid simile, as 'corset strings' for the Habsburg forces.[13] In contrast, on the Italian front, Austro-Hungarian troops were able to hold their own for most of the war. Yet here too, during 1917, the results of prosecuting total war with inadequate resources were beginning to emerge. The army's cohesion in 1917–18 was to be subjected to new dangers, stemming from both the hinterland and the enemy (indeed, the two increasingly interacted), and the AOK was to find it impossible to bind the wounds. By the summer of 1917, for example, there were alarming signs on the Italian front; these can serve us with a basis for studying the wide-ranging threats to the morale of the Austro-Hungarian forces. During the year, from the Tyrolian region commanded by Conrad von Hötzendorf, the number of desertions to the enemy had grown dramatically: from 115 in the first six months to a total of 82 for the months of July and August alone. Moreover, while in the past the deserters were usually 'Slavs and Romanians', this was no longer precisely the case. Conrad ordered a thorough investigation since the phenomenon had to have, 'apart from nationalist agitation and war-weariness, its own special causes'.[14]

The results, which Conrad dispatched in a short report to the AOK on 15 September 1917, illustrate amply the degree to which the military by this time saw events within Austria-Hungary as the major threat to army morale and discipline.[15] General war-weariness or the rigours of life in the front line appeared to be side issues. Above all, the report, based upon the views of corps commanders and their subordinates, put the blame for the rise in desertions upon the amnesty for political prisoners which Emperor Karl had granted in July 1917. It went on to highlight insufficient discipline as a key problem: Conrad criticized the Emperor's decision to abolish two forms of punishment (tying up and chaining up) which were felt to be vital as a means of controlling the ranks. Since the commanders would only be left with the option of punishing recalcitrants by placing them in 'labour units', the AOK petitioned energetically to have the ban rescinded: and in February 1918, after the notorious naval mutiny at Cattaro, Arz managed to persuade the Emperor to permit the two punishments 'under extra-ordinary conditions'.[16] A tightening of discipline seemed all the more necessary because (the third major point in Conrad's report) of the low calibre of troops now reaching the war zone. Conrad complained about the steady influx of 'unreliable elements' from the hinterland, specifying these as men of Serb, Czech, Romanian and Ruthene nationality, who then had to be mixed with 'reliable' German or Magyar troops. Not only should this mixing be avoided, since the new recruits were unsettled by serving next to troops speaking a different language, but the assignation of unreliable elements must stop: 'for otherwise in a short time there will be no units left which we can characterize as *absolutely* reliable'. One officer at the AOK minuted alongside this, 'yes, but where then can we send them?' It had, after all, been normal procedure at least since the behaviour of IR 28 to place known 'unreliable' elements under firm supervision. And as the army was reorganized from May 1917, it was becoming standard practice to create nationally mixed regiments as an extra check upon suspect nationalities. More fundamentally, the military's criteria for judging troops as 'unreliable' were highly suspect. It might still be true that Germans, Magyars, Croats, Slovenes and Poles made, on the whole, the most disciplined soldiers; but in 1917 the list of deserters to Italy was beginning to contain German and Hungarian names, a sign that crude generalizations about 'reliability' could not continue for much longer.

Indeed, the reality, at least according to Italian sources, was that during the summer of 1917 over a third of deserters to the enemy from the Tyrolian front were Slovenes or Croats, hitherto regarded by both the Austrian and Italian High Commands as patriotic 'Austrians'.[17] The AOK probably first had an inkling of this development at the same time as they received Conrad's report. For in the night of 17–18 September, there took place the most notorious case of 'treachery' by an Austro-Hungarian officer: the plot by a Slovene reserve officer, Ljudevit Pivko, to betray the position at Carzano to the Italians.[18] The subsequent investigation revealed that domestic Czech and Slovene nationalism had fermented the plotters' ideas: this seemed obvious from their back-ground and particularly from the numerous radical nationalist and socialist newspapers to which they had subscribed. Conrad, in his report on desertions (15 September), had already expressed alarm at the type of information which was permeating the war zone from the hinterland. He had singled out those newspapers which regularly spread rumours of imminent peace and thereby left the men disappointed. He then linked this problem closely to the lack of leave available to the troops: since leave was so infrequent, the troops depended all the more on optimistic sounds from home to maintain their morale. The AOK replied predictably to Conrad that the manpower crisis made leave a luxury; some divisions continued to contain hundreds of men who had never been on leave.[19] But Conrad's logic was also slightly askew: he went on to complain in his report about the nationalist or war-weary agitation which infected those who went on leave, preventing many of them from returning on time to the front. The reality, therefore, was that whether on leave or not, the troops could not be kept in quarantine from the mood of the hinterland. The AOK might impose a ban on leave to certain unsettled regions; they might in mid-1918 create an index of certain radical newspapers which were banned from the war zone. But neither move was foolproof or without harmful side-effects. Only stability within the Monarchy would help, but here the military lacked the means or the influence adequately to affect the situation.[20]

The military's natural reflex was to keep a tight check upon undesirable developments in the hinterland by repressive methods, such as scrupulous censorship of the press and the banning and arrest of nationalist or socialist agitators. Ironically, the highpoint of this response (1914–16) had coincided with the period of the war when it was least necessary; for in the early years, at least until mid-1916, a certain political truce or even Habsburg patriotism had been preserved in many parts of the Monarchy, especially in Hungary where, with parliament still sitting, a kind of *union sacrée* seemed to be developing. The military's draconian behaviour at this time – in Bosnia, Galicia and the Tyrol (but also outside the war zone in Bohemia) – had undoubtedly done much to damage the sense of 'imperial solidarity', cutting off at a stroke any future mobilization of these civilians. On the other hand, it does seem to have been the military, rather than the political authorities, who made the most conscious efforts to boost Habsburg patriotism among the civilian population. Although Count Stürgkh at the start of hostilities had stated that the Austrian government's only aim was to galvanize everybody towards winning the war, there was no subsequent campaign to stir domestic patriotism apart from periodic appeals for war loans.[21] The AOK were immediately more sensitive to the issue because of the dangers to military morale; they commissioned war correspondents to write eulogistic articles or embellish dry official reports from the war zone. Conrad himself, it is true, seems to have had little appreciation of how the press might be used for positive domestic propaganda: he would later write contemptuously of propaganda as 'the greatest example of stupidity which has ever been exhibited by the human race'.[22] But he also belatedly acknowledged its effectiveness, and during the war he had at least made some small efforts to kindle patriotism, notably in the field of education. In 1915–16, the AOK had pressed Stürgkh on a number of occasions to reform 'Austrian' schools, proposing to nurture 'more reliable citizens' not simply by weeding out subversive teachers or by vetting school textbooks (notably in Bohemia where in 1917 the Czechs would express their irritation at this move), but by positive steps: firstly, by 'nationalizing' the many Austrian primary schools which were in private and theoretically nationalist hands; and secondly, by introducing into middle schools a curriculum of pre-military training for all male pupils so as to 'facilitate their education as truly patriotic citizens'. Neither idea made much headway: in the first case – it seems – because it could not be implemented by decree (without parliamentary approval); in the second case because, although the Minister of Education in June 1915 sent out guidelines to all Austrian school councils, the idea of militarizing youth was never compulsory and many teachers were opposed to it. Nor would the AOK's plans ever receive Hungary's blessing, and, as a result, an educational programme for all corners of the empire was never a practical possibility.[23]

When Karl ascended the throne the issue of stimulating imperial patriotism arose once again. In January 1917 the new Emperor appointed Karl Werkmann as his press officer, a sole individual charged with the task of publicizing the dynasty in the press. A few years later the exiled Emperor would admit that this had been inadequate. Indeed, in the words of one Austrian historian, the lack of propaganda by the Habsburg dynasty was 'certainly the gravest sin of omission' during Karl's reign.[24] Like Conrad von Hötzendorf, the Emperor had little understanding of how to shape public opinion, commenting on one occasion that thoughts and ideas 'could not be recommended like laxatives, toothpaste and foodstuffs'.[25] Apart from appointing Werkmann, he seems to have expected that his actions would speak for themselves and, in particular, that personal appearances at the front or in the hinterland could contribute substantially to raising patriotism. Undoubtedly he was encouraged by General Arz to believe that he could personally boost the morale of the army, but if his periodic visits and his solicitude for individuals might convince most soldiers of his inherent good nature, it was also true that many were already beyond salvation for the Habsburg cause.[26] Similarly, in the field of domestic propaganda, Karl appears to have done little but follow the AOK's lead in blaming the education system for weak patriotism and seeking to expand the number of state schools. It was a policy which in 1917 the reinvigorated political parties in Austria could successfully obstruct.[27]

An essential dilemma for the Habsburg dynasty from 1916 centred on how to maintain support for the war effort after three years of hostilities,

when at the same time the dynasty's real inclination (as expressed by
Karl on his accession) was to rally the civilian population behind the
goal of a speedy end to the war. The two rallying cries were
incompatible, and partly because of this they were both inadequately
propagated by the authorities. Ideally, the various nationalities would be
mobilized around the goal of supporting the Monarchy's war precisely in
order to achieve a worthwhile peace; in reality, by 1917 it was becoming
clearer that the peoples of Austria-Hungary did not share the same war
aims and were highly suspicious of each other's peace aims. In the
months after the Austrian Reichsrat had been reconvened (April 1917),
the chasm between the political groupings in Austria began to grow:
while the Viennese government remained adamantly bound to the
German alliance and the rigid dualist structure of the Monarchy, the
Czech and Slovene political leaders were equally obstinate about a
federal restructuring of the empire. From the early summer of 1917, in
the absence of any Habsburg solution apart from the status quo (and, as
we have seen, that in itself was inadequately propagated), a mobilization
of civilians began to materialize in the Czech and southern Slav regions
of the Monarchy, a mobilization which in both cases had an agenda of its
own and one which was increasingly non-Habsburg. In the Czech lands,
what had previously been a small-scale underground agitation run by a
few individuals on instructions from the Czech émigré organization,
began to agitate more openly. In part, popular protest at the deteriorating economic situation – illustrated by mass strikes in Prague from
April 1917 – put pressure on reluctant Czech politicians; in part, radical
Czech leaders began to tap this unrest and lead it in a political direction,
most notably with their Epiphany Declaration (January 1918) demanding Czechoslovak unity and independence, which was soon taken
up at a local level.[28]

Meanwhile, in the south, the Slovene political and clerical elite
initiated an even more vociferous and coordinated 'declaration movement' on behalf of southern Slav unity. By 1918, stimulated by war-
weariness and the food crisis, it was spreading through all sections of
society and all Yugoslav regions of the Monarchy.[29] The 'Austrian'
authorities had neither the military forces nor the legal powers to act
against movements which were increasingly moving into a radical anti-
Habsburg camp. By the summer of 1918 it was still possible to find mass
Christian rallies in Vienna on behalf of the Habsburgs, while in the
Austrian and Hungarian parliaments the prime ministers still spoke out
in praise of the royal couple: Sándor Wekerle, for example, urged all
'well-meaning circles' to work to calm public disquiet at malicious
rumours about the dynasty.[30] But at the same time – July 1918 – the

authorities were fast losing control of regions distant from the capitals: according to official reports, in northern Hungary the Slovak intelligentsia was 'completely poisoned with treasonable ideas'; in Galicia the Polish elite were working openly towards an independent Polish state, the judiciary and clergy of Kraków, for example, being 'wholly indifferent' to the Monarchy; while in the south, the pulpits of southern Styria and Carniola were entirely devoted to 'anti-state propaganda' and the Slovene leaders no longer bothered to mention the Habsburgs at their rallies to proclaim southern Slav unity.[31]

Much of this 'secondary mobilization' had been in its infancy in September 1917 when Conrad made his report on desertions. In the next twelve months it became a widespread phenomenon, but it assumed a different character in each region. Among the Poles of Galicia and the Slovaks of Hungary the nationalist agenda remained primarily in the hands of an educated elite, while among the Slovenes, Czechs and Magyars a nationalist and socio-economic programme was becoming fused together and accepted by a far broader cross-section of the population. As far as the armed forces were concerned, these developments – the threats from the interior – simply strengthened the trends which Conrad had highlighted in his September report. Moreover, they became even more of a danger to army morale when combined with two factors which Conrad mentioned only briefly: first, the underlying food crisis (always the most basic threat to morale), and second, the beginnings of enemy propaganda, the aim of which was to accelerate the social and national disintegration of the empire and its military machine.

The food crisis, which had its roots in the Entente blockade, deepened substantially as the Monarchy entered its fourth year of hostilities; 1918 notoriously became the year when the army was 'living from hand to mouth' while the authorities frantically improvised with short-term solutions. While the army commanders simply blamed bad organization in the hinterland, the outlook and concerns of many front-line troops can be summed up through the words of one Polish soldier of the 10th Army, writing (in a censored letter) to his mother in Galicia. Complaining that rations now consisted of water and a loaf of bread between four men, he wrote:

I think we will die of hunger before a bullet gets us. The bosses say that we should wait a bit as in a short time we will get the grain for 1918. That means we must fight the Italians as we have taken an oath. And the stupid peasant believes that peace is nearer every day. But it won't come so quickly. The people must make peace themselves; meanwhile, for the peasant in East and West music plays in his stomach and he must fight. Dear mother, I have heard that revolution has broken out in Galicia – is it true?[32] Will the grain be requisitioned? If it's going to be taken away, then hide it, for why should it be taken away if I can't eat it . . . Ah! dear mother, our dog is better fed than I am here. In the cabbage there are worms, and we have to live and fight like this.[33]

Apart from its personal commentary on the food crisis, this letter also illustrates the degree to which revolution and peace on the Russian front in the winter of 1917–18 had stimulated rumours and raised hopes elsewhere. The AOK of course fully appreciated these dangers, having witnessed the Russian army's disintegration which they considered to have been accelerated by the Central Powers' own peace propaganda at the front during 1917. They viewed as very serious the possible impact of Bolshevik propaganda upon their own forces and therefore arranged a carefully planned 'reception' for the thousands of Austro-Hungarian prisoners of war who flooded back into the Monarchy after the Treaty of Brest Litovsk (over 500,000 by June 1918). These 'homecomers' were coldly processed, kept in special camps for inspection under miserable conditions, and even when judged 'reliable' were conceded only a few weeks' leave before having to return to their former units.[34] Not surprisingly, the very nature of this apparatus caused much of their discontent; many in the following months swelled the bands of deserters in the hinterland (the so-called green cadres), while those who returned to their units fomented unrest and were, on the whole, responsible for the six major rebellions which took place in the interior in May 1918.[35]

From the spring of 1918, this Bolshevik propaganda from the East was complemented by an increasingly sophisticated propaganda campaign from the Italians, aiming to accelerate nationalist agitation in the Monarchy.[36] If Conrad had noted the first signs of this in his September report, it was nevertheless particularly after the shock of Caporetto that the Italian military were persuaded to use the new 'propaganda weapon', all the more so as they were now responding to a propaganda campaign which Austria-Hungary herself had launched against them that autumn. This 'propaganda duel' on the Italian front was to be the most carefully planned and sophisticated campaign of its kind during the First World War. On the Entente side, it is important to note that it was an operation largely run by the Italians; but they were also stimulated (and the Austrians were thoroughly alarmed) when in February 1918 Great Britain created – again chiefly in response to the Central Powers' use of propaganda in 1917 – a 'Department of Propaganda in Enemy Countries' nominally under the newspaper tycoon, Lord Northcliffe. In the Habsburg empire, the sheer reputation of Northcliffe and his department always vastly outweighed its actual dangers: for although in 1918 the real brains of the organization – Henry Wickham Steed – could successfully influence British policy against the Monarchy, the more poisonous source of propaganda against the Austro-Hungarian army was always in Italian hands.

It was in response to these new threats, within and outside the Monarchy, that the AOK in the spring of 1918 tried to tighten the controls on army morale and discipline. At first it meant extra checks on desertion and sudden inspections of all soldiers' belongings in the war zone.[37] Yet the authorities realized that these defensive measures were not sufficient; as Stöger-Steiner, the Minister of War, noted in a letter sent to all military commands, the Russian army had disintegrated because in late 1917 its 'educational organs' had been insufficiently equipped to withstand revolutionary propaganda. In other words, sharp vigilance and discipline had to be accompanied by well-organized 'patriotic instruction'.[38] Until 1918, it was chiefly the military pastorate in the Austro-Hungarian army who had undertaken the latter task, and at first the AOK simply envisaged an intensification of such work with a suitable officer, who through informal conversations would enquire into a man's background and private life 'in order to gain insight into the psyche, mentality and level of intelligence of his subordinates, to encourage the man's trust in the officer [and at the same time] discover the destructive elements, socialists, anti-militarists, etc., among his subordinates and paralyse their damaging influence upon the other men'.[39] The soldiers would be reminded of their military oath, and taught about the true causes of the war (of how Italy had stabbed Austria-Hungary in the back) and the successes of the Central Powers and their determination to continue fighting until an honourable peace had been concluded.[40] As support for this 'instruction' the AOK ordered the War Press Office (*Kriegspressequartier*) to produce a weekly journal with articles on topical subjects. The first editions appeared on 7 March and a very limited number were dispatched to the Italian front to be presented to troops as a 'privately published' newspaper.[41] In fact from the start there were problems, since only German (*Heimat*) and Hungarian (*Uzenet*) editions were issued; a Czech version when produced was simply a translation of *Heimat*, and specialized Slovene and Croat editions never appeared due to the lack of trained personnel and typesetters. It was a major irony that in a multi-national empire the authorities could not produce a multi-national literature. But it was also the case that to do so, and to appeal realistically to individual national sentiments among the armed forces, could now have the effect of undermining the very patriotic outlook which the AOK wished to instil.

Patriotic instruction as a whole, however, was going to be on a grander scale, for on 14 March Arz proceeded to announce the creation of a special organization to control education in the armed forces. It is unclear how far he moved in this direction because of the example of Germany, where patriotic instruction had already begun in the early summer of 1917; certainly, the AOK was also affected by repeated petitions from commanders at the front and, perhaps even more, by the example of the Italian enemy who seemed to be managing such instruction to good effect among their own troops in the wake of Caporetto. Arz's own declared reasons for the new organization were threefold, reflecting the AOK's prioritization of tangible dangers. First, it would combat those elements, buoyed by war-weariness, which were threatening Austria-Hungary politically and socially from within; second, it would counter Bolshevism, the threat from the East; third, it would fight 'enemy propaganda' since 'Northcliffe's appointment . . . shows most clearly what hopes our enemy sets on its publicity work'.[42] The head of the new organization was to be the invalided Oberstleutnant Egon Freiherr von Waldstätten (brother of the deputy Chief of Staff). A week later he announced that the first task of what became known as the Feindespropaganda-Abwehrstelle (FAst – Enemy Propaganda Defence Agency) would be to organize teacher-training courses in Vienna for specially appointed officers who would then act as FA instructors amongst military units in the field or hinterland.[43] Thus eventually an FA network would evolve throughout the Monarchy with the purpose of protecting the army from subversive influences and instilling into them *Staatsgedanken*, or ideas of state loyalty, as a counter to the nationalist ideas propagated by 'the enemy'.

By the end of April more flesh had been put on to the FA bones. On 26 April all army commands were issued with guidelines on 'patriotic instruction and defence against enemy propaganda'. These specified that the FAst in Vienna would be the coordinating centre, producing propaganda material and training education officers; in turn, each army command should appoint an 'education chief' (*Unterrichtsreferent*) and each division an education officer, so that a hierarchical network would be created. The FA education, to be conducted with the active support of all officers, was to lay particular emphasis upon the viability of the Austro-Hungarian state; the soldiers were to be reminded of the 'freedom and equality' of all citizens of the empire and of the advantages of living in a large state ruled by the Habsburg dynasty.[44] Moreover, in accordance with a decision reached at the inaugural FA meeting, all 'political themes' were to be excluded from the education. Arz's view, that 'only love for the dynasty and mutual respect for all nationalities of both states' need be achieved, was adhered to by the new organization despite the clear difficulties of avoiding any politicized discussion, and despite the fact that by trying to avoid 'political themes' the FAst was

ignoring from the start the widespread evidence of domestic disintegration – a topic which enemy propaganda was quite prepared to discuss
and exploit. Not surprisingly, some of the FA lecturers in Vienna (and
later in Budapest for *Honvéd* units) were to find it very difficult to deal
with the issues of Italian or Romanian irredentism without also touching
on the Monarchy's nationality problems.[45] The FA filled this serious
omission with guidelines which simply encouraged the soldiers' sense of
duty, discipline and order – that desertion was a disgrace with serious
consequences, that indiscipline and laziness had produced the great
defeats of the Russian and Italian armies in 1917, and that Austria-
Hungary should not be allowed to fall into chaos like Russia. It had to be
shown that it was a duty but also worthwhile to hold out for victory,
since the Monarchy was morally superior (Britain was the real originator
of the war, Italy was the traitor) and could look forward with confidence
to a favourable outcome of the conflict before the United States affected
the balance of forces.[46]

By the time of Austria-Hungary's ill-fated Piave offensive of June
1918, two FA training courses had been held in Vienna and about 150
Unterrichtsoffiziere (education officers) had passed through them. While
the first course was primarily for officers from the fronts and occupied
territories, 80 per cent of those on the second course stemmed from
units in the hinterland where FA was to be organized in each military
district in the same way as in the war zone. The numerous lectures at
these courses reflected the themes suggested in the AOK guidelines.
Thus, Karl Werkmann, head of the imperial press office, discussed 'the
dynasty and the war' with the purpose, as he assured the FAst, 'of
destroying the rather widely spread belief that members of the imperial
house do not participate in the duties and suffering of this war to the
same degree as other citizens of the Monarchy'.[47] Then there were
lectures on the real nature of the war and the need to stand firm: 'Why
are we fighting?', 'How to personally see it through' (by the Hungarian
Gyula Gömbös, later to be a notorious anti-legitimist and right-radical);
on optimistic plans for the future: 'Industrial and social reconstruction
after the war', 'Care for the war invalids'; and on the nature of enemy
propaganda and how to combat it: 'Italian propaganda', 'The principles
of propaganda at home and abroad', 'Socialism' (by Max Weber), 'How
a newspaper should be produced and read'.[48] Many of these lectures
were eventually issued as brochures for the benefit of FA personnel and
they were regularly supplemented with new themes ranging from 'The
war aims of England' (forty-seven colour slides) to 'The holy egoism of
the Italians', or even 'The significance of fertilizer in modern agriculture'
(twenty-six slides).

It was with these aids at their fingertips that the education officers proceeded to their work in the armed forces (including the navy). For example, in the predominantly Croat 42nd Honvéd Infantry Division on the Italian front, patriotic instruction began on 1 June in the wake of a number of serious officer desertions to the enemy. The divisional *Unterrichtsoffizier*, a former history teacher named Juraj Sušnjak, discussed with his regimental counterparts the propaganda guidelines which, besides the usual themes, included an explanation of Italy's alleged friendliness towards the south Slavs, the nature of Italy's aspirations to Croatian territory and hence the 'reality' behind the claims of Italian propaganda manifestos. According to Sušnjak, both men and officers revealed a keen interest in the new patriotic education; he painted for the FAst a surprisingly rosy picture of his troops on the eve of the Piave offensive – of men eager to fight against their hereditary enemy – and he went on to claim that if the treasonable agitation in the hinterland could be suppressed and the Monarchy's political problems quickly solved, then all harmful influences would indeed be removed from the army.[49]

Despite such wild optimism, the FAst leaders themselves were aware from the start that there were fundamental obstacles to their work. Not only was Waldstätten allotted a very small budget, but there was – as in most military fields by 1918 – a lack of suitable personnel for the FA network; some of those attending the FA courses were too old and many were far too young. It proved impossible to meet the AOK's specification, that 'only men experienced in war, inspired with ideal energy and capable of expressing their views in eloquent language, were suited to instruct and convey really effective propaganda into the ranks'.[50] Similarly, as we have seen, it proved impossible to find enough translators and specialized personnel to produce a multi-lingual FA literature which might match the carefully targeted material distributed by Italian aeroplanes and propaganda patrols. But apart from these technical difficulties, the FAst faced an uphill struggle because of the timing of its inauguration. By early 1918 it was already too late to begin a campaign of patriotic instruction to combat subversive ideas and raise morale. Since the summer of 1917, nationalist mobilization in diverse regions of the interior had been steadily boosted by the food crisis and the rumours of an end to hostilities. By the summer of 1918, the demoralizing influences from inside and outside the Monarchy were even greater. Waldstätten might well warn his FA personnel that hungry troops would be less receptive to Austrian propaganda, but the military could do little to improve the food situation in the war zone.[51] At the same time many commanders repeatedly stressed that patriotic instruction would only achieve good results if it found 'the proper fertile soil in the hinterland': they appealed in vain for effective censorship of the press and a rigid clampdown on nationalist agitation.[52] Yet above all, Austria-Hungary's defeat in the June offensive on the Italian front was a fundamental blow to the FA campaign. Preparations for the attack in May and June had in any case severely hampered the network of patriotic instruction in the Italian theatre. By July, when instruction could be advanced in all units, the educators found themselves faced with pupils who were thoroughly demoralized.

Morale in the Austro-Hungarian army never recovered from the defeat on the river Piave. The troops faced a return to trench warfare with endless disheartening news from the hinterland and worsening material conditions in the war zone. One divisional commander spoke for many when in mid-July he observed 'on all sides, regardless of nationality, rank or intelligence, a mental and physical depression'.[53] During the summer there was an increasing stream of desertions to Italy or, more commonly, into the hinterland. According to a lengthy report of 10 September by the 10th Army commander, Field Marshal Krobatin, there were two basic factors sapping troop morale: first, the effect of the hinterland (war-weariness and nationalist agitation) and, second, the permanent lack of sufficient food and clothing; both of these evils were then stimulated and nurtured by 'enemy propaganda'.[54] The commanders threatened the usual disciplinary measures even though by this time the backlog of judicial cases, sometimes in arrears by seven months, tempered the effect of this threat upon the men. They also tried some new vigilance: for example, in a significant move, the authorities in early September tried to ensure that the war zone cordon surrounding the Tyrol was patrolled only by Germans or Hungarians (as usual an impossible task because of manpower).[55]

Yet despite the evident dangers of army disintegration, it is worth emphasizing that in the summer of 1918 neither physical hardship nor nationalist agitation nor enemy propaganda caused anything more than desertions or low morale at the front. Until late October there appear to have been no significant open revolts there. Instead, it was the rear areas and the hinterland – admittedly the location of most troops – which witnessed the most blatant examples of insubordination, particularly in widespread desertions from trains bound for the front; in one incident in Galicia, 550 soldiers deserted from a train heading towards the south-west theatre. By the end of the war there were said to be a quarter of a million deserters roaming around the interior and sheltered by the local population, but the AOK always lacked the manpower to tackle the problem; it was a rare show of efficiency when in August 240 deserters were rounded up on the Dalmatian island of Korčula.[56] This anarchy simply reinforced the AOK's view that the hinterland was the main source of indiscipline. It also perpetuated the myth, beloved by the military elite and repeated by some historians, that because many troops fought loyally on the Italian front until November 1918, the army as a whole had held together until the bitter end.[57] In fact, the level of desertion in the Habsburg army by the autumn makes such a contention highly questionable. Reports from the Italian front in September give the impression of an army which was disciplined but at the same time depressed. A staff officer who visited the 7th Corps near the coast (Isonzo Army) found the positions weakly manned and the troops themselves weakened by insufficient food and clothing:

I saw young officers with thin shirts which they will have to wear during the winter as they are not entitled to any more uniforms until the spring. I also saw men with totally ripped shirts and even some without shirts! Even the washing of uniforms has to be strictly limited so that their material does not become worn out.[58]

Another staff officer, who inspected the 20th Corps in the mountains (10th Army) in early September, also reported the chronic lack of manpower, the inadequate food in the severe altitude, and the frequent absence of boots or trousers since the 10th Army's uniform supplies for July had not yet arrived. He concluded in typical fashion:

Enthusiasm for the war is completely missing. Most of the men are apathetic, but they will fulfil their duty bravely and unflaggingly, and will according to their commanders hold out for another year or longer if it is demanded. The longing for peace is widespread . . . (Morale is indeed being damaged by material hardships) but especially by conditions in the hinterland. Again and again one hears complaints among the officers or in the ranks about the total disorganization of the hinterland and the inability of the government to remedy the economic and political misery. Efforts of the company commanders to put heart into the ranks by patriotic instruction are unsuccessful largely because of news which they receive from the hinterland or the impressions which they bring back from their time on leave.[59]

The FA campaigners in their final months were of course facing an uphill struggle with their basic arguments. They might indeed challenge the type of slogans propagated by enemy manifestos, and urge their pupils to treat them like newspaper advertisements for 'hair-restorers, breast cream, facial massage or gout ointment' – which appealed only to the 'stupid and credulous'.[60] They might also attack the hypocrisy of the western Allies, claiming, for example, that Great Britain actually strove for world domination since she ruled 80 per cent of the globe, and that she would never apply her slogan of self-determination to India or Ireland. But it was when the *Unterrichtsoffiziere* turned from attacking the enemy to defending the nature of Austria-Hungary that their arguments looked decidedly weak. In contrast to the enemy who were propagating radical nationalism in tune with agitation in the Monarchy, patriotic instruction was only offering a defence of the old system, alleging the advantages of living in a large state and of the 'national and cultural freedoms' which existed there. It not only failed to offer any adequate alternative solution to the south Slav or Polish questions, but it deliberately avoided any discussion of domestic politics. In the same way, the FA personnel could not fight the realities of the food crisis or the increasingly gloomy news from the Balkans and the western front. They might claim that all was not lost, that as in previous years there could be a sudden change of fortune, but such claims were increasingly at variance with reality.[61]

In its final days, the leaders of the FAst hoped that their organization might have a new peacetime role with the army acting as 'the cement of the Monarchy'.[62] In fact by October 1918 the empire did not exist to be welded together: the regional national councils which had been consolidated during the summer moved to seize power and pulled the regions ever further away from dynastic unity. While some belated patriotic instruction had been possible in the body of the armed forces, it was impossible and never attempted in the Monarchy as a whole. This lack of a 'general propaganda mobilization' was always an underlying threat to the FA campaign within the army, and was recognized as such by many on the spot. But by the time that the military elite began seriously to discuss some coordinated 'hinterland propaganda' – in October 1918 – they realized even more its limitations. As the head of the War Press Office observed only a month before the final dissolution:

Priests, teachers, writers and politicians of the different nationalities are all contributing to a situation where the nationalist goals of the native races take precedence over the imperial ideal . . . Considering the degree of disorganization already present, the goal of domestic propaganda can only be to hold the various nationalities together in a looser association. It can certainly not be a goal of domestic propaganda to try to preserve existing conditions, for this would rapidly cause internal antagonism. In order to begin suitable domestic propaganda, a clear political goal must first be established.[63]

It was this clear political goal which had never been satisfactorily propagated within the Monarchy; indeed, it might be argued that consensus over such an objective could never have been achieved even in 1914. As the fronts multiplied and economic strains emerged, increasing numbers of the civilian population had been mobilized but, ultimately, not on behalf of the Habsburg war effort. Instead, it was counter-mobilization with a nationalist, pacifist and social agenda. This could not fail to undermine the armed forces since they were no longer an exclusive dynastic instrument: they were bound to share the tensions and failures associated with Austria-Hungary's inability to manage 'total war'.

IV

The limits and consequences of mobilization

12 Remobilizing for 'total war': France and Britain, 1917–1918

John Horne

When war broke out in 1914, civil liberties were curtailed and the arbitrary powers of the state were dramatically increased in France and Britain, as in other belligerents.[1] The imposition of military discipline on millions of men completed a huge expansion of the state's repressive capability. Yet the legitimacy of both state and nation in the pre-war period had come increasingly to depend on mass participation, however incomplete, and this was especially true of Britain and France as something approaching democracies. Since the war was immediately held to be a matter of survival for each nation and state, mobilizing the energies of society behind it naturally drew on the broader legitimacy of both. It was a process which could not rely on repression, or even on the state, but entailed the 'self-mobilization' of civil society in the form of a host of semi-official and private agencies. Support for the national effort, especially in the liberal democracies, came from persuasion – and self-persuasion – much more than from coercion.

The crisis of home-front morale which afflicted both France and Britain in 1917 challenged this mobilization process. The interminable war of attrition produced currents of war-weariness which labour and pacifist minorities threatened to radicalize. The consensus on continuing the war until outright victory had been achieved could no longer be taken for granted.[2] The issue of how, and on what terms, to end the conflict re-politicized the war effort and shattered the political truce more decisively than any earlier quarrels over the conduct of the war. Confronted with this crisis, the French and British states faced the problem for the remainder of the war of how to restore and maintain support for military victory and of whether to change the balance between coercion and persuasion. This chapter seeks to evaluate the responses of the state in the two cases, and in so doing to suggest some of the strengths and limits of the mobilization process.

Measuring changes in the level of home-front repression in 1917–18 is not easy. Coercion operated at a number of levels, including media censorship, strike bans and the restriction of 'pacifist' criticism of the

195

war. Normal criminal statistics do not cover many of the offences defined under exceptional wartime legislation and a good deal of state coercion was administrative rather than judicial. Conclusions for either France or Britain must, in the current state of knowledge, remain tentative. Nonetheless, the question here is not whether coercion continued – it clearly did – but how important it was to the state in sustaining home morale in the last two years of the war.

One possible response to the major waves of industrial unrest in 1917–18 was to attribute these to pacifist agitators and enemy subversion, a combination ready-made for repression. Despite advocates of such draconian action, however, the government in both countries recognized the legitimacy of working-class economic grievances and adopted frameworks of bargaining and conciliation to settle strikes even where these were illegal under wartime legislation. In particular, the Clemenceau government in 1918, after a disastrous early experiment in repressing a popular rank-and-file movement in the Loire, adopted the relatively conciliatory approach taken by its predecessors in practice – while maintaining a tough stance in public.[3]

Explicitly anti-war sentiments were a more direct menace. Although perceptible since 1915, circumstances made this danger particularly acute in 1917–18. The attack mounted by Clemenceau against the Ribot and Painlevé governments in 1917, and especially against Malvy, the Minister of the Interior, turned on the latter's supposed failure to pursue pacifist agitators who were felt by much of the High Command and by many right-wing politicians to be German agents and responsible for the spring mutinies in the French army. Likewise in Britain, the war cabinet feared that the strikes of May 1917 might favour the rampant growth of pacifism.

In both countries, governments used the existing panoply of coercive action to meet this threat. In particular, pacifist militants and labour activists who sought to give strikes a political, anti-war edge were subject to arrest while pacifist publications were censored. But the protean nature of 'pacifism' – ranging as it did from the advocacy of alternative war aims or a negotiated peace to active resistance against the state – called for a differentiated and circumspect approach to coercion. So, too, did the difficulty of turning the vague accusation of pacifism into a watertight prosecution. Moreover, the continued existence of a public opinion which, though manipulated by the state, was by no means controlled, meant that repression was far from risk-free. Public trials of leading pacifist dissidents in both countries demonstrated the point. In Britain, the ham-fisted prosecution of Bertrand Russell in 1916 for his role in the Union of Democratic Control (UDC) was abandoned after providing him with an unrivalled public platform for his views.[4] In March 1918, the feminist and syndicalist school teacher, Hélène Brion, was tried by court-martial in Paris for defeatism. Again, the trial afforded an ideal opportunity to publicly restate her beliefs. A by no means unsympathetic court gave her a suspended sentence.[5]

Stringent sentences were still imposed by courts for pacifist activity. The Mayoux couple, both pacifist teachers, were sentenced to two years in December 1917 while, E. D. Morel, secretary of the UDC, was condemned to six months' prison in August 1917.[6] Moreover, in France the prosecution of a few highly publicized cases of treason in 1918 created the deliberate impression of a much tougher line overall.[7] But it is by no means clear that the number of prosecutions for 'pacifist' or 'defeatist' activities increased *substantially* in 1917–18 in France. President Poincaré, for one, accused Clemenceau of being no tougher on pacifism than his forerunners. And in the case of Britain, official willingness to prosecute pacifists may have declined rather than increased in 1917–18, as the Lloyd George government accepted an increased level of pacifist agitation.[8]

Political censorship of the press continued in both countries, although initially at least Clemenceau declared that he was prepared to tolerate a wider range of opinion, including sentiments about the war and peace aims.[9] In both countries, articles about peace and industrial unrest were routinely excised or sanitized by the censors and papers were suspended, while in Britain stricter regulations tightened control over the publication of pamphlets in November 1917. But censorship was far from total and protest against coercive measures was vigorous in parliament and elsewhere. The continued appearance of papers such as the *Labour Leader* (Independent Labour Party) or Pierre Brizon's *La Vague*, both maintaining a highly critical stance on the war, suggests that the range of openly expressed 'pacifist' opinion in 1918 remained considerable.[10]

It is therefore arguable that when allowance is made for the increased volume of industrial unrest and pacifist opinion in 1917–18, neither the French nor British states dramatically increased their reliance on coercion or shifted to a policy of mass repression.[11] One explanation might be that the existing, selective use of repression was adequate to the menace, especially in conjunction with intensive wartime surveillance. The latter allowed the authorities to assess the real threat from war lassitude as against militant pacifism or labour radicalism, and thus to particularize rather than generalize repression.

But though part of the answer, this explanation does not account adequately either for the degree of government concern at the threat from 'pacifism' or for the authorities' desire to influence mass opinion.

There are grounds for suggesting that in both France and Britain the government felt on balance that heavy reliance on coercion would undermine its essential democratic legitimacy and thus prove counter-productive. Malvy was acutely aware of this danger and argued down to his fall in August 1917 that a democracy could only successfully prosecute the war with a discipline that was 'freely consented' rather than 'brutally imposed . . . by violence . . . by repression'.[12] Privately, Clemenceau accepted something of the same logic. 'My weak point is the rear', he declared to a confidant in February 1918. 'I, of all people, cannot use troops. If France wants to russianize herself, she will have to do it without me.'[13] Lloyd George put the point slightly differently when he commented in retrospect that 'entire nations are not yet – not even in war – on the parade ground where Ministers can bellow at them orders which must be implicitly and promptly obeyed on peril of the guard room'.[14]

If coercion was restricted (in practice more than in principle), persuasion was not. And the fact in both cases that the more immediate danger seemed to come from war-weariness, from a detachment of sections of the population from the national effort, rather than from politicized opposition to the war, made it more important to change what was largely a state of mind by persuasion rather than by repression. It is the contention of this chapter that the state in both countries met the crisis of civilian morale in 1917 with a major attempt to remobilize opinion behind the war which drew on the underlying legitimizing values of nation and regime. Indeed, the argument might be taken further to suggest that it was only in the last eighteen months of the war that the importance of a *coordinated* propaganda effort for the home front about the meaning and significance of the war was fully understood. Much of the official propaganda on this theme had hitherto been directed at foreign, and especially neutral, opinion.[15] Earlier domestic propaganda on the broad meaning of the war had been widespread but diffuse, and was often the product of the 'self-mobilization' of agencies such as the press or the churches. Where the state had directly organized or backed home-front propaganda it had tended to focus on specific needs, such as voluntary recruitment (in Britain), war loans or industrial mobilization. In 1917–18, by contrast, the state became involved in a broad-fronted campaign to sustain civilian morale for outright military victory, which displayed distinct similarities in the British and French cases.

In both countries, this campaign took the institutional form of an umbrella organization which, though nominally independent, was loosely attached to the state. In the French case, the Union des Grandes

Associations contre la Propagande Ennemie (UGACPE) received its original and most powerful impulse from the Ligue de l'Enseignement, the voluntary body at the heart of the republican establishment which supported the secularized state primary school system. The Ligue had already begun to establish local leagues 'against enemy propaganda' in November 1916. In January 1917 it convened a meeting of teachers' professional bodies and adult education organizations at its national headquarters at which a message from the president of the Chamber of Deputies, Paul Deschanel, called for 'a kind of intellectual mobilization' in order to remind the French population of the causes of the war and the need to fight it to the bitter end.[16]

The resulting UGACPE marked its inception with an act of national rededication to the war, the 'national oath' held in the Sorbonne on 7 March 1917. Under the presidency of Deschanel, this was attended by President Poincaré, Prime Minister Ribot and his government, the leading republican historian, Lavisse (who became the union's other president), and an array of voluntary and patriotic bodies. The latter included the spokesmen for the main religious communities, republican and nationalist organizations (including those bitter antagonists during the Dreyfus affair, the Ligue des Patriotes and the Ligue des Droits de l'Homme), and the principal patriotic women's organizations. The essential purpose of the meeting was to warn against German peace manoeuvres and the siren calls for a negotiated end to the war, and to rally public opinion to the total defeat of Germany with the slogan 'All of France upstanding for the Victory of Justice'.[17] The first regular meeting of the union was held a fortnight later when Lavisse and the secretary of the Ligue de l'Enseignement, Léon Robellin, presented a basic plan of propaganda for the whole country to a large meeting of notables. Both men outlined the 'reasons for holding on', stressing the 'pangermanist' designs for continental domination and the greater strength of the Allies. The meeting concluded with the screening of army films 'representing' French troops defending Verdun 'which enthused the audience'.[18] In the months that followed, a plethora of voluntary and patriotic organizations (some long-standing, others spawned by the war) joined the UGACPE and hundreds of meetings were organized throughout the country to stiffen civilian morale.[19]

In Britain, the war cabinet responded to the May strikes in 1917 with the resolution that 'the time had come to undertake an active campaign to counteract the pacifist movement, which at the present had the field to itself'.[20] The result was the founding of a National War Aims Committee (NWAC) which, like the UGACPE, aimed to 'strengthen national morale and consolidate the national war aims as outlined by the executive government and endorsed by the great majority of the people' and to 'counteract and, if possible, render nugatory the insidious and specious propaganda of pacifist publications'.[21] Also like the UGACPE, the NWAC began its activity with a national rededication to the war effort, marking the third anniversary of the declaration of hostilities. The meeting, held in Queen's Hall on 4 August 1917, was attended by government ministers, the Archbishop of Canterbury, Lord Crewe, chairman of the London County Council, and 'members of Parliament, metropolitan mayors, members of the London County Council, and many women engaged in local work of national service'. Here, too, premature peace was the central issue. Lloyd George, in the principal address, portrayed Germany as driven by the ambition of continental domination. He warned against deceptive German peace hints and called on the nation to be 'patient, strong and above all united' in order to ensure that war was 'eliminated . . . from among the tragedies of human life'.[22] Like its French counterpart, the NWAC immediately sought to translate this message into publications and meetings.

The difference in the framework used in each country for this remobilization of political support for the war is revealing – as is the ambiguity of the connection with the state. In the French case, the Ligue de l'Enseignement remained one of the two pillars of the UGACPE. Its secretary, Léon Robellin, was also secretary of the union and perhaps half the literature disseminated in 1918 was channelled through the educational network. The other pillar of the union consisted of the dozens of affiliated voluntary patriotic organizations, most of which were republican where they had a political orientation, although some came from the pre-war nationalist right. The UGACPE therefore linked the primary school system, that fundamental agent of republican legitimiza-tion, with the leagues and associations which had characterized the development of a more popular politics in France since the 1880s and with the (usually republican) notables who provided their leadership. In this sense it drew on key features of the political culture of the pre-war Third Republic. This emerges particularly clearly in the committees which were formed in a number of the French departments. Typically, the senior educational figure, the Inspector of the Academy (who was also likely to be the president of the local branch of the Ligue de l'Enseignement) grouped the leading local representatives of the state (prefect, treasurer general), the local patriotic and voluntary associa-tions, representatives of business and occasionally the clergy in a local propaganda drive.

The NWAC was also rooted in a distinctive feature of pre-war British politics – though one with no direct French equivalent – the party system. National party leaders (except for Labour) were honorary presidents of the NWAC and prominent members of parliament played an active role.[23] But above all, the constituency organizations of the Conservative and Liberal Parties provided an unrivalled vehicle of political mobilization. Already used in 1914–15 as the basis of the Parliamentary Recruiting Campaign, they now supplied the structure and much of the local expertise for the broader domestic propaganda offensive in England and Wales (Scotland was covered by two committees and Ireland appears to have been excluded from the NWAC's operations).[24] In many respects, the NWAC conducted its local action on the model of a pre-war election or interest group campaign (such as tariff reform), with the local committee disseminating national literature, organizing set-piece meetings and street corner hustings, and even using the women's organizations (the Liberal Women's Federation and the Conservative Primrose League) for house-to-house publicity.[25]

In both cases, the guiding hand of the state was fundamental. Yet, significantly, this could not be advertised without compromising the 'self-mobilization' which both the UGACPE and the NWAC sought to stimulate. Both organizations maintained close contact with the government. In the autumn of 1917, Sir Edward Carson, cabinet minister responsible for propaganda services, sat on the NWAC, and the committee was often requested by government departments for help with specific campaigns (war loans, economies). By October 1917, the NWAC was financially dependent on the Treasury.[26] Yet the national committee frequently warned speakers that their credibility depended on the appearance of autonomy.[27]

Likewise, the UGACPE was linked to government from the start. Louis Steeg, who directed the foreign propaganda service at the government's Maison de la Presse (established in 1916 principally for foreign propaganda), presided over weekly meetings of the union until June 1918.[28] Clemenceau sent delegates to these meetings, who reported directly to him. And in May 1918, at the juncture of a serious wave of strikes and a critical moment in the German spring offensive, Clemenceau undertook a major reorganization of all propaganda services, in large part as a result of pressure from the UGACPE, appointing a Commissaire Général de la Propagande who presided over the UGACPE and took responsibility for its funding.[29] Robellin greeted this development enthusiastically as representing 'front-line unity in the work of patriotic propaganda in the interior'.[30] Like the NWAC, the UGACPE was used throughout its existence for specific government campaigns.[31] Yet the statutes of the union, approved in

June 1918, affirmed the complete autonomy of all the affiliated bodies.[32]

Both the UGACPE and the NWAC saw themselves as rejecting narrow party politics in their bid to rally the nation behind the long war effort. The statutes of the union forbade 'all political or religious discussion' while the NWAC's 'Instructions for speakers' stated that 'the War Aims Committee knows no party and does not support or oppose any party'.[33] The only condition stipulated by both bodies for participation in the campaign to oppose war-weariness and counter pacifism was rejection of a negotiated peace and belief in the Allied capacity to defeat Germany on the battlefield.

In effect, this meant that the principal opponents of the remobilization campaign lay on the political left. This was not just a question of more or less explicitly 'pacifist' bodies, such as the ILP and the UDC in Britain or the minority socialists and syndicalists in France, who could be seen as aiding the enemy. Mainstream labour and socialism in both countries, by December 1917, also supported the idea (without disavowing the military effort) that a negotiated end to the war ought to be explored.[34] The NWAC tried repeatedly but unsuccessfully to win the adherence of the Labour Party and local trades councils. But it succeeded only in gaining the support of individual Labour and trade union leaders (like Will Thorne of the Gasworkers' and General Workers' Union, and the principal remaining Labour minister, G. N. Barnes) and of nationalist labour bodies.[35] Likewise in France, the socialist and syndicalist majorities organized their own Republican Coalition in 1918 which combined national defence, the exploration of a negotiated peace and a critical stance towards the Clemenceau government.[36] But the UGACPE and the NWAC were both keen to make it clear that socialists and socialism as such were not excluded from the campaign.[37]

This attitude had a determining influence on the nature of the anti-pacifist campaigns. A comparison of the subjects dealt with by the brochures of the two organizations (370 for the UGACPE, 70 for the NWAC) broadly indicates the message which each tried to put across. Unsurprisingly, war aims and the meaning of the war constituted the most important issue. Dominant in the British case (56 per cent), it ranked equally with the conduct of the war in the French case (22 per cent) where the Ludendorff offensive of 1918 had renewed concern with German military behaviour (including 'atrocities') and the harshness of the German occupation. But Alsace-Lorraine (19 per cent of the UGACPE's brochures) can reasonably be added to the category of war aims and the meaning of war, raising this theme to over 40 per cent of the French titles.

Above all else, the question of war aims meant rejecting talk of a negotiated, compromise peace. The real aims of Germany were held to be those of the pangermanists and the military dictatorship, and it was not difficult to find evidence (including the terms of the Brest–Litovsk treaty) which seemed to prove that some form of continental domination had been Germany's goal since 1914, if not before. More insidious were the rumours of peace feelers by the Central Powers and also the more moderate views on a negotiated peace represented by the July 1917 Reichstag peace resolution. The argument had therefore to be extended to demonstrate that even a compromise peace with the apparently democratic parties in Germany would amount to German dominance. The democratization of Germany was presented as unreliable and the Social Democrats as irremediably subservient to Prussian militarism.[38]

Stating what kind of peace the two campaigns supported was more problematic. In both France and Britain, pacifists and mainstream Labour and socialism argued that outright Allied military victory might easily lead to a punitive and even expansionist peace. At least in France, German occupation of national territory gave a tangible logic to the call for military victory. In Britain, the absence of a direct threat made it that much more difficult to explain what military victory was meant to achieve – a point highlighted by the controversy surrounding Lord Lansdowne's call in November 1917 for a negotiated peace. The NWAC conducted its own press survey on the issue and concluded that:

[The] country is looking for a definition and limitation of our War Aims. It is resolved as ever to achieve victory and to break Prussian militarism, but it does not desire to pass an omnibus resolution which will bind us to fight on until every claim of every ally is satisfied . . . The idea in the mind of the ordinary man appears to be that if we push the policy of liberation too far, we shall confirm the power of Junkerdom by lending colour to the contention that the Central Powers are fighting a war of defence.[39]

In fact, in both cases there was considerable variety in the views on peace presented by the anti-pacifist campaign. Lloyd George's speech in Caxton Hall, Westminster, on 5 January 1918, which was specifically designed to supply the more precise definition of war aims demanded by the NWAC, emphasized the idea of the war to end war ('war is a relic of barbarism') and a 'just and lasting peace'. The literature of the NWAC and the UGACPE was just as likely to stress a Wilsonian vision of the League of Nations as a peace based on territorial security against Germany – though the idea of legitimate reparations was a leitmotiv of the French pamphlets. In the same way that the coalition of groups behind the UGACPE and the breadth of party support for the NWAC rebut any idea that these were simply organizations of the political right, so the sense of what peace would mean was diverse. The binding thread was unanimity that only military victory could deliver it.

War aims were inseparable from the wider meaning of the war. The tendency from the outset to see the war in terms of national survival was reinvigorated by the political remobilization of 1917–18. One device used to repudiate a 'German peace' was to imagine the country under German rule (*If the Kaiser ruled Britain,* as one NWAC pamphlet put it). The converse was to evoke the defining characteristics and legitimizing values of nation and regime in order to demonstrate how unthinkable such a fate was. In the French case, this most often took the form of republicanism, interpreted both as the historical foundation of the nation and also the universal democracy which the war was to hasten. Thus, in June 1918, a cluster of 'left republican leagues' within the UGACPE plastered a poster, 'To the People of France' on the walls of Paris and its suburbs which proclaimed civilian solidarity with the soldiers resisting the German offensive in terms of republican values and history. Citing the forebears of 1793 who opposed the 'European coalition which menaced revolutionary France and the future of all democracies', the poster called on 'free and responsible citizens' to proclaim a 'discipline of Public Safety' and to reject any temptation of a peace without victory, which could only prepare 'a defeat without peace, moral degradation . . . economic slavery'. A further 100,000 copies were distributed throughout France by the Ministry of the Interior.[40]

Alsace-Lorraine played a particularly important role in the French case as a source of legitimization for the national effort beyond the immediate goal of its re-annexation. A powerful symbol for the nationalist right, it was simultaneously one of the constituent elements of republican legitimacy through its role in the French Revolution, and thus served to define national integrity across the political spectrum. It also illustrated the pacific credentials of republican France, since the annexation of 1871 had been met with moral resistance not physical violence – most notably by the deputies of Alsace-Lorraine, who made a celebrated protest in the National Assembly at Bordeaux, in March 1871, before assuming their opposition role within the new German Reich. Since the German declaration of war in 1914 nullified the Treaty of Frankfurt, the return of Alsace-Lorraine was seen as the restoration of national territorial integrity. It was beyond negotiation, and the UGACPE sought to popularize this argument at all levels of sophistication (brochures, posters, *images d'Epinal*).[41] Alsace-Lorraine was also the focus of one of the national days of rededication to the war effort organized by the union. On 2 March 1918, the 1871 declaration by the deputies from Alsace-Lorraine was read out in every primary school in the country as well as to a huge gathering in the Sorbonne at which Poincaré, the entire government, and representatives of the two provinces were gathered.[42]

Both the UGACPE and the NWAC devoted a smaller but still significant percentage of their titles to the home effort and also to the Allies. This was partly a celebration of the moral unity of nation and Entente. But there was a practical edge to the two issues, the aim being to demonstrate that if outright military victory was desirable, it was also feasible. Here, the emphasis was on the cumulative industrial build-up and the weight of American intervention, which made victory inevitable. Both campaigns tried to present detailed, persuasive evidence of Allied might and in the French case, at least, there were suggestions that mere platitudes (after the crushed hopes of so many unsuccessful offensives) were no longer enough. The secretary of the main rural propaganda association told the UGACPE that:

The old phrases 'to the bitter end', 'final victory', etc. no longer have any hold on well-informed or distrustful workers and peasants. It would be much better if we could tell them when the Americans will come, how many will come, if we'll have enough to eat next winter . . . in short if we could tell them *truths*.[43]

Overall, the message of both the French and British campaigns was one which assumed a legitimacy for the national and Allied effort beyond the divisions of domestic politics. In this sense it was a reassertion of the *union sacrée*. But it was more than a warmed-up serving of earlier propaganda in that it sought to direct these mobilizing values against the case for a negotiated peace and to persuade wavering or detached opinion that the survival of the nation and its essential values depended on military victory. The means employed were essentially traditional. Both the UGACPE and the NWAC based their campaigns on the kind of material – brochures, tracts, posters, postcards – which formed the conventional medium of pre-war political and commercial communication. But in both cases it was envisaged that public opinion would also be remobilized through meetings. Much turned, therefore, on the model of meeting adopted.

The UGACPE's approach was didactic – whether that of the lecture by a guest speaker in hall or theatre or the humbler *causerie* ('chat') of the village school teachers in the adult education classes which were an essential part of their duties. Thus, in the late spring of 1918, the campaign in the Vendée relied essentially on the local Ligue de l'Enseignement. It included a primary school inspector speaking in Sables d'Olonne on Alsace, in Saint-Gilles on Germany, and in Challans on German *Kultur*. An *institutrice* advised audiences of 'the particular duties of women during the war', and a local *lycée* teacher who was also a decorated war hero addressed a packed theatre in La Roche-sur-Yon. In the Manche, speakers toured all the main towns while the Inspector of the Academy organized little reading groups in most villages every Sunday, maintaining that 'good texts well chosen . . . produce as much or more effect as a lecture painfully learned by heart'. In the Gironde, where the local patriotic associations joined with the Ligue de l'Enseignement in a Comité Girondin de Propagande Nationale, a week of propaganda was mounted early in June on Alsace-Lorraine. Ten meetings were held in Bordeaux attended by 22,000 people, including 1,200 primary school teachers brought in from all over the department. Two exhibitions of propaganda were organized and nearly a million tracts and brochures, 400,000 postcards and 10,000 posters were distributed. In the same month, over 700 people crammed into a cinema in the Landes to be addressed by a professor from the Faculty of Toulouse on 'Total war and moral force' ('everyone, in the rear, at the front, should wage total war').[44]

In all of this, the voices of established authority predominated. The NWAC also organized big meetings and made use of the services of many professional lecturers, but the essential work was done by local party activists and councillors. In keeping with the electoral model adopted by the organization, the emphasis was placed on informal and open-air meetings, often in rivalry with those of the ILP or UDC. Along with main squares, factory gates, and local halls, lunchtime meetings were organized in the works canteens of engineering factories in Coventry while working-class holidaymakers were targeted in resorts like Skegness. Here, the voice of authority was clothed in more popular accents, if possible by speakers 'familiar with Trade Union and Labour matters'.[45]

Yet both the UGACPE and NWAC recognized the potential for constructing new types of mass audience, especially through films, which were frequently used at meetings. The army cinematographic service and commercial distributors lent films to the UGACPE.[46] The NWAC used cinemas as well as film in order to reach random audiences by taking the intermission slot for talks. On 4 August 1918, it arranged for a sealed message from Lloyd George (entitled 'Hold Fast!') to be broken open and read out simultaneously from 5,000 cinemas and music halls around the country, to an estimated audience of two and a half million.[47] The NWAC considered film itself sufficiently important to invest in at least fifteen cinema vans, which toured the country on its behalf. The UGACPE also recognized the potential of cinema vans and by the end of the war a small fleet was in operation.[48] Only the NWAC took the ultimate step of commissioning its own production. Known as 'The National Film', this cost the enormous sum of £23,500, with the script (by a popular novelist, Hall Caine) imagining Britain in the throes of a German invasion. The film was shot on location in Chester, large numbers of whose women citizens resisted brutal hordes of British soldiers dressed in German uniforms who eventually dragged them into lorries ready for mass deportation.[49] Clearly, the cinema offered the potential for reaching beyond the self-selecting audiences of meetings, though it must be remembered that the vast bulk of films seen during the war had nothing to do with the conflict.

There is little doubt that the French and British governments sought to reach and persuade a mass audience in 1917–18. It is also clear that the UGACPE and NWAC operated on a significant scale. In the first year of its existence, the UGACPE distributed five million tracts and two million brochures, postcards and posters, and organized over 3,000 local meetings; and these numbers increased substantially in 1918.[50] Three hundred and sixty propaganda dossiers were circulated every week to prefects, other officials and the secretaries of patriotic associations. In the case of the NWAC, the meetings held during the last ten months of the war, and of which a brief individual report survives, number about 10,000.[51]

Whether the campaigns had the desired effect is another matter. The sceptical pacifist journalist, Michel Corday, commented on the launching of the UGACPE that it 'was a symbol of this war: the privileged classes working up their own enthusiasm for its continuance . . . The *people* of France were the only interests not represented.'[52] The records of the two organizations, together with a longitudinal set of state surveillance reports for each country, allow a tentative assessment of Corday's argument.[53]

Several factors acted against the remobilization campaigns. At one level, popular concern with the question of a negotiated peace was not about real diplomatic possibilities of ending the conflict. Rather it was a coded way of expressing feelings about the war – the horror of combat, the scale of casualties and mass bereavement. There was the danger that the military reality of the war would overshadow the issues for which it was ostensibly being fought, and which had served to articulate the initial mobilization, and 'self-mobilization', behind the national efforts. The British cabinet was informed in May 1917 that:

There is . . . a much more vivid realisation [by industrial workers] of the actual horrors of the war due to the large number of men who have returned home with the experience of it fresh upon them, and of the large number of casualties due to the great number of men now engaged. Further, the essential aims and causes of the war have tended to become obscured and forgotten. Public memory is apt to be short.[54]

This view of the war as a personal and social catastrophe may have been especially prevalent among working-class and peasant women. The French generals noted in November 1917 that 'the women work as hard as ever in the fields; but they do not hide their fatigue or their desire for peace', while the NWAC heard from a pensions inspector (who frequently visited working-class homes) that many women 'regard the war as a gigantic and useless slaughter of men caused by the personal animosities of two or three monarchs. I have heard more than once "I think there's been enough killing. King George ought to go and fight it out with the Kaiser." '[55]

The only serious rejoinder to such arguments by the anti-pacifist campaigns was that of justified sacrifice. One of the affiliates of the UGACPE, the Union of Fathers and Mothers whose Sons have died for the Fatherland, had been founded precisely to articulate 'the voice of the dead' and it reassured Clemenceau of the support of the slaughtered soldiers for outright victory.[56] The same logic is apparent in the report of a mainly female NWAC meeting in Lancashire: 'Although many of these women have made great sacrifice in having their sons and some their husbands away at the front, I find they are very strongly in favour of going on till German militarism is crushed. The watchword of these Lancashire women is "No next time".'[57]

A further problem was that of reaching those who were hostile or indifferent to the campaigns of the UGACPE and NWAC. The question was how to reconnect with the areas of opinion most prone to 'war-weariness' and 'pacifist' contamination when the voluntary circuits of national adhesion had weakened and a sceptical resistance had developed. The problem was compounded by the cultural forms of the anti-pacifist campaigns. In particular, the didacticism of the UGACPE may have excluded in advance many of those whom it was trying to reach. One much-discussed report on rural propaganda depicted the countryside as isolated not from the effects of the war but from any official explanation of it, since newspapers were not bought and soldiers' letters were personal and anecdotal. But urban-style meetings at which a 'clever and competent speaker' addressed an already convinced, elite audience, 'had no chance of succeeding in the country-side'.[58] The same problem faced the school system in working-class districts, with the educational inspectors signalling that 'it is very difficult to reach the workers, and it is always the same people . . . already won over, who form the audience'.[59] Reaching women presented a particular problem, and the NWAC concluded in October 1917 that special meetings were required to reinvolve them in the war effort.[60] In this context, much remains to be discovered about the role of the middle-class women who, individually and in women's organizations, featured in both campaigns.

But it would be unwise to deduce from all this too simplistic a model of state versus society, in which the state sought to remobilize 'from above' a largely refractory or indifferent opinion 'below', albeit one which was insufficiently organized to offer sustained resistance. In the first place, the remobilization of support for the war in 1917–18, even if it was less spontaneously 'self-mobilized' than it was made to appear, involved substantial voluntary participation by notables and dignitaries and by the cadres of the political and administrative systems down to a very local level. The state, in other words, retained the ability to mobilize crucial supporting groups.

Secondly, there is evidence that the campaigns achieved some wider impact. In the British case, in particular, the reports of local meetings in 1918 show working-class audiences ranging typically from a hundred to a thousand supporting government war aims and opposing the calls of rival (usually ILP) meetings for a negotiated peace. NWAC speakers in the textile towns around Rochdale relentlessly argued for Lloyd George's war aims, the rights of small nations and outright victory. They claimed success for reversing ILP influence in the cotton spinners' clubs and for winning the assent of cinema audiences to government war aims.[61] In early 1918, reports on a series of talks in canteens and on the shop floor claimed rapt attention from crowds up to 3,000 strong in Birmingham engineering works.[62] Although partisan, these accounts (and there are thousands more) are corroborated by the more sober assessments of Ministry of Labour intelligence which found in November 1917, for example, that in Yorkshire and the East Midlands 'the efforts of the War Aims Committee have met with uniform success', or that the local War Aims Committee on Clydeside was largely responsible for reducing the influence of the militant Clyde Workers' Committee in early 1918.[63]

In France, there is no comparable record of UGACPE local meetings in industrial areas, and it may be that the state did not have the same success in reactivating working-class support as in Britain. But the union's poster campaign against a negotiated peace in the closing months of the war was sufficiently influential to provoke a bitter reaction by organized labour.[64] And local records show that for all the cultural barriers it encountered in the countryside, the UGACPE was central to the government's partially successful attempt in 1917 and

1918 to turn the annual war savings drive into an 'anti-defeatist' campaign, remobilizing support for the war in the remotest village of every department.[65]

Finally, the circumstances of the war in 1918 rendered the job of persuasion easier. In both cases, state intelligence emphasized the dominant effect on civilian morale of military and diplomatic events and noted that the looming German spring offensive generally raised morale by making the military menace more tangible. In April 1918, the Home Office reported that there had been 'an almost entire cessation of public meetings to advocate immediate peace' and this was corroborated by the Ministry of Labour's view that 'the seriousness of the present position has rallied a large number of men who were previously tending towards pacifism, and bitter hostility to all Government measures'.[66] The reports of the generals commanding the internal regions in the early spring likewise noted the buoyancy of French morale, despite a distinct dip in confidence in April–May, which the UGACPE strove hard to counteract.[67] From mid-summer, morale climbed steadily in both countries with the growing likelihood of outright military victory. Propaganda was not an independent variable which could reverse responses to negative situations and the French and British anti-pacifist campaigns in 1918 had the advantage of working mainly with, rather than against, events.

To return to the observation with which we started: the wartime state in Britain and France was obliged by the kinds of legitimacy which underpinned it to meet the fluctuations of civilian morale in 1917–18 with persuasion rather than generalized coercion. In so doing, campaigns were mounted which sought to reactivate the underlying values of nation and regime in support of specific arguments for 'holding on' until military victory had been achieved. They also made use of more permanent processes of political mobilization and incorporation – state education in France, the party system in Britain – to achieve this end. Success in the terms proposed by the two campaigns – restoration of the national unity of 1914–15 – was illusory. The weight of war-weariness and the clash of opposed moral sensibilities over the war (whether the horrors of the conflict outweighed the disadvantages of a negotiated peace) made this inevitable. So did the impediments to remobilizing the active support of various sectors of the population. By contrast, a range of factors which had nothing to do with the propaganda campaigns (improving military prospects, relative preservation of living standards), operated in the converse sense to underpin French and British civilian morale. Nonetheless, the ability of the state and the social groups on which it drew most closely to *regenerate* a degree of more general commitment to the national cause in late 1917–18 was a significant element in explaining the resilience of French and British support for the war to the end. It stands in sharp contrast to the experience of states, such as Germany and Austria-Hungary, whose popular legitimacy had been irreparably damaged even before the *coup de grâce* of military defeat.

13 Mobilization and demobilization in Germany, 1916–1919

Richard Bessel

Writing shortly after the First World War, in his examination of the economic demobilization in Bavaria, Kurt Königsberger described the German revolution as 'nothing other than the demobilization of the nerves' ('*nichts anderes als die Demobilmachung der Nerven*').[1] While this characterization of the revolutionary upheavals of 1918 and 1919 may have been something of an oversimplification, it has the merit of placing those upheavals into a revealing if often overlooked framework. By relating the revolution to the processes of demobilization in the widest sense, and thus implicitly to the processes of wartime mobilization, it suggests how the events of 1918–19 may have been linked to what had occurred in Germany during the war, and that the revolutionary unrest might be seen as a reaction to wartime political, economic and social mobilization. Viewed from this angle, the German revolution itself might appear a sort of political demobilization, and an expression of the failure of wartime attempts to mobilize the German people.

The aim of this chapter is to discuss the *limits* of wartime mobilization. It proceeds from the suggestion outlined above that one way to understand the 'German revolution' might be to regard it as a political demobilization which followed the extraordinary and ultimately unsuccessful attempts at mobilization of the war years and which paralleled the military, economic and social demobilization at the end of the conflict. Thus the attempts at economic and political mobilization during the second half of the war may be seen to have led directly to the economic and political collapse which followed. The wartime attempts at mobilization aroused expectations which probably never could have been met, even had Germany won the war, and consequently provoked a massive negative reaction when they came to nothing. The mobilization of 1916 and 1917 and the revolution and demobilization of 1918 and 1919 might therefore be seen as a continuum, whereby the latter was a reaction to the former.

The contrasts between the wartime mobilization and the post-war demobilization in Germany are remarkable. Wartime mobilization was an expression of enormous bureaucratic effort and frenetic planning, and ultimately proved a spectacular failure. The hasty post-war demobilization, which caught the planners largely unawares and which was guided by a rough *ad hoc* policy of 'wriggling through', proved a surprising success.[2] Whereas the wartime mobilization failed either to generate solid popular support behind the idea of a 'victorious peace' or to increase weapons and munitions production as had been hoped, the demobilization of Germany after the First World War appeared stunningly successful in the short term. Contrary to many expectations, the soldiers were rapidly brought back to the Reich and were largely integrated into civilian life, and the sudden transition in the economic sphere from the overwhelming concentration on war production was achieved without complete collapse or terribly high unemployment in the immediate aftermath of the war.[3] This juxtaposition of the striking failure of Germany's wartime mobilization with the surprising success of the post-war demobilization presents us with an important question. Was not 'mobilization' in large measure a delusion of Germany's political and military elites who, having lost touch with economic realities and with the population which they allegedly were attempting to mobilize, effectively undermined their own positions? Or, put more generally, is the idea of mobilizing for 'total war' more an expression of the perceptions of political, military and economic elites than a description of what actually happened on the ground?

Of course, observation that the attempt at the extreme mobilization of wartime Germany proved a resounding failure is hardly new. The profoundly disruptive consequences of the political and economic mobilization which took place in Germany during the First World War have been well documented.[4] With the appointment on 28 August 1916 of Paul von Hindenburg as chief of the General Staff and Erich Ludendorff as First Quartermaster-General, the stage was set for an attempt at the 'total mobilization' of the German economy for war. The overwhelming popular support for these appointments by a population which had grown tired of war and hoped for a quick end to privations and sacrifice tended to obscure what had actually happened – that Germany's wartime government had largely abdicated responsibility to radical militarists who were convinced that the way to achieve results was to issue orders.

Under the direction of Hindenburg and Ludendorff, a radical programme was imposed which paid scant attention to the problems faced by a Germany that confronted both a military alliance with superior economic and human resources and military stalemate in the West. Through the Hindenburg Programme, Germany's wartime rulers demanded an enormous increase in weapons and munitions production, and through the Auxiliary Service Law of 5 December 1916 they aimed to compel Germany's civilian population to assist the war effort. Absolute priority was to be given to the needs of the military; huge increases in munitions production were ordered without regard to the consequences or to the lack of the necessary resources – both human and economic – required to bring these increases about. As Gerald Feldman noted more than a quarter of a century ago, the ascendance of Hindenburg and Ludendorff 'represented the triumph, not of imagination, but of fantasy'.[5] German political and economic leaders increasingly took refuge in a fantasy world which allowed them to avoid the narrow constraints within which they had to operate. The flight into fantasy was not limited to the Supreme Army Command but also extended to the boardrooms of industry, where directors could proclaim indignantly (as did a member of the board of the Oberschlesischer Berg- und Hüttenmännischen Verein in June 1917) that they had absolutely nothing to be ashamed of (*'Wir Industrieller haben keinen Fleck auf der Weste'*). Difficulties with and unrest among the labour force allegedly had nothing to do with them but were due instead to the Auxiliary Service Law, 'outside agitators' and pernicious government interference which had led to the payment of higher wages and restrictions on price rises for coal.[6] The more Germany mobilized for 'total war', the more those directing that mobilization became divorced from the economic and political reality around them.

In the event it was not ambitious targets but rather the harsh facts of economic life in wartime Germany – the scarcity of raw materials, the labour shortages, the limits on what could be demanded of employees, and (not least) the greed of German industrialists – which actually determined how many shells rolled off the production lines. In fact, the goals of the Hindenburg Programme had to be brought into line with reality, rather than the other way round. The mobilization of resources envisaged by Germany's military rulers was in large measure an illusion, a paper exercise. As Michael Geyer has observed of the wartime attempts to increase armaments production and mobilize labour resources to their utmost by means of the Hindenburg Programme and the Auxiliary Service Law: 'The War Office administered and organized, but had little influence on what occurred in industry.'[7] However, this does not mean that the attempts at extreme economic mobilization had no effect. If anything, the results were the opposite of those which Germany's wartime rulers had intended. Instead of achieving an effective economic mobilization, the failure of the Hindenburg Programme and the Auxiliary Service Law served to undermine civilian morale further, to provoke growing popular discontent, and to fuel a growing desire for an end to the conflict whether or not Germany might emerge victorious. That is to say, not only were the attempts at economic mobilization largely ineffective in achieving their aim, they also proved profoundly counterproductive.

Similar observations may be made about the attempts at *political* mobilization during the second half of the war. The weakening of morale which resulted from the combination of military stalemate, rising casualties (with no end in sight), worsening living conditions at home, and evidence of obvious mismanagement of the economy by a government attempting to achieve the impossible, provoked renewed concern to bolster patriotic sentiment and popular support for a victorious peace. A victorious peace was to be the means by which to square the circle. Territorial aggrandisement and war booty were to be compensation for the years of privation – the bribe for war enthusiasm and/or grim determination to 'see it through'. Without such a bribe, Germany's rulers were fearful of how the German population would regard the sacrifices they had been called upon to make. As Max Weber observed in the middle of the conflict, Germany's continuation of the war 'essentially was conditioned not by objective political considerations but by the fear of the peace'.[8] The spoils of victory were to compensate for the privations of war – a contract which implicitly underlay the programme of 'patriotic instruction' (*'vaterländischer Unterricht'*) for the troops launched during the second half of 1917, and to which Ludendorff and countless government officials devoted considerable attention. It was a contract which could not be met.

The most resonant expression of 'patriotic' political mobilization in Germany during the second half of the war was the Fatherland Party (Vaterlandspartei), established in August 1917. Formed at the urging of Germany's military leadership and in reaction against the 'Peace Resolution' passed by the Reichstag in July 1917, enjoying official and industry support and with an extreme annexationist programme, the Vaterlandspartei was intended to rally Germans against a compromise peace and political reform. It was, therefore, from the moment of its birth more an expression of the political divisions in Germany than of some unifying 'spirit of 1914' – a point underscored by the contrast between the repressive measures aimed at the Social Democrats and the trade unions on the one hand and the official favour bestowed on the Vaterlandspartei on the other.[9] The new party rapidly attracted an enormous membership – 1.25 million members organized into roughly 2,500 local groups. Impressive though this may have been, however, the most striking characteristic of the support for the Vaterlandspartei, aside from its size, was its ephemeral nature. Mass support for the party evaporated almost as quickly as it had coalesced. Already by the beginning of 1918, well before it had become obvious that Germany was heading for defeat, the party's activities often were successful more in stirring public disquiet than in whipping up support for rabid nationalism. Meetings of the Vaterlandspartei were broken up and many Germans became convinced that it was 'contributing to the prolongation of the war through its demands for a peace from a position of strength (*Machtfrieden*)'.[10] Thus the attempts of the Vaterlandspartei at political mobilization were undermined by the war-weariness which had become widespread among the German population. What remained in the wake of its failure was an unrealistic conviction among many Germans that their country could and should have achieved an annexationist peace, together with a further fragmentation of the political consensus on the meaning and direction of the war.

It was not only the attempts at wartime mobilization by the right which posed political problems and proved counterproductive. On the left, the Social Democrats were weakened and divided by the challenge of the war; the membership of the Social Democratic Party and the Social Democratic trade unions declined steeply as hundreds of thousands of members were called to the colours, and the party split over its attitude to the war.[11] To some degree, the position of the Social Democrats paralleled that of the government, caught between, on the one hand, patriotic sentiment and the desire to 'see it through' and, on the other, growing popular impatience and discontent as a result of the wartime privations and injustices which people had had to suffer. Unlike their political opponents on the right, however, the social democrats could not offer the bribe of annexation to convince a tired and embittered population that the sacrifices had been, and continued to be, worthwhile. Their hope was that the experience of the war, and the loyal contributions of the one-time 'unpatriotic fellows' to the war effort, would lead to a democratization of Germany's authoritarian political system. The prize to which the Social Democratic leadership aspired was full integration into the political system and participation in government – a prize which appeared of questionable value to people suffering extreme privations and whose overriding desire was simply that the war be brought to an end.

One particularly revealing measure of the failure of German political mobilization during the second half of the war was the fate of attempts to sell war loans to the civilian population. Unlike the United Kingdom, Germany did not have access to international (essentially American) capital markets, nor could Germany easily raise more money by direct taxation from a population already suffering severe hardship and serious undernourishment. This left the German government with two main sources of funding for the war effort: printing money and borrowing from the German people through war loans.[12] This, in turn, made the fate of war-loan issues critical. Whereas during the first half of the war the issues of war loans had been oversubscribed, none were fully subscribed during the last two years of the war. Each the last five war-loan issues, from mid-1916 onwards, was undersubscribed to a greater degree than the previous one, and the Eighth and Ninth War Loans (both in 1918) were undersubscribed by 23.9 and 39.0 per cent respectively.[13] It seems clear that 1916 was the turning-point. Not only was the Fifth War Loan, in September 1916, the first to be under-subscribed, but the numbers of Germans who signed up for it (3.8 million) were far below the numbers who had signed up for the Fourth War Loan the previous March (5.2 million).[14] As the Landrat in Rüdesheim noted in November 1917, the poor response to calls to subscribe to war loans demonstrated that 'the patriotic feeling of the ordinary people is declining more and more'. Soldiers urged relatives not to subscribe, and during the final stages of the war, soldiers on leave were warning people at home, 'especially the women', against signing up for the Ninth (and last) War Loan, because the military situation looked so bad.[15] The extreme attempts by the government to mobilize the German population during the last two years of the war were accompanied by declining popular willingness to finance the conflict.

The war-weariness and sullen discontent which spread among the German population during the second half of the war was a world away from the society apparently addressed in official pronouncements. Germany's rulers were trapped by their own propaganda – such as the assertion, contained in the introduction to the German army's guidelines for 'enlightenment and propaganda activity' on the home front in May 1917, that 'the maintenance of a willingness for sacrifice and optimism' [*einer opferfreudigen und zuversichtlichten Stimmung*] among the popula-tion is the first precondition of success'.[16] Of course, such rhetoric was only to be expected. Propaganda is often most effective among its purveyors, and in any event what else were the political and military elites to say? Such exhortations may have had their desired effect during the first two years of the conflict.[17] However, when set against the evidence of public mood in Germany after nearly three years of war, millions of casualties and the severe food shortages during the 'turnip winter' of 1916–17, talk of the 'maintenance of a willingness for sacrifice and optimism among the population' appears to have been the replacement of politics with fantasy.

The attempts at extreme political and economic mobilization in Germany during the second half of the war were carried out against a background first of essentially static and, from the spring of 1917, declining troop levels. Troop levels in the field (the *Feldheer*) had increased fairly steadily from the beginning of the war until the spring of 1916, then rather levelled off until the beginning of 1917, rose again until June of that year (when the *Feldheer* reached its greatest strength), and declined thereafter – and particularly steeply after the failure of the spring offensives of 1918.[18] This was due in part to the high number of casualties, and in part to needs of the wartime economy, as the pressing demand for labour in war industries meant that hundreds of thousands of men declared fit for military service were kept or brought back to work in Germany during the last two years of war.[19] That is to say, the more the German government attempted to mobilize society in the service of the war effort, the less successful it was in putting troops into the field to face the Allies – and this at a time when the Allies were benefiting from increasing numbers of fresh troops arriving every month from the United States. The result was declining morale at home and at the front. Within Germany men who had seen wartime military service, whether on leave or called back to essential war work, often were the most effective agents undermining civilian morale. Within the army, the military mobilization and the failed offensives of the spring of 1918 effectively eroded the German army as a fighting force. Morale plummeted and hundreds of thousands of soldiers avoided duty in what Wilhelm Deist has termed a 'covert military strike'.[20] After the numbers of dead and wounded suddenly increased following a period during which military casualties had been quite low (December 1917–February 1918), Germany's soldiers no longer were quite so willing to be cannon fodder for a lost cause.[21] Once again, wartime mobilization achieved the opposite of its aim. Instead of concentrating Germany's military resources effectively for a knock-out blow, it served essentially to intensify the longing for demobilization – for an end to the conflict and to the sacrifices which mobilization had entailed.

Germany's wartime mobilization was essentially a male affair, in that it was carried out largely by men and reflected their concerns. However, the wartime German society which was to be mobilized was largely female. With between six and seven million men away in uniform during 1917 and the spring of 1918, adult women in Germany far outnumbered adult men.[22] Therefore, while wartime *political* mobilization remained essentially a male concern, since women continued to be denied representation in the political system, wartime economic mobilization during the second half of the war consisted in large measure of the mobilization of women – as workers, as producers of food, as purchasers of war bonds. This effort largely failed, since its aims were at odds with the concerns which dominated the everyday lives of most women (and of most men, for that matter) in wartime Germany. Fairly typical of this was the fate of the campaign, begun in February 1917, to induce women in the cities to take up jobs in agriculture which was desperately short of labour. Despite often desperate food shortages in urban areas, German women ignored War Office appeals stressing the benefits for the nation and for their own health of volunteering to leave their homes for work on farms, and farmers proved unenthusiastic about taking on city women. In November 1917 the campaign was broken off, a complete failure.[23] Far from dutifully following the guidance offered by government bureaucrats, Germany's women turned to the black market and to the theft of food on a massive scale.[24] Among women as well as men exhortations to support the war effort – exhortations which had little connection with the actual, day-to-day concerns of most Germans – increasingly fell on deaf ears, and attempts to mobilize German women ultimately proved no more successful than the attempts to mobilize German men.

Mobilization, whether in the economic or military realm, essentially meant sacrifice. Attempts by the imperial German government to mobilize the population were essentially attempts to promote and channel enthusiasm for further sacrifice – sacrifice which appeared increasingly pointless and indeed counterproductive in that, in the absence of a real prospect of victory, it only served to postpone an end to the conflict. Demobilization, on the other hand, appeared to promise an end to sacrifice. Of course this was an unrealistic estimation of what demobilization actually would entail, by a population which had deluded itself into believing that an end to the war and a successful demobilization somehow could bring about a restoration of the *status quo ante*. However, it highlights the link between failed wartime mobilization and the post-war demobilization, in that the unsuccessful attempts to mobilize the German population behind the war effort fuelled desires for an end to the war and for demobilization. In the popular imagination, the aim of demobilization was to reverse what the government had attempted and failed to impose on German society during the war – sacrifice and state control. Demobilization was to be the end of sacrifice and government controls. The failure of mobilization framed the 'success' of demobilization.

This helps to explain the enormous antipathy to state controls with which Germans emerged from the First World War and the widespread conviction that demobilization was about reducing state interference in social and economic life.[25] Wartime mobilization inevitably had meant the extension of state controls – over the distribution of food and raw materials, over prices. Equally inevitably, the extension of controls guaranteed neither adequate supply of food and raw materials nor stable prices. What it did guarantee, however, was intense anger at state interference in people's everyday lives, and a powerful popular desire that the end of the war and the post-war transition should be accompanied by a jettisoning of the hated controls. Here, too, the wartime mobilization proved counterproductive, in that it undermined the authority of the state and paved the way for revolution and a rapid demobilization.

Alongside sacrifice, the unsuccessful attempts at wartime mobilization had become associated with disorder. War, and wartime mobilization, had been profoundly disruptive of established social and economic relationships, and this gave rise to a widespread desire for the re-establishment of *order*. Although the conviction that it was possible to reconstruct the pre-war social, economic and moral order reflected Germans' misunderstanding of their collective predicament in 1918, this nevertheless framed popular expectations of the post-war demobilization. Wartime attempts to control the economy had given rise to a thriving black market. Wartime attempts to give Germans a common sense of purpose had been overwhelmed by divisive pursuit of selfish interest. Women had been compelled to take on roles conventionally regarded as inappropriate, and youth had been deprived of the 'strong hand of the father' and allegedly were 'running wild'. To many Germans, therefore, an end to the war meant the opportunity to put things right again. Wartime mobilization had signified disruption, and for a lost cause. Post-war demobilization was regarded as the process of putting the pieces of a profoundly disrupted society back together.[26]

The above observations raise the question of the extent to which the 'mobilization' which occurred in Germany during the second half of the war in fact was a mobilization at all. Indeed, in large measure this 'mobilization' consisted of rhetoric aimed at a tired and increasingly alienated and resentful population no longer in a mood to be mobilized to do anything. What actually could a successful 'mobilization' have looked like in 1917–18? Was not the idea that the German people or the German economy could be 'mobilized' further in 1916–18 quite unrealistic – a political statement, and more an exercise in self-delusion than a realistic assessment of what was possible in Germany during the First World War? It is here that one may see the underlying continuity of 1916–19 – in the crumbling and then the complete disintegration of the illusion that either the German people or the German economy *could* be mobilized effectively. The fact was that by the autumn of 1918 the German people, whether at the military front or on the home front, had had enough. By pressing the point, by attempting to mobilize German society without any realistic idea of what this meant or what was possible, Germany's political elites undermined their own position. The attempt to mobilize German society for 'total war' led not to victory but to economic overstretch, military collapse and political revolution. The failed mobilization during the war led to the 'demobilization of the nerves' of 1918–19.

The experience of Germany (and of the other combatants) during and after the First World War illustrates the limits of attempts at wartime mobilization. The sort of mobilization which political and military leaders believed necessary for the successful conduct of the war was probably impossible to achieve. Attempts to achieve it nonetheless either threatened to undermine the existing political order, as in the case of France during 1917, or actually did so as in the case of Russia in 1917 and in Austria and Germany in 1918. Indeed, such mobilization appears to have been essentially counterproductive – more a reflection of official concerns and the preoccupations of government and military planners than of the realities of fighting or living through a war. Consequently it proved a major irritant which served essentially to widen the distance between rulers and ruled and thus to undermine the very war effort which it ostensibly was intended to bolster.

Germany's failure successfully to mobilize society for war suggests that to attempt to mobilize for 'total war' is to chase a dangerous illusion. Notwithstanding the self-serving theorizing of Erich Ludendorff, the real lesson of Germany's experience of the First World War may be that there is no such thing as 'total war' and that mobilizing for such a thing is self-delusion which serves only to deny the fundamental irrationality of conducting industrial war.[27] No wars are 'total wars'; no nation is totally mobilized for war; no people can have its needs totally subordinated to a war effort. Civilian needs and concerns still need to be met. All wartime mobilization is necessarily partial, and the key to waging war successfully involves establishing a sustainable balance between the needs of the military and the needs of society. That is to say, the key is political.

To judge German wartime mobilization as a failure is, of course, easy to do with hindsight. Obviously, the mobilization failed in the sense that Germany lost the war as both the military and the home front cracked. However, given that Germany's rulers *had* embarked on a course which was militarily and politically foolhardy, perhaps the mobilization should not be judged solely by its ultimate failure or success but also by the degree to which it achieved partial goals. Despite the extreme tensions which the First World War created in German society and economy – tensions which ultimately erupted and led to military defeat and destroyed the German empire – Germany did manage to wage war for over four years against a coalition of allies which was superior in both manpower and economic and financial resources. Thus, in a limited sense, the mobilization may indeed have been successful. However, by enabling the German government to prolong a war which they ultimately could not win, that partial success made the inevitable failure that much greater when it arrived.

In an attempt to view the German war economy during the First World War within a comparative perspective, Jay Winter has judged it to have been 'one of the earliest and least successful examples of a "military-industrial complex" in action'. Following Gerald Feldman's devastating examination of the failure of German attempts to organize the wartime economy while meeting the interests of the army, labour and (especially) industry, Winter concludes, correctly, that 'the "corporatist" solution to Germany's economic difficulties was no solution at all. This was because the waging of war – in economic matters as much as in other spheres – is essentially a political matter.'[28] This is the crux of the matter. Germany's attempt to mobilize for and conduct total war – 'to fly in the face of economics', as Avner Offer has put it, and effectively to suspend political considerations in a bid to salvage a hopeless military situation – ended in calamity.[29] Neither economics nor politics ultimately could be suppressed. With the revolution and demobilization, political considerations forced their way back on to centre stage. Successful politics involves recognizing economic and social realities and, on the basis of that recognition, making choices about priorities. This is precisely what German wartime leaders, in their attempts to mobilize the German economy and society especially from 1916 onwards, were unable to do. Their attempt to mobilize for total war was a reflection of a denial of politics, and that proved a recipe for disaster.

14　The Italian experience of 'total' mobilization 1915–1920

Paul Corner and Giovanna Procacci

Introduction

Anyone making even a fairly cursory examination of Italian reactions to the experience of the First World War cannot fail to be struck by the paradoxical nature of certain of the political positions of 1919. It seems strange, at least in terms of the final outcome, that Italy fought a successful war yet emerged psychologically a loser. A further anomaly is that although it was ranged with the victorious Allies whose institutions did not seem threatened by revolution, Italy in the immediate post-war period seemed likely to follow the path of the defeated and succumb to popular revolt. And, in contrast with the joyful reactions of France, Britain and the United States, it is surprising that large parts of the Italian population, civilian and combatant alike, greeted the final victory with repeated denunciations of the war effort and derisive attacks on its consequences, despite enormous sacrifices.

These anomalies are highly indicative of the unique experience of the First World War in Italy. As in the rest of Europe, mobilization produced enormous and radical changes in Italian society – in political and economic structures in particular. But the nature of these changes, and their immediate effects, were largely determined by factors which were peculiar to Italy and which reflected many of the difficulties the country had faced in the decades preceding the conflict.

In fact, the shock of 'total' war exposed many of the weaknesses of the liberal Italian state. In Italy, as in all belligerent countries, mass mobilization and the total commitment to the war effort necessitated a new relationship between state and civil society. This is an aspect of the impact of modern warfare on society which has already received considerable attention. Yet, while all nations involved in the conflict experienced many of the same pressures, not all of them experienced them on the same terms. The specificity of the Italian case is provided by the fact that the national objectives of what was essentially for Italy a war of aggression were imposed on the majority of the population who from the outset had been hostile to Italian participation in the war. This hostility was determined in part by the pacifist tradition of Italian socialism which, unlike the socialism of other countries, did not rally to the flag once war was declared, but continued to argue that workers and peasants had nothing to gain from a war between competing imperialisms. But it came in even greater measure from the persistence of a great divide between the Italian state and the mass of the population – a divide which liberal governments had never managed to overcome.

The extreme diffidence which existed between the majority of the population and government was a reflection of the fact that most Italians had never been in any sense 'integrated' into the new Italian state. Nor had most governments sought to win any popular consensus. There was, as a consequence, a constant, if latent, distrust of the governed for all government. The strong anti-state sentiment in the country – which the liberal-democratic regime of the turn of the century had only managed to allay in part and for short periods – had emerged powerfully again after 1913 when the economic crisis put in question the fragile systems of political and social equilibrium. What can only be termed a sense of national non-identification showed itself in popular risings which openly proclaimed anti-state sentiments – the most significant among many being the insurrections in much of central and northern Italy during the so-called 'Red Week' of June 1914, when in many cases 'independent republics' were declared. In parallel with explicit hostility to the state went a reinforcement of localisms and family loyalties. This was a defensive phenomenon which tended to increase the internal division of a society already geographically, culturally, politically and economically extremely diverse.

The Italian war effort took place against this background of always latent, sometimes open, social conflict and division. The anomalous attitude of many Italians to victory was determined by the manner in which government dealt with the pressures of war in the light of these already existing divisions. This was no easy task, especially for a 'latecomer' to the political and economic scene of Europe, but the behaviour of government during the conflict provoked a popular response which goes a long way towards explaining the dramatic extremism of the social and political struggles of the immediate post-war period.

The position of government. The illusion of the 'short war'

Italy entered the war after almost ten months of neutrality and a wearing and divisive 'interventionist crisis'. The decision to intervene was made without any general agreement being reached among the various groups of the governing elite, as had occurred in the other belligerent countries. It was a decision imposed on the country and on parliament by the executive, which used the public demonstrations organized by small, violent but undisturbed bands of young interventionists to justify its position. While in line with the expansionist hopes of a consistent section of the economic, financial and political worlds, it was a decision made in spite of the hostility of the majority of public opinion – a public opinion formed not only by workers and peasants, but also by a sizeable part of the middle class of employees and professional people.

Limited social and political support for the decision to intervene in the conflict facilitated a military policy of aggressive war and the renewal of a repressive domestic policy, restricting individual and collective liberties. These restrictions had typified the authoritarian governments of the nineteenth century but corresponded nonetheless with the requisites of a modern state capitalism. By 1915, this repressive approach also extended to various mechanisms of intervention in the realm of industrial relations. Many of these were innovative compared with previous practices, but were nonetheless marked by reactionary intentions, as was the case with the imposition of military control over the principal industries and the regulation of labour disputes by arbitration.[1]

These repressive choices – made by a government headed by a representative of the old agrarian right, Salandra, and supported at the Foreign Ministry by another leading political conservative, Sonnino – resembled those made by the Central Powers (to which Italy was linked by the Triple Alliance) much more than those taken by the democracies of the Entente, whose wartime alliance Italy had entered. In political terms, these choices meant the clear supremacy of the executive over the legislative, widespread military influence in civilian affairs, and an accentuated recourse to strong solutions in order to resolve social and political conflicts. It was no accident that all the new mechanisms of regimentation and control which the Italian state introduced during the war were inspired by the model of the continental powers. In particular, Italy seemed very close both to Austria-Hungary in the way she curbed the powers of the legislature and limited civil rights, and to Germany in the level of state intervention in the spheres of industrial production and labour. In other respects Italy resembled another European empire. If one considers the degree of division existing within the political class, the level of opposition to the war among the civilian population and the inadequate preparation for war, the country which seems most similar to Italy is Russia. This explains why the terror of an outcome to the war like that experienced in Russia pervaded the Italian ruling class from

1917 onwards, to a degree unknown in any other allied or enemy country.

Thus, the natural inclination of government, and the knowledge that the war was unpopular in the country, favoured the tendency to prefer repressive forms of social control to those which aimed to win the population over to the cause of the war. This line was followed not only because of the convictions of Salandra and those forces who approved of his project for an authoritarian restoration, but also because of the certainty among the politicians and the military that the war would be extremely short. It was this illusion of a quick victory in 1914–15 that made the lack of an adequate military apparatus seem a secondary consideration, just as the absence of consensus among the population did not appear to be an insuperable barrier. According to interventionist forecasts, the rapid end to the war would permit the country to do without the necessary military and civil preparation, while the glory of the anticipated victory would ensure that the lack of consensus for the war would be transformed into a generalized favourable plebiscite. In this way the defeat of the political opposition could be guaranteed, finally realizing the end of the detested regime of Giolitti and the ruin of the socialists who had achieved some prominence under that regime. Indeed, the list of probable advantages was long. The enforced end to internal conflicts, the revival of the war industries, the reconquest of hegemony on the part of the conservative groups, the isolation of the Giolittian opposition and the marginalization of the socialists, the assumption by Italy of the role of great power – all these considerable prizes, it seemed, could be won simply by fighting a brief offensive against Austria-Hungary (Italy did not declare war on Germany until August 1916). Nevertheless, even a brief war was seen to be likely to pose some social problems, given the general opposition to the conflict. It was the way in which these problems were faced which did so much to accentuate the pre-existent divisions in Italian society.

Government and social control

In the expectation of a short war, the government considered that the best way of dealing with possible social unrest was through special repressive legislation and the delegation of a large number of powers to the military, which implemented its new-found authority in a harsh and rigorous manner. At the front, where General Cadorna dictated behaviour, the first law seems to have been the application without question, and often apparently without reason, of the most savage regulations. Decimation by lot was widely encouraged as a reply to acts of indiscipline; executions by firing squad after summary courts-martial were common. Inside Italy, the extension of military authority was also the main method of restricting and repressing dissent. A large part of the country was removed from the control of the civil authorities – both national and local – and placed firmly under the exclusive jurisdiction of the army. In the so-called 'war zones' – initially only the border areas, but progressively extended to all parts of the country which had seen popular anti-war demonstrations or where the socialist party was strong – civil law was substituted by military regulations dictated by the Supreme Command. In many spheres military courts assumed competence for civil crimes. Besides applying a penal code which was much more rigid than the civil code, these courts were made up of judges subject to the military command structure and therefore easily controlled by their superiors. Military power in the civilian sphere was therefore much greater in Italy than in England or France; nor was it held in check by efficient parliamentary control, given that the operation of parliament in Italy was drastically limited from the outset of the conflict.

Repression by the military authorities appeared in other sectors as well. The Ministry of Arms and Munitions, which included the Mobilitazione Industriale (Industrial Mobilization, the institution which looked after the organization of labour in factories), was entrusted to the military. In the factories, where the workforce was made up of enlisted personnel, military regulations were applied and discipline was imposed by army officers. Strikes or the temporary abandoning of the workplace became the equivalent of desertion, and disobedience to a superior civilian official, such as the head of a workshop, was punished on the basis of the military penal code, and so on. The military authorities also attempted to control public opinion through censorship of all correspondence to and from the front as well as of that coming from areas considered 'at risk' – which meant those in which there were strong socialist and anarchist movements. Those people considered to be 'offending' by their opinions could be deferred to military courts.[2]

Although these measures were justified by the appeal to the necessity of national emergency, the almost obsessive fear of public disorder and disobedience produced a war machine which worked in an irregular and often contradictory manner. Not infrequently the widespread authority of the military hierarchy clashed with political interests, slowing down the realization of objectives. The multiplication of mechanisms of control, the construction of an elephantine military and civil bureaucratic apparatus, the overlapping of inconsistent regulations and offices – all served to produce a dysfunctional structure. Thus, repression often struck in a random and arbitrary way, increasing the popular sense of inefficiency and injustice.

On the whole, the government showed itself relatively unconcerned to discover the real causes of popular discontent. The lack of interest in the mentality of the population – or rather, perhaps, the division which existed between ruling class and country – is demonstrated by the fact that the government only infrequently asked local authorities to hold enquiries into the state of 'public opinion' in the country at large and into the 'morale' of the troops at the front. And on these rare occasions when prefects were asked to report on public opinion, it was generally because the level of protest had increased and the authorities had begun to get worried. The February Revolution in 1917 was of great concern to the Italian authorities, who clearly feared the Russian example in a rapidly worsening military and economic climate. But since repression was always seen to be the answer to protest, understanding the causes of discontent was never considered particularly important.[3]

It was not until after the rout of the Italian armies at Caporetto in October 1917 that the government began to rethink its policies and started to try to meet some of the most obvious problems faced by both army and civilian population. While repression became even harsher and often assumed the characteristics of an out-and-out witch-hunt, greater use was made of the tools of propaganda and assistance in order to achieve some kind of remobilization of energies for the conflict. Until Caporetto, the government had not considered the question of war propaganda to be relevant. From the period of neutrality the propaganda which was put out had been directed towards the bourgeoisie with the intention of repairing the internal division in the ruling class between interventionists and neutralists, as is demonstrated by the emphasis placed on the war as the last war of the Risorgimento, for the liberation of the 'unredeemed lands' from the Austrians – all principles which could only have success with the bourgeoisie. Reflecting this lack of state initiative, all propaganda – such as social assistance – was in effect delegated to private initiatives. As a result, a myriad of patriotic associations sprang up right from the start of the war. Slowly they began to unite, until in 1917 they formed a single organization (the Opere Federate di Assistenza e di Propaganda Nazionale) – a private body, but one headed by a minister, the republican U. Comandini.[4]

It was only from the middle of 1917 that it was considered opportune to recoup the consensus of the peasants (who were the backbone of the army), while the attempt to propagandize the factory workers began only in 1918. The institution of the 'P' Office (P for propaganda) saw civilians (intellectuals and politicians) mobilized together with military personnel (preferably the severely and visibly war-wounded or returned prisoners) to give public lectures on patriotic subjects to the soldiers serving at the front. Thousands of patriotic posters, leaflets and newspapers were printed and distributed throughout Italy. At the same time provisions were made which gave material benefits to soldiers (a free life insurance, the formation of an institute for assistance – the Opera Nazionale Combattenti – to help widows and orphans, the handicapped, the disfigured, etc.) and some improvement was made in food, uniforms and the frequency of leave.

Assistance directed towards the civilian population had also remained largely in the hands of private organizations from the beginning of the war. State assistance for poor families had been limited almost exclusively to an allowance which was much less than that handed out in other countries. Eroded by inflation (which removed about 80 per cent of its value), it was insufficient for survival, particularly if families lived in the towns and none of the women and children had a job. Peasants, on the other hand, lost their right to the allowance if they owned even a handkerchief of land. After February 1918 the actions of private organizations were coordinated by a Commissariat for Civilian Assistance and Propaganda. The work of the committees of assistance was sporadic and often ineffectual, however, and was never really separated from the objective of maintaining social control. Thus, for example, summer schools for children were in fact designed to permit their mothers to work even harder, and teachers had to 'teach everyone the virtues of silence'. Above all, assistance was irregular and unpredictable. As the commission of enquiry on the rout of Caporetto was to say later: 'The work of civil assistance, even though encouraged and subsidized by the state, always remained connected to local and individual initiatives', and it therefore varied from place to place.[5]

The popular response to war

As already made clear, the soldiers who left to fight in May 1915, who were mainly conscripts, had never been especially convinced of the necessity for war. From the beginning it was, for the majority, a war for *signori* ('the gentlemen'). The conscript soldiers, who were mostly peasants, knew and cared little about Italy, and even less about Trento and Trieste. Their experience of the senseless massacres of the trenches, of rigid discipline imposed by incompetent officers, of decimation, of hunger, cold and thirst, only served to confirm them in their beliefs. The Supreme Command – reflecting its reading of morale among the troops

– appears for much of the war to have been motivated principally by the fear that the army would desert *en masse* if given the chance. This, for example, became the more or less official explanation for the disastrous defeat at Caporetto in October 1917. Despite the heavy military censorship noted above and the refusal to give home leave to soldiers (thus impeding contact between soldiers and their families), there is little doubt that the situation at the front became widely known in the country.

The same level of anti-war feeling seems to have been present among many of those left behind to work in the fields and the factories. As the economically and industrially weakest of the powers, it was to be expected that Italy would experience internal problems and that these would be felt by civilian workers and peasants. In this respect it has to be remembered that the war provoked a massive increase in the working class (an increase proportionately greater in Italy, a latecomer to the industrial scene, than in other countries). At the same time it gave women a role in factory production on a scale not experienced before. Workers and peasants were subject to the fierce discipline of the Industrial Mobilization or to the requisitioning of their hard-won produce on the land. Both groups frequently responded by declaring their opposition to the war and to the government, very often suggesting that only a revolution at home could put an end to the slaughter at the front.

The problems created by popular hostility to the conflict, and by the consequences of the conflict for the working population, became obvious in August 1917 with the insurrection in Turin. Riots which began as a protest against food shortages soon escalated to express revolutionary intention. This was the high point of civilian protest during the war, but it was soon reflected on the military scene. It is not surprising that after the rout of Caporetto in 1917 there were many official reports of peasants and workers throughout Italy, and not just in the north, invoking the arrival of the Austrians. A journalist reported that around Milan, 'in many areas they have prepared risotto and got drunk in order to celebrate the arrival of the Austrians in Italy – who have come, according to the peasants, to chop off the heads of the gentlemen who wanted the war, and then to help the poor'.[6] Contacts between retreating soldiers and civilians in this period were likely to be particularly damaging to national morale.

In the last year of the war, the worsening living conditions (with frequent requisitions, absence of basic foodstuffs, price increases and rationing), the obvious injustices in the load imposed by the war both at the front and at home, the disappointment that peace had not followed military defeat, and the general weariness with the war, its sufferings and its losses, all tended to accentuate the alienation of the population from the state. Discontent, although masked by repression, was apparent everywhere. It was registered in the reports on public opinion both at the front and at home, and it was visible in the rare, but still significant, demonstrations of peasants and workers. It was also obvious, in unpunishable form, in the innumerable anonymous letters sent to the government which expressed general insubordination towards the authorities ('the generals', 'the gentlemen', 'those in charge', 'those in parliament'), and which complained of injustice and deceit ('the draft-dodgers', 'the speculators', 'the suppliers', 'the profiteers', etc.).

In broad terms, therefore, the consequences of mass mobilization appear to have been quite the opposite of those envisaged by the authorities. The government had seen war as an opportunity for imposing discipline and reducing internal division. Yet, at both military and civilian levels, popular response was negative and hostile. Instead of a patriotic apotheosis, sufferings and injustices experienced by individuals had accentuated feelings of mistrust in respect of the government, whose incompetence – both at the front and at home – was frequently emphasized. Propaganda was unable to compensate for hardships and sacrifices, and repression of dissent, rather than the creation of consensus, remained the overriding characteristic of government behaviour. For the majority of Italians the war was something to which they submitted. It was a repressive experience and certainly not one which reconciled them with nationalist ambitions or which served to consolidate patriotic sentiment.

Demobilization did nothing to remedy the situation. The process was slow and haphazard. The military authorities had no particular desire to relinquish the power they had wielded during the conflict. Even in peacetime they continued to behave as though their charges were more to be feared and restrained than rewarded. It was at this point that the horrifying treatment accorded to the Italian prisoners of war in Austria and Germany by their own government became known. Out of 600,000 more than 100,000 had died, many as a consequence of the refusal of the Italian authorities to send them food parcels, clothes and medical assistance, as required by the Geneva Convention. This policy sought to discourage front-line soldiers from the temptation to desert. Those who returned were treated little better. They were frequently interned and interrogated on suspicion of desertion, and many were released only at the end of 1920. Their feelings towards the Italian state can easily be imagined.[7]

Anti-state sentiment: accentuation and acceleration

The critical factor in the Italian situation was the failure of mobilization to reinforce national sentiment and to involve the population in the war effort on fundamentally favourable, even if begrudging, terms. Instead the war was experienced in the context of a popular opinion which had for long been characterized by strong anti-state feelings. In this context, mobilization revealed itself something of a boomerang for the authorities. Far from relieving social tensions, the experience of 'total war' – the first really mass, national effort in Italian history – caused an accentuation of previously held popular beliefs in respect of the state. It is to be stressed that this was a fundamentally different attitude from that of British or French soldiers, who, while criticizing the war in a great many ways, did not extend their complaints to the state itself. This did happen in Italy, as it always had done, and in this sense the war represented a continuity in popular reaction to authority rather than rupture. But the magnification of popular hostility to the state was combined with a dawning awareness among soldiers and industrial workers that they had become in some sense indispensable. This made them protagonists rather than onlookers and turned a change of scale into one of quality. For the first time the war brought large groups of the population into open conflict with the state itself. What, before the war, had been agitation, rebelliousness and civil unrest, became in 1919 quite clearly revolutionary in intent. Indeed, the striking feature of the behaviour of the intransigent majority of the Socialist Party in 1919 and 1920 (and their principal error) is the extent to which they assumed that the liberal state was already on its death bed and that the socialist takeover of power was only a matter of time.[8]

It was, of course, precisely from this that the bitterness of the post-war conflict sprang. Fear of popular insurrection became one of the decisive elements of the post-war *biennio rosso*, or two-year period of post-war upheaval and revolutionary threat. Unlike many other countries, mass society in Italy was not created around a common objective which inspired mediation and conciliation between groups but around a divisive and lacerating experience which inspired conflict. The immediate popular perception of the war was not that of the achievement of common objectives (however much criticized or disputed) for the whole community but rather of the opposite – of the achievement of the objectives of one class through the sacrifices of another. The war confirmed long-held opinions of the true nature of the Italian state among much of the population and encouraged a final assault on that state in the name of what was termed the 'inevitable socialist future'.

Right-wing feeling and political polarization

On the right, of course, mobilization had an equally dramatic effect, but in the opposite direction. The war had finally permitted the *petite bourgeoisie* to find the role it had been seeking ever since the frustrating years of Giolitti and *Italietta*, when nationalist sentiment had seemed to be disregarded in favour of more mundane wage negotiations and social legislation. The interventionist crisis of 1914–15, which appeared to give victory to the nationalist minority, encouraged high hopes, but the lack of success of the first years of the war, poor troop morale, and the growing unrest at home, had all served to exacerbate patriotic hysteria, culminating in a witch-hunt for the alleged 'internal enemy'. Caporetto brought calls for the final effort and the supreme sacrifice, effectively collapsing the more moderate positions of the pro-war democratic centre and left into those of the nationalist right. Here 'total' war meant complete polarization, either for or against the supposed national 'values' of the conflict. Those who refused the logic of the right were naturally classified as anti-national and against the Italian state.

The intense political hatreds which developed in the latter phase of the war, when everything (including the Risorgimento itself) seemed at stake, were then transferred to reconstruction in 1919. Here it seemed that anti-state socialism – that socialism which continued to denigrate the war effort – had in the end emerged with the upper hand. When the experience of war was combined with the first experiences of the peace – socialist triumphs in 1919 and what the Italians considered the 'mutilated victory' accorded to them by the Versailles peace treaty – it is unsurprising that many were attracted to a ferociously anti-socialist, anti-liberal and nationalist movement such as fascism. Again there were elements of continuity. Right-wing nationalism had always despised socialism and had always been highly critical of liberal institutions. What was new was the depth of feeling and the disposition to do something about it. D'Annunzio's activities at Fiume, performed in the name of Italy, were deeply subversive of the Italian state and represented a radical challenge from the right. This was the same spirit as that expressed by the first fascists, many of them officers and soldiers who felt betrayed by the apparently impotent and incompetent state they had fought for: 'A revolution at any price, just as long as we don't have to return to the world of Giolitti.'[9] Actions like those of D'Annunzio, just as statements like this last, indicate that both mobilization and demobilization had been realized on terms which the civilian and military authorities had been unable to control.

Whether one chooses to stress breach or continuity in this polarization is in part a question of emphasis. The reactions of both military and civilians to mobilization and the war effort clearly depended on opinions and attitudes which had already largely been formed before the conflict. War accentuated these opinions and, in doing so, gave them a new and much more destabilizing significance. Revolutionary attitudes were not exclusively products of a negative experience of mobilization, therefore, but were built on previous ideas of opposition to liberal Italy, both on the left and the right. The discontinuity was, in a sense, provided by the very intensity of the post-war clash – a new scale of division prompted new responses to what were essentially old problems. Fascism was one of these responses.

Institutional failure and the new role of the state

The depth of division provoked by the conflict had further and unhappy consequences for Italian institutions. If Italy had been no more than a fragile and artificial democracy before the war, many of the pretences of democracy were abandoned during the struggle. Maximum effort required a streamlining of decision-making for which parliament seemed ill-adapted. More important, parliament risked being simply a sounding board for Giolittian and socialist opposition to the war. As a result, parliament was called very rarely and power fell in fragmented and arbitrary fashion into the hands of ministers, generals and industrialists. It would be mistaken to see Italian participation in the war as a defence of her fragile democracy – Salandra's intention was hardly that – but certainly the experience of the conflict weakened the possibilities of democratic restoration after 1918. The irony of the post-war situation was that the first real mass participation in politics was realized at a moment when socialist and Catholic attitudes to parliament were ambiguous and uncertain. Again this was not exclusively a consequence of war; such attitudes had existed before, but the tensions provoked by war had served to give them new substance. As a result, parliament never really managed to regain the central ground in Italian politics and extra-parliamentary solutions to problems became more attractive and more credible.

However, while the war provoked a weakening of democratic institutions, it also saw a widening and strengthening of the role and influence of the state. This was perceived by all groups, although each placed its own significance on the phenomenon. A feature of the last years of the war and the immediate post-war period, in fact, is that all political, social and economic groupings appeared to accept the increased role of the state, but wished the state to act for their benefit rather than for that of others. The interventionist middle classes continued to assume an ambiguous position – one which had always distinguished their campaign. On one hand they supported the state which had decided to fight the war, but on the other hand they disputed its actions, which they thought to be too indulgent towards opposition groups and too little appreciative of their own contribution. They considered themselves penalized by inflation and the downgrading of the professions and asked for recognition which would revalue their social and economic position. And above all they aspired to a different type of representation, no longer mediated through parliamentary institutions (considered incompetent), but based on direct participation in power by the groups which represented the various interests and professions. This desire to engage personally in the running of public affairs and to reduce the place of parliament was to be reflected in the corporatist and syndicalist drive of the 1920s.

For their part, workers, aware of their contribution to production, wanted to be rewarded for their pains and for the humiliations they had experienced in the militarized factories. The peasants, and more generally those who returned from the front, wanted to be repaid for their sufferings and demanded that promises which had been made should be maintained. The big landowners, on the other hand, considered that they had lost ground during the war to policies which favoured the industrial sector, and asked for compensation, while the industrialists, who considered their role to have been fundamental in achieving victory, had no intention of giving up the favours of the state in the economic sphere or the state's powerful intervention on their behalf in disciplining the workforce.

The assumption by the state of a new role during the war coincided, therefore, with a great increase in social fragmentation. As a result, the divisiveness of the war was translated, first implicitly then ever more explicitly, into a struggle for the control of the state. At the same time, the response of government and nationalist middle-class opinion to divisiveness was often made in terms of the repression and coercion which had operated throughout the conflict. The fact was that those features of increased state authority and competence – heavy state intervention in the economy and the organization of labour, the establishment of limits and controls, the centralization of decision-making – which had appeared in Italy during the war (albeit in a haphazard and confused manner) and which many on the right wished to see confirmed in peacetime, had appeared under the sign of repression and coercion and were assumed to work only because of that. Again it seemed that the lessons of war should be remembered.

As a consequence it was businessmen and industrialists who were least ambivalent in their attitude to the state. For them, the war taught lessons which were remembered not only in 1919 and 1920, but throughout the entire fascist experience. Possibly the greatest continuity between the war and the post-war period is provided by this interweaving of state and industry – again something which had been a feature of Italian industrial development, but which had been raised to new levels by the war itself. For, if the Great War taught that the state could be all-embracing and provided the ideology of repression, it also indicated more concrete policies, particularly in the field of labour organization. In the war years, the Industrial Mobilization had shown industrialists the benefits of rigid control of the workforce through the intervention of the state. The harsh conditions enforced in the factories had opened the eyes of employers to the advantages which could accrue from state-backed control of the workforce. The real results were seen in 1925 and 1926 – after the establishment of the regime – when the fascist government decided it was in a position to define its attitude to labour relations. At this point the legislation of the war, which had been abandoned in early 1919, was reviewed and in part exhumed. Strikes became illegal, the disciplinary powers of employers in respect of the workforce were greatly increased (even if the working class was not militarized), and the place of unions was much reduced. Here, very clearly, the experience of the war had been highly instructive. As in the war, workers found themselves virtually defenceless in their struggle with their bosses.

There was, however, an important difference. In a further significant way, the attitude of the industrialists to fascist policy reflected very accurately their experience of the war. While they welcomed state control of the workforce which fascism had, in practice, provided from the outset, they rejected attempts by fascism to influence the internal workings of industry. Just as many industrialists had in fact been keen to see the Industrial Mobilization dismantled in 1919 because they objected to too much state control of production (e.g. arbitration boards, wage indexing, which threatened the free hand of the employer), so after 1925 they were very careful to keep control of essential matters in their own hands and to frustrate the attempts to place fascist representatives on the factory floor. In respect of the workers, fascist authority finished at the factory gates. Clearly, for the industrialists, repressive labour legislation was one thing but political interference with industrial autonomy was another. To put it another way, industrialists welcomed the social aspects of state control of the workforce which they had learned with the war; they were much more wary – precisely because of their experience during the war – of the implications of the extension of state authority to production.

The legacy of failed mobilization

Yet the greatest element of continuity between the war and the post-war period perhaps remains that of ideology – the right-wing nationalist ideology which was forged in the conflict and which permeated Italian life for the following twenty years. Here the response to the failure of national mobilization is very apparent, particularly if the time span is extended beyond 1920. In many ways, in fact, Italian fascism can be viewed as an effort to create, on its own terms of course, the national unity which had been absent during the conflict and which mobilization had been intended to create. The identification of the citizen with the nation, which the war should have brought about, but patently did not, was to be realized by other means. This meant the defeat and elimination of that factor which was thought to have prevented unity and provoked division – socialism. The analogy with Germany is striking. During the 1920s in Germany, right-wing apologists were to explain defeat by pointing to the alleged working-class 'stab in the back' of November 1918. In Italy, in a sense, the 'stab in the back' legend had been developing ever since the beginning of the war, and certainly from 1916, when the spectre of the 'internal enemy' was raised to explain military failure. Moreover the myth was embraced by a new young officer class created by the war; in Italy there was no strong military tradition and no well-established officer caste, as in Germany, to counterbalance the extremism of the younger officers. Despite victory, therefore, the divisions generated by the war were to inflict a permanent scar on Italian society. The ambitions and the resentments which resulted from the conflict were to remain embedded in the fascist consciousness as the fascists attempted to realize what had not been realized in the war and to destroy what had not been destroyed.

For these reasons, fascism became in a way the mirror image of total mobilization in war. In the areas in which it acted with particular vigour, it did so because it was in those areas that wartime mobilization had been seen to fail. Realizing a new and genuine mobilization thus stood at the very centre of fascist aspirations. The 'new fascist man', which fascism intended to create, was someone who, to fascist eyes, would have been the perfect mobilized combatant of the Great War – courageous, obedient, ready for the final sacrifice. He stood in sharp contrast to the defeatist, the deserter, the draft-dodger. In fact, it was the war which really provided the moral imperatives which fascism would later adopt ('believe, obey, fight'). It was for this reason that fascism attempted to maintain that military commitment which had characterized the conduct of the war itself. The fascist action squads organized themselves on military lines from the beginning, thus distinguishing themselves from the paid thugs who had often been used by employers before the war. For many of the early fascists, the systematic violence of *squadrismo* was undoubtedly a means of reliving the camaraderie and the excitement of the trenches – usually on far more favourable terms. After the seizure of power, fascism invented the Milizia Volontaria di Sicurezza Nazionale (the militia) in order to keep the tradition going, and similar paramilitary organizations were soon set up for women and children. Uniforms, salutes, drill, wooden rifles and marches became the order of the day. Through miming war, fascism was attempting to create something that the war itself had not been able to. This was permanent mobilization which had no place for demobilization. It was an absurd parody of conflict born of the frustrations of the conflict itself.

The persistent reference to combat went even further, of course. Whatever fascism set out to achieve was described as a 'battle'. There was the 'battle for wheat' to achieve self-sufficiency in food supplies; there was the 'battle of the lira' to permit the heavy revaluation of the currency in 1927; and there was the demographic battle, which aimed to produce more soldiers for future conflicts. The military metaphor was present throughout and constantly referred to. This was much more than simple rhetoric. Fascism, through its style, its language and its ideology, tried to recreate the psychological tensions of war in time of peace. This was not only because war appeared to provide the correct moral imperatives, which peacetime could not. It was also because constant reference to the war seemed to provide a legitimation of the fascist position. For fascism, the great lesson of the war had been that patriotic and nationalist objectives could provide the ideological justification for repressive social policies and authoritarian government. The 'internal enemy' of the war years had been defeated (or so they liked to think) by tough measures which wartime permitted; in the same way the enemies of fascism would be crushed by the resolute action of a government on a permanent war footing. Thus, the accentuated nationalism, which fascism attempted to emulate from the experience of the war, served to legitimize violence, coercion and repression, just as it had done during the war itself. In addition, in a time of great changes, it helped to reassure the bourgeoisie that the disorder of social conflict and technological change, which had emerged with such rapidity with the war and which seemed to threaten all the old-established values of a stable world, could legitimately be controlled and brought to order. The values apparently destroyed by the war could be saved by resort to the values of the war itself – discipline, hierarchy, male domination, patriotism. Again, the trauma of 'total war' – indeed the failure of 'total war' – dictated the perception of the peace.

Although Italian society was deeply divided even before the war, the kind of reaction which fascism represented is inconceivable without the experience of the war itself. The unsystematic and spasmodic repression of dissent and revolt which had been a feature of Italian politics before the conflict was replaced by systematic and highly organized state repression, reproducing in its methods what had been learned in the war and attempting in its ideology to overcome the divisions and apparent weaknesses of Italian society which had been revealed by the experience of total mobilization. As resistance to fascism waned during the 1920s, it was this second aspect which assumed greater importance. Nationalist and patriotic ideals developed during the war provided the moral basis of fascist domination throughout the *ventennio*. Not only did they suggest the objectives of the regime but they also gave legitimacy to those objectives. Opposition to fascism thus became automatically opposition to the nation and to legitimate national objectives, and thus tantamount to treason. It was this inner logic which fascism created for itself, largely based on the experience of the mobilization of the war, which paved the way for totalitarianism. In some ways, 'total' mobilization for war had been the unsuccessful preview of the new totalitarian concept. What should have happened in time of war was what was now going to happen in time of peace.

Conclusions

It is clear that, in all countries, mass mobilization was likely to be a difficult and unpleasant experience for the population, creating complaints, tensions, resistance and conflict. Those societies which stood up to these pressures did so for four reasons. Firstly, they had long-established institutions which were able to withstand the crisis and reimpose their authority after the end of the war. Secondly, there was some underlying sense of common cause which limited the extent of protest. Thirdly, governmental conduct of the war itself was such that previously existing social tensions were not pushed beyond breaking-point by the conflicts born of the mobilization process. Fourthly, they won the war – and with some tangible benefits.

Italy fulfilled none of these conditions. There were no strong institutions, few ideas of common cause, nor were there palpable benefits of victory. And the conduct of the war was such as to enlarge social and political divisions rather than to bridge them. In a sense, therefore, the story is one of historical continuity rather than rupture. The war confirmed and accentuated the tensions which had developed during the difficult decades following unification and served to magnify many already existing problems. But it was the unprecedented change in scale of these problems, the vastly increased bitterness of the divisions, which constituted the real, uncontrollable, novelty provoked by the war. The accentuation of positions of ideological and class conflict beyond the point at which mediation was possible represented the fundamental difference between the pre-war and post-war eras. In this sense, fascism was neither purely parenthesis nor simple continuity. It was the product of the war, just as the changes wrought by the war were in large measure the reflections of problems which had their origins further back in Italian history.

Notes

1 INTRODUCTION: MOBILIZING FOR 'TOTAL WAR', 1914–1918

1 See J. P. Nettl, *Political Mobilization. A Sociological Analysis of Methods and Concepts* (London: Faber and Faber, 1967), esp. chs. 4 and 5. It should be noted, however, that political mobilization in wartime and even the political uses of military mobilization are not dealt with in any theoretical detail in this work, which remains important by virtue of its conceptualization of political mobilization as a whole. On the more general reluctance of political scientists to tackle war as a category for conceptualization or even as a significant focus of empirical research outside the framework of international relations, see G. J. Kasza, 'War and Comparative Politics', *Comparative Politics*, April 1996, pp. 355–73.

2 E. J. Hobsbawm, 'Mass-Producing Traditions: Europe, 1870–1914', in E. J. Hobsbawm and T. Ranger (eds.), *The Invention of Tradition* (Cambridge: Cambridge University Press, 1983), pp. 263–307; R. Samuel and P. Thompson (eds.), *The Myths We Live By* (London: Routledge, 1990).

3 For a discussion of this process in the German case, see G. Mosse, *The Nationalization of the Masses. Political Symbolism and Mass Movements in Germany from the Napoleonic Wars through the Third Reich* (Ithaca, NY and London: Cornell University Press, 1975).

4 Especially J.-J. Becker, *1914: Comment les français sont entrés dans la guerre* (Paris: Presses de la Fondation Nationale des Sciences Politiques, 1977). See also G. Krumeich, 'L'Entrée en guerre en Allemagne', in J.-J. Becker and S. Audoin-Rouzeau (eds.), *Les Sociétés européennes et la guerre de 1914–1918* (Paris: Centre d'Histoire de la France Contemporaine, Université de Paris X-Nanterre, 1990), pp. 65–74; J. T. Verhey, 'The "Spirit of 1914". The Myth of Enthusiasm and the Rhetoric of Unity in World War I' (Ph.D. thesis, University of California at Berkeley, 1991); W. Kruse, *Krieg und nationale Integration. Eine Neuinterpretation des sozialdemokratischen Burgfriedensschlusses 1914–15* (Essen: Klartext, 1993).

5 L. L. Farrar, *The Short War Illusion. German Policy, Strategy and Domestic Affairs, August–December 1914* (Santa Barbara and London: ABC Clio, 1973); P. Kennedy, *The War Plans of the Great Powers, 1880–1914* (London: Allen and Unwin, 1979); W. J. Mommsen, 'The Topos of Inevitable War in Germany in the Decade before 1914', in V. Berghahn and M. Kitchen

(eds.), *Germany in the Age of Total War* (London: Croom Helm, 1981), pp. 23–45.

6 J. Horne, 'Soldiers, Civilians and the Warfare of Attrition: Representations of Combat in France, 1914–1918', in F. Coetzee and M. Shevin-Coetzee (eds.), *Authority, Identity and the Social History of the Great War* (Providence and Oxford: Berghahn Books, 1995), pp. 223–49.

7 J. Ellis, *The Social History of the Machine Gun* (London: 1976; new edition, Pimlico, 1993), ch. 5; T. Travers, *The Killing Ground. The British Army, the Western Front and the Emergence of Modern Warfare, 1900–1918* (London: Unwin Hyman, 1987).

8 For a survey of the recent literature on the concept of 'total war', see I. F. Beckett, 'Total War', in C. Emsley, A. Marwick and W. Simpson (eds.), *War, Peace and Social Change in Twentieth Century Europe* (Milton Keynes and Philadelphia: Open University Press, 1989), pp. 26–44.

9 E. Jünger, 'Die totale Mobilmachung', translated into French as 'La Mobilisation totale', in L. Murard and P. Zylberman, 'Le soldat du travail. Guerre, fascisme et taylorisme', *Recherches*, 32/33, 1978, pp. 35–53; E. Ludendorff, *My War Memories 1914–1918* (1919; English translation, London: Hutchinson, 1919); E. Ludendorff, *The Nation at War* (1935; English translation, London: Hutchinson, 1936), esp. ch. 1, 'The Nature of Totalitarian Warfare'.

10 Léon Daudet, the Action Française polemicist, published a book towards the end of the war entitled *La Guerre totale* (Paris: Nouvelle Librairie Nationale, 1918), which proposed a kind of right-wing equivalent of the Jacobin terror in pursuit of total unity behind the war effort. The argument was premissed on the perception that 'it is no longer only armies that fight but also traditions, institutions, customs, codes, states of mind and above all the banks' (p. 8). Daudet himself attributed the formulation of the notion to Clemenceau in the crucial senate speech of 22 July 1917 which launched his bid for the premiership. Clemenceau's inaugural speech, which pivoted on the notion of a renewed moral commitment to the war, opened with the term *guerre intégrale*, meaning above all a total identification of the home with the fighting front (G. Clemenceau, *Discours de guerre* (Paris: Plon, 1934), pp. 157–8). This and 'total war' gained wider currency in 1918 (see chapter 12 below).

11 For a comparative view, see R. Stromberg, *Redemption by War. The Intellectuals and 1914* (Lawrence, Kansas: Regents' Press of Kansas, 1982) and C. Prochasson and A. Rasmussen, *Au Nom de la patrie. Les intellectuels et la première guerre mondiale (1910–1919)* (Paris: Editions la Découverte, 1996). On German intellectuals, in addition to the essay by Wolfgang Mommsen below, see F. Ringer, *The Decline of the German Mandarins. The German Academic Community, 1890–1930* (Cambridge, MA: Harvard University Press, 1969). On French intellectuals, see P. Ory and J.-F. Sirinelli, *Les Intellectuels de l'affaire Dreyfus à nos jours* (Paris: Colin, 1986). On British academics and intellectuals, see S. Hynes, *A War Imagined. The First World War and English Culture* (1990; second edition, London: Pimlico, 1992), and S. Wallace, *War and the Image of Germany. British Academics 1914–1918* (Edinburgh: John Donald, 1988).

12 Nettl, *Political Mobilization*, pp. 253–4.

13 In addition to the essay by Stéphane Audoin-Rouzeau below, see S. Trouvé-Finding, 'French State Primary Teachers during the First World War and the 1920s: their Evolving Role in the Third Republic' (Ph.D. thesis, University of Sussex, 1987). On the 'self-mobilization' of secular and religious identities more broadly, see J.-J. Becker, *The Great War and the French People* (1980; English translation, Leamington Spa: Berg, 1985), chs. 5–7.

14 Ministère de l'Intérieur, *Liste des oeuvres de guerre* (Melun: Imprimerie Administrative, 1918).

15 For the labour and socialist movements, see G. Haupt, 'Guerre ou révolution? L'Internationale et l'union sacrée en août 1914', in G. Haupt, *L'Historien et le mouvement social* (Paris: Maspero, 1980), pp. 199–235; M. Van der Linden, 'The National Integration of European Working Classes (1871–1914)', *International Review of Social History*, 33/3, 1988, pp. 285–311; R. Gallisot, 'La Patrie des prolétaires', *Le Mouvement social*, 147, 1989, pp. 11–25; J. Horne, *Labour at War. France and Britain, 1914–1918* (Oxford: Clarendon Press, 1991), chs. 1 and 2. For feminism and gender, see M. R. Higonnet, J. Jenson, S. Michel and M. C. Weitz (eds.), *Behind the Lines. Gender and the Two World Wars* (New Haven and London: Yale University Press, 1987), esp. pt. 3, 'Wartime Politics and the Construction of Gender'; for Germany, R. J. Evans, *The Feminist Movement in Germany 1894–1933* (London: Sage, 1976), ch. 7, and U. Daniel, *The War from Within. German Women in the First World War* (1989; English translation, Oxford: Berg, 1996); for Britain, S. Holton, *Feminism and Democracy. Women's Suffrage and Reform Politics in Britain, 1900–1918* (Cambridge: Cambridge University Press, 1986), and S. Kingsley Kent, 'Love and Death: War and Gender in Britain, 1914–1918', in Coetzee and Shevin-Coetzee (eds.), *Authority, Identity and the Social History of the Great War*, pp. 153–74; and for France, F. Thébaud, *La Femme au temps de la guerre de 14* (Paris: Stock/Laurence Pernoud, 1986).

16 On the reasons for this choice, see the preface.

17 In addition to the essay by Paul Corner and Giovanna Procacci below, see G Procacci, 'A "Latecomer" in War. The Case of Italy', in Coetzee and Shevin-Coetzee (eds.), *Authority, Identity and the Social History of the Great War*, pp. 3–27 (esp. pp. 5–7).

18 M. Isnenghi, *Il Mito della grande guerra* (1970; new edition, Bologna: Il Mulino, 1989), pp. 77–149.

19 M. T. Florinsky, *The End of the Russian Empire* (1931; new edition, New York: Collier-Macmillan, 1961), chs. 3–5; L. H. Siegelbaum, *The Politics of Industrial Mobilisation in Russia, 1914–17. A Study of the War Industries Committees* (London: Macmillan, 1984), pp. 209–12; F. S. Zuckerman, 'The Political Police, War, and Society in Russia, 1914–1917', in Coetzee and Shevin-Coetzee (eds.), *Authority, Identity and the Social History of the Great War*, pp. 29–56.

20 A. Jacobzone, *14–18. En Anjou, loin du front* (Vauchrétien: Editions Ivan Davy, 1988).

21 For a comparative perspective, see N.-J. Chaline (ed.), *Chrétiens dans la*

première guerre mondiale (Paris: Editions du Cerf, 1993); on Britain, see A. Wilkinson, *The Church of England and the First World War* (London: SPCK, 1978); on France, see J. Fontana, *Les Catholiques français pendant la grande guerre* (Paris: Editions du Cerf, 1990).

22 A. Becker, *La Guerre et la foi. De la mort à la mémoire, 1914–1930* (Paris: Armand Colin, 1994).

23 M. Barrès, *Les Diverses Familles spirituelles de la France* (Paris: Emile-Paul, 1917), translated into English as *The Faith of France* (Boston: Houghton Mifflin, 1918).

24 P. Panayi (ed.), *Minorities in Wartime. National and Racial Groupings in Europe, North America and Australia during the Two World Wars* (Oxford: Berg, 1993); J. Horne, 'L'Etranger, la guerre et l'image de "l'autre", 1914–1918', in *L'Image de l'autre dans l'Europe du Nord-Ouest à travers l'histoire* (Université Charles de Gaulle-Lille III, 1996), pp. 133–44.

25 P. Landau, 'Les Juifs de France et la grande guerre, 1914–1941' (doctoral thesis, University of Paris 7, 1992).

26 M. Levene, 'Frontiers of Genocide: Jews in the Eastern War Zones, 1914–1920 and 1941', in Panayi, *Minorities in Wartime*, pp. 83–117; J.-M. Carzou, *Arménie 1915. Un génocide exemplaire* (Paris: Flammarion, 1975); J. Winter, 'Le Massacre des Arméniens', in Becker *et al.*, *14–18. La très grande guerre* (Paris: Le Monde, 1994), ch. 14.

27 L. Smith, *Between Mutiny and Obedience. The Case of the Fifth French Infantry Division during World War I* (Princeton: Princeton University Press, 1994).

28 D. Stevenson, *The First World War and International Politics* (Oxford: Oxford University Press, 1988).

29 J. Horne, 'Social Identity in War: France, 1914–1918', in T. G. Fraser and K. Jeffery (eds.), *Men, Women and War. Historical Studies XVIII* (Dublin: Lilliput, 1993), pp. 119–35.

30 See S. Audoin-Rouzeau, *Men at War 1914–1918. National Sentiment and Trench Journalism in France during the First World War* (1986; English translation, Oxford: Berg, 1993), ch. 4; J. G. Fuller, *Troop Morale and Popular Culture in the British and Dominion Armies 1914–1918* (Oxford: Clarendon Press, 1990).

31 J. Horne, '"L'Impôt du sang": Republican Rhetoric and Industrial Warfare in France, 1914–18', *Social History*, 14/2, 1989, pp. 201–23. For a study of these issues in the British context, see B. Waites, *A Class Society at War. England 1914–18* (Leamington Spa: Berg, 1987), esp. ch. 1; and for Germany, J. Kocka, *Facing Total War. German Society 1914–1918* (1973; English translation, Leamington Spa: Berg, 1984).

32 Guy Pedroncini demonstrated this in his seminal work, *Les Mutineries de 1917* (Paris: Presses Universitaires de France, 1967), the first on the subject to be based on military archives.

33 In addition to David Englander's essay below, see D. Gill and G. Dallas, *The Unknown Army* (London: Verso, 1985).

34 A. Babington, *For the Sake of Example. Capital Courts Martial 1914–1920* (London: Secker and Warburg, 1983), pp. 228–31.

35 Documentation exists in the Service Historique de l'Armée de Terre, Vincennes (Paris), 5N 363 (the information section at General Head-

quarters) but has not, as far as the author is aware, formed the subject of a study.
36 The crucial study remains G. Feldman, *Army, Industry and Labor in Germany 1914–1918* (1966; new edition, Providence and Oxford: Berg, 1992).
37 See the special dossier on 'Nouvelles pistes de l'histoire urbaine 1914-1918', in *Guerres mondiales et conflits contemporains*, 183, 1996, with essays by Thierry Bonzon on 'La Société, l'état et le pouvoir local: l'approvisionnement à Paris, 1914–18'; by Belinda Davis on 'L'Etat contre la société: nourrir Berlin, 1914–18'; by Jonathan Manning on 'La Guerre et la consommation civile à Londres, 1914–18'; and by L. Tomassini, 'Approvisionnement, protestations et propagande en Italie pendant la première guerre mondiale'. See also J. M. Winter and J.-L. Robert (eds.), *Capital Cities at War: Paris, London and Berlin 1914–1919* (Cambridge: Cambridge University Press, 1996), for the results of a collective project in which the first three of the above-mentioned articles had their origin.
38 J. Winter, 'Some Paradoxes of the First World War', in R. Wall and J. Winter (eds.), *The Upheaval of War. Family, Work and Welfare in Europe, 1914–1918* (Cambridge: Cambridge University Press, 1988), pp. 9–42.
39 On the importance of the former, see A. Offer, *The First World War: An Agrarian Interpretation* (Oxford: Oxford University Press, 1989).
40 R. Aron, *War and Industrial Society* (Oxford: Oxford University Press, 1958).
41 These connections, though often alluded to, seem not to have been the subject of systematic comparative exploration. For some important hints, see M. Howard, 'Total War in the Twentieth Century: Participation and Consensus in the Second World War', in B. Bond and I. Roy (eds.), *War and Society. A Yearbook of Military History* (London: Croom Helm, 1975), pp. 216–26, on the British case; E. Ziemke, 'Strategy for Class War: the Soviet Union, 1917–1941', in W. Murray, M. Knox and A. Bernstein (eds.), *The Making of Strategy. Rulers, States and War* (Cambridge: Cambridge University Press, 1994), pp. 498–533, on the Soviet case; T. Mason, *Social Policy in the Third Reich. The Working Class and the 'National Community'* (Providence and Oxford: Berg Books, 1993), pp. 19–40, and W. Deist, 'The Road to Ideological War: Germany, 1918–1945', in Murray, Knox and Bernstein (eds.), *The Making of Strategy*, pp. 352–92, on Germany.

2 GERMAN ARTISTS, WRITERS AND INTELLECTUALS AND THE MEANING OF WAR, 1914–1918

1 J. Joll, *The Origins of the First World War* (London: Macmillan, 1984); W. J. Mommsen, 'The Topos of Inevitable War in Germany in the Decade before 1914', in V. R. Berghahn and M. Kitchen (eds.), *Germany in the Age of Total War* (London: Croom Helm, 1981), pp. 23–45.
2 G. Mosse, *Fallen Soldiers. Reshaping the Memory of the World Wars* (New York: Oxford University Press, 1990), p. 56.
3 S. George, *Der Dichter und sein Kreis*, p. 262, quoted by R. Stromberg, *Redemption by War. The Intellectuals and 1914* (Lawrence, Kansas: The Regents' Press, 1982), p. 51.

4 *Jahrbuch für die geistige Bewegung*, 2, 1911, p. 25.
5 J. Eltz, *Der italienische Futurismus in Deutschland 1912–1922. Ein Beitrag zur Analyse seiner Rezeptionsgeschichte* (Bamberg: Lehrstuhl für Kunstgeschichte u. Aufbaustudium Denkmalpflege a.d. Universität Bamberg, 1986), pp. 64 ff.
6 S. Holsten, *Allegorische Darstellungen des Krieges 1870–1918* (Munich: Prestel, 1976), pp. 109 ff.
7 See J. T. Verhey, 'The "Spirit of 1914". The Myth of Enthusiasm and the Rhetoric of Unity in World War I Germany' (Ph.D. thesis, Berkeley: University of California at Berkeley, 1991); W. Kruse, *Krieg und nationale Integration* (Essen: Klartext Verlag, 1993).
8 T. Grochowiak, *Ludwig Meidner* (Recklinghausen: Bongers, 1966), p. 99.
9 Stromberg, *Redemption by War*, p. 46.
10 T. Mann, 'Gedanken im Kriege', in *Gesammelte Werke*, 13 vols. (Frankfurt-am-Main: S. Fischer, 1974), vol. XIII, p. 533.
11 Franz Marc, quoted in W. J. Mommsen, *Bürgerliche Kultur und künstlerische Avantgarde 1870–1918* (Berlin: Ullstein, 1994), p. 143.
12 'Arsenal für eine Schöpfung'. See R. Cork, *A Bitter Truth. Avant-Garde Art and the Great War* (New Haven: Yale University Press, 1994), p. 110.
13 E. Barlach, *The Avenging Angel*, in the Hirschborn Museum, Washington, DC.
14 G. Simmel, *Der Krieg und die geistigen Entscheidungen* (Munich: Duncker und Humblot, 1917), pp. 60–2.
15 A. Möser, 'Der Krieg als "Wohltat". Kunstkritik im 1. Weltkrieg am Beispiel der Zeitschrift "Kunst und Künstler" ', *Jahrbuch der Hamburger Kunstsammlungen*, 24, 1979, p. 165.
16 *Ibid.*
17 *Ibid.*, p. 164.
18 P. Paret, ' "The Enemy within"– Max Liebermann as President of the Prussian Academy of Arts' (New York: Leo Baeck Institute, 1984), pp. 7 ff.
19 V. H. Miesel, 'Paul Cassirer's *Kriegszeit* and *Bildermann* and some German Reactions to World War I', in *Michigan Germanic Studies*, 2, 1976, pp. 148 ff; also M. F. Deshmukh, 'German Impressionist Painters and World War I', *Art History*, 4, 1981, pp. 66 ff.
20 L. Corinth, *Selbstbiographie* (Leipzig: Hirzel, 1926), p. 129.
21 M. Beckmann, *Briefe* (Munich: Piper, 1993), vol. I, *1899–1925*, p. 18 (24 May 1915).
22 O. Conzelmann, *Der andere Dix – sein Bild vom Menschen und vom Krieg* (Stuttgart: Klett-Cotta, 1983), p. 133; F. Löffler, *Otto Dix und der Krieg* (Leipzig: Reclam, 1986), p. 12.
23 *Ibid.*
24 M. Eberle, *Der Weltkrieg und die Künstler der Weimarer Republik* (Stuttgart: Belser, 1989), p. 31.
25 S. George, *Gesamtausgabe*, 18 vols. (Berlin: Bondi, 1927–34), vol. IX, pp. 28 ff. See also Stromberg, *Redemption by War*, p. 151.
26 F. Meinecke, *Die deutsche Erhebung von 1914. Aufsätze und Vorträge* (Berlin and Stuttgart: Cotta'sche Buchhandlung, 1914), pp. 29 ff.
27 See B. vom Brocke, 'Wissenschaft und Militarismus. Der Aufruf der 93 "An die Kulturwelt" und der Zusammenbruch der internationalen Gelehrten-

republik im Ersten Weltkrieg', in W. M. Calder III (ed.), *Wilamowitz nach 50 Jahren* (Darmstadt: Wiss. Buchgesellschaft, 1985), pp. 649 ff.

28 K. Böhme (ed.), *Aufrufe und Reden deutscher Professoren im Ersten Weltkrieg* (Stuttgart: Reclam, 1975), pp. 49 ff.

29 R. Borchardt, *Der Krieg und die deutsche Selbsteinkehr* (Heidelberg: R. Weissbach, 1915), pp. 10 ff.

30 W. Sombart, *Händler und Helden. Patriotische Besinnungen* (Leipzig and Munich: Duncker und Humblot, 1915), p. 92.

31 'das erste revolutionslose Großvolk des organisierten Lebensspielraums' (T. Schieder (ed.), *Friedrich Naumann, Werke. Politische Schriften*, vol. II, *Schriften zur Verfassungspolitik* (Opladen: Westdeutscher Verlag, 1964), p. 460).

32 M. Scheler, *Der Genius des Krieges und der Deutsche Krieg* (Leipzig: Verlag der Weissen Bücher, 1915), p. 65.

33 *Ibid.*, p. 353.

34 W. Goetz, *Deutschlands geistiges Leben im Weltkrieg* (Gotha: J. Perthes, 1916), p. 44.

35 See G. Hübinger, 'Eugen Diederichs' Bemühungen um die Grundlegung einer neuen Geisteskultur', in W. J. Mommsen (ed.), *Kultur und Krieg. Schriften des Historischen Kollegs: Kolloquien, 34* (Munich: Oldenburg, 1995), pp. 259 ff.

36 D. Schmidt, '"Bitte mit dem Weltkrieg aufzuhören, ich möchte arbeiten!". Oskar Kokoschka in Dresden 1916 bis 1923', *Pantheon*, 44, 1986, p. 125.

37 H. Richter, *Dada – Kunst und Antikunst* (Cologne: Dumont Schauberg, 1964), p. 12.

38 Now at the Württembergische Staatsgalerie, Stuttgart.

39 See note 36 above.

40 T. Mann, *Tagebücher 1918–1921*, ed. P. de Mendelsohn (Frankfurt: Fischer, second edn, 1979), p. 7.

3 CHILDREN AND THE PRIMARY SCHOOLS OF FRANCE, 1914–1918

1 Quoted by Madame Hollebecque, *La jeunesse scolaire de France et la guerre* (Paris: Didier, 1916), p. 91.

2 *Revue de l'enseignement primaire*, 1, 30 September 1917, p. 3.

3 E. Récéjac, *Sur-hommes et bandits. Discours de distribution des prix* (Alençon: Imprimerie Moderne, 1915), p. 3.

4 J. Guirbal, *La Grande Guerre en compositions françaises* (Paris: F. Nathan, 1915), p. 5.

5 G. Merlier, 'Les bataillons scolaires en France, 1882–1892', *Bulletin de la Société d'histoire moderne*, 19, 1977, pp. 19–27.

6 T. W. Margadant, 'Primary School and Youth Groups in Pre-War Paris: les petites A's', *Journal of Contemporary History*, 2, 1978, pp. 323–36.

7 J.-P. Bertaud, *La vie quotidienne en France au temps de la Révolution (1789–1795)* (Paris: Hachette, 1983); *J'étais enfant en 1789* (Paris: Centre National de Documentation Pédagogique, Dossier de documentation no. 16, 1989).

8 *L'Ecole*, 11, 9 January 1915, p. 47.
9 *Revue pédagogique*, 10–11, October–November 1914, p. 124.
10 Circular from Albert Sarraut to academic governors, *Bulletin administratif du Ministère de l'Instruction Publique (BAMIP)*, 2143, 12/19/26 September 1914, p. 366.
11 *BAMIP*, 2143, 12/19/26 September 1914, p. 374.
12 Circular on the new school year addressed to governors, 29 September 1914, in A. Sarraut, *L'instruction publique et la guerre* (Paris: Didier, 1916), pp. 3–4.
13 Circular on the approaching new school year, to governors, 10 September 1915, *Revue de l'enseignement primaire*, 2, 10 October 1915, pp. 11–12.
14 *BAMIP*, 2158, 30 January 1915; 2163, 6 March 1915; 2192, 2 October 1915; 2200, 27 November 1915.
15 *Revue pédagogique*, 1–2, January–February 1915, p. 109. The article was first published in the *Bulletin de l'enseignement primaire du Finistère*.
16 *Revue pédagogique*, 11, November 1916, p. 536.
17 *Ibid.*, 1, January 1917, p. 90.
18 A. Prost, *Histoire de l'enseignement en France, 1800–1967* (Paris: A. Colin, 1968), p. 336.
19 M. Ozouf, *L'Ecole, l'Eglise et la république, 1871–1914* (Paris: A. Colin, 1963); B. Singer, 'From Patriots to Pacifists: The French Primary School Teachers, 1880–1940', *Journal of Contemporary History*, 12/3, 1977, pp. 413–34; J. and M. Ozouf, 'Le Thème du patriotisme dans les manuels primaires', *Le Mouvement social*, 49, October–December 1964, pp. 5–31.
20 Singer, 'Patriots to Pacifists', pp. 413–34; P. Caspard, *La Presse d'éducation et d'enseignement, XVIIIème–1940*, 3 vols. (Paris: INRP, Ed. CNRS, 1981, 1984, 1986), vol. III, pp. 417–18. A police report dating from 1912 moreover credited the *Revue de l'enseignement primaire et primaire supérieur* with having 'a very great influence in teaching circles' (F7 12844, report of 15 February 1912).
21 Paradoxically, *La Revue pédagogique*, founded in 1878 and very close to the administrative circles of the Ministry of Public Instruction, appeared less engaged. Refusing to move away from a relatively moderate tone, it never made the war its exclusive preoccupation. Rather than the patriotic framing of childhood in wartime, the *Revue* preferred the construction of a highly stabilizing image of the teaching world, particularly in the primary sector. Further, in the picture drawn by the *Revue* from 1915 onwards of the French school in wartime, the descriptive element prevailed over the hortatory; apart from 'inspection notes', direct advice was rare on how to bring the war into the heart of traditional teaching. While remaining stoutly patriotic (as can be seen by the strong presence of the theme of Alsace-Lorraine), the *Revue* retained a moderate tone and continued to promote traditional educational concerns without direct relevance to the war.
22 G. Bruno, *Le Tour de l'Europe pendant la guerre. Livre de lecture courante. Cours moyen* (Paris: Belin, 1916).
23 *Ibid.*, pp. 3–4.
24 Collections of the Historial de la Grande Guerre, Péronne (Somme).
25 Prize certificate, illustration by J. Geoffroy, 1916.
26 See in particular the exhibition 'L'école et la guerre' organized by the Ligue

de l'Enseignement in Paris in 1917, described in the *Revue pédagogique*, 10, October 1917, pp. 340 ff.

27 Report by P. Duval, *Revue pédagogique*, 6, June 1915, p. 455.

28 *Ibid.*, p. 449.

29 *Revue de l'enseignement primaire*, 12, 19 December 1915, p. 142.

30 *Ibid.*, 1, 3 October 1915, pp. 1–2.

31 *Revue pédagogique*, 6, June 1915, p. 472.

32 Such as those preserved by the Musée national de l'éducation, Institut National de la Recherche Pédagogique, Rouen, Série 3-4.01 (1910–19).

33 *Revue de l'enseignement primaire*, 1, 19 September 1918, pp. 22–4.

34 *Revue pédagogique*, 6, June 1915, pp. 472–3.

35 Hollebecque, *Jeunesse scolaire*, pp. 1, 7.

36 P. Gerbod, 'L'enseignement secondaire public en France de 1914 à 1920', *L'Information historique*, 1, January–February 1971, pp. 18–28.

37 *Revue de l'enseignement primaire*, 1, 30 September 1917. The same evolution can be seen in the *Revue pédagogique* from 1916 onwards, but above all in 1917–18.

38 It was also from 1916 onwards, in the Somme, that school 'propaganda' abandoned most of its initial excesses (V. Dehay, 'L'Enfance et l'école dans la Somme pendant la guerre de 1914–1918', thèse de maîtrise, Université de Picardie, 1992, pp. 130 ff.).

39 Circular to teachers in the Basses-Alpes by the school inspector, *Revue pédagogique*, 1, January–June 1916, p. 88.

40 E. Petit, *Revue de l'enseignement primaire*, 1, 30 September 1917, p. 1.

41 *Nos enfants et la guerre. Enquête de la société libre pour l'étude psychologique de l'enfant* (Paris: F. Alcan, 1917), p. 75.

42 *Revue pédagogique*, 6, June 1917, and 3, March 1918.

43 For problems of the child in society and in the family, see M. Crubellier, *L'Enfance et la jeunesse dans la société française, 1800–1950* (Paris: A. Colin, 1979).

44 Dehay, 'L'Enfance et l'école', pp. 41 ff.

45 S. Lesmanne, 'L'Ecole et la guerre (1914–1918)', *Mémoires de la Société d'histoire et d'archéologie de Pontoise*, 1985–86, p. 274.

46 *BAMIP*, 2295, 13 October 1917, p. 723.

47 R. Wall, 'English and German Families and the First World War, 1914–1918', in R. Wall and J. Winter (eds.), *The Upheaval of War. Family, Work and Welfare in Europe, 1914–1918* (Cambridge: Cambridge University Press, 1988), pp. 43–106. In the department of the Seine, the number of minors between thirteen and eighteen years referred to the children's tribunal doubled between October 1915 and September 1916, reaching 2,419 cases against 1,178 for the period 1 October 1915–30 September 1915 (*Larousse mensuel illustré*, 125, July 1917, p. 168).

48 Circular on school attendance, *BAMIP*, 2295, 13 October 1917.

4   WAR, 'NATIONAL EDUCATION' AND THE ITALIAN
PRIMARY SCHOOL, 1915–1918

This chapter was translated from the Italian by Shirley D'Ardia Caracciolo and
John Horne.

1 G. Rochat, *L'Italia nella prima guerra mondiale. Problemi di interpretazione e
   prospettive di ricerca* (Milan: Feltrinelli, 1976), pp. 82–6; A. Fava, 'Assistenza
   e propaganda nel regime di guerra (1915–1918)', in M. Isnenghi (ed.),
   Operai e contadini nella grande guerra (Bologna: Cappelli, 1982), pp. 174–212;
   P. G. Zunino, *L'Ideologia del fascismo. Miti, credenze e valori nella stabilizza-
   zione del regime* (Bologna: Il Mulino, 1985) esp. pp. 99–121; E. Gentile,
   Storia del partito fascista, 1919–1922. Movimento e milizia (Rome/Bari:
   Laterza, 1989); E. Gentile, *Il Culto del littorio. La sacralizzazione della politica
   nell'Italia fascista* (Rome/Bari: Laterza, 1993), esp. pp. 64–103; R. Vivarelli,
   Storia delle origini del fascismo, vol. I, *Il Dopoguerra in Italia e l'avvento del
   fascismo (1918–1922): Dalla fine della guerra all'impresa di Fiume* (Naples:
   Istituto Italiano per gli Studi Storici, 1977); vol. II, *L'Italia dalla grande
   guerra alla marcia su Roma* (Bologna: Il Mulino, 1991); N. Tranfaglia, *La
   Prima guerra mondiale e il fascismo* (Torino: Utet, 1995).
2 The history of Italian education has, of course, always recognized the
   influence of the Great War and the crisis it produced in the primary school
   system as, for example, in the classic study of D. Bertoni Jovine, *La Scuola
   italiana dal 1870 ai giorni nostri* (Rome: Editori Riuniti, 1958, second edn,
   1967), pp. 197–221. But this recognition has not stimulated any substantial
   analysis of school life during the war. The tendency even now to obscure the
   material experience of the war is illustrated by S. Soldani and G. Turi (eds.),
   Fare gli italiani. Scuola e cultura nell'Italia contemporanea, 2 vols. (Bologna: Il
   Mulino, 1993). The specific role of the war is equally ignored by G. Chiosso,
   L'Educazione nazionale da Giolitti a Mussolini (Brescia: La Scuola, 1983),
   except for a discussion of the propaganda work in 1918 of Professor
   Lombardo Radice, already analysed pertinently in M. Isnenghi, *Giornali di
   trincea, 1915–1918* (Turin: Einaudi, 1977). For an effective overview and up-
   to-date bibliography, see G. Cives, 'La Scuola elementare e popolare', in
   G. Cives (ed.), *La Scuola italiana dall'Unità ai nostri giorni* (Florence: La
   Nuova Italia, 1990), pp. 55–103.
3 For the law of 1911, see G. Bonetta, *Scuola e socializzazione fra '800 e '900*
   (Milan: Angeli, 1989), pp. 17–115, and for the ministerial decree of 11
   November 1923, see G. Lombardo Radice, *Lezioni di didattica e ricordi di
   esperienza magistrale* (Palermo/Rome: Sandron, 1925), pp. 429–76. A partial
   reproduction of ministerial teaching programmes for primary schools from
   1859–60 to 1934 can be found in the appendix to I. Zambaldi, *Storia della
   scuola elementare in Italia. Ordinamenti, pedagogia, didattica* (Rome: LAS,
   1975). The best outline of the institutions of the fascist school system
   remains M. Ostenc, *La Scuola italiana durante il fascismo* (Bari: Laterza,
   1981).
4 F. Pesci, 'Cronologia, grafici, statistiche', in Cives (ed.), *La Scuola italiana
   dall'Unità*, pp. 512–14.
5 For the need to pay attention to the multiple levels and forms of mobilization

in different national contexts, see J. Horne, 'La Società britannica e la prima guerra mondiale. Alcune tendenze della storiografia recente', in *Ricerche storiche*, 3, 1991, pp. 603–4; L. Veray, 'La Propagande par les actualités cinématographiques pendant la Grande Guerre', in *Guerres mondiales et conflits contemporains*, 173, 1994, pp. 20–1; Fava, 'Assistenza e propaganda'; A. Fava, 'I Vescovi italiani e il governo Salandra. Un episodio di propaganda di guerra nel giugno 1915', in *Chiesa e società dal secolo IV ai nostri giorni. Scritti in onore di P. Ilarino da Milano*, 2 vols. (Rome: Herder, 1979), vol. II, pp. 610–11.

6 See A. Fava, 'Il Fronte interno e la propaganda di guerra', in *Fronte Interno. Propaganda e mobilitazione civile nell'Italia della Grande Guerra* (Rome: Biblioteca di Storia Moderna e Contemporanea, 1988), pp. 9–22.

7 V. Scialoja, scion of a well-known political family, was a university professor and senator whose ministerial career spanned several governments between 1909 and 1920. For many years, he participated in the consultative Superior Council of Public Instruction, over whose central committee he presided in 1906–8 and 1911–13 (Archivio Centrale dello Stato, *Il Consiglio superiore della Pubblica Istruzione, 1847–1928* (Rome: Ministero per i Beni Culturali, 1994)). U. Comandini was a Mazzinian republican deputy and leading member of the Italian freemasons who enjoyed exceptional prestige among primary school teachers owing to his having played a leading part in the battle for improved professional contracts and for educational reform, both as a member of parliament and as president of the UMN from 1907 to 1913 ('Ubaldo Comandini. Nel cinquantenario della morte', in *Archivio Trimestrale*, 2, 1975, pp. 147–84, esp. pp. 166–70).

8 A. Fava, 'All'Origine di nuove immagini dell'infanzia. Gli anni della grande guerra', in M. C. Giuntella and I. Nardi (eds.), *Il Bambino nella storia* (Naples: ESI, 1993), pp. 145–200 (esp. pp. 160–71).

9 The origins went back to the previous autumn. See Archivio Centrale dello Stato (ACS), Rome, series PCM-Guerra Europea, 34, 35 and 63.

10 ACS, MI-DGPS, series A5G, 28–9 (42); G. Padulo, 'Contributo alla storia della massoneria da Giolitti a Mussolini', in *Annali dell'Istituto italiano per gli studi storici*, 8, 1983–4, pp. 269–89.

11 Over the following months, the government ordered the prefects to coordinate the response to Salandra's appeal, but specified that this should be done through local deputies, associations, influential individuals, etc. Salandra's appeal also resulted in a national subscription for soldiers' families and the funds thus gathered were administered by the Ministry of the Interior. See ACS, MI-DGAC, Division III, Comitati di Assistenza Civile-Gestione Salandra/Boselli. A national card system for civilian volunteers was established by the Presidency of the Council of Ministers, which is to be found in PCM-Guerra Europea, 60–72.

12 UGII, *Atti della Presidenza Generale (Maggio 1915–Ottobre 1917)* (Rome: Tipografia dell'Unione Editrice, 1917). For the programme and early development, see UGII, *Atti della Presidenza Generale (Maggio 1915–Aprile 1916)* (Rome: Regia Università-Biblioteca Giuridica, n.d., but 1916). Publications, conference proceedings and propaganda material produced by the UGII are to be found in the National Libraries of Rome and Florence and in the

Biblioteca di Storia Moderna e Contemporanea in Rome, which has a complete collection of the publications of the Lombard Committee of the union. The 'speaker's notes' produced by this committee for national distribution are in ACS, PCM-Guerra Europea, Propaganda Guerra, 40 (22).

13 For the official announcement of these extended activities, ministerial circular no. 77, 20 December 1916, in *Bollettino Ufficiale*, 8 February 1917–8 November 1918.

14 Decree no. 417, 22 February 1917, and law no. 1143, 18 July 1917.

15 L. Tosi, *La Propaganda italiana all'estero nella prima guerra mondiale. Rivendicazioni territoriali e politica delle nazionalità* (Udine: Del Bianco, 1977), for the official side of Scialoja's activities.

16 E. De Fort, 'L'Associazionismo degli insegnanti elementari dall'età giolittiana al fascismo', in *Movimento operaio e socialista*, 4, 1981, pp. 375–404, and E. De Fort, 'Gli Insegnanti', in Cives (ed.), *La Scuola italiana dall'Unità*, pp. 199–261.

17 Padulo, 'Contributo alla storia della massoneria', pp. 301–4, for the text of the letter and for the influence of the Grand Orient of Italy on the April 1916 UMN conference. For the conference proceedings, see *I Diritti della Scuola*, 30 April 1916. For the connections between the new orientation of the UMN under Comandini and the latter's future ministerial career, see Fava, 'All'Origine di nuove immagini dell'infanzia', pp. 162, 167–8.

18 The Federated Society grouped voluntary associations going back to the late nineteenth century – such as the Lega Navale Italiana (Italian Naval League), the Società Nazionale 'Dante Alighieri' (National Dante Alighieri Society), and the Consiglio Nazionale delle Donne Italiane (National Council of Italian Women) – together with organizations generated by the war, the most important of which were the UGII and the Federazione Nazionale dei Comitati di Assistenza Civile (National Federation of Committees of Civil Assistance). On the pre-war associations, see B. Pisa, *Nazione e politica nella Società 'Dante Alighieri'* (Rome: Bonacci, 1995), and P. Salvetti, *Immagine nazionale ed emigrazione nella Società 'Dante Alighieri'* (Rome: Bonacci, 1995).

19 ACS, CGACPI, series Fascicoli Nominativi, 32 (2892), for the list of these local officials. The list of the eighty provincial secretaries, although less complete, is richer in information (*ibid.*, 22 (52-578)).

20 The weekly review, *I Diritti della Scuola*, contains a wealth of detail on the school teachers' involvement in works of social assistance. For archival sources, see ACS, PCM-Guerra Europea, series 19.1, and *ibid.*, MI-DGAC, Pubblica assistenza e beneficenza, 1913–15, 1916–18.

21 *Assistenza Civile*, the review of the Federazione Nazionale dei Comitati di Assistenza Civile, and especially the supplement, *Notiziario dei Comitati* (Milan, January 1917–December 1918), for this local activity; also S. Bartoloni, 'L'Associazionismo femminile nella prima guerra mondiale e la mobilitazione per l'assistenza civile e la propaganda', in A. Gigli Marchetti and N. Torcellan (eds.), *Donna lombarda. 1860–1945* (Milan: Angeli, 1992), pp. 65–91; C. Dau Novelli, *Società, Chiesa e associazionismo femminile. L'Unione fra le donne cattoliche d'Italia (1902–1919)* (Rome: AVE, 1988), pp. 233–77.

22 For an example of this kind of programme, see *Bollettino* of the Piedmontese committee of the UGII, June–July 1916.

23 Whereas in 1912, only 105 municipal administrations and 315 'auxiliary institutions' received state subsidies for school meals, by early 1918 1,600 communes benefited from such subsidies: UGII, *Relazione finanziaria* (Milan: UGII, 1918), p. 17.

24 The quotation comes from the founder of Young Italy, Professor Ettore Cozzani, as he sought official backing from the Ministry of Public Instruction in August 1918 for the diffusion of the movement throughout the school system. Although this was never given, already in September 1917, Young Italy had received the support of the UGII and the Federated Society so that by the summer of 1918 it could count on the support of fifty-eight committees in as many cities (ACS, PCM-Guerra Europea, 19.1, 62 (28, 30 and 37); 63 (38); 19.11.10, 135 (38)). For the connections with fascism, see A. Fava, 'La Guerra a scuola. Propaganda, memoria, rito (1915–1940)', in *Materiali di lavoro*, 3–4, 1986, pp. 53–126.

25 Almost alone as a protest against the contamination of young minds by patriotic indoctrination through the school was the speech made in parliament by the socialist deputy, Fabrizio Maffi (*Atti Parlamentari, Camera dei Deputati*, 4 March 1916, pp. 8897–9).

26 M. G. Rosada, *Le Università popolari in Italia, 1900–1918* (Rome: Editori Riuniti, 1975); E. Decleva, *Etica del lavoro, socialismo, cultura popolare. Augusto Osimo e la Società Umanitaria* (Milan: Angeli, 1985).

27 The article appeared as an 'open letter' on the front page, 18 November 1917. It bore the pen-name of the leading liberal intellectual and contributor to the *Corriere della Sera*, Luigi Einaudi. The article, which had considerable resonance, was the first in a series later published as *Lettere politiche di Junius* (Bari: Laterza, 1920).

28 For the implications of this debate and its connections with the fascist period, see G. Tognon, *Benedetto Croce alla Minerva. La politica scolastica italiana tra Caporetto e la marcia su Roma* (Brescia: La Scuola, 1990).

5 MOBILIZING LABOUR AND SOCIALIST MILITANTS IN PARIS DURING THE GREAT WAR

This chapter was translated from the French by John Horne.

1 J.-L. Robert, 'Ouvriers et mouvement ouvrier parisiens pendant la grande guerre et l'immédiat après-guerre. Histoire et anthropologie' (thèse d'état, University of Paris I, 1989), and also J.-L. Robert, *Les Ouvriers, la patrie et la révolution. Paris 1914–1919* (Besançon: Annales Littéraires de l'Université de Besançon no. 592, Série Historique no. 11, 1995).

2 J. Horne, *Labour at War. France and Britain, 1914–1918* (Oxford: Clarendon Press, 1991), esp. ch. 3.

3 Syndicat Général des Ouvriers Terrassiers, *Rapport moral et financier du 1er août 1914 au 1er janvier 1918* (Paris: La Cootypographie, 1918); communiqué by Hubert in *La Bataille syndicaliste*, 3 July 1915; *Le Prolétaire du Bâtiment*, May 1917.

4 Meetings of the Syndicat des Maçons-Pierre, 7 and 21 February 1915, Archives Nationales (AN), Paris, F7 13655.

5 Meeting of the Syndicat des Maçons-Pierre, 12 December 1915, *ibid.*

6 Report of Cezan to the meeting of the typographers' union, 7 April 1918, in AN, F7 13753; and 'Chambre syndicale typographique parisienne, secours versés aux chômeurs, aux femmes et aux enfants des mobilisés depuis le début de la guerre', *Bulletin du ministère du travail*, May–June 1915, p. 127.

7 Notice of branch meeting, January 1915, in Archives de la Préfecture de Police de Paris (APP), BA 1535.

8 Fete organized by the unions of Noisy-le-Sec, Pantin and the Gare de l'Est, 10 February 1918, AN, F7 13673.

9 Atsushi Fukasawa, 'Histoire du syndicalisme cheminot en France – des grèves générales à la grande guerre' (doctoral thesis, University of Paris I, 1992).

10 Meeting of delegates of the unions of the Seine, 3 April 1916, in AN, F7 13617.

11 Meetings of the building labourers and craft building workers' unions, 25 July, 26 September and 28 November 1915, AN, F7 13657.

12 Tract announcing the 'very familial meeting' of the two craft unions, 2 January 1916, AN, F7 13649.

13 Meeting of the Métro union, 10 February 1918, AN, F7 13830.

14 Meeting of the metalworkers' union, 31 March 1917, AN, F7 13366.

15 Négrillat, meeting of the unions of stone masons, 7 February 1915 in AN, F7 13655; Lallemand, meeting of the typographers' union, 22 April 1918, in AN, F7 13753.

16 Montagne, meeting of the executive council of the union of postal employees (sous-agents des postes), 10 October 1916, in AN, F7 13803.

17 Meeting of the union of aviation and automobile workers, 13 January 1918, AN, F7 13367; on the same meeting, a report of the Service des Renseignements dans les Usines de Guerre, *ibid.*

18 See appendix I-7 to Robert, 'Ouvriers et mouvement ouvrier parisiens'.

19 Report of the Commission Exécutive of the Fédération de la Seine for the meeting of secretaries of the local sections, 13 December 1914, in APP, BA 1535.

20 See Robert, 'Ouvriers et mouvement ouvrier parisiens', chs. 23 and 24.

21 Report of the Commission Exécutive of the Fédération de la Seine for the meeting of secretaries of the local sections, 13 December 1914, in APP, BA 1535.

22 See Robert, 'Ouvriers et mouvement ouvrier parisiens', ch. 24.

23 Results of the census taken on 8 September 1914 published in *Annuaire statistique de la Ville de Paris et du Département de la Seine, 1914* (section on 'Dénombrement').

24 Section Française de l'Internationale Ouvrière (SFIO), *La XIIème section de la Fédération de la Seine pendant 18 mois de guerre – ses oeuvres de solidarité – son action politique – 1914–1915* (Paris: 1916). See also Lavadeur, *La Vie à Paris pendant la première année de guerre. Etude sociologique* (Paris: Giard, 1915).

25 Statutes of the committee published in SFIO, *La XIIème section.* The bureau of the committee was composed of the members of the executive commission of the section who also envisaged that in case of any anti-socialist reaction, they would make the Socialist Aid Committee into the section's 'legal cover'.

26 Quoted in *La XIIème section*, in bold type in the original.

27 'Notre visite à la Chapelle', *L'Humanité*, 30 August 1914. The socialists dispensed 500 meals each day at Torcy-Palace.

28 'Les Repas populaires – la solidarité ouvrière', by A.-M. M. (Maurel), *ibid.*, series of articles, October 1914.

29 Declaration by Poncet on the occasion of a workers' Christmas at Montreuil, *ibid.*, 1 January 1915.

30 In October 1914, APP, BA 1535.

31 *L'Humanité*, 9, 16, and 27 August 1914.

32 *La XIIème section.*

33 *Ibid.*

34 Thus the fifth section provided help and advice on Mondays, Wednesdays and Fridays from 10.00 to 11.30 a.m. and from 6.00 to 8.00 p.m. (*L'Humanité*, 17 August 1914). The tenth section ran an information service on soldiers missing in action (*L'Humanité*, 5 February 1915).

35 In less than eighteen months, the Vestiaire sent 400 shirts, 732 pairs of socks, 500 handkerchiefs, 100 pairs of underwear, 400 shirt-fronts, 300 mufflers, 60 kgs of chocolate, 3,000 envelopes and sheets of paper, string, tobacco, etc. (*La XIIème section*).

36 *Ibid.* The eighteenth *arrondissement* also had a shelter organized by the local socialist section and by the national labour body, the Comité d'Action (*L'Humanité*, 2 January 1915).

37 R. G. Réau, 'Les Oeuvres socialistes dans le 18ème arrondissement', *L'Humanité*, 13 January 1917.

38 'A Montreuil', *L'Humanité*, 21 March 1915.

39 *L'Humanité*, 15 February 1915. Cf. also in the fifteenth *arrondissement*, *ibid.*, 19 February 1915, the thirteenth *arrondissement*, *ibid.*, 23 January 1915, and the eleventh *arrondissement*, *ibid.*, 6 January 1915.

40 This did happen for several weeks at Villemonble (*L'Humanité*, 15 February 1915), and in the thirteenth section (*ibid.*, 23 January 1915).

41 *L'Humanité*, 19 October, 15 November 1914, and 21 March 1915; and R. G. Réau, 'L'Oeuvre réalisée par une municipalité socialiste', *ibid.*, 19 March 1919.

42 'La Section et la municipalité du Pré-Saint-Gervais', *L'Humanité*, 15 February 1915; for Saint-Denis, *L'Humanité*, 4 September, 26 October 1914 and 29 February 1915.

43 For Courbevoie, *L'Humanité*, 16 January 1915; for Alfortville, *ibid.*, 10 October 1914 (the socialists congratulated the town hall on its actions); at Levallois-Perret, *ibid.*, 14 October 1914 and 5 February 1915 (in this case, the socialist councillors, though in a minority, instigated all the action of social solidarity under the leadership of their elected representative to the department of the Seine, Vendrin); at Malakoff, *ibid.*, 16 January 1915 (following pressure by the local socialist section).

44 *L'Humanité*, 30 February 1915.

45 *Ibid.*, 17 February 1915.

46 *Ibid.*, 15 February 1915.

47 *Ibid.*

48 *Ibid.*, 8 August 1914. The reservations expressed about these proposals in certain quarters, such as the military government of Paris, produced 'very

strong dissatisfaction' among socialists, according to a report of 9 September 1914 (APP, BA 1535).

49 *L'Humanité*, 11 January 1915.
50 *Ibid.*, 22 August 1914.
51 *Ibid.*, 6 January 1915.
52 *Ibid.*, 8 September 1914.
53 *Ibid.*, 30 January 1915.
54 Administrative commission of the twentieth section, 13 September 1915, in APP, BA 1535.
55 Cf., for the tenth section, *L 'Humanité*, 5 February 1915; for the thirteenth section, the municipality was 'very welcoming' (*ibid.*, 23 January 1915); the same sentiment was expressed by the fourteenth section (*ibid.*, October 1914), and by the seventeenth section (*ibid.*, 16 January 1915). Cf. also Fiancette, at a meeting of the nineteenth section on 24 October 1915, in APP, BA 1536; and Berthaut and Reisz at a meeting of the twentieth section on 24 December 1914, APP, BA 1535.
56 Municipal Council, 29 March 1915, *Bulletin municipal officiel de la Ville de Paris et du département de la Seine (BMOVP)*. On the 'yellow' union, see Robert, 'Ouvriers et mouvement ouvrier parisiens', ch. 1.
57 *BMOVP*.
58 Jacquemin, Conseil Général of 26 June 1915, *BMOVP*.
59 Conseil Général of 27 March 1915, *BMOVP*.
60 Federal committee of the socialist federation of the Seine, 20 September 1915.
61 Conseil Général of 26 June 1915, *BMOVP*.
62 *L'Humanité*, 26 September 1914.
63 Cf. also the strong statements made by the elected socialist representatives of the Seine on the subjects of alcoholism and the cinema, or about adolescents. See Robert, 'Ouvriers et mouvement ouvrier parisiens', chs. 5 and 6.

6   BETWEEN INTEGRATION AND REJECTION: THE JEWISH COMMUNITY IN GERMANY, 1914–1918

This chapter was translated from the German by Steven Bileca and Belinda Cooper.
1 P. Panayi, 'Dominant Societies and Minorities in the Two World Wars', in P. Panayi (ed.), *Minorities in Wartime. National and Racial Groupings in Europe, North America and Australia during the Two World Wars* (Oxford and Providence: Berg, 1993), pp. 3–23 (esp. p. 5).
2 See M. Levene, 'Frontiers of Genocide: Jews in the Eastern War Zones, 1914–1920 and 1941', in Panayi (ed.), *Minorities in Wartime*, pp. 83–117.
3 See P. Hyman, *From Dreyfus to Vichy. The Remaking of French Jewry, 1906–1939* (New York: Columbia University Press, 1979), pp. 49–59; C. Holmes, *Anti-Semitism in British Society 1876–1939* (London: Edward Arnold, 1979), pp. 121–40. For a more critical view on the British situation, see David Cesarani, 'An Embattled Minority: The Jews in Britain During the First World War', in T. Kushner and K. Lunn (eds.), *The Politics of Margin-*

ality. Race, the Radical Right and Minorities in Twentieth Century Britain (London: Frank Cass, 1990), pp. 61–81.

4 On the CV, see M. Lamberti, *Jewish Activism in Imperial Germany. The Struggle for Civil Equality* (New Haven and London: Yale University Press, 1978); I. Schorsch, *Jewish Reactions to German Anti-Semitism, 1870–1914* (New York and London: Columbia University Press, 1972), pp. 117–48; J. Reinharz, *Fatherland or Promised Land. The Dilemma of the German Jew, 1893–1914* (Ann Arbor: University of Michigan Press, 1975); A. Paucker, 'Zur Problematik einer jüdischen Abwehrstrategie in der deutschen Gesellschaft', in W. Mosse and A. Paucker (eds.), *Juden im Wilhelminischen Deutschland, 1890–1914* (Tübingen: Mohr, 1976) pp. 479–548; E. Friesel, 'The Political and Ideological Development of the Centralverein before 1914', in *Leo Baeck Institute Year Book*, 31, 1986, pp. 121–46.

5 See P. Pulzer, *Jews and the German State. The Political History of a Minority, 1848–1933* (Oxford: Blackwell, 1992), pp. 106 ff.

6 On the ZVD, see Reinharz, *Fatherland or Promised Land*; R. Lichtheim, *Die Geschichte des deutschen Zionismus* (Jerusalem: Verlag Rubin Mass, 1954); S. M. Poppel, *Zionism in Germany 1897–1933. The Shaping of a Jewish Identity* (Philadelphia: Jewish Publication Society of America, 1976).

7 See E. Zechlin, *Die deutsche Politik und die Juden im Ersten Weltkrieg* (Göttingen: Vandenhoeck and Ruprecht, 1969), pp. 59–85.

8 See M. Lamberti, 'From Coexistence to Conflict. Zionism and the Jewish Community in Germany, 1897–1914', in *Leo Baeck Institute Year Book*, 27, 1982, pp. 53–86.

9 On the Jewish Orthodox in Germany, see M. Breuer, *Jüdische Orthodoxie im Deutschen Reich 1871–1918. Sozialgeschichte einer religiösen Minderheit* (Frankfurt-am-Main: Athenaeum, 1986).

10 *Im deutschen Reich*, 20, 1914, p. 339.

11 *Im deutschen Reich*, 21, 1915, p. 5.

12 *Im deutschen Reich*, 21, 1915, p. 19.

13 *Im deutschen Reich*, 20, 1914, p. 354.

14 *Jüdische Rundschau*, 21 August 1914, p. 349.

15 *Der Israelit*, 55 (32), 1914 (6 August), pp. 1 ff; J. Wohlgemuth, 'Der Weltkrieg', in *Jeschurun*, 1, 1914, pp. 255–72. See also Breuer, *Jüdische Orthodoxie*, pp. 342–50.

16 See Zechlin, *Die deutsche Politik*, pp. 86–100; S. Magill, 'Defense and Introspection: German Jewry, 1914', in D. Bronsen, *Jews and Germans from 1860 to 1933. The Problematic Symbiosis* (Heidelberg: Carl Winter Universitätsverlag, 1979), pp. 209–33.

17 Franz Oppenheimer, 'Antisemitismus', in *Neue Jüdische Monatshefte*, 2, 1917, p. 1.

18 Kurt Alexander, 'Kriegsgedanken eines deutschen Juden', in *Hamburger Familienblatt*, 36, 7 September 1914, quoted in Magill, 'Defense and Introspection', p. 227.

19 Otto Armin (Alfred Roth), *Die Juden im Heer. Eine statistische Untersuchung nach amtlichen Quellen* (Munich: Deutscher Volks-Verlag, 1919), an antisemitic source; Walter Leiser, *Die Juden im Heer. Eine Kriegsstatistik* (Berlin: Philo-Verlag, 1919); Franz Oppenheimer, *Die Judenstatistik des preußischen*

Kriegsministeriums (Munich: Verlag für Kulturpolitik, 1922); Jacob Segall, *Die deutschen Juden als Soldaten im Kriege 1914–1918. Eine statistische Studie* (Berlin: Philo-Verlag, 1922).

20 Oppenheimer, *Judenstatistik*, pp. 40 ff.; Segall, *Die deutschen Juden*, pp. 12, 28.

21 See W. T. Angress, 'Prussia's Army and the Jewish Reserve Officer Controversy before World War I', in *Leo Baeck Institute Yearbook*, 17, 1972, pp. 19–42.

22 See D. Engel, 'Patriotism as a Shield. The Liberal Jewish Defence against Antisemitism in Germany during the First World War', in *Leo Baeck Institute Year Book*, 31, 1986, pp. 147–71 (p. 152).

23 See W. Mosse, *The German–Jewish Economic Elite, 1820–1935. A Socio-Cultural Profile* (Oxford: Oxford University Press, 1989), p. 278.

24 See Zechlin, *Die deutsche Politik*, pp. 101–284.

25 Quoted in Engel, 'Patriotism as a Shield', p. 152.

26 See W. T. Angress, 'The Impact of the "Judenwahlen" of 1912 on the Jewish Question. A Synthesis', in *Leo Baeck Institute Yearbook*, 28, 1983, pp. 367–410.

27 See S. Volkov, 'Antisemitism as a Cultural Code. Reflections on the History and Historiography of Antisemitism in Imperial Germany', in *Leo Baeck Institute Year Book,* 23, 1978, pp. 25–46.

28 Daniel Frymann (Heinrich Class), *Wenn ich der Kaiser wär* (Leipzig: Dieterich, 1912), pp. 74–8. See Zechlin, *Die deutsche Politik*, pp. 46 ff., 545 f.; W. Jochmann, 'Struktur und Funktion des deutschen Antisemitismus', in Mosse and Paucker (eds.), *Juden im Wilhelminischen Deutschland*, pp. 389–477 (464–6); U. Lohalm, *Völkischer Radikalismus. Die Geschichte des Deutschvölkischen Schutz- und Trutz-Bundes* (Hamburg: Libniz, 1970), pp. 27–56.

29 Lohalm, *Völkischer Radikalismus*, p. 63.

30 See W. Jochmann, 'Die Ausbreitung des Antisemitismus', in W. Mosse and A. Paucker (eds.), *Deutsches Judentum in Krieg und Revolution, 1916–1923* (Tübingen: Mohr 1971), pp. 409–510 (p. 415).

31 Houston Stewart Chamberlain, *Kriegsaufsätze* (Munich: F. Bruckmann, 1915, eighth edn), p. 46.

32 Lohalm, *Völkischer Radikalismus*, p. 63; Jochmann, 'Die Ausbreitung des Antisemitismus', p. 411.

33 Theodor Fritsch, 'Burgfrieden', in *Hammer*, 13, 1914, pp. 505–10 (p. 510).

34 E.g. the articles in *Hammer*, 13, 1914, pp. 501, 523 ff., 545 ff., 576–8, 632–5. See also Zechlin, *Die deutsche Politik*, pp. 521–8; Lohalm, *Völkischer Radikalismus*, p. 64; Jochmann, 'Die Ausbreitung des Antisemitismus', pp. 415 ff. After the war, all these accusations were collected in Otto Armin (Alfred Roth), *Die Juden in den Kriegs-Gesellschaften und in der Kriegs-Wirtschaft* (Munich: Deutscher Volks-Verlag, 1921).

35 Anti-semitic leaflet of 1918, quoted in *Deutsche Israelitische Zeitung*, 41, October 1918, p. 12. See also Zechlin, *Die deutsche Politik*, pp. 528–34; Jochmann, 'Die Ausbreitung des Antisemitismus', pp. 422 ff. After the war, the accusations were collected in another book by Otto Armin (Alfred Roth), *Die Juden im Heer.*

36 Jochmann, 'Die Ausbreitung des Antisemitismus', pp. 412 ff.
37 See, for example, Theodor Fritsch, 'Die fremde Rassenflut', in *Hammer*, 14 (319), October 1915; Georg Fritz, *Die Ostjudenfrage. Zionismus und Grenzschluß* (Munich: J. F. Lehmann, 1915).
38 Jochmann, 'Die Ausbreitung des Antisemitismus', p. 417.
39 See *ibid.*, pp. 421 ff..
40 See *ibid.*, p. 420; Saul Friedländer, 'Die politischen Veränderungen der Kriegszeit und ihre Auswirkungen auf die Judenfrage', in Mosse and Paucker (eds.), *Deutsches Judentum in Krieg und Revolution*, pp. 27–65 (p. 40). On the liberal press during the war, see W. Becker, 'Die Rolle der liberalen Presse', in *ibid.*, pp. 67–135.
41 Zechlin, *Die deutsche Politik*, pp. 518 ff.
42 See Konstantin von Gebsattel, 'Judenwahlen und Judenfrieden', in *Deutsche Zeitung*, 21 September 1917.
43 See Lohalm, *Völkischer Radikalismus*, pp. 46 ff.
44 Zechlin, *Die deutsche Politik*, pp. 260–77; T. Maurer, 'Medizinalpolizei und Antisemitismus. Die deutsche Politik der Grenzsperre gegen Ostjuden im Ersten Weltkrieg', in *Jahrbücher für Geschichte Osteuropas*, 33, 1985, pp. 205–30.
45 See W. T. Angress, 'Das deutsche Militär und die Juden im Ersten Weltkrieg', in *Militärgeschichtliche Mitteilungen*, 19, 1976, pp. 77–146; Angress, 'The German Army's "Judenzählung" of 1916. Genesis, Consequences, Significance', in *Leo Baeck Institute Year Book*, 23, 1978, pp. 117–35; Zechlin, *Die deutsche Politik*, pp. 528–41.
46 Georg Salzberger, *Aus meinem Kriegstagebuch* (Frankfurt-am-Main: sp. issue of *Liberales Judentum*, 1916), p. 131.
47 See Angress, 'Das deutsche Militär', p. 103; Zechlin, *Die deutsche Politik*, pp. 534 ff.
48 See Angress, 'Das deutsche Militär', pp. 99–102, 113–17.
49 *Ibid.*, p. 121.
50 *Im deutschen Reich*, 24, 1918, p. 433. See also Zechlin, *Die deutsche Politik*, p. 553.
51 Engel, 'Patriotism as a Shield', p. 159.
52 Quoted in Angress, 'Das deutsche Militär', pp. 106–11, 120.
53 *Ibid.*, pp. 86 ff.
54 *Ibid.*, p. 119.
55 E. G. Reichmann, 'Der Bewußtseinswandel der deutschen Juden', in Mosse and Paucker (eds.), *Deutsches Judentum in Krieg*, pp. 511–612.
56 *Im deutschen Reich*, 23, 1917, p. 395.
57 See Pulzer, *Jews and the German State*, pp. 197, 205.
58 Quoted in Jochmann, 'Die Ausbreitung des Antisemitismus', p. 427.
59 J. Marx, *Kriegstagebuch eines Juden* (Frankfurt-am-Main: Ner-Tamid-Verlag, 1964), p. 32.
60 Salzberger, *Aus meinem Kriegstagebuch*, p. 17.
61 Reinhold Lewin, 'Der Krieg als jüdisches Erlebnis', in *Monatsschrift für Geschichte und Wissenschaft des Judentums*, 63, 1919, pp. 1–14 (p. 6).
62 *Ibid.*, p. 8.
63 See G. L. Mosse, *The Jews and the German War Experience 1914–1918*, Leo

Baeck Memorial Lecture 21 (New York: Leo Baeck Institute, 1977), pp. 13 ff.

64 Quotation from Isaak Heinemann, '"Der Zweck heiligt die Mittel". Eine Betrachtung über die Moral des Krieges', in *Jeschurun*, 3, 1916, p. 421; more generally, see Pulzer, *Jews and the German State*, pp. 202 ff.

65 See Reichmann, 'Bewußtseinswandel', pp. 521 ff.; S. Aschheim, *Brothers and Strangers. The East European Jew in German and German Jewish Consciousness, 1800–1923* (Madison: University of Wisconsin Press, 1982).

66 Ernst Simon, 'Unser Kriegserlebnis', in *Jüdische Jugend*, 1, 1919, pp. 39 ff., quoted in Reichmann, 'Bewußtseinswandel', p. 531.

67 H. Schulze, *Gibt es überhaupt eine deutsche Geschichte?* (Berlin: Siedler, 1989), p. 28.

68 See H.-U. Wehler, *The German Empire 1871–1918* (1973; English translation, New York and Oxford: Berg, 1991, second edn), pp. 90–4, 102–13.

69 Quoted in Jochmann, 'Die Ausbreitung des Antisemitismus', p. 440. See also Zechlin, *Die deutsche Politik*, pp. 558 ff.; Lohalm, *Völkischer Radikalismus*, pp. 51 ff.

7 *WACKES* AT WAR: ALSACE-LORRAINE AND THE FAILURE OF GERMAN NATIONAL MOBILIZATION, 1914–1918

The author would like to thank the Humboldt Foundation, Bonn, for providing essential support for research in French and German archives on this project.

1 M. Spahn, *Elsaß-Lothringen* (Berlin: Ullstein, 1919), pp. 357–9.

2 H.-U. Wehler, 'Unfähig zur Verfassungsreform: Das "Reichsland" Elsaß-Lothringen von 1870 bis 1918', in H.-U. Wehler, *Krisenherde des Kaiserreichs 1871–1918. Studien zur deutschen Sozial- und Verfassungsgeschichte* (Göttingen: Vandenhoeck and Ruprecht, 1970), pp. 30–51.

3 In fact, there was generous provision of French language teaching, and even French-medium teaching in schools with a majority of francophone pupils. Wehler, 'Unfähig zur Verfassungsreform', pp. 51–6. On dialect, see J. Rossé *et al.* (eds.), *Das Elsaß von 1870–1932*, 4 vols. (Colmar: Alsatia, n.d. (1936–8)); vol. I: *Politische Geschichte*, pp. 138–9 and 175.

4 D. Schoenbaum, *Zabern 1913. Consensus Politics in Imperial Germany* (London: Allen and Unwin, 1982); H.-U. Wehler, 'Symbol des halbabsolutistischen Herrschaftssystems: Der Fall Zabern von 1913/14 als Verfassungskrise des Wilhelminischen Kaiserreichs', in Wehler, *Krisenherde*, pp. 65–84. *Wackes* was the insulting term for Alsatians at the centre of the Zabern affair.

5 H. Hiery, *Reichstagswahlen im Reichsland. Ein Beitrag zur Landesgeschichte von Elsaß-Lothringen und zur Wahlgeschichte des Deutschen Reiches 1871–1918* (Düsseldorf: Droste, 1986).

6 Wehler, 'Unfähig zur Verfassungsreform'. On the structure of the Kaiserreich, see W. J. Mommsen, *Der autoritäre Nationalstaat. Verfassung, Gesellschaft und Kultur im deutschen Kaiserreich* (Frankfurt-am-Main: Fischer, 1990).

7 This was argued by the French socialist Marcel Sembat, *Faites un roi, sinon faites la paix* (1913), cited in Karl Kautsky, *Elsaß-Lothringen. Eine historische*

Studie (Stuttgart: Dietz, 1917), p. 73; and also by the Alsatian industrialist F. Lamey in Württembergisches Hauptstaatsarchiv-Militärarchiv (HStA-MA Stuttgart), M30/1-89, Kriegspresseamt – Oberzensurstelle to Chef IIIb, 17 October 1918.

8 Friedrich Lienhard, *Das deutsche Elsaß*, vol. XVII of Ernst Jäckh (ed.), *Der Deutsche Krieg. Politische Flugschriften*, 97 vols. (Stuttgart and Berlin: Deutsche Verlags-Anstalt, 1914–17), pp. 14–20; C. Baechler, 'L'Alsace entre la Guerre et la Paix: Recherches sur l'opinion publique (1917–1918)' (thèse de troisième cycle, University of Strasbourg, 1969), pp. 24–5.

9 Spahn, *Elsaß-Lothringen*, p. 346.

10 Konrad Jarausch, *The Enigmatic Chancellor. Bethmann Hollweg and the Hubris of Imperial Germany* (New Haven and London: Yale University Press, 1972), p. 159. For von Gleich, see HStA-MA Stuttgart, M660, Gleich papers, Book 153, p. 4, April 1915.

11 Baechler, 'L'Alsace', p. 131. This is almost certainly an overestimate which includes *Altdeutsche*, i.e. citizens of other German states, and other German volunteers.

12 E. Huber, *Deutsche Verfassungsgeschichte seit 1789*, 7 vols. (Stuttgart: Kohlhammer, 1957–84), vol. V (1978), pp. 43–4. The 'simple state of war' applied in the interior of Germany.

13 Cf. W. J. Mommsen, 'Der Geist von 1914: Das Programm eines politischen "Sonderwegs" der Deutschen', in Mommsen, *Der autoritäre Nationalstaat*, pp. 407–21.

14 Lienhard, *Das deutsche Elsaß*, p. 23. He published these remarks also in the *Frankfurter Zeitung*, 7 October 1914.

15 *Straßburger Post*, 8 August 1914, cited in Baechler, 'L'Alsace', pp. 39–40; *ibid.* for further examples.

16 G. Wolfram (ed.), *Verfassung und Verwaltung von Elsaß-Lothringen 1871–1918*, 3 vols. in 4 (Berlin/Frankfurt-am-Main: Selbstverlag des Elsaß-Lothringen-Institutes, 1931–7), vol. II/1 (1936): *Das Reichsland Elsaß-Lothringen 1871–1918*, p. 84.

17 Baechler, 'L'Alsace', p. 41.

18 *Deutsche Tageszeitung*, 19 August 1914.

19 *Kölnische Zeitung*, 25 August 1914.

20 Baechler, 'L'Alsace', p. 43.

21 Cf. HStA-MA Stuttgart, M30/1-117, 6th Army to Army Group Crown Prince Rupprecht, 22 June 1918, which recommended that the Alsatian men from country areas made the best soldiers; also Guard Reserve Corps to 4th Army, *ibid.*, 19 June 1918.

22 Rossé *et al.*, *Das Elsaß*, vol. I, pp. 296 f.; vol. IV, tab. 30 a/b. The figure 8,000 represents the number of volunteers in the 14th, 15th, 16th and 21st army corps.

23 Bundesarchiv-Militärarchiv, Freiburg (BA-MA), PHD7/60, 'Das Verhalten der Elsaß-Lothringer in drei Kriegsjahren', ed. Quartermaster-General (i.e. General Hahndorff), Berlin, 1917, p. 59. There may have been as few as 6,000 volunteers from Alsace-Lorraine, including many *Altdeutsche*: Charles Schmidt, *Die geheimen Pläne der deutschen Politik in Elsaß-Lothringen (1915–1918)* (Paris: Fischbach, 1923), p. 10.

24 Archives Départementales du Bas-Rhin (ADBR) Strasbourg, AL87 5607, Hauser. Cf. also Heck in the same file, and several cases in *ibid.*, AL87 5928, e.g. Thomas.

25 Schmidt, *Die geheimen Pläne*, pp. 9–10.

26 BA-MA Freiburg, N21/1, Falkenhausen 'Erinnerungen', p. 60.

27 E.g. Lieutenant-General von Bodungen, commander of the Upper Rhine fortifications, BA-MA Freiburg, N559/16, 'Denkschrift der Armee-Abteilung B', p. 140: report 28 October 1914.

28 Bundesarchiv, Abteilungen Potsdam (BA Potsdam), 07.01, 2465/3, fol. 6: Chancellor to *Statthalter* von Dallwitz, undated, apparently not sent, probably late August 1914.

29 E.g. Bayerisches Hauptstaatsarchiv, Abt. IV Kriegsarchiv (KA) Munich, HS 3411/1, war diary Major-General von Clauss, 3 August 1914.

30 BA Potsdam, 07.01, 2465/3, fol. 45: von Wandel, War Ministry, to Chancellor, Chief of General Staff, etc., 11 December 1914. On Landtag members Zimmer and Weber, see fol. 21: Chancellor at GHQ to Reichskanzlei Berlin, 23 September 1914. On the notables in Upper Alsace, cf. HStA-MA Stuttgart, M30/1-89, Armee-Oberkommando B: 'Kurzer Bericht' p. 2.

31 Evidence for this comes from a wide variety of sources: *Vorwärts*, 2 September 1914; Rossé *et al.*, *Das Elsaß*, vol. I, p. 238; Archives du Ministère des Affaires Etrangères, Paris, (MAE) Film P1463, vol. MXCVII, pp. 101–2 (report by Alsatian woman, 20 August 1914); HStA-MA Stuttgart, M1/7-20, extradition list, 17 February 1920; Anon., *Wie die Elsass-Lothringer während des Krieges behandelt werden* (n.p., n.d., (1918)), in HStA-MA Stuttgart, M30/1-89.

32 KA Munich, HS 2373, 'Die Augusttage von 1914 in Weiler' – diary Emilie Dietz.

33 HStA-MA Stuttgart, M660, Gleich papers, 'Meine Erlebnisse im Feldzug 1914', 4–5 August, Book 153, pp. 10–13.

34 BA-MA Freiburg, PHD7/60, 'Verhalten', p. 17.

35 *Ibid.*, p. 18.

36 Cf. Helmuth von Moltke, *The Franco-German War of 1870–71* (1891; English translation, London and Novato, CA: Greenhill, 1992), pp. 167–72.

37 Cf. BA-MA Freiburg, PHD7/60, 'Verhalten', p. 16.

38 HStA-MA Stuttgart, M30/1-89, Armee-Oberkommando B: 'Kurzer Bericht', pp. 7–13.

39 *Ibid.*

40 Hiery, *Reichstagswahlen*, p. 41.

41 Wehler, 'Unfähig zur Verfassungsreform', pp. 51–6.

42 Language map in Rossé *et al.*, *Das Elsaß*, vol. IV, p. 16; table 94, p. 198.

43 BA Potsdam, 07.01, 2465/3, fol. 22: press cuttings 29 September and 8 October 1914.

44 *Saargemünder Zeitung*, 29 September 1914.

45 *Straßburger Post*, 7 October 1914.

46 BA-MA Freiburg, N21/1, 'Erinnerungen', p. 62.

47 Rossé *et al.*, *Das Elsaß*, vol. I, pp. 301 and 326. There may have been as

many as 36,000 Alsace-Lorraine citizens who moved to France in the war (Schmidt, *Die geheimen Pläne*, p. 10).

48 BA-MA Freiburg, PHD7/60, 'Verhalten', pp. 56–7.

49 Rossé *et al.*, *Das Elsaß*, vol. I, p. 295. This is a minimum, since the authors were anxious to stress the Alsatians' loyalty to Germany.

50 E.g. Generallandesarchiv (GLA) Karlsruhe, 456-F8-66, Bezirkskommando I Mülhausen to 14th Army Corps, n.d. (June 1917).

51 HStA-MA Stuttgart, M30/1-89, Armee-Oberkommando B: 'Kurzer Bericht', preface and p. 1.

52 GLA Karlsruhe, 456-F8-65, Bezirkskommando I Mülhausen to 14th Army Corps, 19 June 1917.

53 HStA-MA Stuttgart, M30/1-107, Armee-Abteilung Falkenhausen to 15th Army Corps, 26 August 1915. No figure is given, but the 'very high number' included those who refused to return to Germany and those who left the Reich before or during their call-up.

54 GLA Karlsruhe, 456-F8-65, v. Wrisberg, War Ministry to 15th Army Corps, 31 August 1915. The area was that bounded by Donon–Haslach–Oberehnheim–Schlettstadt–Kestenholz–Leber au–Markirch.

55 E.g. ADBR Strasbourg, AL87 5633, 2 July 1915, Bierot; *ibid.*, 23 March 1916, Bantze.

56 E.g. *ibid.*, *passim*. Cf. the results of postal control in HStA-MA Stuttgart, M30/1-20, 21, 73, 106, 107, etc.

57 BA-MA Freiburg, PHD7/60, 'Verhalten', pp. 55–6. However, no absolute figures are cited, and the proportions given may therefore be the result of statistical manipulation. Missing Alsace-Lorraine soldiers were no doubt more likely to be regarded as deserters than others. It seems to have been assumed that there were only 125,000 Alsace-Lorraine soldiers. According to another estimate, no fewer than 3,465 Alsace-Lorraine men had deserted from Army Department B alone by the end of 1916 (BA-MA Freiburg, N559/16, 'Denkschrift der Armee-Abteilung B', p. 165).

58 HStA-MA Stuttgart, M30/1-77, calculated from reports by Quartermaster-General at GHQ and Army Group Duke Albrecht. These figures are incomplete and provisional. Further statistics for October 1915 to November 1917, in M30/1-117, 106 and 107, *passim*. On deserters see the forthcoming dissertation by Christoph Jahr, Freie Universität, Berlin.

59 The 14th and 16th Army Corps, 14th Reserve Army Corps, Department von Bodungen, and Army Department von Falkenhausen. BA-MA Freiburg, PHD7/60, 'Verhalten', pp. 47–8.

60 *Ibid.*, p. 50, citing War Ministry to army commands, 13 March 1915.

61 Cf. Dominik Richert, *Beste Gelegenheit zum Sterben. Meine Erlebnisse im Kriege 1914–1918* (Munich: Knesebeck and Schuler, 1989), pp. 98–289, *passim*.

62 *Ibid.*, p. 88.

63 *Ibid.*, p. 91.

64 HStA-MA Stuttgart, M30/1-117, 10th Army Corps to 4th Army, 20 June 1918.

65 Richert, *Beste Gelegenheit*, pp. 20–1.

66 *Ibid.*, p. 38.

67 *Ibid.*, p. 42.

68 *Ibid.*, pp. 224–5.

69 E.g. HStA-MA Stuttgart, M30/1-21, Bride, 22 April 1918.

70 BA-MA Freiburg, PHD7/60, 'Verhalten', pp. 42–6.

71 HStA-MA Stuttgart, M30/1-106, Army Department A to Army Group Herzog Albrecht, 26 December 1917; *ibid.*, 21, Bride, 22 April 1918.

72 *Ibid.*, Army Department C to Army Group Herzog Albrecht, 14 August 1917. Cf. HStA-MA Stuttgart, M30/1-107, War Ministry to army commands, 4 July 1917.

73 BA-MA Freiburg, PHD7/60, 'Verhalten'.

74 HStA-MA Stuttgart, M30/1-107, War Ministry to army commands, 4 July, and press release 15th Army Corps, Strasbourg, 7 July 1917.

75 HStA-MA Stuttgart, M30/1-106, War Ministry to all army commands, etc., 30 January 1917.

76 *Ibid.*, 201st Infantry Division to Gruppe Metz, 22 December 1917.

77 HStA-MA Stuttgart, M30/1-117, 1st Garde-Reserve-Division 14 July, 6th Army to Gruppe Queant, 31 July and 10 August, 6th Army to Gruppe Vimy, 11 August 1917.

78 *Ibid.*, Infantry Regiment 403, 19 December 1917.

79 HStA-MA Stuttgart, M30/1-106, Army Group Duke Albrecht to OHL Operations Department, 28 December 1917. The Army Group Duke Albrecht formally became responsible for centralizing all material on Alsace-Lorraine by a decree of the Prussian War Ministry of 21 June 1918. I am grateful to Christoph Jahr for pointing this out. However, the idea was proposed on 1 May – cf. HStA-MA Stuttgart, M30/1-117, War Ministry to 15th Army Corps, and it was sent material dating back to mid-1917.

80 *Ibid.*, Army Department A to Army Group Duke Albrecht, 26 December 1917.

81 GLA Karlsruhe, 456-F8-65, War Ministry, 12 January 1918.

82 HStA-MA Stuttgart, M30/1-106, von Stein, War Ministry to Army Group Duke Albrecht, 23 August 1917.

83 Spahn, *Elsaß-Lothringen*, p. 363. On the plans see Wehler, 'Unfähig zur Verfassungsreform', pp. 56–60. Many of the plans are printed in Schmidt, *Die geheimen Pläne*, which also summarizes the press debate on the plans, pp. 8–14.

84 HStA-MA Stuttgart, M30/1-106, Geheime Feldpolizei Dendermonde, 22 October 1917, to Geh. Feldpolizei 4th Army.

85 Schmidt, *Die geheimen Pläne*, pp. 181–2.

86 Fritz Fischer, *Germany's Aims in the First World War* (1961; English translation, London: Chatto and Windus, 1967), pp. 342–63. Minutes of the Bingen conference on 15–16 June 1917 in Schmidt, *Die geheimen Pläne*, pp. 23–93.

87 K. Epstein, *Matthias Erzberger und das Dilemma der deutschen Demokratie* (Frankfurt-am-Main: Ullstein, 1976), pp. 134–6.

88 Dietrich Schäfer, *Das Reichsland* (Berlin: Grote, 1917), p. 115. Cf. also Lujo Brentano, *Elsässer Erinnerungen* (Berlin: Reiß, 1917); Kautsky, *Elsaß-Lothringen*, p. 74.

89 BA Potsdam, W-10/50366. The memorandum was written in March 1918. This is incorrectly entitled 'Abschrift der Stellungnahme von Generalfeld-

marschall Hindenburg', but the marginal comments are signed 'W', and style and content clearly indicate that the author was the Kaiser.

90 HStA-MA Stuttgart, M30/1-107, Chief of General Staff, 1 February 1918, to Chancellor.

91 HStA-MA Stuttgart, M30/1-73, War Ministry decree, 20 October 1917; *ibid.*, Postüberwachung XV. Armeekorps, 27 February 1918.

92 HStA-MA Stuttgart, M30/1-107, Postüberwachungsstelle Mülhausen to XIV. Armeekorps, 13 April 1918.

93 *Ibid.*, Kalbert, 1 April 1918.

94 HStA-MA Stuttgart, M30/1-106, Ludendorff to Army Group Duke Albrecht and all ministries of war, 28 February 1918.

95 *Ibid.*, Ludendorff to Oberbefehlshaber Ost, all Army Groups, etc., 8 March 1917.

96 HStA-MA Stuttgart, M30/1-117, 2nd Army to Army Group Duke Albrecht, 21 June 1918; 107th Infantry Division [to 2nd Army?], 15 June; 10th Reserve Corps to 4th Army, 20 June.

97 *Ibid.*, Chief of General Staff, Army Group Duke Albrecht to Quartermaster-General, GHQ, 31 March 1918.

98 Richert, *Beste Gelegenheit*, editorial postcript, p. 385.

99 HStA-MA Stuttgart, M30/1-117, 5th Army to 84th Infantry Division on 21 April 1918; reply by 84th Infantry Regiment, 24 April.

100 BA-MA Freiburg, Deimling papers, N559/v. 29: *Straßburger Post*, 4 October 1917. See Christoph Jahr, 'Berthold von Deimling: Vom General zum Pazifisten. Eine biographische Skizze', in *Zeitschrift für die Geschichte des Oberrheins*, 142, 1994, pp. 359–87.

101 BA-MA Freiburg, N559/v. 29, Deimling to Hindenburg, 2 November 1917.

102 *Ibid.*, 22 June 1918.

103 HStA-MA Stuttgart, M30/1-117, 46th Landwehr Division to Army Group Duke Albrecht, 24 July 1918.

104 *Ibid.*, 107th Infantry Division [to 2nd Army?] 15 June 1918.

105 *Ibid.*, 29 June 1918.

106 *Ibid.*, 20 June 1918.

107 *Ibid.*, 19 July 1918.

108 HStA-MA Stuttgart, M30/1-107, Eschmann, mid-March 1918.

109 HStA-MA Stuttgart, M30/1-106, Akten Beverloo.

110 HStA-MA Stuttgart, M30/1-21, Heitz, 3 June 1918.

111 *Ibid.*, Botems, 16 August; Ancel, 29 August; Wantz, 12 September 1918.

112 *Ibid.*, War Ministry to Army Group Duke Albrecht, 26 June 1918.

113 *Ibid.*, Ludendorff to Army Group Duke Albrecht, 9 September 1918, reproduced by the Heeresgruppe and sent to the divisions. Extracts from such letters in *ibid.*, Postüberwachungsstelle Hagenau, 19 June 1918.

114 *Ibid.*, Chief of Staff, Army Group Duke Albrecht to Quartermaster-General, 18 September 1918.

115 HStA-MA Stuttgart, M30/1-89, Chief of Staff, Army Group Duke Albrecht to OHL, Military-Political Department, 10 October 1918. This self-serving report seems to have been intended to absolve the Army Group of blame for the impending loss of Alsace-Lorraine by claiming it had argued for a more liberal and less repressive regime.

116 *Ibid.*
117 *Ibid.*, Army Group Duke Albrecht [probably] to OHL, 11 October 1918.
118 Wehler, 'Unfähig zur Verfassungsreform', p. 58.
119 BA-MA Freiburg, N559/v. 29, Hindenburg to Deimling, 8 October 1917.
120 HStA-MA Stuttgart, M30/1-91, Minutes of meeting in Berlin, 2 November 1917. Also present were Minister of the Interior Wallraf, Minister of Finance Helfferich, Foreign Secretary Kühlmann, Chancellor Hertling, Hindenburg and Ludendorff.

8   DISCIPLINE AND MORALE IN THE BRITISH ARMY, 1917–1918

1 W. Robertson, *Soldiers and Statesmen*, 2 vols. (London: Cassell, 1926), vol. I, p. 283.
2 See T. Travers, *The Killing Ground: the British Army, the Western Front and the Emergence of Modern Warfare 1900–1918* (London: Routledge, 1987).
3 I. Hamilton, *The Soul and Body of An Army* (London: Edward Arnold, 1921) p. 209.
4 E. John Solano (ed.), *Drill and Field Training* (London: John Murray, 1914), p. 8.
5 H. R. Sandilands, *The 23rd Division 1914–1919* (Edinburgh: William Blackwood, 1925), pp. 58–9; E. Wyrall, *The History of the 62nd (West Riding) Division 1914–1919*, 2 vols. (London: John Lane, 1924–5), vol. I, p. 67; J. H. Boraston and E. O. Bax, *The Eighth Division in War, 1914–1918* (London: The Medici Society, 1926), p. 56.
6 D. Hannay, 'Conscript Armies', *The Edinburgh Review*, 230, 1919, pp. 56–7.
7 J. H. Boraston (ed.), *Sir Douglas Haig's Despatches* (London: J. M. Dent, 1919), p. 347.
8 On Austrian and German methods, see the contributions to this volume by Mark Cornwall and Wilhelm Deist.
9 See I. L. Child, 'Morale: A Bibliographical Review', *Psychological Review*, 38, 1941, and I. McLaine, *Ministry of Morale, Home Front Morale and the Ministry of Information in World War II* (London: Allen and Unwin, 1979), pp. 7–11.
10 E. Campion Vaughan, *Some Desperate Glory: The Diary of a Young Officer, 1917* (London: 1982; Macmillan Papermac edn, 1984), p. 121; SS 408, *Some of the Many Questions a Platoon Commander should ask himself on taking over a Trench and at intervals afterwards* (General Staff, 1916). See too, E. Wyrall, *The Die-Hards in the Great War*, 2 vols. (London: Harrison and Sons, 1926), vol. I, pp. 319–20.
11 SS 143, *Instruction for the Training of Platoons for Offensive Action* (General Staff, 1917), p. 12.
12 See, for example, Public Record Office, London (PRO) WO 71/669, court-martial of no. 204232 Pte. Robert Young, 11th Worc., Regt, September 1918.
13 Vaughan, *Some Desperate Glory*, pp. 78, 181, 219–220; G. Seton, *Footslogger* (London: Hutchinson, 1934), pp. 207–8; Imperial War Museum (IWM),

Maxse Papers, 69/53/6, 'Notes on a Conference', 4 August 1915; H. Gough, *The Fifth Army* (London: Hodder and Stoughton, 1934), pp. 243, 247–8.

14 See Vaughan, *Some Desperate Glory*, pp. 25, 126, 141, 147; Major-General J. Vaughan to Sir Ivor Maxse, 9 August 1918, IWM, Maxse Papers, 69/53/11; also D. Englander and J. Osborne, 'Jack, Tommy and Henry Dubb: the Armed Forces and the Working Class', *Historical Journal*, 21, 1978, p. 603.

15 'The Platoon Commander', IWM, Maxse Papers, 69/53/14.

16 See J. G. Fuller, *Troop Morale and Popular Culture in the British and Dominion Armies, 1914–1918* (Oxford: Clarendon Press, 1990), pp. 81 ff.; I. Beckett and K. Simpson (eds.), *A Nation in Arms, A Social Study of the British Army in the First World War* (Manchester: Manchester University Press, 1985), pp. 24–5.

17 C. Falls, *The History of the 36th (Ulster) Division* (Belfast: M'Caw Stevenson and Orr, 1922), pp. 135–7.

18 Sandilands, *23rd Division*, pp. 163–4; Vaughan, *Some Desperate Glory*, p. 106; Fuller, *Troop Morale*, p. 102.

19 Boraston and Bax, *Eighth Division in War*, pp. 8–9.

20 Solano, *Drill and Field Training*, p. 4.

21 Hamilton, *Soul of an Army*, p. 120.

22 PRO WO 32/5461, Haig to Secretary, War Office, 2 June 1919.

23 M. Messerschmidt, 'German Military Law in the Second World War', in W. Deist (ed.), *The German Military in the Age of Total War* (Leamington: Berg, 1985), p. 324.

24 See W. Moore, *The Thin Yellow Line* (London: Leo Cooper, 1974); A. Babington, *For the Sake of Example* (London: Leo Cooper, 1983); J. Putkowski and J. Sykes, *Shot at Dawn* (Barnsley: Wharncliffe Publishing, 1989).

25 M. Weber, 'Bureaucracy and Politics', in G. Roth and C. Wittich (eds.), *Economy and Society: An Outline of Interpretive Sociology by Max Weber*, 2 vols. (Berkeley and London: University of California Press, 1978), vol. I, p. 1393.

26 See, for example, C. Pugsley, *On the Fringe of Hell: New Zealanders and Military Discipline in the First World War* (Auckland: Hodder and Stoughton, 1991), p. 132.

27 On mismanagement of the records relating to the BEF by the director of the official war history in collusion with the cabinet secretariat, see D. Winter, *Haig's Command* (Harmondsworth: Penguin Books, 1992), pp. 225–61.

28 Cf. R. H. Ahrenfeldt, *Psychiatry in the British Army in the Second World War* (London: Routledge, 1958), p. 273.

29 J. Keegan, *The Face of Battle* (London: Jonathan Cape, 1976), pp. 270–2; A. Farrar-Hockley, *Goughie: the Life of General Sir Hubert Gough* (London: Hart Davis MacGibbon, 1975); M. Middlebrook, *The Kaiser's Battle* (London: Allen Lane, 1978); J. Toland, *No Man's Land: The Story of 1918* (London: Methuen, 1980).

30 Appendices to 5th Army War Diaries, 1917–18, PRO WO 95/524–5.

31 Hardie Papers, IWM, 'Report on Complaints, Moral etc.', 5 December 1916, p. 6.

32 *Ibid.*, pp. 10–11.

33 PRO WO 95/524-5, 5th Army Routine Orders March–July, 1917; Englander and Osborne, 'Jack, Tommy and Henry Dubb', p. 601.
34 Hardie Papers, 'Report on Complaints, Moral etc.', 23 November 1916, p. 4; D. Englander, 'The French Soldier 1914–1918', *French History* , 1, 1987, p. 62.
35 Hardie Papers, 'Report on Moral etc.', III, May, 1917, p. 10.
36 Hardie Papers, 'Report on Complaints, Moral etc.', 23 November 1916, p. 12.
37 Hardie Papers, 'Report on Moral etc.', III, May 1917, para. 2.
38 Hardie Papers, 'Report on Moral etc.', III, February, 1917, pp. 6–7.
39 Hardie Papers, 'Report on Moral etc.', IV, 25 August 1917, p. 3.
40 Hardie Papers, 'Report on Peace', V, 19 November 1917, pp. 1–2.
41 *Ibid.*, p. 4.
42 Falls, *History of 36th (Ulster) Division*, pp. 178–9.
43 See, for example, Maxse Papers, 69/53/11, Hewlett to Maxse, 18 July 1918.
44 Figures from Putkowski and Sykes, *Shot at Dawn*.
45 D. Englander, 'Military Intelligence and the Defence of the Realm: the Surveillance of Soldiers and Civilians in Britain during the First World War', *Bulletin of the Society for the Study of Labour History*, 52, 1, 1987, pp. 24–32.
46 On military unrest see Englander and Osborne, 'Jack, Tommy and Henry Dubb', pp. 593–621; G. Dallas and D. Gill, *The Unknown Army: Mutinies in the British Army in World War I* (London: Verso, 1985); S. P. Mackenzie, *Politics and Military Morale. Current Affairs and Citizenship Education in the British Army 1914–1950* (Oxford: Clarendon Press, 1992), p. 13; on political propaganda in the 16th Division, see PRO Cab 45/140, Gough to Edmonds, 3 May 1941.
47 E. Ludendorff, *The General Staff and its Problems: The History of the Relations between the High Command and the German Imperial Government as recorded by Official Documents*, 2 vols. (London: Hutchinson, 1920) vol. II, pp. 385–400.
48 PRO WO 95/2706, Memorandum of Sir John French, November 1915.
49 Boraston (ed.), *Despatches*, p. 342. See also Mackenzie, *Politics and Military Morale*, pp. 6–7.
50 On the YMCA's role in army education, see Ministry of Reconstruction, *Final Report of the Adult Education Committee*, Cmd 321 (1919), pp. 336–50.
51 F. Maurice, *Life of General Lord Rawlinson of Trent* (London: Cassell, 1928), pp. 184–5.
52 The campaign, which involved lectures and addresses dealing with labour unrest and cognate matters, can be traced in the Air I materials at the Public Record Office. I am grateful to Dr Nicholas Hiley for this point. On preparations for citizenship education, see Mackenzie, *Politics and Military Morale*, pp. 16–31.
53 ABCA (Army Bureau of Current Affairs) was the organization which provided political and civic instruction for British troops during the Second World War.
54 Monk Gibbon, *Inglorious Soldier* (London: Hutchinson, 1968), p. 248; L. Macdonald, *They Called It Passchendaele* (London: Michael Joseph, 1978), p. 64; H. Butler, *Confident Morning* (London: Faber, 1949), p. 122; D. Briscoe (ed.), *Brigadier General Sir Archibald Home, The Diary of a World*

War I Cavalry Officer (London: Costeiio, 1985), p. 171; Falls, *The History of the 36th (Ulster) Division*, p. 71.

55 Gibbon, *Inglorious Soldier*, p. 333; SS 143, *Instruction for the Training of Platoons for Offensive Action* (General Staff, 1917), p. 12. Quotation from E. Wyrall, *The History of the 62nd (West Riding) Division, 1914–1919* (London: Bodley Head, 1925), p. 60.

56 See Maxse Papers 69/53/11, paper by Sir Hubert Gough, General Officer Commanding 5th Army, 2 September 1917. 'Notes on Inspection, August to October 1918', and useful discussion in E. K. G. Sixsmith, *British Generalship in the Twentieth Century* (London: Armour Press, 1973).

57 Attempts to liberalize allotments, improve monitoring procedures and overcome officer resistance were undertaken at the beginning of 1918. Ironically, the implementation of these policies was subsequently upheld as a critical weakening influence in the 5th Army where, on 21 March 1918, 70,000 men were on leave. On liberalization, see, PRO WO 95/527, 5th Army Routine Orders (1874), 2 January 1918; Routine Orders (1955), 14 February 1918; and Routine Orders (1978), 19 February 1918. On rationale and extent of leave, see W. Shaw Sparrow, *The Fifth Army in March 1918* (London: Bodley Head, third edn, 1923), p. 300.

9 REMOBILIZING THE CITIZEN-SOLDIER THROUGH THE FRENCH ARMY MUTINIES OF 1917

1 This explanation originated with the senior command itself, as shown below. Anglophone historians, more concerned than French historians with 1940, continued to emphasize this view. See J. Williams, *Mutiny 1917* (London: William Heinemann, 1962) and R. M. Watt, *Dare Call it Treason* (New York: Simon and Schuster, 1963).

2 G. Pedroncini, *Les Mutineries de 1917* (Paris: Presses Universitaires de France, 1967).

3 J. Keegan, 'An Army Downs Tools: Mutiny in the First World War: Theory and the Poor Bloody Infantry', *Times Literary Supplement*, 13 May 1994. This is a frequently cranky, but not actually unfavourable, review of the author's book *Between Mutiny and Obedience: The Case of the French Fifth Infantry Division during World War I* (Princeton: Princeton University Press, 1994).

4 See M. Howard, *Clausewitz* (Oxford: Oxford University Press, 1983).

5 A cross-section of this terminology may be found in 'Mutineries de 1917 et incidents', Grand Quartier Général, 1e Bureau, Service Historique de l'Armée de Terre, Château de Vincennes (hereafter referred to as SHA), 16 N 298. Unless otherwise noted, all translations from documents in this archive are my own.

6 Pedroncini, *Les Mutineries de 1917*, pp. 135–42.

7 'Rapport du Capitaine Victor Jean, commandant la 9e compagnie au chef de bataillon commandant le 109e RI sur les événements de la nuit du 1er au 2 juin 1917', in G. Pedroncini (ed.), *1917: les mutineries de l'armée française* (Paris: Julliard, Collection 'Archives' no. 35, 1968), p. 177.

8 See Pedroncini, *Les Mutineries de 1917*, pp. 183–5.

9 'Le général Féraud commandant le 1er CC à Monsieur le général

commandant la IIIe Armée', 1er Corps de Cavalerie, Etat-Major no. 3560, 1 June 1917, in Pedroncini (ed.), *1917: les mutineries*, pp. 229–31.

10 Pedroncini, *Les Mutineries de 1917*, pp. 159–62. See also Pedroncini (ed.), *1917: les mutineries*, pp. 180–2.

11 SHA, 16 N 298, 'Note aux Groupes d'Armées et Armées', GQG des Armées du Nord et du Nord-Est, Etat-Major, 1e Bureau, 11 June 1917.

12 SHA, 19 N 277, 'Réponse à la Note du GAC en date du 30 juin 1917', 16 July 1917, IIe Armée, 1er Bureau.

13 Pedroncini, *Les Mutineries de 1917*, pp. 194, 215.

14 SHA, 16 N 1522, Télégramme chiffré, général commandant en chef à l'Etat-Major, no. 2.433 et 2.434, 8 June 1917, in GQG, 2e Bureau, Service Spécial Morale.

15 Smith, *Between Mutiny and Obedience*, p. 211.

16 *Ibid.*, p. 210. Pedroncini estimated a figure of 10 per cent for the army as a whole (*1917: les mutineries*, p. 236).

17 See Pedroncini, *Les Mutineries de 1917*, pp. 183–231.

18 Smith, *Between Mutiny and Obedience*, pp. 212–14.

19 Télégramme chiffré, 8 June 1917.

20 See Smith, *Between Mutiny and Obedience*, pp. 204–5.

21 Untitled report, GQG, Etat-Major, 3e Bureau, no. 18022, 19 May 1917, in Pedroncini (ed.), *1917: les mutineries*, p. 260.

22 SHA, 18 N 298, 'Bulletin confidentiel no. 2, Résumant la situation morale aux armées dans la semaine du 9 au 15 juillet 1917', 15 July 1917, in Group des Armées de l'Est, 1e Bureau.

23 See L. V. Smith, 'Confronting Mutiny: French Generals, Spring 1917', in H. Cecil and P. Liddle (eds.), *Facing Armageddon: The First World War Experienced* (London: Leo Cooper, 1996), pp. 79–92.

24 Quoted in Pedroncini, *Les Mutineries de 1917*, p. 282.

25 SHA, 18 N 37, 'Le Général de Division Franchet d'Esperey commandant le Groupe d'Armées du Nord à M. le général commandant en chef (SRA)', no. 9,426, 13 June 1917.

26 SHA, 6 N 53 (Fonds Clemenceau) 'Le Général Commandant en Chef à Monsieur le Ministre de la Guerre', GQG des Armées du Nord et Nord-Est, Cabinet, no. 28.042, 29 May 1917.

27 SHA, 19 N 1037, 'Le Général Commandant en Chef à Monsieur le Ministre de la Guerre (Cabinet) à Paris', 23 August 1917, in VIe Armée, 2e Bureau.

28 'Le Général Commandant en Chef à Monsieur le Ministre de la Guerre', 29 May 1917.

29 SHA, 18 N 37, 'Le Général de Division Franchet d'Esperey, Commandant le Groupe d'Armées du Nord au Général Commandant en Chef (Cabinet)', no. 9.154, 10 June 1917, in Groupe des Armées du Nord, 1e Bureau.

30 Watt, *Dare Call it Treason*, p. 186.

31 'Le général Taufflieb commandant le 37e CA à Monsieur le général commandant la VIe Armée', 37e CA, Etat-Major, 1er Bureau, no. 1071/C, in Pedroncini (ed.), *1917: les mutineries*, p. 181.

32 SHA, 19 N 1093, untitled response dated 30 May to report by 3rd Army Corp commander General Lebrun on the mutinies in the 36th and 129th Regiments, in VIe Armée, 3e Bureau.

33 On the origins of this tension see K. M. Baker, *Inventing the French Revolution: Essays on French Political Culture in the Eighteenth Century* (New York: Cambridge University Press, 1990).

34 I. Woloch, *The New Regime: Transformations of the French Civic Order, 1789–1820s* (New York: W. W. Norton, 1994), p. 433.

35 R. D. Challener, *The French Theory of the Nation in Arms: 1866–1939* (New York: Columbia University Press, 1955), p. 4.

36 J. Jolinon, 'La Mutinerie de Cœuvres', *Mercure de France*, 15 August 1920, p. 82.

37 See M. Perrot, *Workers on Strike: France, 1871–1890* (1984; abridged English translation by C. Turner *et al.*, New Haven: Yale University Press, 1987).

38 Quoted in Smith, *Between Mutiny and Obedience*, p. 194 (author's italics).

39 Untitled report, IIIe Armée, 2e Bureau, 2 June 1917, in Pedroncini (ed.), *1917: les mutineries*, p. 69.

40 'Rapport du Capitaine Victor Jean', *ibid.*, pp. 174–5.

41 Quoted in Smith, *Between Mutiny and Obedience*, p. 192.

42 Untitled report, IIIe Armée, Etat-Major, 2e Bureau, Service de Renseignements, 2 June 1917, quoted in Pedroncini (ed.), *1917: les mutineries*, p. 68.

43 Quoted in Smith, *Between Mutiny and Obedience*, p. 188.

44 Pedroncini, *Les Mutineries de 1917*, p. 150.

45 Quoted in *ibid.*, p. 125.

46 SHA, 19 N 305, confiscated letter from J. B. to 'Monsieur Pugliesi-Conti, Député', undated but postmarked 31 May 1917, IIe Armée, 1e Bureau.

47 SHA, 16 N 1418, 'Compte-Rendu' (Postal Censors, 5th Division), 20 June 1917, GQG, 2e Bureau, SRA, Contrôle Postal, VIe Armée.

48 Pedroncini, *Les Mutineries de 1917*, pp. 128–9.

49 Smith, *Between Mutiny and Obedience*, p. 194.

50 *Ibid.*, pp. 201–3.

51 'Le Général de division Guillaumat à Monsieur le général commandant en chef', IIe Armée, Etat Major, 1er Bureau, no. 7895/J, 15 July 1917, in Pedroncini (ed.), *1917: les mutineries*, pp. 203–8.

10   THE GERMAN ARMY, THE AUTHORITARIAN NATION-STATE AND TOTAL WAR

1 See Kuno Graf Westarp, *Das Ende der Monarchie am 9 November 1918* (ed. W. Conze), (Stollhamm: Helmut Rauschenbach, 1952), p. 46.

2 G. Krumeich, 'Verdun: Ein Ort gemeinsamer Erinnerung', in H. Möller (ed.), *Deutsch-französisches Lesebuch* (forthcoming).

3 See H.-U. Wehler, *The German Empire, 1871–1918* (1973; English translation, Leamington Spa: Berg, 1985), pp. 62 ff. See also the stimulating article by G. Schramm, 'Militarisierung und Demokratisierung. Typen der Massenintegration im Ersten Weltkrieg', in 'Forschungen zur westeuropäischen Geschichte', *Francia*, 3, 1975, pp. 476–97. I feel, however, that his comments on the Third High Command might need further nuances.

4 G. Ritter, *The Schlieffen Plan. Critique of a Myth* (1956; London: Wolff, 1958); S. Förster, *Der doppelte Militarismus. Die deutsche Heeresrüstungspolitik zwischen Status-quo-Sicherung und Aggression 1890–1913* (Wiesbaden: Steiner,

1985); and S. Förster, 'Der deutsche Generalstab und die Illusion des kurzen Krieges 1871–1914. Metakritik eines Mythos', *Militärgeschichtliche Mitteilungen*, 54, 1995, pp. 61–l95.

5   W. Petter, 'Der Kompromiß zwischen Militär und Gesellschaft im kaiserlichen Deutschland', in *Revue d'Allemagne*, 11, 1979, pp. 346 ff.; W. Deist, *Militär, Staat und Gesellschaft. Studien zur preußisch-deutschen Militärgeschichte* (Munich: Oldenbourg, 1991), pp. 19 ff., 103 ff.

6   Deist, *Militär, Staat und Gesellschaft*, pp. 113 ff.; see also D. Schoenbaum, *Zabern 1913. Consensus Politics in Imperial Germany* (London: Allen and Unwin, 1982).

7   W. Mommsen, 'Die latente Krise des Wilhelminischen Reiches. Staat und Gesellschaft in Deutschland 1890–1914', in W. Mommsen, *Der autoritäre Nationalstaat. Verfassung, Gesellschaft und Kultur im deutschen Kaiserreich* (Frankfurt-am-Main: Fischer, 1990), p. 295.

8   Förster, *Der doppelte Militarismus*; V. R. Berghahn and W. Deist (eds.), *Rüstung im Zeichen der wilhelminischen Weltpolitik. Grundlegende Dokumente 1890–1914* (Düsseldorf: Droste, 1988).

9   Förster, *Der doppelte Militarismus*, pp. 208 ff.

10 Letter from Falkenhayn to Bethmann Hollweg, 8 July 1914, in Berghahn and Deist (eds.), *Rüstung im Zeichen der wilhelminischen Weltpolitik*, pp. 418 ff.

11 See the summarizing article by G. Krumeich, 'L'Entrée en guerre en Allemagne', in J.-J. Becker and S. Audoin-Rouzeau (eds.), *Les Sociétés européennes et la guerre de 1914–1918* (Paris: Publications de l'Université de Nanterre, 1990), pp. 65–74; J. T. Verhey, 'The "Spirit of 1914". The Myth of Enthusiasm and the Rhetoric of Unity in World War I Germany' (University of California at Berkeley: Ph.D. thesis, 1991); W. Kruse, *Krieg und nationale Integration. Eine Neuinterpreation des sozialdemokratischen Burgfriedensschlusses 1914–15* (Essen: Klartext, 1993); B. Ziemann, 'Zum ländlichen Augusterlebnis 1914 in Deutschland', in B. Loewenstein (ed.), *Geschichte und Psychologie. Annährungsversuche* (Pfaffenweiler: Centaurus, 1992), pp. 193–203.

12 See B. Ulrich, 'Kriegsfreiwillige. Motivationen, Erfahrungen, Wirkungen', in *August 1914. Ein Volk zieht in den Krieg* (Berlin: Berliner Geschichtswerkstatt, 1989), pp. 232 ff., and the press reports quoted therein.

13 For Bethmann Hollweg's political course, see F. Fischer, *Germany's Aims in the First World War* (1961; English translation, London: Chatto and Windus, 1967), pp. 95–119; W. J. Mommsen, '1914: The Topos of Inevitable War', in V. R. Berghahn and M. Kitchen (eds.), *Germany in the Age of Total War* (London: Croom Helm, 1981), pp. 23–45; and the letter of the Prussian Minister of War, 25 July 1914, reprinted in W. Deist (ed.), *Militär und Innenpolitik im Weltkrieg 1914–1918*, 2 vols. (Düsseldorf: Droste, 1970), vol. I, no. 77, pp. 188–92.

14 Deist (ed.), *Militär und Innenpolitik*, no. 78, pp. 192–3, no. 79, pp. 193–4, and no. 81, pp. 196–7.

15 *Schulthess' Europäischer Geschichtskalender, Neue Folge* 30, 1, 1914, p. 382.

16 A. Kramer, ' "Greueltaten". Zum Problem der deutschen Kriegsverbrechen in Belgien und Frankreich 1914', in G. Hirschfeld and G. Krumeich in collaboration with I. Renz, *"Keiner fühlt sich hier mehr als Mensch . . ."*

Erlebnis und Wirkung des Ersten Weltkriegs (Essen: Klartext, 1993), pp. 85–114; and especially S. Remus, 'Das "Franc-tireur-Problem" im sundgau während der 1. und 2. Schlacht um Mülhausen im Elsaß, August 1914. Zum Verhältnis zwischen Militär und Zivilbevölkerung' (M.A. thesis, University of Freiburg, 1994).

17 Förster, 'Der deutsche Generalstab'.

18 See documents in B. Ulrich and B. Ziemann (eds.), *Frontalltag im Ersten Weltkrieg. Wahn und Wirklichkeit. Quellen und Dokumente* (Frankfurt: Fischer, 1995), pp. 50 ff.; K. Unruh, *Langemarck. Legende und Wirklichkeit* (Koblenz: Bernard and Graefe, 1986).

19 Deist (ed.), *Militär und Innenpolitik*, no. 85, pp. 202–4, and no. 81, pp. 196–7.

20 *Ibid.*, no. 78, fn. 6.

21 *Ibid.*, no. 86.

22 See K. Riezler, *Tagebücher. Aufsätze. Dokumente* (ed. with introduction by K. D. Erdmann), (Göttingen: Vandenhoeck and Ruprecht, 1972), p. 183.

23 B. Ulrich, 'Die Desillusionierung der Kriegsfreiwilligen von 1914', in W. Wette (ed.), *Der Krieg des kleinen Mannes. Eine Militärgeschichte von unten* (Munich: Piper, 1992), pp. 110 ff.; Unruh, *Langemarck*; K. Schwabe and R. Reichardt with R. Hauf (eds.), *Gerhard Ritter. Ein politischer Historiker in seinen Briefen* (Boppard: Boldt, 1984), pp. 200 ff. (letter of 7 March 1915); W. Deist, 'Le Moral des troupes allemandes sur le front occidental à la fin de l'année 1916', in J.-J. Becker, J. Winter, G. Krumeich, A. Becker and S. Audoin-Rouzeau (eds.), *Guerre et cultures 1914–1918* (Paris: A. Colin, 1994), pp. 91–102 (esp. 93 ff.).

24 Deist (ed.), *Militär und Innenpolitik*, pp. XL ff.; W. Deist, 'Kiel und die Marine im Ersten Weltkrieg', in J. Elvert, J. Jensen and M. Salewski (eds.), *Kiel, die Deutschen und die See* (Wiesbaden: Steiner, 1992), pp. 143 ff.

25 W. Gutsche with B. Kaulisch (eds.), *Herrschaftsmethoden des deutschen Imperialismus 1897/98 bis 1917. Dokumente zur innen- und außenpolitischen Strategie und Taktik der herrschenden Klasse des Deutschen Reiches* (Berlin: Ost, 1977), pp. 198 ff. (esp. pp. 207 ff.).

26 G. Ritter, *The Sword and the Sceptre. The Problem of German Militarism*, 4 vols. (1959–68; English translation, London: Allen Lane, 1972–3), vol. III, *The Tragedy of Statemanship. Bethmann Hollweg as War Chancellor, 1914–1917*, pp. 40 ff.; Fischer, *Germany's Aims in the First World War*, pp. 95–119; B. Thoß, 'Nationale Rechte, militärische Fuhrung und Diktaturfrage in Deutschland 1913–1923', *Militärgeschichtliche Mitteilungen*, 42, 1987, pp. 27 ff.

27 See K. Lange, *Marneschlacht und deutsche Öffentlichkeit 1914–1939. Eine verdrängte Niederlage und ihre Folgen* (Düsseldorf: Bertelsmann, 1974), pp. 35 ff.

28 A. Schérer and J. Grunewald, *L'Allemagne et les problèmes de la paix pendant la première guerre mondiale*, 3 vols. (Paris: Presses Universitaires de France, 1962), vol. I, no. 13, pp. 15 ff.; Ritter, *The Sword and the Sceptre*, vol. III, pp. 41–6; F. Fischer, *War of Illusions: Geman Policies from 1911 to 1914* (1969; English translation, London: Chatto and Windus, 1975), pp. 543–5, and recently the thorough study by H. Afflerbach, *Falkenhayn. Politisches Denken und Handeln im Kaiserreich* (Munich: Oldenbourg 1994), pp. 179 ff.

29 Heeres-Sanitätsinspektion des Reichswehrministers, *Sanitätsbericht über das Deutsche Heer im Weltkriege 1914/1918*, 3 vols. (Berlin: Mittler, 1934–5), vol. III, *Die Krankenbewegung bei dem Deutschen Feld- und Besatzungsheer*, table 147.

30 For the losses among officers, see *ibid.*, tables 130–3. Relative to the overall strength of the army, losses were highest in August and September 1914; in absolute figures, they were only surpassed during March and April 1918.

31 M. Brown and S. Seaton, *Christmas Truce* (London: Secker and Warburg, 1984); M. Eksteins, *Tanz über Graben* (Hamburg: Rowohlt, 1990), pp. 150 ff.

32 See notes 11, 12 and 18 above.

33 This development on the German side is now documented in Afflerbach, *Falkenhayn*, pp. 190 ff.

34 For the mobilization of the material resources, see L. Burchardt, *Deutschlands kriegswirtschaftliche Vorbereitungszeit vor 1914* (Boppard: Boldt, 1968); G. Hecker, *Walther Rathenau und sein Verhältnis zu Militär und Krieg* (Boppard: Boldt, 1983); W. Michalka, 'Kriegsrohstoffbewirtschaftung. Walther Rathenau und die "kommende Wirtschaft"', in W. Michalka (ed.), *Der Erste Weltkrieg. Wirkung. Wahrnehmung. Analyse* (Munich: Piper, 1994), pp. 485 ff.; G. D. Feldman, *Army, Industry and Labor in Germany 1914–1918* (1966; new edn, Providence and Oxford: Berg, 1992); G. D. Feldman, *The Great Disorder. Politics, Economics and Society in the German Inflation, 1914–1924* (New York: Oxford University Press, 1993).

35 Deist (ed.), *Militär und Innenpolitik*, nos. 184 to 245, pp. 461–647.

36 As an example see A. Roerkohl, *Hungerblockade und Heimatfront. Die kommunale Lebensmittelversorgung in Westfalen während des Ersten Weltkrieges* (Stuttgart: Steiner, 1991); and for the official line of the military, see Deist (ed.), *Militär und Innenpolitik*, nos. 95, 97, 104, 106, 115, pp. 222 ff.

37 See the instructive article by G. Krumeich, 'Der deutsche Soldat an der Somme, 1914–1916. Zwischen Idylle und Entsetzen', in S. Quandt and H. Schickel (eds.), *Der Erste Weltkrieg als Kommunikationsereignis* (Giessen: Köhler, 1993), pp. 45 ff., which underlines in an original way what effect the theory of a defensive war had on the soldiers.

38 E.g. the letter of the Bavarian Ministry of War to the Bavarian Minister of State, dated 1 February 1916, in: Deist (ed.), *Militär und Innenpolitik*, no. 126, pp. 294–9; Deist, 'Le Moral des troupes allemandes', pp. 95 ff.

39 Fischer, *Germany's Aims in the First World War*, pp. 95–279.

40 See Deist (ed.), *Militär und Innenpolitik*, nos. 127–9, pp. 300–8.

41 *Ibid.*, nos. 121 (27 December 1915) and 56 (28–9 February 1916), pp. 279 ff. and 110 ff.; see also n. 36; Deist, 'Kiel und die Marine'; I. Materna, H.-J. Schreckenbach with B. Holtz (eds.), *Berichte des Berliner Polizeipräsidenten zur Stimmung und Lage der Bevölkerung in Berlin 1914–1918* (Weimar: Böhlan, 1987).

42 For the material resources of the so-called Hindenburg Programme, see Feldman, *Army, Industry and Labor*, pp. 150 ff.; Deist (ed.), *Militär und Innenpolitik*, nos. 188 and 189, pp. 482–91.

43 See Feldman, *Army, Industry and Labor*, pp. 197 ff.; Deist (ed.), *Militär und Innenpolitik*, nos. 184 ff., pp. 461 ff. For the Third High Command see also

M. Kitchen, *The Silent Dictatorship. The Politics of the German High Command under Hindenburg and Ludendorff, 1916–1918* (London: Croom Helm, 1976).

44 R. Patemann, *Der Kampf um die preußische Wahlreform im Ersten Weltkrieg* (Düsseldorf: Droste, 1964); S. Miller, *Burgfrieden und Klassenkampf. Die deutsche Sozialdemokratie im Ersten Weltkrieg* (Düsseldorf: Droste, 1974), esp. pp. 240 ff.; H.-J. Bieber, *Gewerkschaften in Krieg und Revolution. Arbeiterbewegung, Industrie, Staat und Militär in Deutschland 1914–1920* (Hamburg: Christians, 1981), pp. 168 ff.

45 Riezler, *Tagebücher*, p. 183.

46 See Thoß, 'Nationale Rechte', pp. 35 ff.

47 Deist (ed.), *Militär und Innenpolitik*, no. 190, pp. 492 ff., quotation p. 495.

48 *Ibid.*, no. 198, pp. 511 ff., esp. p. 513.

49 *Ibid.*, nos. 256, 258, 267, 276, 281, 296, 308, pp. 570 ff., as well as W. J. Mommsen, 'Die deutsche öffentliche Meinung und der Zusammenbruch des Regierungssystems Bethmann Hollweg im Juli 1917', in Mommsen, *Der autoritäre Nationalstaat*, pp. 422 ff.

50 Deist (ed), *Militär und Innenpolitik*, no. 275, pp. 700–2.

51 *Ibid.*, no. 314, pp. 782 ff., in particular pp. 783 ff.

52 *Ibid.*, no. 319, pp. 790–8.

53 *Ibid.*, pp. 793 ff.

54 *Ibid.*, no. 371, pp. 989–93.

55 *Ibid.*, nos. 331 and 332, pp. 841 ff., as well as no. 337, pp. 860 ff. See also D. Stegmann, 'Die deutsche Inlandspropaganda. Zum innenpolitischen Machtkampf zwischen OHL und ziviler Reichsleitung in der Endphase des Kaiserreiches', *Militärgeschichtliche Mitteilungen*, 12, 1972, pp. 75 ff.; G. Mai, ' "Aufklärung der Bevölkerung" und "Vaterländischer Unterricht" in Württemberg 1914–1918', *Zeitschrift für Württembergische Landesgeschichte*, 36, 1977, pp. 199 ff.

56 See notes 38 and 40.

57 *Das Werk des Untersuchungsausschusses der Verfassunggebenden Nationalversammlung und des Deutschen Reichstages*, series 4, *Die Ursachen des deutschen Zusammenbruchs im Jahre 1918*, 12 vols. (Berlin: Deutsche Verlagsgesellschaft, 1927–31), vol. XI/1, pp. 17ff. (testimony of Hobohm); *ibid.* vol. XI/II (testimony of Volkmann), and the sources indicated there; see also B. Thoß, 'Menschenführung im Ersten Weltkrieg und im Reichsheer', in *Vorträge zur Militärgeschichte* (Herford: Mittler, 1982), vol. III, pp. 113 ff.

58 See Ludendorff's order dated 15 September 1917, in Deist (ed.), *Militär und Innenpolitik*, no. 337, pp. 860–4.

59 *Ibid.*, no. 331, pp. 841 ff., esp. p. 845.

60 *Ibid.*, no. 388, pp. 1048 ff.; no. 410, pp. 1101 ff.; Thoß, 'Nationale Rechte', pp. 51 ff.

61 See the sources in *Das Werk des Untersuchungsausschusses*, vols. XI/I and II; Deist (ed.), *Militär und Innenpolitik*, nos. 333 ff., pp. 848 ff.

62 *Ibid.*, nos. 359–61, pp. 943–53.

63 H. Meier-Welcker, 'Die deutsche Führung an der Westfront im Frühsommer 1918. Zum Problem der militärischen Lagebeurteilung', in *Welt als Geschichte*, 21, 1961, pp. 164 ff.; W. Meier-Dörnberg, 'Die große deutsche Frühjahrsoffensive 1918 zwischen Strategie und Taktik', in *Vorträge zur*

Militärgeschichte, vol. IX, (Herford: Mittler, 1988), pp. 73 ff.; W. Deist, 'The Military Collapse of the German Empire: the Reality behind the Stab-in-the-Back Myth', *War in History*, 3/2, 1996, pp. 186–207.

64 Deist, 'Le Morale des troupes allemandes', pp. 97 ff.; see also Ulrich and Ziemann, *Frontalltag im Ersten Weltkrieg*, pp. 117 ff.
65 Deist (ed.), *Militär und Innenpolitik*, no. 458, fn. 1.
66 Philip Witkop (ed.), *Kriegsbriefe gefallener Studenten* (Munich: Müller, 1918), p. 341 (letter dated 14 March 1918).
67 *Der Weltkrieg 1914–1918*, ed. by the Kriegsgeschichtliche Forschungsanstalt, 14 vols. (Berlin: Mittler, 1925–44), vol. XIV, p. 283; Crown Prince Rupprecht von Bayern, *Mein Kriegstagebuch*, ed. Eugen von Frauenholz, 3 vols. (Berlin, Deutscher Nationalverlag, 1929), vol. II, p. 382 (14 April 1918).
68 Deist, 'The Military Collapse'; see also W. Deist, 'Verdeckter Militärstreik im Kriegsjahr 1918?', in Wette (ed.), *Der Krieg des kleinen Mannes*, pp. 146 ff.
69 K.-J. Müller, *General Ludwig Beck. Studien und Dokumente zur politisch-militärischen Vorstellungswelt und Tätigkeit des Generalstabschefs des deutschen Heeres 1933–1938* (Boppard: Boldt, 1980), pp. 323 ff., esp. p. 326.
70 See the memorandum by the head of the War Press Authority, Deutelmoser, dated 5 October 1916, in Deist (ed.), *Militär und Innenpolitik*, no. 175, pp. 431 ff.; as well as *ibid.*, nos. 181 ff., pp. 450 ff.
71 Schramm hardly considers this combination of political and military offensive on the part of the Third High Command, which brought about this particular form of collapse (Schramm, 'Militarisierung und Demokratisierung').
72 Deist (ed.), *Militär und Innenpolitik*, no. 119, pp. 271 ff., this quotation, p. 276.
73 See W. Deist, 'The Road to Ideological War: Germany, 1918–1945', in W. Murray, M. Knox and A. Bernstein (eds.), *The Making of Strategy. Rulers, States, and War* (Cambridge: Cambridge University Press 1994), pp. 352 ff., this quotation p. 360.

11 MORALE AND PATRIOTISM IN THE AUSTRO-HUNGARIAN ARMY, 1914–1918

1 K. F. Nowak, *Der Weg zur Katastrophe* (Berlin: Verlag für Kulturpolitik, 1926), p. xix.
2 Quoted in M. Rauchensteiner, *Der Tod des Doppeladlers. Österreich-Ungarn und der Erste Weltkrieg* (Graz, Vienna and Cologne: Styria, 1993), p. 384.
3 *Ibid.*, p. 369.
4 See for example, Arhiv Hrvatske (Croatian State Archives), Zagreb, Sarkotić MSS, General Viktor Weber to Sarkotić, 10 March 1918.
5 R. Plaschka, H. Haselsteiner and A. Suppan, *Innere Front. Militärassistenz, Widerstand und Umsturz in der Donaumonarchie 1918*, 2 vols. (Vienna: Verlag für Geschichte u. Politik, 1974), vol. I, pp. 159–66; A. Arz von Straussenburg, *Zur Geschichte des Grossen Krieges 1914–1918*, (Vienna: Rikola, 1924), p. 222.

6 *Ibid.*, pp. 144–5, 147.

7 N. Stone, *The Eastern Front 1914–1917* (London: Hodder and Stoughton, 1975), p. 314, note 16.

8 C. Führ, *Das K.u.K. Armeeoberkommando und die Innenpolitik in Österreich 1914–1917* (Graz, Vienna and Cologne: Böhlau, 1968), pp. 63–4.

9 For a detailed study see R. Plaschka, 'Zur Vorgeschichte des Überganges von Einheiten des Infanterieregiments Nr. 28 an der russischen Front 1915', in *Österreich und Europa. Festgabe für Hugo Hantsch zum 70. Geburtstag* (Vienna: Institut für österreichische Geschichtsforschung, 1965), pp. 455–64.

10 Arz, *Zur Geschichte des Grossen Krieges*, p. 54.

11 Führ, *Das K.u.K. Armeeoberkommando*, p. 48.

12 L. Palla, *Il Trentino Orientale e la Grande Guerra* (Trento: Museo Trentino del Risorgimento e della Lotta per la Libertà, 1994), p. 133.

13 Rauchensteiner, *Der Tod des Doppeladlers*, p. 372.

14 Kriegsarchiv Vienna (hereafter KA), AOK Op. Abt 1917, Op. Nr. 44599, Kommando der SW Front to AOK Op. Abt, Op. Nr. 17480, 2 September 1917.

15 *Ibid.*, Op. Nr. 45286, Heeresgruppekommando (HGK) Conrad to AOK Op. Abt, Op. Nr. 31165, 15 September 1917.

16 Arz, *Zur Geschichte des Grossen Krieges*, p. 135.

17 KA, Evidenzbüro (EvB) 1918, Faszikel (Fasz.) 5746, Nr. 9089, Beute no. 38 Austrian deserters (statements of Italian interrogations of deserters, captured after Caporetto).

18 A full edition of Pivko's memoirs has recently been republished in Slovenia: Ljudevit Pivko, *Proti Avstriji* (Maribor: Zalžba Obzorja, 1991). A useful summary in Serbo-Croat is Pivko's *Naši dobrovoljci u Italiji* (Maribor: Klub Dobrovoljcev, 1924).

19 For example, in the largely Croat 42nd Honvéd Division, by 1918 there were 254 men in one regiment who had never had any leave: Hadtörténeti Intézet és Levéltár (Hungarian War Archives), Budapest, 42nd Honvéd divisional records, Fasz. 1659.

20 For a fuller discussion of this subject and the military's frustrations, see M. Cornwall, 'News, Rumour and the Control of Information in Austria-Hungary, 1914–1918', *History*, 77, 249, February 1992, pp. 50–64.

21 Führ, *Das K.u.K. Armeeoberkommando*, p. 27.

22 C. von Hötzendorf, *Private Aufzeichnungen. Erste Veröffentlichungen aus den Papieren des k.u.k. Generalstabs-Chef*, ed. Kurt Peball (Vienna and Munich: Amalthea, 1977), p. 111.

23 Führ, *Das K.u.K. Armeoberkommando*, pp. 132–8; Rauchensteiner, *Der Tod des Doppeladlers*, pp. 274–5.

24 Erich Feigl, *Kaiserin Zita. Legende und Wahrheit* (Vienna and Munich: Amalthea, 1977), pp. 380–2.

25 L. Windischgrätz, *Helden und Halunken. Selbsterlebte Weltgeschichte* (Vienna, Munich and Zurich: Wilhelm Frick, 1965), pp. 134–5.

26 See, for example, Ljudevit Pivko's vivid description of an inspection by the Emperor in Pivko, *Vulkanska Tla* (Maribor: Klub Dobrovoljcev, 1924), pp. 80–4, and Arz's own rather excessive remarks about Karl's influence, *Zur Geschichte des Grossen Krieges*, p. 133.

27 F. Höglinger, *Ministerpräsident Heinrich Graf Clam-Martinic* (Graz and Cologne: Böhlau, 1964), p. 144.

28 See Cornwall, 'News, Rumour', pp. 58–61; and for a recent basic synthesis with useful economic and social data: H. Louis Rees, *The Czechs during World War I. The Path to Independence* (New York: Columbia University Press, 1992).

29 A detailed discussion is to be found in M. Cornwall, 'The Experience of Yugoslav Agitation in Austria-Hungary 1917–1918', in H. Cecil and P. Liddle (eds.), *Facing Armageddon: the First World War Experienced* (London: Leo Cooper, 1996), pp. 565–76.

30 Erich Feigl, *Kaiserin Zita*, pp. 336–42.

31 KA, EvB 1918, Fasz. 5756: Nrs 22824 (Beilage 3), Nr. 23510; KA, Feindespropaganda-Abwehrstelle (FAst) 1918, Fasz. 5994, Res. Nr. 185.

32 This was not true, but the Monarchy's separate peace with the Ukraine in February 1918 had had a devastating effect on Polish public opinion in Galicia.

33 KA, FAst 1918, Fasz. 5994, Res. Nr. 113, Beilage: letter to Anna Dutkiewicz, 22 March 1918.

34 The AOK's fear of the homecomers is well expressed in M. Ronge, *Kriegs- und Industriespionage. Zwölf Jahre Kundschaftsdienst* (Zurich, Leipzig and Vienna: Amalthea, 1930), pp. 327 ff.

35 A small but significant nationalist ingredient was also present in these rebellions, as it had been in the naval mutiny at Cattaro in February 1918: see Plaschka, Haselsteiner and Suppan, *Innere Front*, vol. I, pp. 324 ff.

36 The weapon of military propaganda, as used by and against Austria-Hungary during the First World War, is the subject of my monograph, *The Undermining of Austria-Hungary. The Role of Military Propaganda* (forthcoming).

37 See for example, KA, EvB 1918, Fasz. 5743, Nr. 3584, Arz to military commands, 25 February 1918.

38 *Ibid.*, Fasz. 5743, Nr. 4041, Stöger-Steiner to AOK (NaAbt), Präs. Nr. 672, 8 February 1918.

39 R. G. Plaschka, 'Contradicting Ideologies: the Pressure of Ideological Conflicts in the Austro-Hungarian Army of World War I', in R. A. Kann, B. K. Király and P. S. Fichtner (eds.), *The Habsburg Empire in World War I* (New York: Columbia University Press, 1977), p. 111.

40 KA, 11AK (11th Army Command) 1918, Fasz. 449, Pr. Nr. 2145, 11AK Op. Nr. 1766, pp. 6–8.

41 *Ibid.*, Fasz. 448, Pr. Nr. 2099, AOK to 11AK, Op. Nr. 140566, 7 March 1918.

42 KA, FAst 1918, Fasz. 5994, Res. 18, Arz Op. Geh. Nr. 1219, 'Aufklärungsarbeit in der Wehrmacht', 14 March 1918.

43 *Ibid.*, Fasz. 5994, Res. 13, Kriegspressequartier to FAst, Adj. Nr. 1162, 21 March 1918: minutes of meeting held on 20 March.

44 *Ibid.*, Fasz. 6003: 'Richtlinien für vaterländischen Unterricht und Abwehr des Feindespropaganda', AOK zu Op. Nr. 141676, pp. 3, 7–8, 12 ff.

45 See Edmund von Glaise-Horstenau, *Ein General im Zwielicht*, ed. Peter Broucek, 3 vols. (Vienna: Böhlau, 1980–8), vol. I, p. 497.

46 KA, FAst 1918, Fasz. 6003, 'Richtlinien', pp. 8–11.

47 *Ibid.*, Fasz. 5994, Res. 46, Werkmann to FAst, 21 April 1918.

48 *Ibid.*, Fasz. 5995, Res. 278/I, *Vaterländische Bildungsarbeit, Mitteilungen der FAst*, Nr. 1, 10 July 1918, pp. 4–6.

49 *Ibid.*, Fasz. 5995, Res. 273/6, 42 HID (Oblt Juraj Sušnjak) to XIII KK, 20 June 1918.

50 *Ibid.*, Fasz. 5994, Res. 263, AOK to FAst, Op. Nr. 146335, 19 July 1918.

51 *Ibid.*, Fasz. 6003, 'Vaterländische Unterricht Heft Nr. 1 – Einleitungsvortrag zu 1. Informationskurs, von Oberst Egon Frh. v. Waldstätten', p. 6.

52 See for example, *ibid.*, Fasz. 5995, Res. 330, 6AK to AOK, Op. Nr. 900/Ev-4, 6 July 1918.

53 KA, XIII KK 1918, Fasz. 182, 48 ID Kmdo (GM Gärtner) to I KK, Op. Nr. 707/16, 10 July 1918.

54 KA, AOK 1918 Op. Akten, Fasz. 376, Op. Nr. 112195, FM Krobatin to HGK GO Erzherzog Joseph, Op. Nr. 5495, 10 September 1918. Krobatin gave as secondary evils some habitual problems: the lack of adequate disciplinary measures, the lack of good officers, the lack of leave and rest (all leave from the war zone had been suspended in mid-August), and the irregularity of the postal system.

55 *Ibid.*, Fasz. 374, Nr. 111806, FML Willerding to AOK, Na Nr. 158, 2 September 1918.

56 *Ibid.*, Fasz. 375, Nr. 111877, Kmdo General BHD [Sarkotić] to AOK, tel. Op. Nr. 4757, 9 September 1918; Edmund von Glaise-Horstenau, *The Collapse of the Austro-Hungarian Empire* (London: Dent, 1930), p. 236.

57 See for example, Arz von Straussenburg, *Kampf und Sturz der Kaiserreiche* (Vienna and Leipzig: Günther, 1935), p. 110; O. Regele, *Gericht über Habsburgs Wehrmacht* (Vienna and Munich: Herold, 1968), pp. 112 ff; and more recently, Alan Sked, *The Decline and Fall of the Habsburg Empire 1815–1918* (London and New York: Longman, 1989), p. 264.

58 KA, AOK 1918 Op. Abt, Fasz. 377, Nr. 112802, Report of Hptm Geza Schwarz, 21 September 1918.

59 KA, AOK 1918 Org. Gruppe, Fasz. 380, Nr. 113801, Report of Hptm Alfred von Marquet (no date). Further illuminating reports from the final days are to be found in Hugo Kerchnawe, *Der Zusammenbruch der österr.-ungar. Wehrmacht im Herbst 1918* (Munich: Lehmann, 1921), pp. 21 ff.

60 KA, FAst 1918, Fasz. 5999, Res. 962, 11AK, 'Beitrag zum vaterländischen Unterrichte', Nr. 7 (FA165).

61 See for example, *ibid.*, Fasz. 5998, Res. 892, 11AK to AOK, FA Nr. 158, 13 October 1918.

62 *Ibid.*, Fasz. 5998, Res. 875, FAst to AOK Op. Abt, 15 October: 'Gegenwartsaufgaben des vaterländischen Unterrichtes'.

63 *Ibid.*, Fasz. 5998, Res. 839, Oberst Eisner-Bubna (KPQ) to FAst, Adj. Nr. 14600, 7 October 1918.

12 REMOBILIZING FOR 'TOTAL WAR': FRANCE AND BRITAIN, 1917–1918

1 P. Renouvin, *The Forms of War Government in France* (New Haven: Yale University Press, 1927), pp. 27–97; A. Marwick, *The Deluge. British Society and the First World War* (London: Macmillan, 1975), pp. 36–9.

2 P. Renouvin, 'L'Opinion publique et la guerre en 1917', in *Revue d'Histoire Moderne et Contemporaine*, 15/1, 1968, pp. 4–23; J.-J. Becker, *The Great War and the French People* (1980; English translation, Leamington Spa: Berg, 1985), pp. 193–248. There is no adequate study of British public opinion during the war, but see T. Wilson, *The Myriad Faces of War. Britain and the Great War 1914–1918* (Cambridge: Polity, 1986), pp. 507–18.

3 J. Horne, 'The State and the Challenge of Labour in France 1917–20', in C. Wrigley, (ed.), *Challenges of Labour. Central and Western Europe 1917–1920* (London: Routledge, 1993), pp. 239–61; C. Wrigley, 'The State and the Challenge of Labour in Britain 1917–20', in *ibid.*, pp. 262–88.

4 B. Wasserstein, *Herbert Samuel. A Political Life* (Oxford: Clarendon Press, 1992), pp. 188–9.

5 J. Maitron (ed.), *Dictionnaire biographique du mouvement ouvrier français* (Paris: Editions ouvrières, 1973), vol. XI, pp. 60–1.

6 Maitron, *Dictionnaire biographique* (Paris: Editions ouvrières, 1976), vol. XIII, p. 84; C. Cline, *E. D. Morel 1873–1924. The Strategies of Protest* (Belfast: Blackstaff, 1980), p. 113.

7 D. R. Watson, *Georges Clemenceau. A Political Biography* (London: Eyre Methuen, 1974), pp. 286–7.

8 D. Hopkins, 'Domestic Censorship in the First World War', *Journal of Contemporary History*, 1970, 5/4, p. 167, who suggests that the number of prosecutions declined; Cline, *E. D. Morel*, p. 113, and J. M. Turner, *British Politics and the Great War. Coalition and Conflict, 1915–1918* (New Haven: Yale University Press, 1992), pp. 248–52, on the greater 'respectability' of pacifist advocacy of a negotiated peace by the winter of 1917–18.

9 Service Historique de l'Armée de Terre, Vincennes (SHA), 5N 334, 'Directives à la censure de province', 23 November 1917; M. Berger and P. Allard, *Les Secrets de la censure pendant la guerre* (Paris: Editions de la Portique, 1932).

10 D. Hopkins, 'Domestic Censorship', p. 161.

11 Ireland, as so often, is a case apart and the British attempt to impose conscription there in 1918 is the exception which proves the rule.

12 *Journal Officiel, Chambre des Députés, Débats parlementaires*, 7 July 1917, p. 1710.

13 A. Ferry, *Les Carnets secrets d'Abel Ferry, 1914–1918* (Paris: Grasset, 1957), p. 220.

14 D. Lloyd George, *War Memoirs of David Lloyd George*, 2 vols. (London: Odhams Press, 1938), vol. II, p. 1587.

15 M. L. Sanders and P. Taylor, *British Propaganda during the First World War* (London: Macmillan, 1982); J.-C. Montant, 'L'Organisation centrale des services d'informations et de propagande du Quai d'Orsay pendant la grande guerre', in J.-J. Becker and S. Audoin-Rouzeau (eds.), *Les Sociétés européennes et la guerre de 1914–1918* (Paris: Centre d'Histoire de la France Contemporaine, University of Paris X-Nanterre, 1990), pp. 135–43.

16 *La Ligue de l'Enseignement pendant la guerre*, 2 vols. (Paris: Ligue de l'Enseignement, 1919), vol. II, *Janvier 1917–décembre 1918*, pp. 5–6.

17 *La Ligue de l'Enseignement pendant la guerre*, vol. II, pp. 6–8; *Le Temps*, 8 March 1917.

18 *La Ligue de l'Enseignement pendant la guerre,* vol. II, pp. 8–9.

19 In addition to *La Ligue de l'Enseignement pendant la guerre,* the principal sources for the UGACPE are the printed minutes of the regular national committee meetings, a partial collection of which (covering February to December 1918) survives in the Bibliothèque de Documentation Internationale et Contemporaine (University of Paris X-Nanterre), and the daily paper, *Toute la France debout pour la victoire du droit,* published from 1 November 1918.

20 Public Record Office, London (PRO), CAB 23/3/154 (22), 5 June 1917.

21 PRO T 102/16 (undated memorandum, also cited in 'Home Publicity during the Great War: National War Aims Committee', compiled by the Ministry of Information in 1939, PRO INF 1/317). The archives of the NWAC are in PRO T 102/1–26.

22 *The Times,* 6 August 1917, p. 4.

23 PRO T 102/5. By October 1918, Lloyd George, Asquith, Bonar Law and the chief Labour figure remaining in government, G. N. Barnes, were the NWAC presidents.

24 PRO INF 1/317, 'Home Publicity during the Great War', p. 4, on Scotland. By the end of 1917, there were 184 local committees, though the aim was one in every constituency (PRO T 102/16, report of 8 December 1917).

25 PRO T 102/14, correspondence with Mrs McArthur of the National Women's Liberal Federation.

26 The Treasury granted the six-month budget from October 1917 (PRO T 102/16).

27 E.g. meeting of the NWAC, 4 April 1918 (PRO T 102/16).

28 Until May 1918, the UGACPE actually met in the Maison de la Presse, when it reverted to the headquarters of the Ligue de l'Enseignement (minutes of the UGACPE, 4 June 1918, pp. 4–5, valedictory speech by Steeg).

29 UGACPE minutes, 14 May 1918, in which Commandant Chaix, one of Clemenceau's representatives on the union's committee and the official responsible for the reorganization, maintained that he was doing no more than implementing the UGACPE's ideas on coordinated home-front propaganda. The demand for such a reorganization had been expressed by a two-day convention held by the union, 9–10 February 1918. For the reorganization, see SHA 5N 372, instructions to the Commissaire, 30 May 1918.

30 UGACPE minutes, 14 May 1918, p. 4.

31 E.g. in July 1918, the UGACPE dispatched 90,000 letters to local mayors and school teachers to prepare public opinion for the requisitioning of 200,000 horses (UGACPE minutes, 2 July 1918, p. 6).

32 UGACPE minutes, 25 June 1918, pp. 15–16.

33 *Ibid.*; PRO T 102/16, NWAC report, 12 December 1917.

34 J. Horne, *Labour at War. France and Britain, 1914–1918* (Oxford: Clarendon Press, 1991), ch. 8.

35 The Meetings Committee reported that, locally, organized labour shunned the NWAC on the grounds that 'our war aims are not defined' (PRO T 102/16, report of 10 October 1917). Nor is there any evidence that the situation improved in 1918, when Lloyd George gave government war aims greater

precision, for the Labour Party and TUC were deeply involved in their own peace diplomacy. Only the patriotic National and Democratic Labour Party supported the NWAC (PRO T 102/5).

36 Horne, *Labour at War*, pp. 174–6.

37 In the case of the UGACPE, the socialist former minister, Albert Thomas, put the socialist case for support for military victory (*Le Temps*, 10 February 1918). Also, when some affiliated associations tried to condemn the celebration of the centenary of Marx's birth in 1918 by certain French socialist groups as 'pro-German', the protest was considerably toned down (after a long debate) for fear of offending pro-war socialists (UGACPE minutes, 30 April 1918, pp. 7–9).

38 E.g. two UGACPE brochures, G. Blondel, *Ce que voudraient les allemands* (1918), which asked whether 'a real democratization of the German race was not utopian' (p. 5), and *Pourquoi la guerre a éclaté. Comment elle doit finir* (Editions de la Ligue Républicaine de la Défense Nationale, Droit et Liberté, 1918), which argued that even a peace on the *status quo ante* would be illusory since Germany would retain a position of potential dominance. For the NWAC, see W. Stephen Sanders, *Germany's Two Voices* (London: n.d.).

39 PRO T 102/16, report on Landsdowne letter (n.d., but December 1917).

40 UGACPE minutes, 18 June 1918 for the initial poster campaign; Archives Départementales, Tarn, 10R 1/2, telegram of the Minister of the Interior to all prefects, 3 July 1918, for nationwide circulation.

41 See, for example, the basic historical catechism in *L'Alsace-Lorraine est-elle Française ou Allemande?* edited by the Conférence au Village for the UGACPE in 1917 or 1918.

42 UGACPE minutes, 9 April 1918; *Le Temps*, 2 and 3 March 1918; R. Poincaré, *Au Service de la France*, 11 vols. (Paris: Plon, 1926–33), vol. X, *Victoire et Armistice 1918*, p. 66.

43 UGACPE minutes, 28 May 1918, p. 10.

44 UGACPE minutes, 25 June 1918.

45 PRO T 102/4, correspondence of Lynden Macassey, director of the Admiralty's Shipyard Labour Department, with Cox, secretary of the NWAC, December 1917.

46 *La Ligue de l'Enseignement pendant la guerre*, vol. II, p. 11; UGACPE minutes, 9 April 1918, p. 11. Popular titles included *La Bataille de la Somme* (of which the union was offered the première), *En Alsace française*, *L'Effort militaire français*, *Le Réveil économique*, *La Femme et le sourire de la France*, *Le Traitement des prisonniers allemands*, *La Vie à Paris pendant la bataille de Verdun* and *L'Enfance pendant la guerre*.

47 PRO T 102/5, letter first suggesting the idea December 1917; *The Times*, 29 July and 6 August 1918.

48 UGACPE minutes, 12 March 1918, p. 5; *ibid.*, minutes, 14 January 1919.

49 N. Reeves, *Official British Film Propaganda during the First World War* (London: Croom Helm, 1986), pp. 125–32.

50 UGACPE minutes, 12 March 1918, pp. 10–11.

51 PRO T 102/22–26. These standardized reports indicate the time, place and date of the meeting, the numbers present, and often the theme of the address with an assessment of audience reaction.

52 M. Corday, *The Paris Front. An Unpublished Diary 1914–1918* (1932; English translation, London: Gollancz, 1933), p. 235.

53 Particularly useful as a substantial sequence are the monthly reports of the generals commanding the internal military regions of France, August 1917–April 1919 (SHA 6N 147) and the Ministry of Labour's weekly *Reports on the Labour Situation*, from May 1917 (PRO CAB 24).

54 PRO CAB 24/832, Labour situation, 23 May 1917.

55 SHA 6N 147, generals' report, 15 December 1917, p. 2; PRO T 102/5, letter of G. Hodgson of Chesterfield, 17 December 1917.

56 UGACPE minutes, 26 February 1918.

57 PRO T 102/22, meeting at Littleborough, with 150 present.

58 UGACPE minutes, 9 July 1918.

59 UGACPE minutes, 16 July 1918.

60 PRO T 102/16, report of Meetings Department, 10 October 1917.

61 PRO T 102/22–24, various reports on the Royton division.

62 PRO T 102/23, various reports.

63 PRO CAB 24/2716, Labour situation, 21 November 1917, p. 5; PRO CAB 24/3677, Labour situation, 20 February 1918, p. 1.

64 Corday, *Paris Front*, pp. 382–3; Horne, *Labour at War*, p. 175.

65 Archives Départmentales, Tarn, 10R/5, various reports on both years.

66 PRO CAB 24/4/4199, report of 10 April 1918; PRO CAB 24/4239, Labour situation, 17 April 1918.

67 E.g. with the Paris poster campaign 'To the People of France'.

13 MOBILIZATION AND DEMOBILIZATION IN GERMANY, 1916–1919

1 K. Königsberger, 'Die wirtschaftliche Demobilmachung in Bayern während der Zeit vom November 1918 bis Mai 1919', *Zeitschrift des bayerischen statistischen Landesamts*, 52, 1920, p. 196.

2 This is the oft-quoted and apposite phrase of Joseph Koeth, who headed the Reich Demobilization Office in late 1918 and early 1919. See J. Koeth, 'Die wirtschaftliche Demobilmachung: Ihre Aufgaben und ihre Organe', in *Handbuch der Politik*, 6 vols. (third edition, Berlin and Leipzig: W. Rothschild, 1920–6), vol. IV, *Die wirtschaftliche Wiederaufbau*, p. 167. See also G. D. Feldman, 'Economic and Social Problems of the German Demobilization 1918–19', *Journal of Modern History*, 37, 1975, pp. 1–23; R. Bessel, *Germany After the First World War* (Oxford: Oxford University Press, 1993), pp. 106–7.

3 On the return of the soldiers, see Bessel, *Germany after the First World War*, pp. 69–90. On post-war unemployment, see R. Bessel, 'Unemployment and Demobilisation in Germany after the First World War', in R. J. Evans and D. Geary (eds.), *The German Unemployed: Experiences and Consequences of Mass Unemployment from the Weimar Republic to the Third Reich* (London and Sydney: Croom Helm, 1987), pp. 23–43.

4 See, especially, the classic work by G. D. Feldman, *Army, Industry, and Labor in Germany 1914–1918* (Princeton: Princeton University Press, 1966; new edn, Providence and Oxford: Berg, 1992).

5 Feldman, *Army, Industry, and Labor*, p. 150.

6 Archiwum Panstwowe w Wroclawiu (State Archives, Wroclaw), Rejencja Opolska I, 10051, ff. 90–105: 'Aktenvermerk über die Verhandlungen in der Vorstandssitzung des Oberschlesischen Berg- und Hüttenmännischen Vereins vom 2. Juni 1917', dated 3 June 1917. For further outbursts by directors of the Upper Silesian coal and smelting combine, see Feldman, *Army, Industry and Labor*, pp. 360–1.

7 Michael Geyer, *Deutsche Rüstungspolitik 1860–1980* (Frankfurt-am-Main: Suhrkamp, 1984), p. 110.

8 M. Weber, 'Zur Frage des Friedenschließens', in W. J. Mommsen (ed.), *Max Weber. Zur Politik im Weltkrieg. Schriften und Reden 1914–1919 (Max Weber Gesamtausgabe. Abteilung I: Schreiben und Reden,* vol. XV*)* (Tübingen: Mohr, 1984), p. 65.

9 See Feldman, *Army, Industry, and Labor*, pp. 429–32.

10 W. Deist (ed.), *Militär und Innenpolitik im Weltkrieg 1914–1918*, 2 vols. (Düsseldorf: Droste, 1970), vol. II, pp. 1144–5, doc. 431: 'Entwurf einer Weisung des bayerischen Kriegsministeriums an die stellv. kommandierenden Generale der bayerischen Armeekorps betr. Einschränkung der Veranstaltungen der Deutschen Vaterlandspartei', Munich, 30 January 1918.

11 See especially S. Miller, *Burgfrieden und Klassenkampf. Die deutsche Sozialdemokratie im Ersten Weltkrieg* (Düsseldorf: Droste, 1974).

12 See C.-L. Holtfrerich, *The German Inflation 1914–1923. Causes and Effects in International Perspective* (New York: De Gruyter, 1986), pp. 108–19; G. D. Feldman, *The Great Disorder. Politics, Economics and Society in the German Inflation 1914–1924* (New York: Oxford University Press, 1993), pp. 37–51.

13 See the table in Holtfrerich, *The German Inflation*, p. 117.

14 Feldman, *The Great Disorder*, p. 43.

15 Hessisches Hauptstaatsarchiv Wiesbaden, 405/6359, f. 86: The Landrat to the Regierungspräsident in Wiesbaden, Rüdesheim, 16 November 1917; Generallandesarchiv Karlsruhe, 465/E.V.8, Bund 86: Stellv. Generalkommando, XIV. Armeekorps, to the Grossh. Ministerium des Innern, Karlsruhe, 1 October 1918.

16 Deist (ed.), *Militär und Innenpolitik im Weltkrieg 1914–1918*, vol. II, p. 816, doc. 324, 'Richtlinien für die Aufklärungs- und Propagandatätigkeit im Bereich des stellv. Generalkommandos des X. AK.', 10 May 1917.

17 However, even the apparent war enthusiasm which accompanied the outbreak of war in 1914 is now the subject of critical and sceptical analsysis. See W. Kruse, 'Die Kriegsbegeisterung im Deutschen Reich zu Beginn des Ersten Weltkrieges. Entstehungszusammenhänge, Grenzen und ideologische Strukturen', in M. van der Linden and G. Mergner (eds.), *Kriegsbegeisterung und mentale Kriegsvorbereitung. Interdisziplinäre Studien* (Berlin: Duncker und Humblot, 1991), pp. 73–87; J. T. Verhey, 'The "Spirit of 1914": The Myth of Enthusiasm and the Rhetoric of Unity in World War I Germany' (Ph.D. thesis, University of California at Berkeley, 1991); B. Ziemann, 'Zum ländlichen Augusterlebnis 1914 in Deutschland', in B. Loewenstein (ed.), *Geschichte und Psychologie. Annäherungsversuche* (Pfaffenweiler: Centaurus, 1992), pp. 193–203; Bessel, *Germany after the First World War*, pp. 2–4;

B. Ulrich and B. Ziemann (eds.), *Frontalltag im Ersten Weltkrieg. Wahn und Wirklichkeit* (Frankfurt-am-Main: Fischer, 1994), pp. 29–47.

18 See the table in *Sanitätsbericht über das Deutsche Heer (Deutsches Feld- und Besatzungsheer) im Weltkriege 1914/1918*, 3 vols. (Berlin: Mittler, 1934–5), vol. III, *Die Krankenbewegung bei dem Deutschen Feld- und Besatzungsheer*, p. 8. See also Bessel, *Germany after the First World War*, pp. 5–6.

19 See Bessel, *Germany after the First World War*, pp. 13–14.

20 W. Deist, 'Der militärische Zusammenbruch des Kaiserreichs: Zur Realität der "Dolchstoßlegende" ', in U. Büttner (ed.), *Das Unrechtsregime. Internationale Forschung über den Nationalsozialismus. Ideologie, Herrschaftssystem, Wirkung in Europa* (Hamburg: Christians, 1986), pp. 101–29; W. Deist, 'Verdeckter Militärstreik im Kriegsjahr 1918?', in W. Wette (ed.), *Der Krieg des kleinen Mannes. Eine Militärgeschichte von unten* (Munich: Piper, 1992), pp. 146–67. See also E. O. Volkmann, *Der Marxismus und das deutsche Heer im Weltkriege* (Berlin, 1925), pp. 192–5; Bessel, *Germany after the First World War*, pp. 45–7.

21 A good indication of the monthly ebb and flow of military casualties may be gained from figures from the city of Leipzig, in Statistisches Amt (ed.), *Statistisches Jahrbuch der Stadt Leipzig. Band 1915–1918* (Leipzig, 1921), p. 73. In all four years of the war, the winter months generally saw the lowest casualties.

22 For more detailed figures on the absent soldiers, see Bessel, *Germany after the First World War*, pp. 5–6. The case of Leipzig illustrates the feminization of the home population where, out of a total recorded population of 542,845 in 1917, 326,797 (60.2 per cent) were female and 216,048 (39.8 per cent) male. See *Statistisches Jahrbuch der Stadt Leipzig 1915–1918*, p. 10.

23 See U. Daniel, *Arbeiterfrauen in der Kriegsgesellschaft. Beruf, Familie und Politik im Ersten Weltkrieg* (Göttingen: Vandenhoeck and Rupprecht, 1989), pp. 98–100.

24 See Daniel, *Arbeiterfrauen in der Kriegsgesellschaft*, pp. 224–32; A. Roerkohl, *Hungerblockade und Heimatfront. Die kommunale Lebensmittelversorgung in Westfalen während des Ersten Weltkrieges* (Stuttgart: Franz Steiner, 1991), pp. 261–75.

25 See R. Bessel, 'State and Society in Germany in the Aftermath of the First World War', in W. R. Lee and Eve Rosenhaft (eds.), *The State and Social Change in Germany, 1880–1980* (New York, Oxford and Munich: Berg, 1990), pp. 200–27.

26 On these themes, see generally S. Rouette, *Sozialpolitik als Geschlechterpolitik. Die Regulierung der Frauenarbeit nach dem Ersten Weltkrieg* (Frankfurt-am-Main and New York: Campus, 1993), and Bessel, *Germany after the First World War*.

27 E. Ludendorff, *The Nation at War* (1935; English translation, London: Hutchinson, 1936). See the suggestive comments of M. Geyer, *Aufrüstung oder Sicherheit. Die Reichswehr in der Krise der Machtpolitik 1924–1936* (Wiesbaden: Steiner, 1980), pp. 484–9.

28 J. Winter, 'Some Paradoxes of the First World War', in R. M. Wall and J. M. Winter (eds.), *The Upheaval of War. Family, Work and Welfare in Europe, 1914–1918* (Cambridge: Cambridge University Press, 1988), p. 40.

29 A. Offer, *The First World War: An Agrarian Interpretation* (Oxford: Oxford University Press, 1989), p. 352.

14   THE ITALIAN EXPERIENCE OF 'TOTAL' MOBILIZATION 1915–1920

1 On the repressive policies followed in Italy, see G. Procacci, 'State Coercion and Worker Solidarity in Italy (1915–18): the Moral and Political Content of Social Unrest', in L. Haimson and G. Sapelli (eds.), *Strikes, Social Conflict and the First World War. An International Perspective* (Milan: Annali Fondazione Giangiacomo Feltrinelli, 1991), pp. 145–78; L. Tomassini, 'Industrial Mobilization and State Intervention in Italy in the First World War. Effects on Labor Unrest', in *ibid.*, pp. 179–212; and L. Tomassini, 'Industrial Mobilization and the Labour Market in Italy during the First World War', *Social History*, 16, 1, 1991, pp. 59–87.

2 The daily average for correspondence, which at the beginning of the war (May–June 1915) was around 1,600,000 pieces (700,000 from the country and 900,000 from the army), increased constantly in the following years, reaching its peak in June 1917 of 2,780,000 letters and postcards daily from the front and 1,500,000 from the country. Considering the correspondence between soldiers as well, the total – for the whole period of the war – was almost 4,000 million pieces, with an average of around 3,000,000 per day. See G. Procacci, *Soldati e prigionieri italiani nella grande guerra* (Rome: Editori Riuniti, 1993), p. 12.

3 G. Procacci, 'Popular Protest and Labour Conflict in Italy, 1915–18', in *Social History*, 14, 1, 1989, pp. 31–58.

4 See chapter 4 in this volume by A. Fava.

5 *Relazione della Commissione d'inchiesta. Dall'Isonzo al Piave. 24 ottobre–9 novembre 1917*, 2 vols. (Rome: 1919), vol. II, *Le cause e le responsabilità degli avvenimenti*, p. 419.

6 Letter of the journalist Tullio Giordana, 31 October 1917, from Milan, in Archivio Centrale dello Stato, Rome, Presidenza del Consiglio dei Ministri, Prima Guerra Mondiale, 19.6.5.

7 Procacci, *Soldati e prigionieri italiani*, pp. 330–58.

8 For examples of socialist errors in this sense, see P. Corner, *Fascism in Ferrara 1915–1925* (Oxford: Oxford University Press, 1974), ch. 5.

9 The phrase is that of the fascist leader Italo Balbo in his *Diario del 1922* (Milan: Mondadori, 1932), p. 6.

Index

CPSIA information can be obtained at www.ICGtesting.com
Printed in the USA
BVOW08s1533220114

342676BV00001B/96/A